Changing
Public Sector
Values

Garland Reference Library of Social Science
Volume 1045

_R_

Changing Public Sector Values

Montgomery Van Wart

Garland Publishing, Inc.
A member of the Taylor & Francis Group
New York & London
1998

Library of Congress Cataloging-in-Publication Data

Van Wart, Montgomery, 1951–
     Changing public sector values / Montgomery Van Wart.
        p.   cm.
     Includes bibliographical references and index.
     ISBN 0-8153-2071-X (hardcover : alk. paper). —
ISBN 0-8153-2072-8 (paperback)
     1. Public administration—Moral and ethical aspects. 2. Values.
I. Title
JF1525.E8V36   1998
351—dc21   97-44078
                                    CIP

Printed on acid-free, 250-year-life paper
Manufactured in the United States of America

To my parents,
Mary and Franklin Van Wart

CONTENTS

Foreword xiii
Introduction xvii
    The Importance of Clarifying Contemporary Values xvii
    Purpose of the Book xix
    Structure of the Book xx
    Audiences xxii
    Definition of the Subjects of This Study xxiii
    Acknowledgments xxiv
        Notes xxv

PART I
Values Endorsed in Public Administration

CHAPTER 1

The Five Value Sources Used in Decisionmaking in the Public Sector 3
    Problems in Identifying Sources of Decisionmaking 4
        Which Are the Key Sources or Value Sets? 4
        The Problem of Source Definition 6
        Which Source Takes Precedence When Sources Compete? 7
    The Five Major Sources of Values 8
        Individual Values 8
        Professional Values 12
        Organizational Values 14
        Legal Values 18
        Public Interest Values 20
    Conclusion 23
        Notes 26

PART II
An In-Depth Look at Values Endorsed in Public Administration

CHAPTER 2

The Role of Individuals' Values 33
    The Individual Values Environment in American Society 34
        A Contemporary View of Moral Development 35
    Individual Values in the Public Sector 38
        Strong Civic Integrity Is Critical for Public Employees 38
        Public Servants Have Basic Rights As Citizens 42
        Public Administrators Are Capable of Unique Contributions 45
    The Potential Contributions of Individual Values 46
        Civic Integrity Increases Citizens' Trust That Their Interests
        Are Being Faithfully Executed 47
        Civic Integrity Reduces Reliance on Laws and Rules 47
        Individual Values Challenge the Excesses of the State
        and Other Value Sets 48
        Acknowledgment of Individual Contributions and Leadership
        Is Both Practical and Humane 48
    Problems with Excessive Reliance on Individual Values 48
        Substitution of Legal Values by Personal Values 49
        Usurpation of the Public Interest by Individual Values 50
    Conclusion 51
        Notes 53

CHAPTER 3

The Role of Professional Values 61
    The Professional Values Environment 62
        A Systematic Body of Knowledge 62
        A Professional Culture 62
        Sanctions of the Community 63
        A Regulative Code of Ethics 63
        Substantial Professional Authority 64
        The Evolution of Professions 64
    What Are Professional Values in the Public Sector? 68
        Determinants of Professionalism and the Public Sector 70
    What Are the Potential Contributions of Professional Values? 74
    What Are the Problems of Excessive Reliance on Professional Values? 76
    Conclusion 77
        Notes 78

CHAPTER 4

The Role of Organizational Values 81
    The Organizational Values Environment 81
        Environmental Conditions 83

Effectiveness Criteria 85

Culture Types 87

Leadership Types 91

What Are Public Sector Organizational Values? 94

Evolution of the Hierarchical Culture in the Public Sector 94

The Movement Away from Bureaucratic Hierarchies 95

Emerging Organizational Culture Values 97

What Are the Potential Contributions of Organizational Values? 107

What Are the Potential Problems of Excessive Reliance
on Organizational Values? 107

Notes 108

CHAPTER 5

The Role of Legal Values

The Role of Legal Values 117

The Role of Legal Values in Public Administration 118

Four Basic Assumptions About Legal Values 119

What Is "Subordination," and How Much Is Enough? 122

The Contributions of Legal Values in the Public Sector 124

The Problems of the Legal Values of Public Administration 126

Conclusion 128

Notes 129

CHAPTER 6

The Role of Public Interest Values

The Role of Public Interest Values 135

The Public Interest Values Environment 136

Systematic Governance 137

Representational Democracy 137

Division and Separation of Political Power
Through Federalism 138

Protection and Celebration of Individualism 139

Protection of Religious Choice as an Individual Right 141

A Relatively Pure Form of Capitalism 142

Public Administration and Public Interest Values 144

Implementing Policy but Not Usurping the Process
or Amassing Power 144

Being Efficient and Effective with the Public's Resources 146

Supporting the Public's Right to Know 148

Supporting the Public's Right to Be Involved 149

Contributions of Public Interest Values for Public Administrators 151

Potential Problems of Public Interest Values
of Public Administrators 151

Conclusion 152

A Summary of the Five Sources and Part II 153

Notes 155

PART III
Analyzing Values Using a Cultural Framework Perspective

CHAPTER 7

The Cultural Framework and an Analysis of the Origins
of Basic Assumptions in Public Administration 163
    The Four Levels of the Cultural Framework 165
        The Tangible Levels of Culture 167
        The Values Levels of Culture 167
    The Four Levels as Determinants of Actions 170
    Basic Assumptions as a Determinant of Action 172
        Assumptions Flowing from General Philosophy 172
        Assumptions Flowing from Political Philosophy 174
        Assumptions Flowing from the Ethical Subsystem 176
    Conclusion 177
        Notes 179

CHAPTER 8

Decisionmaking Paradigms for Public Administration:
Values at Level 3 187
    What Do the Three Paradigms Look Like? 189
        A Four-Point Comparison of the Paradigms 193
    Conclusion 196
        Notes 197

CHAPTER 9

Selection of a Decisionmaking Process: Values at Level 2 199
    Twelve Types of Rationality and Decisionmaking Processes 202
        Market (Rational Choice) Rationality 202
        Reasoned Choice Rationality 204
        Nonlinear Systems Rationality 206
        Human Needs Rationality 208
        Coercive Rationality 209
        Traditional Rationality 211
        Religious Rationality 212
        Altruistic Rationality 214
        Elite Rationality 215
        Democratic Rationality 218
        Legal Rationality 219
        Anarchic Rationality 221
    Conclusion 222
        Notes 227

CHAPTER 10

Using a Decisionmaking Process: Reasoned Choice Models (Level 1) 233
    Characteristics of Values in Practical Decisions 234

Strengths and Weaknesses of Values in Practical Decisionmaking 235
An Example of Decisionmaking and Values in the Public Sector 236
Decisionmaking Models 237
Instinctive Models 238
Simple Models 238
Reasoned Choice Decisionmaking Models 240
A Contingency Approach 243
Reasoned Choice Decisionmaking at Other Levels 244
The Special Nature of Decisionmaking in
American Public Administration 246
Excessive Discretion 249
Insufficient Discretion 249
Moderate Discretion 250
Conclusion 251
Notes 252

PART IV
Shaping and Managing Values to Ensure Coherence and Legitimacy

CHAPTER 11

Encouraging the "Right" Values

Encouraging the "Right" Values 257
Consensus About Values 258
Determining the Environment of Current Values 260
Supporting a Consensus on Values When It Exists 270
Establishing a Consensus on Values When Significant
Disagreement Exists 271
Education About Values 273
A Prerequisite for Consensus: Knowledge and Awareness 273
A Simple Model for Evaluating Consciousness of Values 274
Use of Incentives and Disincentives in Value Systems 278
Goals of Incentive Plans for Values 278
Transmittal of Organizational Culture 279
Common Elements of Incentive Plans for Values 280
Conclusion 282
Notes 283

CHAPTER 12

Identifying the "Right" Controls to Monitor and Limit Administrative Discretion

Identifying the "Right" Controls to Monitor and Limit
Administrative Discretion 289
The Functions of Controls of Public Organizations 290
The Types and Sources of Control 292
Examples of the Seven Types of Control 292
Control by Laws 294

Control by Rules 295
Control by Public Opinion 296
Control by Virtue 297
Control by Norms 298
Control by Competition 299
Control by Comparison 301
Current Shifts in Emphasis 303
Laws and Rules 303
Public Opinion 306
Virtue 307
Norms 308
Competition and Comparison 308
Conclusion 309
Notes 310

CHAPTER 13
Conclusion 315
A Summary of the Main Points of the Book 316
Notes 320
Index 321

FOREWORD

Consider Miami. Miami at the end of the millennium would seem to represent the full gamut of public sector values. In 1957, Miami and Dade County created a unique structure of local governance (known in the literature as "two-tier," or "federative government") that set up a system designed to build responsiveness, effectiveness, and efficiency into the structure itself. Under this plan, the Miami metropolitan area is governed by smaller urban governments, which deliver those services that can be delivered most responsively and effectively on a small scale, and by a single, metro-wide, county government, which delivers those services that can be provided most efficiently on a large scale. As a structure, Miami–Dade County remains a unique governmental form in the United States, and one that, at least at the time, reflected the most advanced thinking about local government in scholarly and practitioner circles.

In 1980, the Dade County metropolis exploded in the most violent race riot since the 1960s. This "insurrection," as it was called, indicated to some that the governmental structures which Miami and Dade County had erected for purposes of being more responsive and effective had, at best, failed.

In the late 1990s the federal investigation Operation Greenpalm uncovered a governance system rife with corruption of the type that we now associate with the nineteenth century. This investigation indicated to some that the government structures which Miami and Dade County had erected for purpose of being more efficient had failed.

I mention Miami–Dade County because this metro-area dramatizes a diverse spectrum of public sector values. Nevertheless, the governmental values represented by South Florida's largest metropolis are by no means all the values that could be represented.

Here is where Montgomery Van Wart helps those of us concerned with why government does what it does come to a much fuller understanding of this question. The Chinese have a saying that to understand something, first we must name things correctly. Van Wart does precisely this. Discussions of "values" in the public sector are often confused with discussions of "ethics." As Van Wart makes clear, however, ethics is but a small slice of values; he notes toward the close of his book that ethics is both acting on the right values and not acting on the wrong ones. In other words, there are a lot of values, and these values can be ethical, unethical, or simply nonethical. In any event, values underlie ethics, and, as such, constitute a much larger universe than that occupied by ethics.

The largest segment of this universe is likely nonethical values—that is, values which are neither "right" nor "wrong" but which have real and often moral results when acted upon. Consider a small example: In our age of cutback management, most public administrators tend to cut back unilaterally. In other words, all agencies are cut back by the same proportion. There is nothing unethical in this approach, but there is something stupid in it. A more intelligent approach to cutting back agency programs, and the people in them, is to determine which programs are the most pertinent to the long-term public interest, and which are less so. This is not an easy task, but it is one certainly laden with an array of values from which the public administrator may choose in making his or her decision.

Van Wart both simplifies and clarifies these choices on a much broader scale than I can here. I would suggest to the reader that he or she begin the book by referring, first, to the table that closes Part II, The Five Value Sources and Seventeen Basic Assumptions Used in Decision Making in Public Administration (Table 6.1). These assumptions are at the core of *Changing Public Sector Values* and referring to this table initially might be helpful.

Van Wart has continued the estimable tradition in the field of ethics represented by John Rohr, Terry Cooper, and Hal Gortner, among others. But he goes beyond a relatively narrow treatment of ethics in the public sector by, as the title of this book indicates, treating the larger field of values. This is new, and his approach will introduce readers to some literatures of which they are unlikely to be knowledgeable. Most notably, perhaps, these include philosophy and anthropology, which make up much of the discussion in Part III. Discussions that may be more familiar to most readers (and I am assuming that most readers will be scholars, students, and practitioners of public administration) will be found in Part II.

Chapter 4, The Role of Organizational Values, is one of the richest portraits that I have come across on the role of values in organizational cultures. I am among those who like matrices to illustrate discussions, and Chapter 4 is replete with matrices. They are good ones. The penultimate chapter, Chapter 12, likely would be most appreciated by practitioners, as it is a hands-on approach to the subject of values in public administration. It is fun to read.

In sum, here is what you will gain from reading *Changing Public Sector Values:* It is a systematic treatment of public sector values, and perhaps the first one ever explicitly done; it provides a renewed discussion of ethics, and is possibly among the more balanced treatments of ethics to appear in recent years; it weds in unique ways the literatures of public administration, anthropology, and philosophy, and it does so in an entertaining fashion, largely by using good, substantive examples.

This is an important book. Van Wart goes back to the basics and builds a logical, thoughtful argument from those basics. But perhaps its even more lasting value is the fact that it clarifies this chaotic and ill-understood field. Few phenomena are messier than values, and Van Wart brings discipline and clarity to this ongoing discussion. We owe him a debt.

Nicholas Henry

The Importance of Clarifying Contemporary Values

The complexity of prioritizing public administration values is difficult even in relatively stable times. In these times of major change, the challenge is exceptionally difficult, but exceptionally important. Administrative competence is seriously affected by administrators' ability to clarify their values environment in at least three respects: administrative effectiveness, ethical decisionmaking, and political-judicial alignment.

First, being clear about and managing values is an organizational priority of the highest order. In his book In Search of Excellence, Tom Peters wrote that "every excellent company we studied is clear on what it stands for, and takes the process of value shaping seriously."[1] Evan Berman and Jonathan West assert that the same is true for the public sector: "[Public] institutions are beginning to take seriously the possibility of deliberate and systematic management of values."[2] Lack of clarity about the values to be endorsed, their priority, their application in different situations, their support, and their enforcement leads to ineffectiveness as employees work at cross-purposes. Other side effects of poor clarity about values are well-meaning but out-of-step individuals, diminished team spirit and camaraderie, organizational turmoil, poor alignment among agencies within governmental systems, and poor integration and communication with the values of the public.

Second, values are the foundations of ethical systems. Values determine what is right and what is wrong. Murkiness about values invites unnecessary ethical dilemmas and encourages an environment in which ethical lapses flourish. Core social values such as honesty and forthrightness are relatively easy to comprehend, as are public administration values like abiding by the law and attending to the public interest. But in many situations, the shifts in emphasis (such as from risk avoidance to moderate risk taking) and the competition between values (such as between personal convictions and organizational dictates) make decisionmaking exceedingly hard. Public employees want to do the right thing, but it is not always clear what that right thing is. This is made more difficult because of the complexity and size of modern public administration, as well as its penetration in the economy at large. Questions about how to use extensive regulatory discretion, how aggressive to be in promoting economic development through government, how extensive or competitive to make government services, and how to balance constituent interests are only a few of the issues that are not only of practical concern but of ethical concern as well.

Third, values are important in the political-judicial context. Public administration is a part of the political system in which societal values are authoritatively determined. Although there is much disagreement about the degree to which public administrators actually play a role in choosing values as expert analysts, decisionmakers, implementers, and evaluators, there is little disagreement that they do play a large and vital role in the political system.[3] Of course this role is constantly being reinterpreted and reshaped by the judicial system, as well as by the other two branches, as a part of the overall system of governance. Thus, clarity about values is necessary to play an appropriate role in the ever-changing political system. Examples of important contemporary issues here include the degree to which administrators can be programmatically responsive to constituent needs and demands without short-circuiting democratic governance, the restructuring of agencies and whole governmental systems to suit political initiatives, and the degree to which competitive or public choice models of administration should add to or replace command-and-control models.

However, managerial, ethical, and political values are not separate. Decisions must be based on a single set of values that blends all three considerations simultaneously. The challenge of public administration is to achieve a mixture of values in a workable gestalt or whole. This requires a never-ending dialectic because of legitimate competition of values and inevitable shifts in priorities. Indeed, for organizational leaders and managers there may be no more important task in today's turbulent environment than to provide the means to clarify values, support values consensus, and, ultimately, to provide systems to monitor appropriate compliance within accepted parameters.

Purpose of the Book

The single most important purpose of this book is to create *a field of public administration values,* a field that currently does not exist in a recognizable form. Surely values are discussed significantly and usefully by the fields of ethics, management, decisionmaking, and organization behavior and theory, to mention only a few. But these discussions are inevitably narrower in scope than is necessary for a true field of *values.* Such a field is needed to help bridge the seeming chasm about discussions of values among the established fields.

A second purpose of this text is to provide a comprehensive treatment of values. To undertake this comprehensive treatment, not one but three separate perspectives are fully articulated. The first looks at values analytically from the bottom up, that is, from the individual administrator's perspective. The second perspective looks at values from the top down, using a cultural framework. The third perspective looks at values from a practical and functional standpoint. I have also tried to be comprehensive by including not only all the major relevant subfields of public administration but also significant perspectives from sociology, anthropology, political science, philosophy, and business.

A third purpose of the text is to provide a balanced treatment, giving all the major schools of thought roughly the same coverage so that their values can be compared as dispassionately as possible. This is always appreciated by practitioners and students who are groping to understand the private languages and silently loaded arguments that are the natural tendency of those writing from a single perspective or for a single approach. However, since a balanced treatment of the many schools of thought is overdue at the scholarly level as well, this treatment should be useful in facilitating serious cross-perspective discussions.

A fourth purpose of the book is to make the subject accessible to and interesting for practitioners and students. This has required a number of features. I have tried to simplify the language where possible, avoiding difficult (if occasionally useful) terms such as *Anti-Federalists, praxis, neoinstitutionalism,* and others. I have also used an endnote system, a minor inconvenience for scholars but a placement generally appreciated by nonscholars. I have drawn examples from all levels of government. The emphasis on general values means that the discussions usually have more practical values than are discussed by ethicists but more rigorous analyses of values than are common in the work of management theorists and advocates. Surely the most common question practitioners ask after reading important texts in the ethics field is, What's the connection? The connection is there, of course, but the extrapolation process is often long and tedious. This work aims to suit those practitioners (many of whom populate MPA and DPA programs) with a less lengthy process of application.

A fifth but related purpose is to emphasize topical issues and debates. This in turn has meant a much fuller treatment of value changes than in the ethics literature in the past, and a more rigorous analysis of change (with regard to values) than is typical in the management literature. Thus I try to discuss and compare classical, entrepreneurial, institutionalist, and postmodern public administration approaches, even as I seek to find where common ground seems to exist among them. I do not seek to synthesize the approaches, however, for their differences are as important as their similarities, and I am not trying to offer an amalgamated approach. Fortunately for this text, the topical issues with which we must grapple today are likely to be with us for decades. For example, the values incipient in current trends, such as downsizing, detenuring, management reductions, organizational redesign, job restructuring, service provision shifts, privatization, internal competition, and so on are just beginning to heat up. No matter what practitioners or academics view as appropriate or responsible, the public and public officials are showing an ever-increasing appetite to experiment with fundamental change in both scope and depth of services offered by the public sector as well as the actual mechanisms of delivery and accountability. No matter whether we see the onslaught of major changes as inevitable trends, curses, or mixed blessings, we need to understand them in order to channel, challenge, or explore change in the most productive ways possible.

Structure of the Book

Part I and Part II both analyze the universe of public administration values from an individual administrator's perspective. Part I introduces a framework of five value sources: individual or personal values, professional values, organizational values, legal values, and public interest values. These five value sources are the same as those used in ASPA's current Code of Ethics, on which I was fortunate to work with others in the Committee on Professional Ethics.[4] The discussion should be useful for those wanting either a relatively succinct review of the field of values and ethics or an additional insight into the ASPA Code.

In Part II each of the five value sources is discussed in separate chapters. While complementing Part I, the chapters elaborate an analysis of basic assumptions even denser than that represented by the ASPA Code. The ASPA Code has 32 principles; the analysis of the five value domains reveals 17 fundamental assumptions that are largely agreed upon by all the schools at an abstract level. Each chapter in Section II begins by looking at the broad cultural assumptions in society-at-large and then using this as a springboard for the narrower analysis of the assumptions in public adminstration. Because the 17 fundamental assumptions often counterbalance one another, and therefore are in competition or a dynamic tension with one another, their "strengths" and "weaknesses" are also discussed. Because agreement about the fundamental basic assumptions breaks down as soon as any level of operationalization is attempted, the discussions reflect these beliefs about different ways to conceptualize administrative functions, which is where the schools of thought differ. The emphasis in this section is not on the schools of thought, however, but rather on the differences in the operational beliefs on an assumption-by-assumption basis.

Part III introduces the cultural framework perspective. This framework looks at values from four levels: a grand, cultural level (basic assumptions); a conceptual but more operational level (the beliefs level); a level in which basic assumptions and beliefs produce general standards of behavior (the patterns of action level); and the level at which actual individual decisions are made and behaviors are exhibited, which uses all the preceding levels as guides but which also incorporates the individual's unique interpretation and priorities as well (the individual decision-making level). Chapter 7 introduces the cultural framework and discusses the grand cultural level of basic assumptions. Chapter 8 discusses the differing beliefs about public administration in a sustained discussion of the three paradigms currently competing for dominance. Chapter 9 discusses patterns of actions as different forms of rationality. Different cultures and cultural subsystems give very different priorities to types of rationality in different situations. This chapter gives the best tools for practitioners and academics to get inside different approaches and to compare the values espoused. Chapter 10 uses the most common type of rationality in public administration as an example as it analyzes the decisionmaking that occurs in a reasoned choice model.

Part IV moves the general discussion from analytic understanding into an action mode. How do you deal with changing values, large value divergences in a single organizations, and ignorance about simple, moderate, or sophisticated values? Also, how do you ensure that the authorized and agreed-to value systems are appropriately monitored and controlled in a way that reflects both the needs of the organization and a healthy balance of mechanisms? Chapter 11 talks about how organizations can identify the "right" values, which may change over time, and then how to encourage those values as good practical and ethical behavior. Chapter 12 examines seven possible means of controlling administrative behavior, and the contemporary trends in that area. Chapter 13 reviews and concludes the book.

Audiences

The genesis of this book began many years ago as a monograph for *practitioners*. I attempted not to lose sight of this audience in the successive expansions and revisions in the text. Because of the length of the book, practitioners and those teaching classes or seminars for practitioners many simply want to be more selective in their use of parts of it. Chapter 1 and Chapters 8 through 12, as well as Figure 6.1 summarizing Part II, are likely to be of greatest interest. Throughout the text, practical issues are discussed relating to the tough decisions that organizational members and leaders are experiencing in public agencies today.

As an instructor myself, I hope this text will have unusually wide appeal for *faculty* teaching courses in issues affected by values and change. Its straightforward language and extensive use of figures and exhibits should make the text accessible to all students, even at the undergraduate level. I hope the book will be a candidate as a core text in ethics classes because it provides a comprehensive overview. However, I also hope that it will be a strong candidate as a core or auxiliary text in management, organization behavior and theory, and even introductory classes in public administration because of its important discussions about values and value changes. MPA and DPA curricula are urged to have a strong ethics component, yet this has proven difficult because most ethics treatments do not blend well in general classes, and special classes in ethics are generally electives taken by only a small portion of the total student population. This text can supplement other core classes because of its general treatment of values and its topical discussions, which are of wide appeal.

Finally, I hope that *scholars* will appreciate the contribution to the field of values and ethics because of the many gaps in the field. I have published parts of the book, as answers to questions that I was working on, in *Public Administration Review* (Chapters 1 and 11), *Public Integrity Annual* (Chapter 12), and *Public Administration Quarterly* (Chapter 4). While the framework undergirding Parts I and II is not my own, it does considerably extend this perspective, especially by offering scholars a discrete list of basic assumptions to use as a focal point for discussion (and debate) or as a research platform. Part III extends the pioneering work of Edgar Schein, Steve Ott, and others. I hope scholars will appreciate my efforts to integrate the various perspectives used in the book. The individual administrator perspective and the cultural framework are linked by a similar use of basic assumptions, although basic assumptions in Part II tend to be a bit narrower than they are in the discussion of the cultural framework because they are confined to the *culture* of public administration (not subculture as in Part III). The practical portions in Part IV are linked to the other Parts because they assume that practitioners have the skills to analyze the values framework within and outside the organization (which is provided by the earlier sections). Without these analytic skills, practitioners will be poorly prepared to take advantage of the advice given there. Yet perhaps the most important scholarly contribution is to facilitate discussion about a separate field of values.

Definition of the Subjects of This Study

One's responsibilities vary according to position, accountability mechanisms, and social expectations. This is certainly true for the elected official/appointed official/civil servant spectrum. In fact, even this spectrum is too coarse to gather even the most common distinctions. For example, elected officials vary from those with pure legislative-policy responsibilities (for example, a U.S. senator), those with executive-policy responsibilities (such as a governor), and those with executive-operational responsibilities (an elected recorder from a rural county with two staff members, for example). It goes without saying, elected officials with substantial operational responsibilities are far more similar to civil servants than are elected officials confined to policy responsibilities. Among administrators, not only are there those who are appointed and who are frequently responsible for policy considerations,[5] but there are also a number of managers who are exempt from civil service regulations. This last group, exempt managers, are generally culled from the civil service. They have the indocrination and mindset of merit employees but enhanced political responsiveness because of their "at-will" status.

This study focuses on the values of those who consider themselves public *administrators*. That certainly includes those covered by civil service systems, but to some degree it may include exempt managers, appointed officials, and even some elected officials in their administrative capacities. It does not focus on elected officials in their policy roles. This study largely applies to judicial employees and employees of legislative agencies, especially in their administrative roles.

Acknowledgments

The genesis of this book has been so long that many have contributed to my efforts, more than I can probably acknowledge here. General intellectual debts are certainly owed to John Rohr, Terry Cooper, Carol Lewis, and Bob Golembiewski. Specific intellectual debts are owed to Hal Gortner, Edgar Schein, and Steven Ott, whose work was especially important in the conceptualization of various parts of the book.

I owe great personal debts to those who encouraged me in the task, which often were daunting. Chet Newland encouraged me to expand the original monograph into a more ambitious book-length treatment on values. Joe Cayer, a long-time intellectual partner, was enormously helpful through his discussions and advice. David Rosenbloom was very supportive through his auspices as the editor for *Public Administration Review* and his encouragement of specific pieces of the manuscript. A number of people took the time to carefully review the entire text at various stages, always a time-consuming task when done properly. Some of the people who did so and offered extensive and useful critiques included Chet Newland, Carolyn Ban, Jorgen Rasmussen, Nick Henry, Stuart Gilman, Barbara Sherman, Paul Suino, Dwight Ink, and a number of anonymous reviewers who were all conscientious in their assistance. Innumerable people reviewed individual chapters at various times, offering much assistance. They include Pat Percival, Leslie Dornfeld, Michael Hawthorne, Ken Holland, Zed Lanham, Ina Wintrich, Jim Coffman, Lou Weschler, and Colin DeWitt. Bev Christenson designed the figures. I am sure that this list is incomplete since there were so many who helped. Of course I must thank the students who suffered through early versions of the chapters and who also made helpful suggestions.

Ultimately, without a good editor—one who is both rigorous and compassionate, understanding yet demanding—an author is in great jeopardy. I have been privileged to have a great editor, David Estrin, who has worked with me quietly and insistently for several years as this book was expanded and reshaped.

Notes

1. Thomas J. Peters and Robert H. Waterman, Jr., *In Search of Excellence: Lessons from America's Best-Run Companies* (New York: Warner Books, [1982]/1984), p. 280.

2. Evan Berman and Jonathan West, "Values Management in Local Government: A Survey of Progress and Future Directions," paper delivered at the National Conference of the American Society for Public Administration, San Francisco, June 1993.

3. David Rosenbloom and Bernard H. Ross, "Administrative Theory, Political Power, and Government Reform," in Patricia Ingraham and Barbara S. Romzek, eds., *New Paradigms for Government* (San Francisco: Jossey Bass, 1994), pp. 145–168.

4. The subcommittee that did the bulk of the work was composed of April Hejka-Ekins, Gail Topolinsky, and Jack Goldsmith. Some of the others in the committee who were particularly active in the efforts at reforming the Code were Stuart Gilman, Don Menzel, Willa Bruce, Mylon Winn, Robert Kweit, Fran Burke, and Howard Balanoff.

5. I omit the small class of appointed officials who support other appointed officials as personal staff.

Values Endorsed in Public Administration

Part I briefly examines the domains of values competing for an individual administrator's attention. Depending upon the circumstances, the administrator may have to look carefully at the following questions:

- What is the legal thing to do?
- What is best for the organization?
- What is best for the public at large?
- What best meets professional standards?
- What is an appropriate role for me to play and to what extent should my interests influence the decisionmaking process?

Answers to these questions require value assessments, which always have practical concern. That is, even when there is no question of impropriety or moral judgments, decisions are based on values that should be understood and explainable. If the administrator is trying to meet minimum standards or to improve performance and standards, answers to the above questions may also encompass ethical concerns. Whether ethical issues are simple or complex, it is imperative that the values be ascertained clearly.

The following chapter presents a framework for understanding the values inherent in both practical *and* ethical decisions.

CHAPTER 1

The Five Value Sources Used in Decisionmaking in the Public Sector*

Individuals facing difficult decisions and trying both to do the right thing and to avoid doing the wrong thing must generally consider a number of factors, ranging from society's mandates to personal convictions. If those individuals work in the public sector they may feel the pinch of competing values even more acutely than others do, for several reasons:

1. They have implicitly (and sometimes explicitly) sworn to higher ethical standards of commitment to the nation and their organizations.
2. Decisions and actions may have more complex countervailing values to consider.
3. Their personal standards may be more keenly honed because of their strong civic commitments, while their personal needs may be among the least considered in the family of professional organizations because of an ethic of subordination of personal benefit to the public good.

In making decisions, individuals must consider their own standards and needs, the principles of their professional disciplines, the precepts of their specific organizations, and the dictates of the law, all the while trying to accomplish what is in the overall public good. Juggling these differing sets of interests is only made more difficult by the fact that none of them is constant over time. Even the most basic assumptions of public administrators are being subtly redefined and reinterpreted, just as new constitutional amendments subtly redefine society and Supreme Court decisions reinterpret old ways of behaving. In this current era of great value shifts, the decisions public administrators must make are not only more profound but also more open to debate and disagreement. Given this context, a clear understanding of the underlying values of those decisions and actions is both essential and reflected in some of the typical questions administrators ask today, including these: What are the underlying values implicit in a new organizational structure? To what degree should personal concerns for career and security play a role in agency downsizing? How best should a new, more austere social policy be implemented? This book aims to assist in the analysis and explanation of the many decisions that administrators make, and one of its major premises is that *it is the responsibility of administrators not only to be able to understand the values implicit in their important decisions, but to be able to articulate those values clearly for others in the organization—especially subordinates, clients, and legitimate overseers outside of the organization.*

This chapter examines decisionmaking from an individual's perspective. It begins with an overview of the various—and sometimes competing—taxonomies of decisionmaking sources that have been described in the literature, and the derivation and rationale for the one underlying the discussion in this text. It also discusses some of the major considerations in using each source and provides some examples. (A full chapter is dedicated to each source in Part II.) The five sources (and their constituent basic assumptions) that guide administrative behavior are as old as the Republic, but, as is typical of each new era in any evolving society, these sources can and are undergoing significant reinterpretation, leading to new emphases within and among them.

The aim here is not only to examine the decisionmaking affecting ethical problems and conundrums, but to extend that examination to *all* decisionmaking—both traditional and more explicitly ethical—by public administrators.[1]

Problems in Identifying Sources of Decisionmaking

Which Are the Key Sources or Value Sets?

There is widespread agreement that administrators have numerous *value sets,* or roles, which are sources for the decisions they make. An administrator may, for example, concentrate quite appropriately on legal issues at one point, organizational issues at another, and personal interests at still another. This agreement quickly dissipates when one tries to identify and name the specific sources or value sets that are crucial for public administrators.

Researchers have divided an administrator's major value sets in many ways. Some specialize in a single area, even though their views are broad, as John Rohr did in concentrating on regime values (law and legal tradition) and George Frederickson did in giving attention to social equity (public interest).[2] Many researchers have consciously divided the sources to cover all the major decisionmaking bases. Both Darrell Pugh and April Hejka-Ekins divided legitimate sources into bureaucratic ethos and democratic ethos.[3] Barry Posner and Warren Schmidt compared the rugged-individualism ethic to the community and cooperation ethic.[4] Some have defined three critical value sets, as Patrick Dobel did in identifying regime accountability, personal responsibility, and prudence as the keys to the ethical decisionmaking mix; Kathryn Denhardt similarly distinguished honor, benevolence, and justice as the three "moral foundations."[5] Terry Cooper classified four sources—individual attributes, organization structure, organization culture, and societal expectations.[6] Donald Warwick's four sources were public interest, constituency interests, bureaucratic interest, and personal interest.[7] Carol Lewis, Stephen Bonczek, and Harold Gortner each detailed five sources; Gortner's is a particularly thorough analysis of role classification.[8] Depending on the narrowness of the values and the degree to which they are allowed to overlap, other researchers have catalogued more numerous sources; for example, Jonathan West, Evan Berman, and Anita Cava identified 11 popular ethics roles, and Dwight Waldo found a dozen.[9]

The fluidity of administrative value sets can encompass all these classifications, so the acid test for an analysis may be the purpose to which it is applied. ASPA's Professional Ethics Committee and its subcommittee that redrafted the Code of Ethics selected five role sources as the organizing basis for the 32 principles used in ASPA's Code.[10] Those five are likewise used here: They are *personal values, professional values, organizational values, legal values,* and *public interest values.* Five is a number that allows for adequate differentiation of sources without undue overlap. A discussion of each of these sources, however, would be premature without first considering some of the problems related to clear and consistent definition of roles or sources.

The Problem of Source Definition

Source definition (or role definition) varies significantly in light of the decisionmaking context, a phenomenon Rohr calls *role morality:* "The limited (or particularistic) character of role morality immediately challenges the universal quality of most moral propositions."[11] In other words, all roles or value sets, even legalistic ones, lose much of their universal appeal when applied to the details of specific cases. This is clear in a classic example: Killing someone is considered immoral in the eyes of the law, but it is sanctioned in a variety of exceptional circumstances, such as war-time combat, self-defense, and the state's execution of prisoners. Two even more controversial possible exceptions to the universal rule are abortion, which is partially legally sanctioned, and euthanasia, which is not currently legally sanctioned. Moreover, the specific details of cases rarely enable "clean" decisions, even when a general rule has been established. For example, when is withdrawing a patient from life-support systems mercy killing? When is doing so restoring the natural condition?

A second issue for source or role definition is that the values in roles (value sets) change during the lives or evolution of individuals, organizations, countries, and civilizations. The foremost value-researcher, Milton Rokeach, commented,

> If values were completely stable, individual and social change would be impossible. If values were completely unstable, continuity of human personality and society would be impossible. Any conception of human values, if it is to be fruitful, must be able to account for the enduring character of values as well as for their changing character.[12]

Public administration has undergone value changes associated with Federalists, Jacksonians, civil-service reformers and Progressives, New Dealers, and the Civil Rights and Great Society movements of the 1960s.[13] Such changes clearly represent a great challenge to public administration because "'reinventing government' involves a profound commitment to new ideas, values, and roles."[14] Thus, while each source has been an important value set since the beginning of the republic, the way these sources have been defined has varied significantly with successive eras. The current sea shift of values (at the beliefs level) will subtly but profoundly alter not only the definition of, say, legal values (changing the values in the value set), but also the emphasis placed on one source in comparison to other sources. How, then, can administrators choose among competing sources when making decisions?

Which Source Takes Precedence When Sources Compete?

The problems of source identification and source definition may be largely intellectual, but when legitimate sources compete, the challenge of decisionmaking for practitioners becomes acute. At a minimum, competing sources mean tough decisions; they may also provide fertile ground for ethical predicaments. Empirical studies indicate that "management's toughest dilemmas occur in trying to strike a balance between competing objectives."[15]

To use a prosaic example, it is clear to government employees that government vehicles are for official use only. If employees are traveling on government business for several weeks, do personal needs, such as traveling to a restaurant or dry cleaner, then become "official"? If not, is the employee expected to absorb the cost of renting a taxi or using a hotel laundry service? Or is the employee expected to use discretion in considering critical personal needs to be official because of their full-time service function while away from home? This is a dilemma for management because even government employees who do not want to give the appearance of impropriety may be upset when expected to go to what they may consider to be unnecessary lengths.

For different reasons, neither popular perceptions nor agency training generally recognizes the complexity of decisionmaking in the public sector, with its competing mandates, missions, customers, and stakeholders. Popular perception often conceives of the public sector as rife with the graft associated with $300 hammers and with brazenly lazy and obstructive employees. Such perceptions are wildly inaccurate and lead to misdiagnosis of other problems, such as bureaucratic pathologies, poor policymaking by politicians, and unrealistic public expectations.

In the case of agency training, a simplistic do-not approach is often used because of time and resource constraints. Agency ethics classes often focus on ethics legislation or the "do nots" such as: conflict of interest, competitive bidding, discrimination, nepotism, political activity by employees, open meeting laws, disclosure and public record laws, whistleblowing statutes, proper use of facilities and equipment, and gifts and favors. Such classes offer critical help in assisting employees to avoid ignorant or unmindful wrongdoing. However, they often succumb to time pressures and offer no assistance with pursuing "right-doing," a perspective critical to both high integrity and performance. Unlike the narrower perspective of a short ethics-training class, professional codes of ethics are generally broader, addressing not only broad prohibitions but also the aspirational aspects of right behavior. What professional codes of ethics may lack in technical details they can counterbalance with a richer context. Yet, like any other tool for good decisionmaking, a code of ethics has little effect if it is not: (1) realistic and coherent; (2) encouraged through training, education, and the organizational culture, and (3) monitored and supported through sanctions as well as rewards.[16]

In sum, the values used in decisionmaking in the public sector can be very complex. Defining clear-cut prohibitions that are largely limited to legal values is useful for neophytes, but it is only a first cut at the problem. Entangled within complex problems and issues are five major sources of values. Comprehending them better prepares an individual for the complex decisionmaking administrators face daily.

The Five Major Sources of Values

Five major sources influence administrators' decisionmaking for both the prohibitions and aspirations of the public sector: inidvidual, professional, organizational, legal, and public interest values. Each is discussed here in a separate section, and at the conclusion of each section, the relevant portion of ASPA's Code of Ethics provides a concrete example.

Individual Values

To paraphrase Alexander Hamilton, good government needs honest people who are encouraged to remain honest.[17] More recently, Terry Cooper and others have reinvigorated the discussion of virtue as a motivating factor for public administrators.[18] Without individuals with integrity, government agencies fall prey to a variety of problems. But how is this integrity to be exercised when there are competing values? Or more specifically, when and to what degree should personal interests and values play a role in difficult decisions?

Integrity has been defined as "the state of being complete; unbroken condition; wholeness."[19] People with integrity generally have lives that are complete and that are characterized by harmony within the various aspects of their lives and among their beliefs and actions. Such people practice what they preach, and are unlikely to change what they believe and do for temporary convenience. Integrity for public servants brings an unusually weighty responsibility, then, because acceptance of public employment implies active acceptance of the civic principles that society generally endorses. Public administrators are expected to have "civic integrity," which means an appreciation of the Constitution and the laws of the land and a respect for the political-legal system. Without honor for the general system of authoritative decisionmaking and an appreciation for its underlying legitimacy, public officials could view the laws as nuisances to be overlooked or skirted when no one is paying attention. Ironically, occasionally political bureaucrats and civil servants disregard the law because they think it is inefficient or ineffective in accomplishing the public good. Civic integrity requires working through the law and the "system" to make necessary changes in the law if it is ineffectual. Only the most extreme and rare cases would admit violating one civic principle (such as technical compliance with the law) for another principle (such as safety, when technical compliance might lead to an unanticipated death).

Generally, civic integrity also includes universally held cultural values as well:

- *Honesty*—If people are not honest, no possibility of valid communication exists and all other values remain a mystery to be discovered by observation.[20] In nearly every study on the topic of U.S. values, *honesty* is at the top of the list, even before competence.

- *Consistency*—A reasoned attempt to act from principle rather than from whim; as used here, the term does not mean unchanging or rigid.

- *Coherence*—A reasoned attempt to connect principles to examples of those principles and to make them as harmonious as possible.

- *Reciprocity*—A reasoned attempt to act toward others as you would have them act toward you under similar conditions.

When these four values are in place, a high-trust culture is established, which characterizes both high-performing teams and organizations.[21]

The ramification of this reasoning, then, is that not only is dishonesty unethical, but so too are inconsistency, incoherence, and nonreciprocal behavior. This is a rigorous test and is akin to principle-centered decisionmaking, the level of ethical consciousness ranked highest by psychologist and ethicist Lawrence Kohlberg.[22] (Kohlberg's theory of moral development is explored more fully in Chapter 2.) Administrators who base decisions on principles exercise the most powerful form of control, because their control comes from within.[23]

Public servants are not public slaves; they have the rights belonging to all citizens in a democratic state. They have the right *to strive for* adequate income, job stability, and job advancement. Public employees cannot be expected simply to forego interest in their own needs. However, the way they exercise their rights is key to this discussion. On one hand, it is generally true that good pay, low job turnover, and job advancement possibilities produce the conditions for an excellent organization to exist. On the other hand, it is equally true that many public sector organizations have unfunded mandates, unpleasant working conditions causing high turnover, and few job advancement possibilities.

To cite just one example, what actions can a public employee take when faced with pay well below the market average? The employee can quit, ask for a raise, engage in union negotiating, and pursue raises through the political system, although doing so must be highly restrained because of various "Hatch Acts." Is it ethical, however, (if not legally prohibited) to engage in a strike, a work slowdown, a reduction of hours worked (but not hours paid), or a refusal to accept customary assignments to force the issue or "make the organization pay" in informal ways? A purist might argue that employment in the public sector is a privilege, not a right, so the only right the employee ultimately has is to quit. But when do employees suffering substantial and widespread inequities have the right to do more? The question becomes increasingly pertinent as ever larger numbers of public sector employees qualify for food stamp assistance and are being moved to a less secure status.

Another difficult question for public administrators is personal conviction. Unless we want a government of yes-people, we must allow a range of statements and actions based on personal belief. The Nuremberg trials established the precedent of private conviction over public weal in extraordinary cases. Americans should not be so naive as to believe that their government has never committed atrocities (although one can hope they are seldom and on a much smaller scale).[24] Thus the range of values to examine here extends from freedom of speech and personal convictions of human dignity at one extreme, to civil disobedience at the other.

In speaking out for the right to voice personal convictions, Elliott Richardson said, "Integrity requires of you the consistent pursuit of the merits, your willingness to speak up, to argue, to question, and to critique is as essential to determination of the merits as the readiness to invite ideas, encourage debate, and accept criticism."[25] Although he was talking about the policy level, his sentiments apply equally to organizational issues at the supervisory level. Hopefully most conflicts between personal convictions and organizational directives can be worked out through improvements, consensus building, and compromise. When they cannot, the individual may elect to pursue higher levels of dissent. Dennis Thompson identifies four such levels:

1. Protest and possibly a request for reassignment
2. Carrying the protest outside the organization while otherwise performing duties
3. Open obstruction to the policy
4. Covert obstruction, such as leaks to the press[26]

Dissent, especially at higher levels identified by Thompson, should not be taken lightly. Both the organization and the individual will probably pay some price for the conflict of values. In the case of the individual, it may be loss of either job or reputation—possibly both.

A final aspect of individual values is the importance of appearances in government work. Not only is rectitude important, but the appearance of rectitude is also essential if government work is to be carried out effectively.[27] This criterion establishes a higher standard not only for conduct but also for consensus and communication, than that which is uniformly found outside public administration.[28] Politicians have been involved in so many scandals in the last quarter of a century that, through guilt by association, public opinion has deteriorated dangerously for public administrators as well.[29]

While appearances are important because of the confidence they instill and the pride they promote, an overemphasis on appearances can sap energy applied to problems, lead to undue attention to "show," and promote a climate of secrecy or cover-up. President Richard Nixon, for example, was forced to resign not for the misdeed of the Watergate break-in but for the subsequent cover-up, which was an abortive attempt to protect appearances.

The ASPA Code of Ethics Section III is titled Demonstrate Personal Integrity. It urges members to "demonstrate the highest standards in all activities to inspire public confidence and trust in public service." Its guidelines urge members to

1. maintain truthfulness and honesty and to not compromise them for advancement, honor, or personal gain.
2. ensure that others receive credit for their work and contributions.
3. zealously guard against conflict of interest or its appearance: [for example] nepotism, improper outside employment, misuse of public resources, or the acceptance of gifts.
4. respect superiors, subordinates, colleagues, and the public.
5. take responsibility for their own errors.
6. conduct official acts without partisanship.

Professional Values

Professional values are a subtle but important source for administrative decisionmaking. No single definition exists for a profession but one researcher suggests six characteristics:[30]

- A cast of mind or self-awareness
- A corpus of theory and knowledge
- A social ideal
- A formal organization to promote its interests
- A national academy to revere and celebrate its leading practitioners
- Ethical standards

The most "successful" professions (such as medicine and law) tend to be those that have a narrow enough scope to enhance identity but a broad enough range to help define legal standards for admission to the field. Yet characteristics of professions are seen in an increasing number of occupations from intellectual to manual. The challenge for the public sector, with its 19 million employees, is diversity of disciplinary interests. Thus while there are numerous "professionals" within the public sector, the public sector can be considered a profession itself only by using the flimsiest standards.

Professionalism has characteristics that are attractive to public sector organizations. Professionals tend to have clear and extremely specific ideas about required education and training, and tend to push for higher levels of education as the profession matures. High expectations for the comprehension of the theory, knowledge, and skills considered state-of-the-art in the field become preliminary standards for entry into the field. High expectations for continuing education may be mandatory. This in turn leads the profession to promote higher standards in general and sophisticated skills leading to independent decisionmaking. James Stever, among others, sees professionalism as the best means for inculcating similar, appropriate, and high ethical standards.[31] However, the heterogeneity of the public sector provides a vigorous challenge, either for the individual professions or for the entire public sector as a profession, to perform to the high standards that have been suggested.

The values of the professions are not without their critics or problems, even if one were able to assume a uniform identity in the public sector (which as noted earlier is nonexistent). The two most relevant problems are unrealistic standards and self-serving tendencies. Professions can become so set upon high standards of education, admission to the field, and practice that they come to have little sympathy for the practical realities facing public sector organizations. For example, the practice of medicine is restricted to so few with such expensive training that people with limited incomes are denied access to the profession, and public sector medical budgets have swollen disproportionately. In practical terms, when relatively high medical standards cannot be achieved, medical treatment is frequently barred altogether. A constellation of factors contributes to the enforcement of high-end standards, but it remains true that professions often devote little energy to practical nonelitist standards.

A second problem of the professions is their similarity to interest groups, with their self-interested behaviors. Professionals, like any interest group, can come to consider high standards of pay, support, or deference their due. They may stifle policy discussion because their self-interested political influence quashes any ideas that do not advance their interests. In such cases, professions argue that they must compete for resources in a market-oriented, pluralistic society. This argument, however, is nearly opposite that used by the professions when they declare themselves the standardbearers of values and ethics because of their civic virtue.[32]

The ASPA Code of Ethics Section V, Strive for Professional Excellence, states that members should "strengthen individual capacities and encourage the professional development of others"; its guidelines urge members to

1. provide support and encouragement to upgrade competence.

2. accept as a personal duty the responsibility to keep up to date on emerging issues and potential problems.

3. encourage others, throughout their careers, to participate in professional activities and associations.

4. allocate time to meet with students and provide a bridge between classroom studies and the realities of public service.

Organizational Values

The placement of organizational interests as the third source for administrative decisionmaking and discretion is not meant to minimize their role in decisionmaking. Gortner, in fact, suggests that they might be the second most heavily used value set.[33] Similarly, Cooper identifies two of four factors inducing responsible conduct as organizationally related—organizational structure and organizational culture. The focus here, however, is whether and how organizational interests should play a role when there is a conflict with other appropriate value sets such as the law, personal integrity, or the public interest.

Organizational Health

The need for a dynamic and healthy organization is a primary consideration. To what extent should the organization be viewed as a valuable tool in implementing the public good? If the organization itself is badly treated, it will probably be a less effective tool for public policy execution. For example, what weight should be given to employee interests when they conflict with other appropriate values? In many agencies, corrections and social service directors fight with legislative bodies to put new funds into increased salaries rather than into new facilities or expanded mandates. Is the reputation of the agency itself ever a valid consideration? If not, then perhaps public agencies should publish their mistakes as well as their successes? Yet it is a truism that agencies that lack a good reputation have a hard time recruiting highly qualified personnel and just as hard a time in retaining them.

The importance of maintaining a proper balance between organizational values and other value sets is probably best illustrated by the extreme case that occurs when organizational values overwhelm all others. This condition, often called *bureaupathology,* characterizes totalitarian states that come to exist for the purpose of the administrative system rather than to serve the people. Such extreme cases rarely occur in the

American system, but more subtle forms of bureaupathology are not so rare, as when the convenience of the organization's members outweighs the convenience of the public it serves. Gerald Caiden, a prominent researcher in this area, noted that when bureaupathologies grip systems, the problems caused "are not the individual failings of individuals who compose organizations but the systematic shortcomings of organizations that cause individuals within them to be guilty of malpractices."[34] Further, Peter Drucker has argued that, if allowed too free a rein in balancing its interests against other interests, any organization will usually rationalize that the protection of the organization is for the public good and that organizational interests are coterminous with the public good.[35]

Organizational Design

Many organizational values are embedded in the organizational design. At the macro level, organizations have values relating to how the organization is supposed to interact with the environment. Should it, for example, use regulation or market incentives in interacting with the public?

The structure of the organization expresses another set of values, the design values. For instance, jobs may be designed around as few functions as possible to keep them simple; wages for such jobs are probably inexpensive and employees are easily replaceable or perhaps jobs are made multidimensional (with correspondingly more expensive wages and less easily replaceable professional employees). Values about work are also incorporated in the organizational design. Is work organized around fixing current "problems," or is the structure proactive, anticipating future possibilities and encouraging an entrepreneurial spirit? Finally, the organizational design will reflect many values about employees: Are they seen primarily as an expense or as an asset? Design values tend to cluster into organizational types. If an organization uses market incentives more than regulation and if it relies primarily on professionals as its front-line production operators, then it probably will tend to emphasize forward-looking behaviors (because the professionals will be competent themselves to do so) and to view those behaviors as an important asset. Chapter 4 discusses organizational design models in depth, but two aspects of organizational design—productivity and expertise—are relevant here.

Productivity values such as efficiency and effectiveness are highly regarded in the public sector, as they are in the private. Organizations exist to produce services or goods and government organizations are no exception, even if the service is sometimes indirect, as in the case of regulation or national defense. Unlike the private sector, however, the public sector does not generally consider efficiency and effectiveness cardinal values.

The high value placed on due process in the American system of governance, for example, is embodied in the extensive and overlapping appeals processes that generally characterize the public sector as a safeguard against the power of administrative decisionmaking. Robert Denhardt, noting that efficiency is but one of a number of values to consider, stated, "Organizations and their members must not be moral only when it is efficient to do so, they must be efficient only where it is moral to do so."[36] Efficiency wins in the competition against other values when, for example, an intake worker overburdened by organizational rules and workload assignments encounters a family with solvable problems but is unable to devote the extensive time that would be needed for an effective intervention.

Expertise, the second aspect of organizational design considered here, tends to bestow additional discretion, especially at a technical level. Thus, issues such as bridge safety, public health protection, and military security tend to be left to the experts. Expertise can bring much insight to decisionmaking, especially with regard to options, cost-benefit, and likely impact on the future. Therefore, because public sector "experts" often select the options to choose from, conduct the cost-benefit analysis, and estimate future effects, they have significant power. When delegated decisionmaking is added (such as responsibility for alternative selections), these people are extremely powerful. Because all decisions, even technical ones, have implicit values, the matter of expert power is no small consideration in the discussion of values or ethics. Technical experts can easily fall into the "we-know-best" trap in which customer or client interests are relegated to a childlike status.

Total Quality Management (TQM) and the management revolution of which it is a part are not only radically redefining the role of the manager, they are changing the role of the expert as well. This is probably one of the areas of greatest value shift currently under way in both the private and public sectors. As organizations attempt to understand who their customers are, they are carefully questioning them about their preferences. Many are discovering that their organization's assumptions are outdated and their customers are more discriminating than they had realized. Thus the role of expertise in decisionmaking is a challenging one. The challenge is to ensure that organizations have expertise and are informed by it while also ensuring that experts do not exercise undue power.

Leadership Style

A final important set of organizational values is embedded in leadership style, which has many possible manifestations. Does the leadership style lean toward the use of hierarchy or teams? Do leaders consider the driving force in the organization to be tradition, money, inspiration, or participation? Is operational decisionmaking considered optimal when it is by command, mutual agreement, or consensus? (Chapter 4 identifies common value clusters that show a great range of values in this particular area.)

In sum, organizational interests are a major aspect of the cultural framework of public administration and a potent factor influencing practical decisionmaking. Organizational values include a vast array of factors from organizational health to organizational design to leadership styles. There is always a threat of organizational factors overwhelming other interests, especially the public interest values and individual values. However, excessive constraints (which are thought to have made so many public organizations rigid, highly bureaucratic, inflexible, and uncreative in recent decades) have led to a powerful management revolt, as witnessed by the reinvention, TQM, and reengineering movements.

The ASPA Code of Ethics, Section IV, Promote Ethical Organizations, encourages members to "strengthen organizational capabilities to apply ethics, efficiency, and effectiveness in serving the public"; its guidelines urge members to

1. enhance organizational capacity for open communication, creativity, and dedication.

2. subordinate institutional loyalties to the public good.

3. establish procedures that promote ethical behavior and hold individuals and organizations accountable for their conduct.

4. provide organization members with an administrative means for dissent, assurance of due process, and safeguards against reprisal.

5. promote merit principles that protect against arbitrary and capricious actions.

6. promote organizational accountability through appropriate controls and procedures.

7. encourage organizations to adopt, distribute, and periodically review a code of ethics as a living document.

Legal Values

Legal values can be broadly defined as the Constitution; the federal, state, and local laws; the rules and regulations that articulate the laws; judicial rulings interpreting laws; and the ethic that celebrates the United States as a nation of laws and holds due process as a basic human, as well as political, value. The great respect afforded the law and due process in U.S. society is equally evident in the academic literature and in practitioner views. The law is a symbol of politically agreed-upon values, which has special significance for those who have dedicated themselves to defining, upholding, and implementing the laws through public service. So strong is the respect for the law and due process that even an entrepreneurial and cost-cutting advocate such as Tom Peters warns against excessive streamlining of legal proceduralism because of the delicately balanced public trust that administrators must protect. He notes, "I'm all for an elite corps running government, local or federal, as long as it's *my* elite corps . . . [but] since I can't ensure that my elite corps will always hold sway, inefficiency (from excessive red tape) as an alternative begins to sound like an acceptable price to pay."[37]

Discussions about legal interests as a source of ethical decision-making for administrators sometimes unfortunately exaggerate the positions to sound as though legal interests are the only truly legitimate source for those who have sworn an oath to uphold the Constitution. In contrast, others say legal interests are a legal baseline, and have little to do with ethics, which deals on a much higher, and more idealistic plane. Despite overstatement, each position is largely true, and administrators must balance the two conceptions simultaneously.

Common sense and empirical studies[38] have demonstrated that the law and due process are never far from an administrator's central thoughts when ethical dilemmas occur. The law is often the central point of the dilemma. An extreme example is the predicament of an appointed administrator who has to execute a law that will abridge "rightful" benefits for a poorly organized group. Another is the dilemma of a supervisor ordered to perform an act of highly questionable legality by a powerful superior who, if opposed, may fire the supervisor. At a minimum, the law, regulations to support laws, and due process constitute a baseline for other competing values. However, in many cases legal interests play little or no role because the law is either silent or does not address the values competing in the specific situation.

It is almost axiomatic, then, that in cases of little discretion, the law and its appurtenances loom large; in situations with much administrator discretion, the law becomes secondary. Total administrative discretion is zealously guarded against, and complete lack of discretion is almost impossible to construct, so the law and due process are generally among, although not always the foremost, competing values in the decisionmaking problems and ethical conundrums that administrators at all levels experience.

Despite legal interest being a pivotal value source, many respected commentators warn against legalism—the unreasonable and excessive reliance on the law. For example, in discussing legal controls on the bureaucracy, Joel Fleishman, Lance Liebman, and Mark Moore note, "We can only set procedures in response to perceived failings; and we are certainly not equipped to reappraise with evidence the mechanisms we invent to combat abuse."[39] An increasingly common protest is that legalism reduces productivity and innovation because "existing procedures are frequently punitive toward productive innovators."[40]

In one of the best overall critiques of legalism, Dobel cites five limitations of what he calls the legal-institutional model:[41]

1. It promotes timid, reactive, and rule-bound public officials.
2. It undermines initiative and dissent.
3. It invites an excessive narrowing of concern or legalism.
4. It ignores the inescapable discretion that public officials must exercise.
5. It overrepresents the interest of wealthy and well-organized groups.

To illustrate Dobel's critique, an eminent administrator, Elliott Richardson, reported,

> In recent years the federal government has placed increasing reliance on specific laws, regulations, and rules to guide the behavior of its officers and employees . . . Their primary purpose, however, is not to promote high ethical standards, but to dispel the suspicion of unethical behavior. Moreover, some current restrictions go too far.[42]

The ASPA Code of Ethics, Section III, Respect the Constitution and the Law, enjoins members to "respect, support, and study government constitutions and laws that define responsibilities of public agencies, employees, and all citizens"; guidelines urge members to

1. understand and apply legislation and regulations relevant to their professional role.
2. work to improve and change laws and policies that are counterproductive or obsolete.
3. eliminate unlawful discrimination.
4. prevent all forms of mismanagement of public funds by establishing and maintaining strong fiscal and management controls, and by supporting audits and investigative activities.
5. respect and protect all privileged information.
6. encourage and facilitate legitimate dissent activities in government and protect the whistleblowing rights of public employees.
7. promote constitutional principles of equality, fairness, representativeness, responsiveness, and due process in protecting citizens' rights.

Public Interest Values

The public interest is a value set of much fervor for many who work in the public service. It goes far beyond mere compliance to the politically determined will (which is often vague, conflicting, or silent). For most public administrators, "the common good is, so to speak, their specialty."[43] Empirical studies have also indicated that public sector managers "agree that fairness, justice, and equity are more important than in business."[44] Unfortunately, although there is a great deal of agreement that public interest values are of special importance to public administrators, there is an unusual amount of disagreement about just what the public interest is.

Theoretical Definitions and Their Implications

Some analysts seem to define the public interest as the long-term values of the society. Some of these broad values would include democracy; the individual pursuit of happiness; capitalism; commercial rather than state ownership, except for special cases; division of church and state; and protection from harm with the least government intervention possible. The public sector becomes the *custodian of society's values* in this perspective. If this perspective is modestly interpreted, public administrators should be sensitive to and careful of society's values. If this perspective is aggressively pursued, public administration becomes quite statist.

A second definition of the public interest focuses on individual citizens. It comes from the long, Western, individualist tradition that fostered the American Bill of Rights. This perspective's focus on individuals fosters a concern for "tyrannical" majorities, unanticipated harm to individuals, and active inclusiveness of all of society. Defined this way, public administrators become *protectors of the rights of individuals* who are or have been unfairly treated.

A third perspective defines the public interest as the public's right to be a part of government, not only in the electoral process but also through administrative processes. In this role, public administrators become *stewards of the public's government* by keeping them informed and involved.

Those who interpret the public interest as promoting society's values sometimes express concern that the public interest will be used as a source of administrative discretion. As Rohr notes cautiously, "He who defines the *public interest* surely governs."[45] To Rohr, when a public administrator makes the point that the public interest is a basis of decisionmaking (discretion), that administrator is then making a claim to govern. This concern is frequently voiced by politicians and political scientists. That point of democratic theory is illustrated clearly by two perspectives of city managers. Richard Box recounts the story of a city manager in Savannah, Georgia, who stated that a manager may "advise on policy matters and recommend policy actions, but must not forget that his constituents are council members and not the public."[46] That city manager's view starkly contrasts to that of Michael Cody and Richardson Lynn, who argue that officials (appointed and merit) owe first allegiance to all citizens rather than to elected officials.[47] Because of major shifts in values at all levels of American society, this is an area of important popular and academic debate (see Chapter 9).

Practical Definitions and Their Application

Public interest is also difficult to define at the practical level when it is most frequently interpreted as promoting fairness to individual citizens or citizen groups. This perspective became especially popular during the period of the New Public Administration during the late 1960s.[48] At least two conceptualizations seem to exist. One defines public interest primarily in terms of social equity and justice.[49] The social-equity definition of public interest seems to further divide into an external focus and an internal focus. The external focus concentrates on those less fortunate, those less powerful, those deserving of compassion, and those in urgent need. Sometimes such an external focus is termed benevolence. The internal focus concentrates on those in the organization or those who conceivably have a right to be in the organization. Nicholas Henry gives a well-known example of giving minority groups hiring preference because of past obstacles and current employment imbalances.[50] Willa Bruce notes the current interest in this focus as represented by work force diversity, organizational democracy, and empowerment.[51]

Another definition of public interest relates to the concept of disinterest. Disinterest appeals to an important sense of impartiality as opposed to self-interest. Disinterest is necessary to combat individual self-interest, but the logic applies equally well to organizational self-interest, which is often as pervasive and much more powerful. The logic even applies to political self-interest in which disinterest is a counterbalance to the overweening power of self-absorbed political masters, aggressive majorities, and powerful interest groups.[52] Nonetheless, the idea of disinterest is closer to the neutrality of the traditional politics-administration dichotomy than it is to the notion of protector that is often advanced by advocates of social equity.

Finally, there is the concern for the public's ability to understand, use, and be involved with the administration that is a part of its government. Public interest in this perspective encourages open administration and constant communication with the public, as in the use of public newsletters and newspaper pages on government issues. It takes the task of assisting the public with its own administration aggressively, assuming that the public may not be aware of its own needs or may be poorly suited to use (or defend itself from) a sophisticated and technocratic set of institutions. This perspective encourages the use of ombudspersons and similar measures, and it promotes involvement of the public in administration when possible, as in the use of citizen advisory boards and public forums.

Even when the argument about the merits of public interest as a value source is settled affirmatively, the issue ultimately shifts—as it does with all other competing sources of administrative decisionmaking—to the situations in which the source applies, the degree to which it applies, and the practical aspects of placing the values represented.

The ASPA Code of Ethics, Section I, Serve the Public Interest, counsels members that in public sector employment, it is honorable to "serve the public, beyond serving oneself"; its guidelines urge members to

1. exercise discretionary authority to promote the public interest.
2. oppose all forms of discrimination and harassment, and promote affirmative action.
3. recognize and support the public's right to know the public's business.
4. involve citizens in policy decisionmaking.
5. exercise compassion, benevolence, fairness, and optimism.
6. respond to the public in ways that are complete, clear, and easy to understand.
7. assist citizens in their dealings with government.
8. be prepared to make decisions that may not be popular.

The complete text of ASPA's current Code of Ethics follows. Its 32 principles form five value clusters or sources. Part II of this book will use the same five sources but condenses the 32 principles into 17.[53]

Conclusion

Most people would acknowledge that extremely few administrators *will-fully* break the law, violate public interests, damage their organization, transgress professional norms, or wantonly superimpose personal interests such as greed. As Gary Brumback has noted, "Government scandals notwithstanding, corruption is not the primary problem."[54] When egregiously unethical behavior does occur, as when public officials abscond with public money, such behavior is easy to label unethical. Much more challenging and relevant to most administrators are the situations in which they must discharge a vague law, balance rival public interest groups, sort out the appropriate organizational interests from organizational ego, consider a higher but costly professional standard, and not overstate or abandon personal interests. For the most part, the really tough administrative decisions are those involving two or more legitimate value sources competing for consideration. Administrative "moral choice involves the competing pulls of routine and reason, obedience and initiative, narrow interest and the public interest,"[55] so no single formula or set of rules automatically takes precedence. When various sources compete, administrators' decisions cannot be determined to be appropriate and ethical simply based on the content of their final actions. Rather,

American Society for Public Administration

Code of Ethics

The American Society for Public Administration (ASPA) exists to advance the science, processes, and art of public administration. The Society affirms its responsibility to develop the spirit of professionalism within its membership, and to increase public awareness of ethical principles in public service by its example. To this end, we, the members of the Society commit ourselves to the following principles:

I Serve the Public Interest

Serve the public, beyond serving oneself.
ASPA members are committed to:

1. Exercise discretionary authority to promote the public interest.
2. Oppose all forms of discrimination and harassment, and promote affirmative action.
3. Recognize and support the public's right to know the public's business.
4. Involve citizens in policy decision-making.
5. Exercise compassion, benevolence, fairness and optimism.
6. Respond to the public in ways that are complete, clear, and easy to understand.
7. Assist citizens in their dealings with government.
8. Be prepared to make decisions that may not be popular.

II Respect the Constitution and the Law

Respect, support, and study government constitutions and laws that define responsibilities of public agencies, employees, and all citizens.
ASPA members are committed to:

1. Understand and apply legislation and regulations relevant to their professional role.

III Demonstrate Personal Integrity

Demonstrate the highest standards in all activities to inspire public confidence and trust in public service.
ASPA members are committed to:

1. Maintain truthfulness and honesty and to not compromise them for advancement, honor, or personal gain.
2. Ensure that others receive credit for their work and contributions.
3. Zealously guard against conflict of interest or its appearance: e.g., nepotism, improper outside employment, misuse of public resources or the acceptance of gifts.
4. Respect superiors, subordinates, colleagues and the public.
5. Take responsibility for their own errors.
6. Conduct official acts without partisanship.

IV Promote Ethical Organizations

Strengthen organizational capabilities to apply ethics, efficiency and effectiveness in serving the public.
ASPA members are committed to:

1. Enhance organizational capacity for open communication, creativity, and dedication.

2. Work to improve and change laws and policies that are counter-productive or obsolete.
3. Eliminate unlawful discrimination.
4. Prevent all forms of mismanagement of public funds by establishing and maintaining strong fiscal and management controls, and by supporting audits and investigative activities.
5. Respect and protect privileged information.
6. Encourage and facilitate legitimate dissent activities in government and protect the whistleblowing rights of public employees.
7. Promote constitutional principles of equality, fairness, representativeness, responsiveness and due process in protecting citizens' rights.

V Strive for Professional Excellence

Strengthen individual capabilities and encourage the professional development of others.
ASPA members are committed to:

1. Provide support and encouragement to upgrade competence.
2. Accept as a personal duty the responsibility to keep up to date on emerging issues and potential problems.
3. Encourage others, throughout their careers, to participate in professional activities and associations.
4. Allocate time to meet with students and provide a bridge between classroom studies and the realities of public service.

2. Subordinate institutional loyalties to the public good.
3. Establish procedures that promote ethical behavior and hold individuals and organizations accountable for their conduct.
4. Provide organization members with an administrative means for dissent, assurance of due process and safeguards against reprisal.
5. Promote merit principles that protect against arbitrary and capricious actions.
6. Promote organizational accountability through appropriate controls and procedures.
7. Encourage organizations to adopt, distribute, and periodically review a code of ethics as a living document.

Enforcement of the Code of Ethics shall be conducted in accordance with Article I, Section 4 of ASPA's Bylaws.
In 1981 the American Society for Public Administration's National Council adopted a set of moral principles. Three years later in 1984, the Council approved a Code of Ethics for ASPA members. In 1994 the Code was revised.

The American Society for Public Administration: 1120 G Street, NW Suite 700, Washington DC 20005 202/393-7878

such a determination can flow only from the thorough consideration administrators give—or fail to give—to all legitimate values in formulating the best possible decision. Part II will examine in more detail the five value sources identified in this chapter.

Notes

* This chapter is based on "The Sources of Ethical Decision Making for Individuals in the Public Sector," in *Public Administration Review* 56 (November–December 1996): pp. 525–534. Used with permission.

1. Ethicists disagree on the scope of "ethical" decisionmaking. The range of usage varies from an extremely narrow scope to an extremely broad one. (1) Ethical decisionmaking in some contexts seems to imply violating explicit prohibitions only, such as laws and rules. (2) It also means violating explicit prohibitions and widely accepted cultural prohibitions, such as lying. (3) In other cases, ethical decisionmaking focuses on both the prohibitions and the ideals. What is wrong behavior and what is very good behavior, given the values adopted? This third position assumes that most decisionmaking involves neither egregious wrongdoing nor courageous rightdoing. This is the idea of ethical decisionmaking that I prefer. (4) Some seem to argue that there is an ethical component to all decisions. That is, one must make sure that selfish interests (personal or organizational) do not distort legal and public interests. I do not care for this perspective because, although it has an element of truth, I believe it subtly denigrates personal and organizational values and overemphasizes legal and public interest values. (5) Finally, more recently some analysts seem to imply that all decisions are based on ethics and that decisionmaking and ethical decisionmaking are synonymous terms. While I like the idea that the same framework of sources be used in both ethical and general decisionmaking situations, and have provided such an interchangeable framework here, I do have a problem broadening the meaning of *ethical* to mean too much. In its classical sense, it referred to right and wrong, and was clearly thought of as a guide for the individual in a social setting; how should the individual act (or not act) relative to other individuals and society? Having ethical refer to the boundaries of behavior (where there is usually fairly good social consensus) is very useful: What is wrong behavior and what is very good behavior? To suggest that all decisions are ethical seems to me to stretch all the meaning out of the term. It implies that selecting the color of the furniture for the office, or processing a routine application (perhaps one of hundreds or thousands that day) is most usefully analyzed in right-wrong terms. Again, I prefer the traditional meanings of ethics and values. Values are used in all decisions; ethics, having to do with right and wrong, is most usefully confined to narrower decision sets about the lower limits and upper thresholds of individual behavior in a social context.

2. John A. Rohr, *Ethics for Bureaucrats: An Essay on Law and Values,* 2nd ed. (New York: Marcel Dekker, 1989); George H. Frederickson, "Public Administration and Social Equity," *Public Administration Review* 50, no. 2 (March/April 1990), pp. 228–237.

3. Darrell L. Pugh, "The Origins of Ethical Frameworks in Public Administration," in *Ethical Frontiers in Public Administration,* James Bowman,

ed. (San Francisco: Jossey-Bass, 1991); April Hejka-Ekins, "Teaching Ethics in Public Administration," *Public Administration Review* 47, no. 5 (September/October 1988), pp. 885–891.

4. Barry Z. Posner and Warren H. Schmidt, "An Updated Look at the Values and Expectations of Federal Government Executives," *Public Administration Review* 54, no. 1 (January/February 1994), pp. 20–24.

5. J. Patrick Dobel, "Integrity in the Public Service," *Public Administration Review* 50, no. 3 (May/June 1990), pp. 356–366; Kathryn G. Denhardt, "Unearthing the Moral Foundations of Public Administration: Honor, Benevolence, and Justice," in *Ethical Frontiers in Public Administration,* James Bowman, ed. (San Francisco: Jossey-Bass, 1991).

6. Terry Cooper, *The Responsible Administrator* (San Francisco: Jossey-Bass, 1990).

7. Donald P. Warwick, "The Ethics of Administrative Discretion," in *Public Duties: The Moral Obligations of Government Officials,* Joel L. Fleishman, Lance Leibman, and Mark H. Moore, eds. (Cambridge, MA: Harvard University Press, 1981).

8. Carol W. Lewis, *The Ethics Challenge in Public Service: A Problem-Solving Guide* (San Francisco: Jossey-Bass, 1991); Stephen Bonczek, "Ethical Decision Making: Challenge of the 1990s—a Practical Approach for Local Governments," *Public Personnel Management* 21, no. 1 (Spring 1992), pp. 75–88; Harold F. Gortner, *Ethics for Public Managers* (New York: Praeger, 1991).

9. Jonathan P. West, Evan Berman, and Anita Cava, "Ethics in the Municipal Workplace," *Municipal Year Book 1993* (Washington, DC: ICMA) pp. 3–16; Dwight Waldo, *The Enterprise of Public Administration* (Novato, CA: Chandler and Sharp, 1981).

10. As a member of ASPA's Professional Ethics Committee and the subcommittee assigned to the redrafting of the Code of Ethics, I was fortunate to be able to play a role in reorganizing the new code.

11. John A. Rohr, "The Problem of Professional Ethics," *Bureaucrat* (Spring 1991), p. 9.

12. Milton Rokeach, *The Nature of Human Values* (New York: Free Press, 1973), pp. 5–6.

13. Zhiyong Lan and David H. Rosenbloom, "Public Administration in Transition?" *Public Administration Review* 52, no. 6 (November/December 1992), p. 535; David H. Rosenbloom, "Have an Administrative Rx? Don't Forget the Politics!" *Public Administration Review* 53, no. 6 (November/December 1993), p. 505.

14. Evan M. Berman and Jonathan P. West, "Values Management in Local Government: A Survey of Progress and Future Directions," Paper delivered at the National Conference of the American Society for Public Administration (San Francisco, June 1993), pp. 16–17.

15. Posner and Schmidt, op. cit., p. 21. For a sampling of others who concur, see Elliott Richardson and the Council for Excellence in Government, "Ethical Principles for Public Servants," *Public Manager* 4 (Winter 1992–1993), p. 38; Linda Dennard, "Recognizing the Right Thing to Do," *Public Administration Review* 51, no. 5 (September/October 1991), pp. 451–453; Gortner, 1991, op. cit.; Robert S. Kravchuk, "Liberalism and the American Administrative State," *Public Administration Review* 52, no. 4 (July/August 1992), p. 374; Cooper, op. cit., p. 19.

16. The application of sanctions and rewards varies tremendously based on the context. Fairly specific codes in agencies can be strong at providing the basis for sanctions, while codes for professional organizations are poorly suited for providing specific sanctions. Basing rewards on codes of ethics is an often-missed opportunity.

17. "The aim of every political constitution is, or ought to be, first to obtain rulers who possess most wisdom to discern, and most virtue to pursue, the common good of society; and in the next place to take the most effectual precautions for keeping them virtuous." Quoted in Ralph Chandler, "The Problem of Moral Reasoning in American Public Administration," *Public Administration Review* 43, no. 1 (January/February 1983), p. 35.

18. See for example, Terry L. Cooper and N. Dale Wright, eds., *Exemplary Public Administrators: Character and Leadership in Government* (San Francisco: Jossey-Bass, 1992). While Cooper focuses on the role of the public administrator, this is part of a larger discussion of the role of virtue and citizenship that has direct roots to Aristotle (*Politics*). Recent commentators in this larger discussion include James Q. Wilson, *The Moral Sense* (New York: Free Press, 1993); Alasdair MacIntyre, *After Virtue,* 2nd ed. (Notre Dame: University of Notre Dame Press, 1984); and William Bennett, *The Book of Virtues* (New York: Simon & Schuster, 1993).

19. *Webster's New World Dictionary* (New York: World Publishing Co., 1978).

20. An interesting exception to this generalization occurred in the summer 1996 Gallup polls that reviewed the favorability ratings of Bill Clinton and Bob Dole. Generally, political candidates who do not have strong honesty ratings cannot succeed. However, in a preelection poll, Bill Clinton had substantially lower honesty ratings than Bob Dole yet was overwhelmingly favored (by approximately 20 percent) for election, based on much higher competency ratings.

21. For teams, see Jon R. Katzenbach and Douglas K. Smith, *The Wisdom of Teams: Creating the High Performance Organization* (Boston: Harvard Business School Press, 1993); for organizations, see Stephen R. Covey, *Principle-Centered Leadership* (New York: Simon & Schuster, 1991).

22. Lawrence Kohlberg, *The Philosophy of Moral Development: Moral Stages and the Idea of Justice,* vol. 1 (New York: HarperCollins, 1981).

23. Charles Manz and Henry P. Sims, Jr., *SuperLeadership: Leading Others to Lead Themselves* (New York: Berkeley Books, 1990).

24. One such government action recently discussed is the use of radioactive materials on retarded children in the 1950s and 1960s, without the parents' knowledge but with government knowledge and support.

25. Richardson, op. cit., p. 38.

26. Dennis Thompson, "The Possibility of Administrative Ethics," *Public Administration Review* 45, no. 5 (September/October 1985), pp. 555–561.

27. Beverly Cigler notes "What was once just an image problem for the national bureaucracy has evolved into morale, recruitment, and retention problems that ultimately affect government employees at all levels and the quality of services offered to citizens." Beverly A. Cigler, "Public Administration and the Paradox of Professionalism," *Public Administration Review* 50, no. 6 (November/December 1990), p. 638.

28. Dennis Thompson, "Paradoxes of Government Ethics," *Public Administration*

Review 52, no. 3 (May/June 1992), p. 256, for example, notes that instead of finding lower standards of conduct in government, elected and appointed officials are shocked to find higher standards, or at least more restrictive standards.

29. Yet to blame politicians solely for this complex phenomenon would be inaccurate. See Cigler's analysis, cited in note 27, for a fuller analysis of the complex reasons leading to a declining opinion of public administration.

30. Pugh, op. cit., p. 9.

31. James A. Stever, *The End of Public Administration: Problems of the Profession in the Post-Progressive Era* (Dobbs Ferry, NY: Transnational Publishers, 1988).

32. Curtis Ventriss, "Reconstructing Government Ethics: A Public Philosophy of Civic Virtue," in *Ethical Frontiers in Public Management,* James Bowman, ed. (San Francisco: Jossey-Bass, 1991).

33. Gortner, op. cit.

34. Gerald E. Caiden, "What Really Is Public Maladministration?" *Public Administration Review* 51, no. 6 (November/December 1991), p. 490.

35. Peter F. Drucker, "What Is Business Ethics?" *Public Interest,* no. 63 (Spring 1981), pp. 18–36.

36. Robert B. Denhardt, "Morality As an Organizational Problem," *Public Administration Review* 52, no. 2 (March/April 1992), p. 105.

37. Tom Peters, "Excellence in Government? I'm All For It! Maybe," *Bureaucrat* (Spring 1991), p. 6.

38. Gortner, op. cit.

39. Joel L. Fleishman, Lance Liebman, and Mark H. Moore, *Public Duties: The Moral Obligations of Government Officials* (Cambridge, MA: Harvard University Press, 1981), p. x.

40. Walter L. Balk, "Productivity Improvement in Government Agencies: An Ethical Perspective," *Policy Studies Review* 4, no. 3 (1985), p. 482.

41. Dobel, op. cit.

42. Richardson, op. cit., p. 37.

43. Waltzer, reported in Cooper, op. cit., p. 41.

44. West, Berman, and Cava, op. cit., p. 16.

45. Rohr, op. cit., p. 12.

46. Richard C. Box, "The Administrator As Trustee of the Public Interest: Normative Ideals and Daily Practice," *Administration and Society* 24, no. 3 (November 1992), p. 5.

47. Michael W.J. Cody and Richardson R. Lynn, *Honest Government: An Ethics Guide for Public Service* (Westport, CT: Praeger, 1992).

48. See Frank Marini, ed., *Toward a New Public Administration* (Scranton, PA: Chandler, 1971).

49. For a distinguished set of essays concerning public interest, see George H. Frederickson, ed., "A Symposium: Social Equity and Public Administration," *Public Administration Review* 34, no. 1 (January/February 1974), pp. 1–51.

50. Nicholas Henry, *Administration and Public Affairs,* 3rd ed. (Englewood Cliffs, NJ: Prentice-Hall, 1986), p. 351.

51. Willa M. Bruce, "Ethics and Administration," *Public Administration Review* 52, no. 1 (January/February 1992), pp. 81–83; and "Rejoinder to Terry Cooper's

Response to the Review of 'The Responsible Administrator: An Approach to Ethics for the Administrative Role,' " *Public Administration Review* 52, no. 3 (May/June 1992), pp. 313–314.

52. The notion of disinterest and "other-regarding" is probably most fully developed by Brent Wall, "Assessing Ethics Theories from a Democratic Viewpoint," in *Ethical Frontiers in Public Management,* James S. Bowman, ed. (San Francisco: Jossey-Bass, 1991).

53. Because some principles can be organized under several sources, my organization of the principles is not identical to ASPA's Code.

54. Gary B. Brumback, "Institutionalizing Ethics in Government," *Public Personnel Management* 20, no. 3 (Fall 1991), p. 362.

55. Warwick, op. cit., p. 115.

An In-Depth Look at Values Endorsed in Public Administration

Part II examines in more detail the five value domains identified and briefly discussed in Part I. It starts with the values closest to the individual, then addresses professional values, organizational values, legal values, and public interest values. Each chapter summarizes the most basic assumptions underpinning public administration and looks at the discussions shaping their interpretation. In all, 17 basic assumptions are identified and discussed.

CHAPTER 2

The Role of Individuals' Values

In a sense, public administrators' personal values affect all the value clusters within the perspective of the individual administrator. Other chapters cover such topics as the relationship between individual values and professional values, or individual values vis-à-vis organizational needs (environment) and culture (history).[1] This chapter limits its discussion to the values of individuals with regard to their role as *members* of the political–public-interest system. That is, it asks, at the most basic level, what is the proper role for public administrators who are not only the responsible stewards of the laws and public interest, but who are also legitimate subjects of the laws and public interest themselves, and oftentimes, one of the most valuable assets as individuals and a class? The discussion of the balance of these three factors—the individual's roles as steward, citizen, and contributor—is the focus of this chapter.

In this context, the values of individuals therefore refer only to the personal values of public administrators regarding:

- their acceptance of strong *civic integrity* (their stewardship role). This value emphasizes the need for public administrators to strongly support not only the system of which they are a part but also the generally held values surrounding that system.
- their retention of *basic rights* (as citizens and humans). This value qualifies the first. It assumes that "basic" rights (however defined) are not swept away by the high level of civic integrity required.

- their role as unique *personal contributors* in the policy community.[2] This value also qualifies the first. It assumes that despite their strong support of the "system," public administrators' personal contribution is always important in a limited administrative sense, and sometimes in a significant policy leadership role as well.

These three values—civic integrity, basic rights, and personal contribution—are widely held when their purview is limited.[3] Yet as the intensity of these values increases, perspectives diverge. When, for example, does civic integrity become blind technocratic compliance? When do personal rights become negotiated privileges? And when do the unique contributions of public administrators begin to supplant representative government? The answers depend to some extent on the school of thought.

Most modern schools of thought have brought new attention to the upper thresholds of individual values, both in terms of emphasis and expansion. Richard Green and Kathryn Denhardt noted that the study of virtue or character ethics has been relatively underdeveloped in American public administration but that it "is currently enjoying a renaissance in various academic subjects and political circles."[4] In addition, the swelling popular debate about increased individual responsibility and higher personal standards is likely to have a major effect on public administration.[5] A similar belief arises from the postmodernists, a philosophical school based on existential and phenomenological beliefs about the inescapability of personal responsibility and the imperative for genuine discourse in a world increasingly splintered into smaller interests and one in which language itself has been much debased.[6] Another group, the entrepreneurial leadership school of thought, has brought much attention (often quite controversially) to this area from the management perspective.[7]

Further attention to the specific individual values and the discussions shaping their interpretation would be premature, however, without first examining the place of individual values in American society at large.

The Individual Values Environment in American Society

Western civilization, unlike the Asian, Middle Eastern, and other civilization basins, has tended to give greater emphasis to individual rights and perspectives than to those of social groups. In Western tradition, individual voters or citizens are a primary focus. In the United States, this concern for individual rights shows up in two great principles—the right of the individual to pursue happiness to the greatest extent without impeding others' rights, and the right to be free of intrusive governmental power. The first of these principles appears in the Declaration of Independence's assertion for the right to the pursuit of individual happiness, the Constitution's Bill of Rights, the Emancipation Proclamation, antitrust legislation, and civil rights legislation, to mention only a few more prominent examples.[8] The second principle is demonstrated by the concern for the proper and bounded use of public power in the separation of powers, the principle of least possible government, competitive elections, disciplinary measures against public officials (such as impeachment and recalls), trial by a jury of one's peers, and other similar measures.

Yet these two principles collide when the citizens are themselves government workers. To what extent should the rights of citizens at large be protected from the oppressiveness of public functionaries, and when do these protections become oppressive to public employees (and potentially dysfunctional as well)? Sorting out the proper balance of responsibilities and rights is key to defining which values to elevate.

A Contemporary View of Moral Development

Few Americans hold that morality is always a simple bifurcation between good and bad or right and wrong.[9] Psychologist Lawrence Kohlberg developed a six-stage model of moral development that is useful in describing the value nuances of the different schools of thought relative to individual values. Kohlberg's model, which is based on his extensive research with children, divides moral development into three levels: preconventional, conventional, and postconventional or principled. Each level has two sequential stages.[10]

The Preconventional Level

At the *preconventional level*, according to Kohlberg, humans are motivated primarily by the immediate or potential consequences of their actions.

- Stage 1. In the *stage of punishment and obedience*, humans act because of the physical or psychological consequences of being good or bad. There is a tendency to unquestioning deference to power. "What is right is to avoid breaking rules, to obey for obedience's sake, and to avoid doing physical damage to people and property."[11]

- Stage 2. At the second stage, the *stage of individual instrumental purpose and exchange*, "right action consists of that which instrumentally satisfies one's needs and occasionally the needs of others. Human relations are viewed in terms like those of the marketplace."[12] While there is an element of fairness and reciprocity involved at this stage, the focus is on concrete, pragmatic exchange. The individual seeks goodwill at this stage only because others have rights not to engage in the exchange, and a reputation for fairness is valuable in later dealings.

The Conventional Level

At the *conventional level*, social conformity becomes valued as a necessary element in orderly and coherent social order, regardless of the immediate or obvious consequences of actions as was true of the preconventional level.

- Stage 3. At the *stage of mutual interpersonal expectations and relationships*, good behavior is generally focused on gaining social approval. Intentions become important and others' feelings matter. Living up to what is expected of you, whether as a family member, neighbor, or organizational colleague, is valued. The Golden Rule is followed in concrete terms but is not necessarily generalized from a system perspective.

- Stage 4. At the *society-maintaining orientation stage*, duty to good behavior broadens from immediate relationships to one's society at large. Also called the "law and order orientation," behavior at this stage focuses on the "viewpoint of the system, which defines the roles and rules."[13] Thus, there is a respect for authority, fixed rules, and the maintenance of social order. This is the most common perspective in American society according to Kohlberg's research.

The Postconventional or Principled Level

At the *postconventional or principled level*, "there is a clear effort to define moral values and principles that have validity and application apart from the authority of the groups or people holding these principles and apart from the individual's own identification with these groups."[14]

- Stage 5. At the *stage of prior rights and social contract*, right moves beyond an authority or "duty" mode to focus on critically examining standards. Procedural rights for reaching consensus are valued. Impartial and rational modes of decisionmaking, arriving at the greatest good for the greatest number, stress due process. Kohlberg considers this the official morality of the United States which is reflected in the Constitution.[15]

- Stage 6. At the *stage of universal ethical principles*, "right is defined by the decision of conscience in accord with self-chosen principles appealing to logical comprehensiveness, universality, and consistency. These principles are abstract and ethical . . . ; they are not concrete moral rules such as the Ten Commandments."[16] At this stage, universal principles of justice take precedence over the concrete laws of societies when the two significantly conflict. The equality of human rights and the dignity of human beings is given primary importance because they are upon what laws should be founded.

Kohlberg's theory clearly expresses the belief that moral development proceeds from an internal (selfish) focus to an external (altruistic) focus, and from an involuntary motivation (such as the threat of force) to a voluntary one. The strengths of his work are its clear steps or stages and its emotional appeal as a theory placing responsibility and pride in humanity's ability for advanced moral growth. Kohlberg's work is not without its critics, however. Some philosophers hold that universalism is dead and that grand schemes in the Kantian tradition are misplaced in a postmodern world.[17] Other philosophers hold that Kohlberg's beliefs are not sufficiently intellectually grounded and that he ultimately is guilty of "philosophical primitivism."[18] Undoubtedly he jumps from *is* to *ought* and back again rather conveniently, saying at first that the development of children proves his contention of inherent moral development (the contention itself being extremely vulnerable to cultural bias), and then using the argument to stress that where it does not hold in society, it should. Yet, even if its intellectual foundation is not universally agreed upon, Kohlberg's overall scheme is so similar to the implicit moral theory used by educational institutions, voluntary organizations, and civic groups that it is a useful working model.[19]

The dilemmas that this theory exposes in public administration re-volve around the problem of the public servant as autonomous or depen-dent moral agent. If public administrators are totally dependent moral agents, as the classical orthodox model has suggested, then public admin-istrators should focus on Kohlberg's fourth stage of development, the so-ciety-maintaining stage. If public administrators are modest participants in the public policy process, they should be contributing to Kohlberg's fifth stage, that of prior rights and social contracts, and should be recom-mending and interpreting policy at a high level. However, if public ad-ministrators are themselves fully autonomous moral agents empowered by their moral development and public trust to act in the public's behalf, then they are entitled to engage their own application of universal ethical principles (Kohlberg's final stage) in the unique problems that they en-counter.

These three conceptualizations range roughly from the proceduralist functionary, to the limited discretion of an executor, to the full discretion of a judge bounded by both the law *and* right reasoning to contextualize unique circumstances. Part of the challenge is, of course, that good ex-amples of each of these conceptualizations can be found and that public administrators seem to have a broad range of moral authority, affected by hierarchical position, leadership style, historical precedent, and the type of public agency.

Individual Values in the Public Sector

As noted earlier in this chapter, three overarching values for individuals are generally prized in the public sector: (1) strong civic integrity, (2) access to basic citizen and human rights, and (3) belief in the right of public administrators to make unique contributions and provide civic leadership.

Strong Civic Integrity Is Critical for Public Employees

David Norton has pointed out that integrity in the Greek tradition meant "actualizing one's unique potential excellence," "integration of the separable aspects of the self," and "wholeness as completeness."[20] When individuals have strong *civic* integrity, they seek to fulfill their potential within and through the civic community, their civic involve-ment is well integrated with other aspects of their life, and the integration of civic and personal beliefs brings a sense of wholeness. For public employees in the U.S. system, this means that they must have certain beliefs about the political-administrative system in which they serve and certain beliefs about the generally held principles of their communities that they must model.

Belief in the Representative-Democratic Social Contract

First, civic integrity means there is a belief in the representative-democratic social contract and willingness to subordinate private convictions and preferences to it. That is, there is an expectation that public administrators will not use their power or position to deny or change basic legal values inherent in our political-administrative system. Examples of legal values (discussed in detail in Chapter 5) include the law as the will of the people; due process; subordination of public administrators to legislative intent, political bureaucrats, and court decisions; and administrative articulation of laws. In other words, one aspect of civic integrity is to believe in the social contract (the Constitution and the laws) so strongly that personal convictions and values are subordinated to it. To work *for* the government is *to be* the government, with its mighty respect for democratic processes of determining public good through political institutions and their supporting administrative institutions. This aspect of civic integrity enhances the notion of different public and private persona, with the public persona scrupulously adhering to a purely instrumental role.

Using the Kohlbergian stages discussed earlier, this belief is anchored in either Stage 4 (society-maintaining) or Stage 5 (social contract). A minimum interpretation of civic integrity as belief in representative democracy translates into a compliance orientation to authority (Stage 4). "Administrative responsibility can be viewed as simply following policies and directions of hierarchical supervisors."[21] Yet some critics argue that such a limited notion can lead to an unresponsive state at best, and allow for an Eichmann phenomenon in extreme cases.[22] Most commentators hold a more robust interpretation, and believe that many public administrations should be acutely aware of the democratic social contract within which they work (Stage 5). Those who believe that the primary inspiration is study of the Constitution and legislative intent would tend to fall into this camp. Yet as Kohlberg himself acknowledged when he noted that a social contract mentality is the official approach of the U.S. government, this aspect of civic integrity generally refrains from encouraging individual civic autonomy (Stage 6).

Belief in Universal Ethical Principles

The second aspect to civic integrity is a belief in universal ethical principles. If the first aspect of civic integrity stresses the specific role of public administrators as special members of the political-administrative community, the second aspect stresses their role as member-citizens of society at large. Civic integrity in this sense means adhering to the values generally agreed upon in society, such as honesty, coherence, consistency, and reciprocity. Public administrators are expected, although not necessarily required by law, to be painstakingly honest about what they say and do.[23] Coherence requires a systematic way of thinking and acting that can be anticipated or rationally explained. Consistency is not meant as uniformity but as harmony and an avoidance of capriciousness. Reciprocity encourages mutuality and even-handedness. Taken as a whole, these values are frequently discussed in terms of being just and fair and instilling a sense of trust. They are so much a part of the bedrock of the American experience that they have a religious fervor, especially in regard to the public sector. From Kohlberg's perspective, this is a slightly higher plane of moral development than social-contract morality.

Theoreticians also discuss another level of nearly universal ethical principles (but perhaps not core values as honesty is). A comprehensive listing of the individual values mentioned in the research literature, and the merits of those categories is beyond the scope of this discussion.[24] However, some of the most common values discussed at this level are competence,[25] commitment,[26] courage,[27] optimism,[28] sacrifice[29] and concern for appearances.[30] Generally they are discussed as a high level of value morality. Competence has been enhanced as an important administrative value in the last century with our merit-based ideology. Yet with today's fast-changing pace, in which whole job classifications disappear quite rapidly as others emerge, and with the tendency to enlarge jobs extensively, competency becomes more challenging to achieve and maintain. Commitment, once nearly a staple in a job environment in which multiple careers in a lifetime were a rarity and job stability was a nearly universal expectation, has become more difficult to attain.[31] Courage is difficult because it is not always clear when an assertion of personal convictions is appropriate or when it is willfulness or a lack of understanding. Optimism, perhaps the most difficult to argue as a general ethical principle, is nonetheless extremely noticeable in its absence when pessimism, apathy, and oppressive orthodoxy prevail. The idea of sacrifice is stated clearly by Stephen Bonczek. "Ethics involves sacrifices and selflessness and becomes the principle criterion of integrity in public officials.

This results in the acknowledgment that personal career aspirations must take second place to furthering the public interest."[32] The concern for appearances is especially important for government because of the power that government has and the people's right to know the people's business. If something looks inappropriate or unethical, there is a responsibility to investigate and to set the record straight or correct the situation. Yet, like all the values in this group, attention to appearances can become dysfunctional if overzealously applied; it can also lead to goal displacement in individuals with poor judgment.

Two Beliefs: Conflicting or Complementary?

These two aspects of civic integrity—the belief in the democratic social contract and the belief in universal ethical principles—can be seen as either conflicting and mutually exclusive or as complementary and integral. If one of these value sources must have absolute primacy, then the individual administrator will experience conflict. If the administrator views strict conformance to due process, law, and legislative intent as not *an* important values source but as *the only* value source, then universal ethical principles will be in a strictly supportive role and cannot trump, or even significantly inform, administrative duties. If the administrator views universal ethical principles as *the* source, the platform upon which social democratic contract was built in the first place, then there is again the potential for conflict. Yet another view, one to which I personally subscribe, is that the two aspects of civic integrity must be held simultaneously and inform each other. This creative tension means that problems of interpretation and balance become a core responsibility of the public administrator. This also means that the public administrator must have the experience, training, and disposition to tackle such problems. But I also believe that this is the robust view that makes sense for professionals who dedicate themselves to the public's work and who have complex tasks with sophisticated dilemmas to handle.

Ultimately, then, one view is that strong civic integrity for public administrators can be seen as two separate values whose bases of legitimacy—one founded on the law and social contract and the other on prior human rights and dignity—can occasionally oppose one another. When this is the view, individuals subtly prioritize the two values in their own minds. Another perspective, suggested by David Norton's vigorous definition of integrity discussed earlier, suggests that civic integrity is a single value melding together social contract and universal ethical principles. While a single, dualistically based value does not ease the tension in resolving many challenges public administrators face, many commentators believe it appropriately balances a respect for the public administrator as an especially responsible legal representative of the people, while still requiring the administrator to be responsible for their individual moral conscientiousness when supported by generally held ethical principles.

Public Servants Have Basic Rights As Citizens

Rights, whether legal or inherent, indicate society's very strong support of a value. Upon accepting employment in the public sector, employees do not forfeit the basic rights afforded to all citizens. However, as with all members of organizations, public employees do have significant constraints on their actions. Michael Harmon comments

> As a condition of employment, public servants sign contracts specifying their formal duties and obligations. In virtually all instances, they do so freely and voluntarily, but in the bargain they give up certain rights, including, but not limited to, avenues of private gain that are otherwise open to ordinary citizens. Public service constitutes a special kind of citizenship—a *public* citizenship—that carries with it a burden of obligations not shared, at least as directly and immediately, by others.[33]

In effect, the individual voluntarily cedes many, but not all, "rights" to the organization. Thus the value of basic rights for public servants is rooted in constitutional principles as well as human rights theory, but determining the proper extent of *basic* legal and human rights tends to be a problem.

Fundamental Political Rights and Exceptions to Them

Some of the rights that are considered fundamental and which cannot be ceded, even voluntarily, are the right to vote, the right to public expression on issues not related to one's job, the right to public expression on job-related issues if the law is being violated, the right to employment selection without political payoffs, and the right to quit. Yet even these very fundamental values have exceptions and have had rather different interpretations over time. The right for the U.S. Armed Forces to vote when off shore was not generally observed until this century. Similarly, public employees have always had the right to public expression on job-related issues but exercising that right inevitably meant demotion, harassment, or firing. Only with the relatively recent whistle-blowing statutes has such expression become a practical option in job-related cases of illegality.[34] Yet another example of circumscribing basic rights is the Armed Forces prohibition on quitting at nonscheduled intervals. National security has generally been allowed to trump the individual's right to pursue happiness in his or her own fashion. Yet individual liberty has been strengthened here, too, with the historically recent move back to volunteer military service.

Do Public Employees Have Basic Work-Related Rights?

Less clear is the extent to which public employees have *basic* rights to adequate physical safety, pay, and job security. The right to physical safety improved significantly in the twentieth century, paralleling society's increasingly higher standards of safety consciousness. Thus while the public sector includes many inherently dangerous jobs—law enforcement, corrections, fire fighting, military action, and so forth—safety concerns for employees have sought to make dramatic improvements and use state-of-the-art precautions to the degree applicable. The right to adequate pay has had a more checkered history over the past century and is probably more open to debate. Benefits across the entire public sector have been among the best in recent decades. Since World War II, the federal government and larger cities have been relatively successful at nearly matching, and occasionally exceeding, market salary ranges. Many states and counties have been much less successful, however; in some cases, salaries for some full-time public employees are below the poverty level. Do public employees have the right to pay that is at the market average, or did they concede those pay rights when they voluntarily accepted employment in the public sector? This value is likely to be more severely tested in the next few decades if the public sector experiences financial cutbacks.

Job security, again paralleling the private sector, has of late suffered greatly as a value. In the public sector (unlike the private sector), job security had come to be more nearly a right than a strong expectation. This expectation evolved for a number of reasons. One was that the idea of protection from political intrusion in all nonexempt (merit) hiring expanded over time to include tenure or property rights by public employees. Another was that due process rights were more meticulously developed and maintained in the public sector than anywhere else. Employment guarantees came to be considered inherent rights because, in practice, firing often required extensive proof of actual incompetence or egregious wrongdoing, and because an ethic of seniority promoted elaborate "bumping-right" practices. A supporting argument was that, while salaries in general were often lower than in the private sector and peak salaries were capped far below the highest range of the market, job security was a compensation. Today of course, job security has diminished significantly in response to the trend toward outsourcing, privatization, reduction of services, transfer of services, various types of competition, and so on. It is likely to continue to diminish as values such as entre-preneurialism and rigorous evaluation after employment become more strongly held.

Finally, there is the issue of the "right" of personal development, the Maslowian notion of self-actualization promoted by the human relations school, which in turn has its basis in human rights theory.[35] Despite the intuitive appeal of this potential right, even its adherents admit to its challenges in definition and execution. Positive arguments about the right to personal development include the idea that individuals who are happier and more fulfilled do better work because they are more moti-vated, creative, knowledgeable, and committed. Further, it is asserted that personal development is simply a form of professional development, and that it contributes significantly to the organization over the long term. Fi-nally, proponents generally argue that government is intended to enhance all of society's ability to lifelong personal development and it would be a crime to overlook those closest under its aegis.[36] Critics of this position do not necessarily disagree that personal development is good; they sim-ply deny it as a right and believe that it quickly becomes an inappropriate perquisite (perk). A well-known example is the occasional controversy that occurs with out-of-state travel for state and local government em-ployees who attend professional conferences that may not have a direct impact on daily operations. Another example is the disagreement about organizational support for individuals to belong to, expend time at, and disperse money for professional organizations. Although personal devel-opment is well established as a significant value in many organizations, it seems rarely to have reached the status of a right comparable to basic citi-zen rights and appropriate physical safety.[37] Many organizations seem to be increasingly torn between the practical good that may be achieved by a strong personal development stance for long-term organization vitality, and the reduction of resources that may be needed to support personal development.

In sum, the belief that public servants have basic rights varies in strength depending on the rights being discussed. Certain basic political rights have been affirmed and strengthened this century. Work-related rights have had more mixed support, with physical safety becoming ever more pronounced and job security being increasingly undermined. Personal development, which has been proposed as a right but has never received wide recognition as one, has received new relevance as organizations search for employees with more creativity, greater flexibility, and broader skills. But tremendous resource pressures (both money and time) are often of equal or greater influence in the decisions of whether personal development is treated as a principal value.

Public Administrators Are Capable of Unique Contributions

In the private sector, the belief that the unique contributions of individuals are critical to organizational success has always been a part of the leadership literature.[38] It was an element of the human relations school dating from the 1960s,[39] but it has been powerfully asserted as a critical value by numerous recent management movements from Peters' and Waterman's excellence, Deming's quality, and Hammer and Champy's reengineering.[40] In these recent management crusades there is a clear emphasis on the importance of leadership activism and employee creativity and energy. This approach stands in sharp contrast to the perception that, in practice, many organizational cultures had leaders who merely managed (maintained) the organization and workers who simply put in their time but not their intelligence.

In the public sector, the value of unique contributions and active leadership has been much more ambivalent. If a strict interpretation of democratic governance assumes that all policy decisions, no matter how small, are the domain of the legislative branch and elected executives, and that career employees are the neutral implementors of that policy, then active leadership and unique contributions may actually be inappropriate. Michael Harmon notes that these commentators, "by attempting to prevent such participation, reduce [the bureaucrat's] role to one of compliant technocrat who bears no personal responsibility for the purposes he or she is supposed to achieve."[41] The strengths and weaknesses of the arguments about the appropriate role of public employees in democratic theory will be covered in Chapters 8 and 9; here we will only examine the value trend in practice.

Lipsky, Gawthrop, and others have argued that even employees very low in the organizational hierarchy often exhibit extensive creativity, discretion, and leadership in fulfilling their duties.[42] More recently, others have noted that active leadership is (and has been) as indispensable for the public sector as for the private.[43] Managers asked to discuss an important contribution they have made to their organization display great difficulty in selecting only one story to tell. When they do tell their stories, they are full of pride at the ingenuity and initiative they used in overcoming all sorts of daunting challenges.[44] No matter what the theoretically appropriate role of public sector workers and leaders is, they generally feel they make unique contributions.

This observation leads to another empirical question. Is the level of unique contribution and active leadership increasing as an important value? Reviewing organizational mission and value statements, promotional materials, newsletters, management initiative materials, training materials, and so forth leads me to say that the evidence is overwhelming that this value is rising sharply,[45] at least as a stated value, or what Argyris and Schön would call an espoused theory.[46] Some of the reasons for increased creativity and more active leadership at lower levels are demands by citizens for more customization, which is now technologically more feasible; far faster response times; more selective use of regulation (which calls for more discretion); and reduced costs (which has translated to more systems design and problem solving with less expensive front-line workers). However, practice usually lags behind newly proposed ideals, and in many cases stated ideals fail to become part of the underlying assumptions of the organization.

The final question about this value cannot be answered here but should be raised nonetheless. To what degree should unique contribution and entrepreneurial leadership be promoted as legitimate values in a democratic bureaucracy? Of course this question assumes that a public employee's contribution *should* be increased, and only asks how much. This clearly seems to be the current trend. How much it *does* increase as an important public sector value remains to be seen and how much it *should* remains open to vigorous debate.

The Potential Contributions of Individual Values

Each value set has its potential contributions as well as its potential liabilities, especially when the value set is relied upon excessively. This section focuses on the potential contributions of strong civic integrity, the belief that public servants have certain basic rights, and the belief that public administrators are capable of unique contributions and civic leadership.

Civic Integrity Increases Citizens' Trust That Their Interests Are Being Faithfully Executed

To the degree that the public sector has a culture of strong civic integrity and appropriate leadership, citizens will tend to trust government more. Government, like almost all institutions, from religious organizations to highly organized professions to financial institutions, has suffered a significant decline in trust since the historic high in the 1940s and 1950s. Thus it is important that both the public sector *be* trustworthy by consistently demonstrating the integrity and leadership of its members and that it ensure that the public *knows about* its trustworthiness.

Mutual trust can play a major role in productivity. As William Ouchi has noted, trust is central to productivity because it allows for subtlety and encourages dedication.[47] David Carnevale explains,

> In high-performing systems, learning is enabled, liberated, and used to gain competitive advantage. In low-trust cultures, learning potential is systematically repressed and destroyed in two ways. First, mistrustful people engage in defensive, self-protective behaviors. Because of their wary posture, they cannot learn effectively. They are not as open to the influence of others or are just plain fearful of disclosing what they know. . . . Second, low-trust work cultures typically feature authoritarian command, an obsession with control, and impoverished, low-discretion work roles. Creative energy is crushed in such climates.[48]

Because of public "ownership" of the public organizations, citizen trust becomes critical for high performance. Without public trust, public organizations cannot act as Carnevale has suggested. Yet as Philip Howard has observed, "We wanted [government] to solve social ills, but distrusted it to do so."[49] This leads to the next point.

Civic Integrity Reduces Reliance on Laws and Rules

Lack of trust generally results in a reliance on rules and external controls. This in turn leads to "bureaucratic behavior in which people focus their efforts only on what is measured and rewarded by the organization, neglecting many other important activities."[50] Obsessive reliance on external control factors is expensive, dysfunctional, and ultimately self-defeating.[51] As James Madison opined, "Is there no virtue among us? If there be not, we are in a wretched situation. No theoretical clerks, no form of government, can render us secure. To suppose that any form of government will secure liberty or happiness without any virtue in the people is a chimerial idea."[52] If the single most important answer is the encouragement of virtue and character rather than a series of "technical" devices, individual values are clearly essential.[53]

Individual Values Challenge the Excesses of the State and Other Value Sets

Because professions, public agencies, and even the state itself can commit practical and moral excesses, it is important to have public employees of character who are willing to stand up to immoderation. Here is that courage which Bailey, Richardson, Thompson, and others have commented upon.[54] Of course, the objections of such employees must fit the gravity of the situation,[55] but if the contribution of their wisdom is not allowed, the government may lose its single most informed voice. As one commentator noted, "Despite our best efforts, then, we have not succeeded in constructing a government system that is independent of the moral qualities of its leaders."[56]

Acknowledgment of Individual Contributions and Leadership Is Both Practical and Humane

The support for acknowledging and honoring individual contributions in organizations and systems is massive and broad based.[57] From the unanticipated results at the Hawthorne Plant, in which attention alone significantly increased results,[58] to Marx's powerful critique about the alienation of many jobs in modern organizations,[59] to the motivation insights of the human relations school, to the ethical arguments advanced by almost all management theorists,[60] the importance of recognizing and encouraging individual contributions is difficult to argue.[61] What can be and is frequently argued, however, is the extent of the role that individual contributions and leadership should play in the unique environment of the public sector, with its critical concern for democratic accountability.

Problems with Excessive Reliance on Individual Values

The two most powerful concerns about excessive reliance on individual values relate primarily to the diminution of legal values (the political-administrative system) and public interest values (those the political-administrative system is supposed to serve).

Substitution of Legal Values by Personal Values

A political-administrative system is inevitably subjected to great pressures from individuals and groups within the society to gain advantages sanctioned or supplied by the state. Those in public administration function as such a group, and their self-serving interests (as individuals and as a group) must be carefully balanced and controlled. Where such controls and balancing do not occur—and here one can point to examples in both the developed and less developed world—then administrators play an "inside game" and profit unfairly. Thus there is a legitimate concern that those in the public sector play *closely* by the legal rules, democratically and authoritatively arrived at, so that they do not profit either by a wholesale misuse of the system for their own selfish gain (such as corruption) or even marginally by manipulating the system (legal but unethical or blatantly selfish practices).

Selfish or personal gain at public expense by public employees (whether it is illegal or should be because of abuse of position) is not an argument against the three individual values discussed but rather is a function of their not operating as they should. Substituting personal gain for legal interests (by abandoning civic integrity) implies a lack of a fundamental conviction in the fairness of the social contract and the public administrator's role to uphold that contract. Likewise, such abuse implies a lack of consistency with generally held ethical principles. The second individual value discussed (that is, the basic rights of public employees) is rarely mistaken for personal gain by unfair use of position. The third individual value discussed—the belief that public administrators are capable of unique contributions and civic leadership—is in many ways the most problematic. As public administrators have increased discretion, an undisputable form of power, the possibility for abuse becomes greater. Therefore, limiting discretion (through laws and rules) also lessens the potential for abuse. This is similar to Hamilton's injunction that although we need to choose virtuous administrators, we must also take precautions for keeping them virtuous.[62] Yet, rule making often becomes rule mongering, which is its own vice, as discussed on numerous occasions in this book.

In sum, substitution of personal values for legal values is not so much an excess of properly understood individual values as a disregard of them. Various types of administrative corruption in public organizations continue to be much on the public's and legislators' minds, but this concern does not seem to square with U.S. reality. Although the corruption of public employees is not unknown, the vast bulk of the corruption is perpetrated by the private sector on the public sector. Legal controls are critical for clarity and public confidence, but strong arguments are being raised about their overuse.[63]

Usurpation of the Public Interest by Individual Values

Usurpation of the public interest is a more subtle but more powerful concern than is outright disregard for legal interests. Here the concern is not about personal financial or physical gains at the public expense, but rather about the warping of the democratic policy process. Groups all along the political spectrum, from civil libertarians to political and administrative scientists in the center to both the populist and elitist conservatives, express concerns about several forms of usurpation.

Ego-Enhancing or Domain-Enhancing Behavior

There is a concern about not only the financial motivations of public administrators but also about their nonfinancial motivations. As Elliott Richardson once declared, "Greed is a far less common corrupter of public servants than ego, envy, timidity, ambition, or a craving for publicity. To know how to manage and keep these in check demands character and discipline."[64] This observation leads to the critique that to the degree that public administrators are given discretion ("public administrators are capable of civic leadership"), their baser instincts can contaminate their civic integrity. Public administrators might be as tempted to be on the winning side of an issue (satisfying ego, ambition, or craving for publicity) as on the "right" side (whether from a legal or ethical standpoint). For example, publicly financed sports stadiums raise a host of legal and ethical problems that demand "right" solutions, yet some administrators may ultimately be more swayed by the "winning" side—politics (which elected officials support the stadium), domain-enhancement (will the stadium expand their administrative purview), or revenue generation for the tax base (will additional revenue bring additional security for government organizations). The point is not that publicly financed stadiums are wrong. The point is that public administrators often play an important role in deciding whether stadiums should be built, and their decisions can be motivated by ego, ambition, self-preservation, or a desire for power.

Substituting Individual Moral Values for Those of the Polity

There is a concern that the moral values of individual administrators may be substituted for those of the polity as represented in the authorized political process. New administrations for example, may be shocked to find out how much the bureaucracy can impede new initiatives or sometimes even find the means to put them aside altogether. Included in this type of concern are frivolous challenges, part of a popular concern about excessive litigiousness and combativeness. Here the argument is that public interests should be argued by the public, not by insiders who have an unfair advantage. Challenges by those in the public sector, this critique holds, should be strictly on legal grounds, or else anarchy reigns.

Growing Statism

There is a growing concern about statism, a condition in which the public apparatus becomes not only a symbol of the state but a personification of it. In some of the most sophisticated statist countries, such as France and Japan, bureaucrats rule on equal terms with elected officials. The United States is far less statist than most countries in the world, but it is far more statist than it was two hundred years ago, simply because of the growth of public sector responsibilities.[65] The current concerns about statism can probably be better addressed through a discussion of the role of government in society[66] than by a discussion of the role of public administrators in governance who are not particularly powerful by world standards.[67]

Conclusion

The values of individual administrators are very important, even within the pantheon of values this book identifies. Because public administrators occupy a unique role in which they use public power in the public's behalf, their individual rights are not identical to, and are usually more restricted than, the rights of other citizens. Even in the private sector, employment often entails a voluntary suppression of classic liberal freedoms, which are subjugated to the corporate good.

This chapter examined Lawrence Kohlberg's moral development scale as a model that can assist with the clarification of individual rights. Kohlberg's scale hypothesizes that moral development proceeds in a series of stages from an externally forced morality that emphasizes self to an internally voluntary morality that emphasizes humanity. His penultimate stage of moral development is a belief in democratically achieved social contract, which recognizes prior human rights. The ultimate stage is morality based on rationally derived universal ethical principles emphasizing human equity and dignity. The intuitive appeal of this argument is that law (social contract) is ultimately based on ethical principles, and therefore ethical principles should trump law when the two collide. The problem then is to determine *who* should decide to put aside (waive, reinterpret, reform, or adjust) the law and *on what* grounds. If this is a difficult issue for society at large, it becomes doubly difficult for those in charge of executing the law.

Three fundamental individual values for public administrators were discussed. All these values have broad support at a very basic level, but that support diminishes significantly as the value is expanded to its logical extreme. The first value discussed was the belief that civic integrity is critical for public employees. Personal integrity, taken by itself, implies an honesty, coherence, and consistency of an individual's values and beliefs; *civic* integrity implies that there is a high degree of coherence between personal and civic ideals of coherence and consistency. Personal integrity is a strong value for society at large; civic integrity is a weaker value and is open to much wider interpretation. For example, most successful business people have, and are expected to have, strong personal integrity, but they may have a weak civic integrity because they are absorbed with financial and personal issues. A strong civic integrity is expected in the public sector. Civic integrity has two elements, roughly equivalent to Kohlberg's highest two stages of moral development: a strong belief in the currently authorized representative democratic system and its administrative apparatus, and a strong belief in the universal principles held by society. These elements exist in a dynamic tension.

The second value for public administrations that was discussed in this chapter is that public sector employees retain their basic rights as humans and citizens. Certainly this is increasingly the case for basic political rights such as the right to vote, express opinions, and be free from patronage obligations. The right to physical safety has also increased in modern times. Yet support for basic rights as a fundamental value (as opposed to merely a situational variable) becomes fuzzier as their demarcation becomes extended to include job-related rights such as adequate pay, security, and personal development.

The third value discussed in the chapter is that public administrators are capable of personal contributions. This seemingly innocuous value challenges the stricter interpretations of administrative roles as "neutral" functionaries whose obligation is to avoid policy and value decisions by passing them up to political superiors. Thus, according to the old politics-administration dichotomy, administrators should do exactly as told, no more and no less, and should certainly abstain from leadership in any but the most technical sense. Although few now hold this extreme position, a new question has arisen: To what degree should public administrators make unique contributions and exercise civic leadership? The calls for increased entrepreneurialism, decentralized leadership, direct partnerships between administrators and citizens, and so on make this issue difficult. Where is the limit, if indeed there is one, on the value emphasis to be placed on the personal contributions of public administrators?

Finally, the strengths and weaknesses of these three value clusters were assayed. The principle strengths were increased citizen trust, reduced reliance on laws and rules, challenges to the excesses of the state and other value sets, and the acknowledgment of individual contributions as both practical and humane. Weaknesses stemmed primarily from a distortion of these values rather than an excess as such. Individual values can lead to goal displacement, not only at a personal financial level but also at a more abstract level involving personal values (ambition, envy, approbation, and so on), or statism—paternalism by a corporatist state.

If anything, emphasis on individual values is clearly increasing as government reexamines its mission, scope, structure, philosophy, and procedures. The practical contemporary question may not be so much *whether* individual values should receive greater emphasis but how much more attention they should receive.

Notes

1. Some readers may find a substantial example useful at this point, even though it will be covered in depth in Chapter 4 on organizational values. As has been pointed out by many scholars and practitioners in the last several decades, the public sector has been highly bureaucratic (as have most of the large corporations) in the twentieth century. Yet as Henry Mintzberg (*The Structuring of Organizations,* [Englewood Cliffs, NJ: Prentice Hall, 1979]) and the advocates of the "competing values approach" (Quinn, McGrath, Rohrbaugh, Hall, and others; see Chapter 4 for bibliography) have observed, bureaucratic organizations are only one type of numerous logical and actual possibilities. The substantially changed environment in the closing decade of this century seems to be a powerful force in encouraging different organizational forms and their concomitant values. Specifically, Quinn and others have noted that some of the values that highly bureaucratic organizations tend to propagate are hierarchy, security, conservatism,

cautiousness, maintenance, control, and specialized expertise. In a stable, noncompetitive environment, this organizational form and these values may work well. But when the environment becomes increasingly dynamic, with rapid and frequent change, and when competition for resources becomes acute, a purely hierarchic bureaucracy may become dysfunctional for both the organization and its members. According to Quinn et al., the organization may respond to the changed environment by moving in one of three directions: toward a market (rational) approach, toward a development (adhocracy) approach, or toward a group (team) approach. The market approach acknowledges the environment's competitive nature but continues to value structure to accomplish specific tasks. But it is much more mindful of results (ends) than its bureaucratic cousin, which emphasizes processes (means). The values such an approach encourages are decisiveness, competition, direction, goal orientation, action, and achievement. Clearly this is one force that has already changed the contemporary private sector and is beginning to affect the public sector. The environment is also being affected by greater ambiguity and rapid change. The structured aspect of the market approach gives way to an adhocracy approach, which values flexibility, rapid structural expansion and contraction to fit environmental needs, risk orientation, inventiveness, and change. A final approach emphasizes the need of individuals to band together in an unpredictable environment to garner the synergies of groups and collectivities. The values of the group approach are integration, team spirit, caring, supportiveness, interaction, and shared fate. Because the public sector is not a monolith, these approaches have been encouraged to different degrees, sometimes even within the same organization. It seems clear, however, that most public sector organizations are trying to mitigate the extreme lock that a highly hierarchical, bureaucratic approach has had in this century, because their environment is no longer stable or noncompetitive.

2. Each of the five value clusters overlaps with others to some degree. Individual values overlap the most with public interest values, which focus on the values that public administrators should have toward those *that they serve,* which includes their roles as custodians, protectors, and stewards. Individual values focus on how public administrators serve and the rights they possess as persons.

3. David Norton called this tendency the "moral minimalism" of modern ethics (David Norton, "Character Ethics and Organizational Life," in *Papers on the Ethics of Administration,* N. Dale Wright, ed. [Provo, UT: Brigham Young University Press, 1988], p. 49).

4. Richard T. Green and Kathryn G. Denhardt, "Preface: Special Issue in Character Ethics in Public Administration" *International Journal of Public Administration* 17, no. 12 (1994), pp. xi–xii.

5. Although initially this theme was primarily conservative, numerous liberals like President Clinton and members of the Left as diverse as Jesse Jackson and Louis Farrakhan are intoning the same point today. Some of the prominent works emphasizing personal responsibility, either on general philosophical and religious grounds, or as a practical counterbalance to the perceived excesses of the welfare state and its concomitant entitlement mentality are William J. Bennett, *The Devaluing of America* (New York: Simon and Schuster, 1992); Alisdair MacIntyre, *After Virtue,* 2nd ed. (Notre Dame, IN: Notre Dame University Press, 1984); and R.N. Bellah, et al., *Habits of the Heart: Individualism and Commitment in American Life* (Berkeley, CA: University of California Press, 1985).

6. The most explicit statement of the ramifications of postmodernism for public administration and policy is Charles J. Fox and Hugh T. Miller, *Postmodern Public Administration: Toward Discourse* (Thousand Oaks, CA: Sage, 1995). Loosely speaking, Michael Harmon's work is in the same camp, although he traveled there via critical theory. See Michael Harmon, *Action Theory for Public Administration* (New York: Longman, 1981); and (with Richard T. Mayer), *Organization Theory for Public Administration* (Boston: Little, Brown, 1986); and most related to the postmodern school, *Responsibility as Paradox: A Critique of Rational Discourse on Government* (Thousand Oaks, CA: Sage, 1995).

7. See Chapter 8 for an extended discussion about the three leading paradigms of public administration.

8. For examples of antitrust legislation, see the Interstate Commerce Act (1887), the Sherman Antitrust Act (1890), and the Clayton Act (1914); notable modern examples of civil rights legislation include congressional legislative acts covering schools, public facilities, and employment (1964), and voting (1957 and 1965).

9. In dozens of workshops on ethics I have found that initially many people can be relatively quick to label as inferior behaviors that stem from a perspective different from their own. Yet usually they are selecting cases of glaring ethical lapses in which generally held principles are being clearly violated. Right-wrong dichotomies are simple in such cases. Workshop participants are much more thoughtful and discriminating when complex situations are presented and in which the most appropriate moral (or truth) base is unclear. This sense of fairness and an ability to appreciate multiple dimensions of morality is seen in the rehabilitation of political leaders, whose quirks, scandals, and documented lapses are generally forgiven if honesty and forthrightness are thereafter demonstrated.

10. Lawrence Kohlberg, *The Philosophy of Moral Development: Moral Stages and the Idea of Justice,* vol. 1 (New York: HarperCollins, 1981).

11. Ibid., p. 409.

12. Ibid., p. 17.

13. Ibid., p. 411.

14. Ibid., p. 18.

15. Ibid., p. 19.

16. Ibid., p. 20.

17. Kohlberg made a strong claim that his research and theory are applicable to all cultures, thus making his claims both essentialist and universal. Postmodernists disagree with the possibility of universalist schemes such as Kohlberg's, but ironically, they would still end up agreeing with him that public administrators have ethical autonomy.

18. Agnes Heller, *General Ethics* (Oxford, England: Basil Blackwell, 1988), pp. 4–5 Another of Kohlberg's main critics argues that his and other universalist schemes are dominated by the male experience. See Carol Gilligan, *In a Different Voice* (Cambridge, MA: Harvard University, 1982).

19. For example, this is essentially the position of Kurt Baier, *The Rational and the Moral Order* (Chicago, IL: Open Court, 1995), pp. 347–350.

20. David Norton, "Moral Integrity, Organizational Management, and Public Education," *International Journal of Public Administration* 17, no. 12 (1994), pp. 2270–2271

21. Carl J. Bellone and Frederick Goerl characterizing what they perceive as excessively limited discretion. "Reconciling Public Entrepreneurship and Democracy," *Public Administration Review* 52, no. 2 (March/April 1992), p. 130.

22. Adolph Eichmann, and most other defendants in the Nuremburg trials, were tried and convicted for war crimes, despite their excuse that they were only following orders. In analyzing the situation, Michael Harmon notes, "Conflicts between conscience and authority are simply conflicts between higher-order and lower-order obligations, in which the Nuremburg defendants and Eichmann were guilty of having obeyed the latter." *Responsibility As Paradox,* op. cit. In other words, a blatantly corrupt state loses its authority as a legitimate source for decisionmaking.

23. For an empirical study on prized values in this regard, see Frances Burke and Amy Black, "Improving Organizational Productivity: Add Ethics," *Public Productivity and Management Review* 14, no. 2 (Winter 1990), pp. 121–133.

24. Milton Rokeach has found that there are approximately 60 to 70 instrumental values. *The Nature of Human Values* (New York: Free Press, 1973), p. 11.

25. Op. cit.; in the Burke and Black study, competence immediately followed honesty, which led the list of values.

26. Often commitment is expressed as duty and obligation by such writers as Carl Friedrick, "Public Policy and the Nature of Administrative Responsibility," in *Public Policy: A Yearbook of the Graduate School of Public Administration, Harvard University,* C.J. Friedrick and Edward S. Mason, eds. (Cambridge: Harvard University Press, 1940), pp. 3–24. It is also expressed as the opposite of not caring enough: "The loss of passion for the public service leads too many into the minimalist habit of simply doing their jobs," said David K. Hart in "To Love the Republic: The Patriotism of Benevolence and Its Rhetorical Obligation," *International Journal of Public Administration* 17, no. 12 (1994), p. 2250. Donna Holmquist states commitment as an ethical imperative when she says that "it is unethical for employees not to give their all," in "Ethics— How Important Is It in Today's Office?" *Public Personnel Management* 22, no. 4 (Winter 1993), p. 540.

27. The most famous single quotation on courage is probably G.K. Chesterton's "that where there is no courage, there is no room for any other virtue." Quoted in Ralph Chandler, "The Problem of Moral Reasoning in American Public Administration: The Case for a Code of Ethics," *Public Administration Review* 43, no. 1 (January/February 1983), pp. 32–39.

28. Emphasized by Stephen Bailey, "Ethics and the Public Service," *Public Administration Review* 24 (December 1964), pp. 234–243; also "The Relationship Between Ethics and Public Service," in *Public Administration and Democracy: Essays in Honor of Paul Appleby,* R. C. Martin, ed. (Syracuse, NY: Syracuse University Press, 1965).

29. A particularly strong statement comes from Stephen Bonczek ("Ethical Decision Making: Challenges of the 1990s—a Practical Approach for Local Government," *Public Personnel Management* 21, no. 1 [Spring 1992], p. 81), "Ethics involves sacrifices and selflessness and becomes the principal criterion of integrity in public officials. This results in the acknowledgement that personal career aspirations must take second place to furthering the public interest."

30. See, for example, Dennis Thompson, "Paradoxes of Government Ethics," *Public Administration Review* 52, no. 3 (May/June 1992), pp. 254–259; Terry Cooper, *The Responsible Administrator* (San Francisco: Jossey-Bass, 1990); Robert N.

Roberts and Marion T. Doss, "Public Service and Private Hospitality: A Case Study in Federal Conflict of Interest," *Public Administration Review* 52, no. 3 (May/June 1992), pp. 260–269.

31. "We are reluctant to close the chapter on safety and begin the one on adventure," Peter Block, *Stewardship: Choosing Service Over Self-Interest* (San Francisco: Berrett-Koehler Publishers, 1993), p. 33.

32. Stephen Bonczek, op. cit., p. 81.

33. Michael Harmon, *Responsibility As Paradox,* op cit., p. 99.

34. P.H. Jos, M.E. Thompkins, and S.W. Hays, "In Praise of Difficult People: A Portrait of the Committed Whistleblower," *Public Administration Review 49,* no. 6 (November/December 1989), pp. 552–561.

35. Abraham Maslow, *Motivation and Personality* (New York: Harper & Row, 1970); "A Theory of Metamotivation: The Biological Rooting of Value-Life," *Humanitas* 4 (1969), pp. 301–343; also, Frederick Herzberg, *Work and the Nature of Man* (Cleveland: World Publishing, 1966), as a modern advocate of this position, Robert Denhardt explains: "It might be suggested that all social institutions, including all large and complex organizations, and especially those in the public sector, should be expected to contribute toward an enhanced moral and ethical climate in which *individual growth and potential* is both valued and encouraged" [italics added]. "Morality As an Organizational Problem," *Public Administration Review* 52, no. 2 (March/April 1992), p. 105.

36. This is an affirmation of positive government, that is, government that actively assists in society building. However, the best-government-is-the-least-government school of thought would not accept this premise in the first place. Recent policy shifts seem to indicate movement in the latter direction.

37. Part of this variation is due to the organizational culture. A strongly hierarchical culture will tend to emphasize personal development as a requirement for a position or a privilege for promotion. Professional bureaucracies may view development as a responsibility and right for professionals only. Adhocracies (flexible organizations in turbulent environments) may view personal development as a necessary element for organizational survival. Henry Mintzberg, *The Structuring of Organizations* (Englewood Cliffs, NJ: Prentice-Hall, 1979). See also the competing values approach of Quinn, Rohrbaugh, and others, which is discussed in Chapter 4. For example, Robert Quinn and Richard Hall, "Environments, Organizations, and Policymakers: Toward an Integrative Framework," in *Organizational Theory and Public Policy,* Richard Hall and Robert Quinn, eds. (Beverly Hills, CA: Sage, 1983).

38. For example, Warren Bennis and Burt Nanus, *Leaders: The Strategies for Taking Charge* (New York: HarperCollins, 1985); James Kouzes and Barry Posner, *The Leadership Challenge: How to Get Extraordinary Things Done in Organizations* (San Francisco: Jossey Bass, 1987); and Rosabeth Moss Kanter, *The Change Masters: Innovation for Productivity in the American Corporation* (New York: Simon and Schuster, 1983)

39. For example, Chris Argyris, *Personality and Organization* (New York: Harper and Row, 1957); Robert Golembiewski, *Men, Management, and Morality* (New York: McGraw-Hill, 1967); and Robert Denhardt, *Theories of Public Organization* (Monterey, CA: Brooks-Cole, 1984).

40. Thomas J. Peters and Robert H. Waterman, Jr., *In Search of Excellence: Lessons from America's Best-Run Companies* (New York: Harper & Row, 1982),

especially Principle Four: "Productivity through people—creating in *all* employees the awareness that their best efforts are essential and that they will share in the rewards of the company's success."; W.E. Deming, *Out of the Crisis* (Cambridge: Center for Advanced Engineering Study, Massachusetts Institute of Technology, 1982); Michael Hammer and James Champy, *Reengineering the Corporation* (New York: HarperCollins, 1993).

41. Harmon, *Responsibility As Paradox,* p 10.

42. Michael Lipsky, *Street Level Bureaucracy* (New York: Russell Sage Foundation, 1980); and Louis Gawthrop, "Images of the Common Good," *Public Administration Review* 53, no. 6 (November/December 1993), pp. 508–515.

43. For example, Jameson W. Doig and Erwin C. Hargrove, *Leadership and Innovation: A Biographical Perspective on Entrepreneurs in Government* (Baltimore: Johns Hopkins Press, 1987); Martin A. Levin and Mary Bryna Sanger, *Making Government Work: How Entrepreneurial Executives Turn Bright Ideas Into Real Results* (San Francisco: Jossey-Bass, 1994).

44. This is a standard part of leadership development workshops. I routinely conduct such workshops as a part of all major management development programs and have experienced this phenomenon hundreds of times.

45. Although this assertion is clearly based on anecdotal evidence, I would point out that it is a mountain of relatively consistent anecdotal evidence based on extensive work in public sector organizations at all levels.

46. C. Argyris and D.A. Schön, *Theory in Practice* (San Francisco: Jossey-Bass, 1974).

47. William Ouchi, *Theory Z: How American Companies Can Meet the Japanese Challenge* (Reading, MA: Addison-Wesley, 1981); and William Ouchi, "Markets, Bureaucracies, and Clans," *Administrative Science Quarterly* 25 (1980), pp. 855–866.

48. David Carnevale, *Trustworthy Government: Leadership and Management Strategies for Building Trust and High Performance* (San Francisco: Jossey-Bass, 1995), pp. xi–xii.

49. Philip K. Howard, *The Death of Common Sense: How Law Is Suffocating America* (New York: Random House, 1994), p. 131.

50. Charles Manz and Henry Sims, Jr., *SuperLeadership: Leading Others to Lead Themselves* (New York: Berkeley Books, 1990), p. 7.

51. See Chapter 12 for a full discussion of this point

52. Reported in Richard T. Green, "Character Ethics and Public Administration," *International Journal of Public Administration* 17, no. 12 (1994), p. 2138.

53. Bruce Payne, "Devices and Desires: Corruption and Ethical Seriousness," in *Public Duties: The Moral Obligations of Government Officials,* Joel Fleishman, Lance Liebman, and Mark Moore, eds. (Cambridge, MA: Harvard University Press, 1981).

54. Stephen K. Bailey, op. cit.; Dennis Thompson, "Paradoxes of Government Ethics," *Public Administration Review* 52, no. 3 (May/June 1992), pp. 254–259; and Terry Cooper, *The Responsible Administrator* (San Francisco: Jossey-Bass, 1990).

55. Dennis Thompson, "The Possibility of Administrative Ethics," *Public Administration Review* 45, no. 5 (September/October 1985), pp. 555–561.

56. Mark Moore, "Realms of Obligations and Virtue," in *Public Duties: The Moral Obligations of Government Officials,* Joel Fleishman, Lance Leibman, and Mark Moore, eds. (Cambridge, MA: Harvard University Press, 1981), p. 5.

57. Currently much of the national discussion is emphasizing the need to acknowledge not only individual contributions but also individual responsibility personally, in civic life, and in public administration. Michael Harmon aptly notes that "Reich and other commentators on both the political left and right are increasingly dismayed by the *atrophy* of individual agency, a loss of a vital sense of personal responsibility, not only *to* others, but also *for* the shaping of the individual's own destiny," *Responsibility As Paradox.* op. cit., p. 149.

58. Fritz Roethlisberger and William Dickson, *Management and the Worker* (Cambridge, MA: Harvard University Press, 1939)

59. Karl Marx, "The Spirit of Bureaucracy," in *Writings of the Young Marx on Philosophy and Society,* Lloyd Easton and Kurt Guddat, eds. (Garden City, NJ: Doubleday, 1967); Karl Marx and Friedrich Engels, *Writings on the Paris Commune,* ed. Hal Draper (New York: Monthly Review Press, 1971).

60. Even the classic management theorists who most strongly advocated closed systems—Weber, Taylor, and Wilson—were more aware of the importance of individual contributions than they are often given credit for. Weber's theoretical ideal may seem cold and hierarchical to some, but it is the basis of the meritocracies today that are generally considered superior to hiring by whim, and giving higher posts according to social rank or ability to buy positions that was common in the early nineteenth century. Taylor's cold-hearted, machinelike efficiency did lead to efficiency increases in places like the Ford Motor Company, which in turn led to wage increases. See Nick Henry, *Public Administration and Public Affairs,* 3rd ed. (Englewood Cliffs, NJ: Prentice-Hall, 1986), pp. 51–52. Richardson and Nigro point out that Woodrow Wilson was keenly aware that good public administration is not achieved solely through hierarchical obedience to legislative interests, but is also achieved through designing public service to contribute to the administrator's "sustenance," "conscience," "ambition," and "interests by advancing his honor and establishing his character." William D. Richardson and Lloyd G. Nigro, "Administrative Ethics and Founding Thought: Constitutional Correctives, Honor, and Education," *Public Administration Review* 46, no. 5 (September/October 1987), pp. 367–377.

61. However, the difficulty of empirically relating organizational effectiveness, itself a difficult idea to conceptualize, with the humanistic model of organizational motivation is not easy. See Frank Gibson and Clyde Teasley, "The Humanistic Model of Organizational Motivation: A Review of Research Support," *Public Administration Review* 33, no. 1 (January/February 1973), pp. 89–96.

62. In Ralph Chandler, "The Problem of Moral Reasoning in American Public Administration: The Case for a Code of Ethics," *Public Administration Review* 43, no. 1 (January/February 1983), p. 35.

63. Howard, op. cit.

64. Elliott Richardson, "Ethical Principles for Public Servants," *The Public Manager* 4 (Winter 1992–1993), p. 38.

65. This is generally true because of its lower level of socialism, its high level of decentralization, and its high level of administrative openness.

66. This discussion of the role of government in society, in terms of the size of government and the depth of the safety net (for all classes and groups), is one of the primary topics of Chapter 6.

67. See for example, Jacques Chevallier, "Public Administration in Statist France," *Public Administration Review* 56, no. 1 (January/February 1996), pp. 67–74.

CHAPTER 3

The Role of
Professional Values

Sociologists have long understood the importance of professional groups in society. Emile Durkheim saw them as important integrating mechanisms between individuals and society in the modern industrial era. Modern society would be much benefited by these formal and informal professional associations, he reasoned, which would aggregate interests and impose self-discipline at a manageable level.[1] Talcott Parsons also stressed the growth of professions in the twentieth century, and noted their particular importance in the United States and Canada.[2] Although their influence is usually subtler than the influence of organizations and the legal system, in some ways it is more pervasive and ingrained, as we shall see when we turn to the characteristics of professionalism.

This chapter first examines the characteristics of professional groups—the professional values environment. What defines a profession and how does it evolve? How does professionalism affect the character of work life for individuals? How does it affect organizational structures and norms? Does it have a significant effect on a society at large? Next, it looks at the nature of professional values in the public sector. How well does the public sector measure up to the ideal profession? Is professionalism growing? What is the effect on public sector individuals and organizations? Finally, the chapter assesses the potential contributions and possible problems of professional values in the public sector.

The Professional Values Environment

Ernest Greenwood describes five attributes for an ideal profession:[3]

1. A systematic body of theory
2. A professional culture
3. The sanction of the community
4. A regulative code of ethics
5. Substantial professional authority

Ernest Greenwood has noted that "strictly speaking, these attributes are not the exclusive monopoly of the professions."[4] In fact, many if not all occupations may be placed somewhere along a continuum between the "ideal" profession at one end and the completely unorganized, occupational categories at the other.[5]

A Systematic Body of Knowledge

Although it is often thought that the key distinction between a profession and a nonprofession is superior skill, most experts agree that the skills that characterize a profession also include mastery of a *systematic body of knowledge*. That mastery in turn leads to the need for more than the skill-based apprenticeships that emphasize mechanical dexterity and memorization that have long been typical of guilds and their successors. In addition to the types of learning common to apprenticeships, professions tend to require extensive, conceptual learning underlying the skill, which in turn requires formal schooling and intellectual practice prior to on-site training. All professionals, whether they practice their professions or do research to advance them, are expected to have a high degree of conceptual mastery.

A Professional Culture

Extended schooling and professional apprenticeships help create a *professional culture*—the group's social values and basic beliefs that are the unquestioned premises upon which its very existence rests. Foremost among those values is the essential worth of the service that the professional group provides to the community. Each profession tends to consider its service a vital social good and believes that the community would be immeasurably impaired by its absence.

Professional cultures are expressed in norms, symbols, and a worldview. Norms serve as guides to behavior in social situations, and they include a range of activities from being admitted into the profession, interacting with others in the profession, and succeeding in the profession. The symbols of the profession include its history and folklore, its vernacular and jargon, and its emblems and dress. True professions are often termed "callings" because they traditionally serve as bases for lifetime careers. Lawyers and doctors, for example, may do things other than practice law and medicine, but their ideas of themselves are usually forever shaped by the professional acculturation process.

Sanctions of the Community

Professions maintain continuity and discipline through external and internal controls. The external control of the professions is represented by the *sanction of the community* in the profession's behalf, which results in special powers and privileges. One of the strongest powers of a profession is the control over its training centers through accrediting processes, which in turn control admission to the profession. When accreditation and admissions standards are rigorous, training and licensing are nearly synonymous, and fellow professionals totally control them. This control results in a virtual monopoly by some professions granted by the community to the professional group.[6] The profession should be careful not to misuse this monopoly by demanding excessive professional wages and perquisites. Professionalization inevitably leads to higher-than-average salaries and benefits, which in the most successful professions may be four or five times the national average income. Other important privileges of professions are client-professional confidentiality, which bestows a special legal status, and the "immunity from community judgment on technical matters."[7] Since only fellow professionals can sit in judgment, self-regulation is easier and scandals are more likely to be averted.

A Regulative Code of Ethics

One of the most powerful internal controls is a *regulative code of ethics.* Codes of ethics are both formal (such as the well-known Hippocratic Oath) and informal (the support of the oath by the medical culture). Formal codes can be enforced by powerful professional associations, whose revocation of membership is tantamount to professional decertification. Informal codes can be enforced both by peer pressure and by economic pressures implicit in jobs and referrals. One of the important elements of professional codes of ethics is the fair and equitable treatment of clients, and the tendency toward what Parsons called "disinterestedness," which leads professionals to give the same high caliber of service to all, regardless of the fee charged.[8] Professional codes tend to emphasize the rapid and nonfinancial dissemination of new knowledge and to discourage blatant competition for clients or the reckless disparagement of colleagues because of the loss of professional standing that would follow such actions.

Substantial Professional Authority

Extensive training, sanction by the community, and self-regulation lead to *substantial professional authority,* bestowing upon professionals a unique position vis-à-vis the people to whom they provide services. Nonprofessionals tend to have *customers*—people who know enough about the service to be able to intelligently "shop around," bargain over prices, and, frequently, ask for service modifications. Nonprofessionals advertise the features of their products and the services in which they excel, and their customers are expected to be able to judge the quality firsthand because of the accessibility of their technical knowledge of the products and services. Professionals are employed (or "retained") by *clients*—parties who, for the most part, are laypersons, without the special training or skills of the professionals they employ. Laypersons cannot be expected to judge the quality of the services that professionals provide. Professionals need therefore to regulate themselves so that their clients may expect consistency and quality from them. Professionals frown on advertising because it would imply inconsistencies in their skills and services. "The client's subordination to professional authority invests the professional with a monopoly of judgment. When an occupation strives toward professionalization, one of its aspirations is to acquire this monopoly."[9] Jargon, highly technical legal requirements, and complex technological processes or equipment greatly enhance professional authority.

The Evolution of Professions

Many professions evolve in a similar pattern. Theodore Caplow suggested that the first step to professionalization is usually a professional association, so that members can be more clearly identified and support for advancement of the profession can be generated.[10] Next, incipient professions tend to change their names, "which serves the multiple function of reducing identification with the previous occupational status, asserting a technological monopoly, and providing a title which can be monopolized, the former one being usually in the public domain."[11] The third step involves the promulgation of a code of ethics, which "asserts the social utility of the occupation, sets up public welfare rationale, and develops rules which serve as further criteria to eliminate the unqualified and unscrupulous."[12] The fourth and final step is the agitation for social approval and public support to maintain occupational barriers. Initially this may only limit the use of specialized titles, but in later stages "the mere doing of the acts reserved to the profession is a crime."[13] The maturation of sophisticated education, training systems, and protocols occurs simultaneously with all these steps and is key to the more highly evolved levels of professionalism.

Professionalism substantially affects the quality of work life. As indicated earlier, professionals tend to enjoy relatively high social esteem and commensurate financial compensation. They tend to view their profession as a lifelong vocation, even though they may change specific jobs. Professionals historically have had a good deal of control over their own work. This was more so in the past, when most professionals were self-employed, as doctors and lawyers were in private practice. However, even in organizational settings, professionals by definition still have substantial job control.

High-esteem professionals also tend to be treated differently in personnel systems in organizations. In fact there are really three major types of personnel systems, although they are often blended in reality. *At-pleasure personnel systems* are employer focused and tend to be the preferred model for much of the competitive or dynamic private sector. *Merit personnel systems* are job and task focused and tend to be preferred in the public sector and the more stable parts of the private sector. *Professional personnel systems* are person focused, so that in some cases rank resides in the person regardless of the job, as it does for the military and university faculty. For many, the explicit or implicit rank associated with being a professional is an attractive feature (in addition to the earning advantages). In merit systems, employees tend to become highly task oriented, but in professional systems, employees tend to be client centered (their historic employers). Also, professional systems tend to hire and promote based on a person's real or potential lifetime contribution, as opposed to the more immediate emphasis on productivity found in true merit systems. Therefore, job tenure historically has been a frequent feature of professional systems.[14]

Professionals are affected by organizational settings, and they in turn affect their organizations. Although that statement applies to all professionals, the discussion here is limited to bureaucratic organizations—organizations that are larger, that have a good deal of formalized behavior, and that do not respond to change rapidly—although other organizational structures do exist.[15] Sometimes professionals work in what Henry Mintzberg called "machine bureaucracies," organizations in which the executive core makes key decisions, most front-line jobs are preferably narrow but not specialized, control is centralized, and mass production is critical.[16] In such organizations, professionals are either unusual exceptions to the hierarchical nature of the organization (such as the organization's in-house doctor, general counsel, or resident expert who serves as an internal consultant) or the professional has assumed a managerial role as well as a professional role. This latter role causes some conflict because managers are expected to give their first loyalty to the organization, whereas professionals are expected to give their first loyalty to their discipline or to their clients.[17] Professionals such as engineers, scientists, lawyers, and educators may not then enjoy reputations as effective managers unless they have had additional training.

In another important organizational model, professionals are at the center of organizational work, as they are in hospitals, universities, public accounting firms, social work agencies, and craft-production firms. According to Mintzberg, the "professional bureaucracy relies for coordination on the standardization of skills and its associated design parameter, training and indoctrination. It hires duly trained and indoctrinated specialists—professionals—for the operating core, and then gives them considerable control over their own work."[18] Because of the prestige of the front-line workers and the nature of the work, professionals exercise critical control over entire organizations, so that much of the decisionmaking is actually bottom-up as compared to the top-down style of the traditional machine bureaucracy. Professional power is often exercised by ensuring that many (or all) of the key executives are fellow professionals. Professionals in organizations usually use general work protocols, but they are always given greater freedom in executing tasks, both because of their expertise and because of the difficulty in completely standardizing their work. Even with their greater freedom, however, conflicts between organizational and professional loyalties may arise, although professional loyalties are inevitably expected to be far stronger in professional bureaucracies.

Professions also affect society at large. As noted earlier, Emile Durkheim and other famous sociologists (such as Max Weber) largely have praised the salubrious aspects of professions as mediating groups in modern society. Professions provide a relatively uniform, high-quality standard of good for society in selected areas with their ethic of protecting the client (as opposed to the attitude of *caveat emptor*—let the buyer beware—of much business) in exchange for esteem and financial comfort.[19] Yet it has long been recognized that professions are capable of abusing privilege or stifling social good for personal or class benefit.[20] Powerful professions are sometimes accused, for example, of restricting entry into the field more to reduce competition than to improve quality. General social trust of professions is important to them because they are allowed to create their own specialized norms, which often vary from those of society at large. One such instance occurs when a lawyer represents a loathed criminal. As John Rohr notes, "The justification for the exceptions the professions demand from universal moral rules is grounded in an implicit, utilitarian assumption that the profession itself can produce sufficient benefits to society to outweigh whatever harm is caused by its departure from customary morality."[21] The contemporary reduction in the levels of trust in all professions (which is mirrored in less trust in institutions as well), should therefore trouble professionals. One likely ramification is additional legislative action to control professional standards and to provide stricter penalties against errant professionals, in a sense regulating their monopoly more tightly.

Professionalism dramatically expanded after World War II. Jobs mirrored the increasing complexity and technological sophistication of society. As some jobs became outdated, those that were left usually demanded greater education and training, with a corresponding need for greater sophistication and better problem-solving skills. Increased professionalism has also been driven by worker interest in the enhanced prestige and income possible. Workers, as much as employers, have fueled the demand for credentialism; but workers alone have pursued external and internal controls over their disciplines in pursuit of professional monopolies.

The trend toward increased professionalism is showing some signs of abatement. Two major factors are countering that trend. First, because professionals demand greater pay, the cost of labor has become an increasingly shrill concern in the current global economy. With an increasing number of jobs classified as professional, labor costs have caused the overhaul of many industries, from manufacturing to service industries. Second, because of the perception of excessive power accruing to many professions, efforts at "deprofessionalization" have increased. For example, the professionalization of management that began after World War II has taken a radical reversal in the last decade. Managers have lost their quasi-tenure status, have seen employment and promotion opportunities decreased, and have been forced to delegate much of their decisionmaking authority to subordinates and customers. The only aspect of professionalism for managers that seems to be increasing is educational standards. Here, as in many other professions, the loss of monopoly over standards and the erosion of a seniority system have produced a sharp increase in the emphasis given to education and training as competitive factors in the job market.

What Are Professional Values in the Public Sector?

In all organizations, occupational groupings differ in the strength of their professional identities and rights; in hospitals, for example, doctors are generally the most highly professionalized, administrators and nurses are the next most fully professsionalized, and clerical and other support staff are the least professionalized. Similarly, in the public sector some groups have relatively strong professional identities, such as

- Teachers
- Land managers and wildlife biologists (in forestry and parks)
- Military
- Public emergency workers
- Fire fighters
- Police and other law enforcement agents
- Lawyers (especially in legal agencies such as attorney general offices)
- Doctors and nurses in medical agencies
- Engineers in transportation agencies
- Accountants in auditing and comptroller departments
- Computer experts in MIS departments
- Librarians
- Purchasing agents and facility managers in administrative agencies

- Scientists in research agencies (such as NASA and the Nuclear Regulatory Commission)
- Foreign service experts (in the State Department, USIA, and USAID)
- Intelligence experts
- Zoologists and botanists in agricultural agencies
- Curators
- Economists
- Environmentalists
- Social workers

Not all of the thousands of occupations in the public sector have strong professional identities. Many are lower-skilled occupations, such as manual laborers, clerical and support workers, and white-collar personnel. Such occupations have narrow functional responsibilities and lack the perquisites of high-esteem professions. Of course, occupations vary in their level of professionalization among themselves and by level of government as well. Some areas, such as corrections (penology) and social assistance occupations at the state level, have been slow to professionalize due to financial constraints and less desirable working conditions.

American public administration has not, by and large, created a professional administrative class per se, as have the British[22] or French.[23] Members of a professional administrative class have generalized management skills, which they have acquired from specific educational and training sources; loyalties to the system greater than those to the organization they currently manage; a sense of career as an administrator; extensive authority; and a strong sense of professional community developed during long years of education and training with other careerists. Professional administrators regularly rotate assignments based on management needs rather than on specialist backgrounds related to the agency mission. In the United States, the Senior Executive Service was created in part to fill this perceived need and is the closest equivalent to a professional administrative class.[24] Although the focus is narrower, the U.S. military also emphasize professional administration through their insistence on management rotation prior to advancement and through extensive education and training that enhances a strong sense of military culture. Some other less pronounced examples of a professional administration ethos are the foreign service at the federal level and law enforcement at all levels. Whether the lack of a strongly defined professional administrative class is a virtue or weakness is disputed. William Richardson and Lloyd Nigro, for example, speculate that the lack of a coherent, professional administrative class may have "seriously eroded the foundations upon which the Founders relied to assure that the regime would be served by publicly virtuous administrators capable of being effectively superintended by public opinion."[25]

Determinants of Professionalism and the Public Sector

If one uses level of education as a primary determinant of professionalism, then the public sector is more highly professionalized than the bulk of the workforce. According to the Census Bureau, the number of professional, technical, and kindred personnel jumped from 2.6 million to 5.4 million from 1960 to 1976.[26] "Nearly 40 percent of all professional, technical, and kindred civilian workers in the United States are employed by a government, a figure that has remained stable since 1970."[27] The level of highly educated workers in the public sector has always exceeded that in the private sector by a substantial amount. "Professional, technical, and kindred public employees account for more than a fifth of all federal civilian employees, 39 percent of all state employees, and 42 percent of all local employees."[28] The especially high figures for state and local governments reflect the high proportion of educators in the personnel systems.

Although professionals in the public sector share many similarities with professionals in the private sector, they also differ from them on a number of characteristics. The following discussion examines these similarities and differences, primarily for the more professionalized groups who have a disproportionate effect on the agencies they serve, especially when they are concentrated in professional bureaucracies.[29]

A Systematic Body of Knowledge

The first of the five professional characteristics identified earlier in this chapter, a systematic body of knowledge, increasingly applies to a large number of positions in government agencies and departments. The case of municipal clerks will illustrate this point. The municipal clerk serves an array of functions, depending on the size of the city or town. In larger jurisdictions, the municipal clerk is primarily a records manager, elections officer, and council minutes taker. Narrow as these functions may be, the clerk of a major city may have hundreds of employees. In the smallest jurisdictions, the clerk may be the de facto town manager, running all town functions for the town council. Most of the approximately 20,000 municipal clerks in the United States historically came to their jobs with limited education, no formal training, and no continuing education. In recent years, the concept of training municipal clerks has spread dramatically, and today there is a formalized and standardized program of study for municipal clerks and their staffs in each of the 50 states (and internationally). The 100-hour curriculum is divided into three segments that are rotated annually. An individual who completes the curriculum receives the CMC (Certified Municipal Clerk) professional designation, assuming he or she has also accumulated the experience and attendance record at professional meetings required by the International Institute of Municipal Clerks. Most states offer an advanced academy each year as well at the same time as their basic institute. This formalized training focuses on both the technical aspects of the municipal clerk's jobs, such as issuing bonds and purchasing insurance, to such general management issues as communication and interpersonal skills. Although relatively few municipal clerks are statutorily required by their councils to be certified, the expectation of certification has risen substantially in the profession and is increasingly becoming a council stipulation for the post.

Public sector professionals, like their private sector counterparts, are highly educated and trained at the "pigeonholing process." "The professional has two tasks: (1) to categorize the client's need in terms of a contingency, which indicates the standard program to use, a task known as diagnosis, and (2) to apply, or execute, that program."[30] Yet the application or execution is rarely identical for professionals (as it might be in a production line) because of the complex nature of the work. A teacher generally handles discipline problems of a particular nature in a similar fashion, but he or she uses professional discretion in the application of the process, depending on the severity of the problem, the background of the child, and the external contingencies of the situation. A heart surgeon uses the same bypass procedure on hundreds of patients, but the fluctuations in each patient's condition and anatomy require expert variation, especially when unusual circumstances dictate immediate remediation.

In addition to the substantive expertise that all professionals bring from their formal education, professionals in the public sector must be especially well versed in the legal ramifications of service provision and the philosophy behind it. Those who work in child protection services must be attuned not only to the problems they uncover—both the children potentially in harm and the parents needing assistance, counseling, and/or restraint—but also to legal restrictions such as citing abuse, removing children from home environments, and maintaining confidentiality.

A Professional Culture

The second attribute of professions discussed earlier was a professional culture. The example of the municipal clerks is again instructive. In the 1950s, before the spread of the municipal clerks' institutes and academies, they were largely indoctrinated by firsthand experience in the town or city government of which they were a part. Thus the organization had the greatest effect on their development as an occupational grouping. Today, standardized training and continuing education provide opportunities to build a professional community and professional ideals. Many experienced clerks serve their professional community by serving as officers in their clerks' association and by attending the annual national convention. As a result, municipal clerks are now affected as much by their national professional culture as by their organizational culture.

Community Sanction on Restricted Title and Function

The third characteristic of professionals is the sanction of the community to restrict the title and functions. In fact, municipal clerks are examples of public administrators who have statutory titles and often have legal authority for given areas, as do many public sector administrators. Municipal clerks must go through a legal authorizing process, even if the process is not a highly rigorous one, as might be the case in very small rural towns. As with all public administrators, access to the field and authority to practice do have legal sanctions, but these sanctions may or may not be guided by the kind of external professional associations that characterize the strong professions. When President Reagan broke the strike by the Air Traffic Controllers, for example, he diminished the profession's influence over its own fate. In another (negative) example, many states are considering decreasing requirements for teachers, in order to "open up" the profession, despite the concerns of teachers' associations. If such changes were enacted, not only would there be public and private sector teachers, there might also be greater access to the profession. This may be a reaction to the "discomfiting influence" of professional associations alleged by many critics. For example, one commentator notes:

> Professional societies are increasingly exercising considerable power in public affairs; the intimate connection between them and public

personnel career systems enhances this power. Studies indicating this growing and discomfiting influence by the professions in government, mostly by political scientists, are too numerous to list, and the variations and subtleties that their influence can assume are limitless. It will suffice to note that the control by private professional associations of a particular sliver of knowledge enables them to have considerable input into those public decisions made in their sphere of expertise. Studies of the decision process in regulatory agencies, studies of the politics of professional licensing procedures in the states, and studies of the raw power and generously funded political activity of some "apolitical" professional societies, such as the American Medical Association, indicate the gravity of the problem not only for public personnel administration but for the public generally.[31]

A Self-Imposed Regulative Code of Ethics

The fourth characteristic of professionalism is a self-imposed regulative code of ethics and standards which, in the strong professions, is administered by fellow professionals. For example, physicians are evaluated by boards composed of other doctors, and professors are granted tenure and promotion by colleagues of a similar or higher rank. Nonprofessionals, on the other hand, are more likely to be regulated by managers than by peer review. Public sector professionals are expected to maintain a higher standard than that accepted for industry, but professional peer review is not the norm.[32] Ethics standards are essentially legislated rather than formulated by professional associations. Instead of professional peer review, public professionals have settled on strong due process rights found in contemporary merit systems, similar to what unions have brought to less professionalized employee groups. Given the recent attacks on seniority-based merit systems (with their quasi-property rights) and on tenure systems, professional self-regulation in the public sector is likely to diminish in the next decade.[33]

Substantial Authority Over Clients

Finally, measured by the attribute of exercising substantial authority or judgment over their clients, public sector professionals clearly have a strong tie to professionalism because of the power and resources of the state vested in them. From the very powerful judges to the lowliest social service intake workers, public administrators have unusual authority over their clients. Control of professional authority is handled differently in the two sectors. Private sector professionals are more likely to be paid, directly or indirectly, by their clients, so there is a natural curb to the power of their expertise and position. In the public sector, however, such curbs on authority are more likely to be administratively determined (not a professional characteristic), since the direct financial link to the client is usually nonexistent. All professionals today are experiencing a more in-formed and more aggressive public; thus the public's quiet acceptance of expertise and position power has diminished. Professionals such as law-yers moving increasingly to advertising for "customers" symbolize this shift; similarly, the public sector has recently accepted the widespread use of the idea of customers.[34]

In sum, the public sector has been more affected than the private sec-tor by rising education and training standards; furthermore, the overall sense of professionalism (standards that are taught and imposed outside specific organizations) has risen significantly. Public sector professionals may have substantial legal position authority, but they are also more circumscribed by bureaucratic controls than are most professionals. Long-term trends advancing professionalism among all occupations are experiencing opposing trends as education and training continue to be advocated but professional power and elitism come under attack for eco-nomic and sociological reasons.

What Are the Potential Contributions of Professional Values?

The rise of professionalism brings many positive values to the public sec-tor.[35] James Stever holds professionalism as one of the great legitimizing factors for public administration in the "post-progressive era."[36] Five will be discussed here: heightened levels of competence, outside review, job satisfaction, innovation, and client satisfaction.

1. *Heightened levels of competence.* In explaining the recent trend toward "learning organizations," Watkins and Marsick note that "in the past, about 80 percent of most jobs involved compliance with clearly developed rules and procedures, whereas about 20 percent of most jobs involved judgment. . . . Today, these proportions are exactly reversed."[37] In other words, as organiza-tions move away from an overwhelming reliance on bureaucratic, hierarchical, organizational structures with their machinelike algorithms, to more flexible structures in order to handle increased

change, more judgment (and thus greater professionalism) will be required. Professionalism brings high levels of both expertise and competence. Philip Howard argues that our current system of regulation stifles the use of professional judgment and produces inflexible decisions that often are counterproductive to the policies they were meant to further.[38]

2. *Outside review.* Professionalism also helps balance inordinate organizational power by providing pressure for general standards. As Nicholas Henry notes, professionalism brings "enforcement of minimal ethical and technical standards" as well as "insulation from pressure to discriminate against clients."[39]

3. *Job satisfaction.* Professionalism increases job satisfaction and organizational democracy. Because of their expertise, professionals have greater control over their work and over administrative decisionmaking than occurs in standard production-line (machine) bureaucracies. This avoids the long-recognized problem of worker alienation and excessive task specialization. Although this control weakens the authorized chain of command frequently associated with democratic accountability, others argue that rigid democratic control adds "doubtful utility in some fields,"[40] especially at the mid- and micro-decisionmaking levels. Professionals also receive great satisfaction from the higher levels of pay and esteem they generally receive for their professional expertise.

4. *Innovation.* Professionalism encourages the dissemination of innovation through the free flow of ideas. Professionals generally make no attempt to patent their ideas for sale (which is not to say that they are not eager for attribution and recognition of their contributions). Surgeons do not sell medical procedures, and professors do not sell new theories (except indirectly through book sales). Because of the ethic of keeping up to date with the state of the field, professionals tend to be avid conference goers, book readers, and seminar takers. They feel embarrassed if their understanding of the field lags behind.

5. *Client satisfaction.* Professionals historically have a special concern for clients, which can be lost in hierarchically oriented bureaucracies with their focus on control and task efficiency, and in market bureaucracies with their focus on competitive responsiveness and profit.

What Are the Problems of Excessive Reliance on Professional Values?

As much as most individuals want to enjoy the perquisites of professionalism, problems may result from an excessive reliance on professional values. Forty or fifty years ago, the excesses of professionalism were noted but were not of much concern because levels of professionalism were far lower and the power of professional groups far less. Today, so many occupations have increased their professional standing, and the strongest professions have become so powerful, that there is an important social debate about the limits of professionalism. The following concerns about professionalism have many variations and are likely to become more hotly debated in the next decade as professionalism advances but collides with growing countervailing forces.

First, professional groups can insist on excessively high levels of education and training. This can lead to supply-side problems. When only high prestige (and high pay) professionals are empowered to provide service for routine or simple needs, the result is a "limitation of public services by the professionals' insistence on the maintenance of unrealistic professional standards."[41] A second concern is that excessive specialization often occurs in advanced professionalism, which may provide some benefits to select clients but can also deter organizational flexibility and adaptability. In talking about this problem, Donald Kettl acknowledges the contributions of specialization in the past but asserts that organizational learning is more often than not inhibited by it today because of the barriers it creates and the lack of communication that follows.[42] Thus advanced professionalism can conflict directly with public interest values.

A third powerful concern about professional values is their tendency toward excessive control and power for a select group in society (the professionals themselves). This tendency leads to a variety of group biases. Professionals (and their unionized cousins) are often accused, as noted earlier in this chaper, of excessively limiting access to their field as a means of keeping demand artificially high. Strong professional occupations are critiqued for providing "undue influence wielded by special publics through professional ties."[43] Professionals like to set their own standards and regulate their own members using the force of law for exclusive rights in an area, so they instinctively and frequently insulate themselves from democratic control and, more ominously, from democratic scrutiny. Again, this conflicts with public interest values.

Fourth, although professional power is supposedly based on individual expertise and group dedication to a socially approved client group, professional power is as often used to promote the concerns of professionals for increased pay, benefits, and superior working conditions. In terms of general social policy, such concerns mean that increasing professionalization costs the public a great deal more in personnel costs, especially since government agencies are historically among the most labor intensive. For example, as cities dramatically expand the professionalism of their sworn peace officers, they are finding public safety (law enforcement and fire service) costs consuming up to 50 percent of their budgets. Internally, professionals often encourage an occupational caste system, which they implicitly believe is necessary because of the virtue of their expertise and for the protection of their privileges. In other words, professionals often believe in organizational democracy for themselves and an authoritarian hierarchy for other workers.

Finally, professionals' concern for clients can become obsessive and unrealistic. This becomes an issue when the costs associated with the attention and care received by selected individuals and small groups must be borne by the state. Although there are endless ways to prolong life, reduce harm, and promote social well-being, all public actions have their associated costs. Professional groups can distort the cost-benefit relationship, such that no cost that the general public must bear is too great for the group they serve.

Conclusion

Professionalism, which springs from the ancient crafts and their guild associations, brings much richness to contemporary society, which needs the expertise and commitment to clients and specific areas of knowledge and practice that they encourage. Professionalism is more than just high levels of education and expertise, however. In its more advanced forms, it entails a professional culture, an ability to self-regulate, some legal control over the discipline, and substantial influence over client options and decisions. Although professionalism in the public sector shares many similarities with that in the private sector, it also varies significantly. Public professionals have the automatic use of public power, but in turn, are generally more circumscribed by hierarchical authority and controls than is normal.

As global competition increases, the public debate about the virtues of professionalism is generally heating up in society, and the public sector variant will not in any way be exempted from this scrutiny. Increased levels of professionalism do bring the virtues of enhanced competence, outside review, job satisfaction, diffusion of knowledge, and client satisfaction. But excessive professionalism can lead to unrealistic standards and training, excessive specialization causing organizational dysfunction, an overly inflated role in public decisionmaking, too much control by professionals as a special interest group seeking advantages for themselves, and an impractical exaggeration of their clients' special concerns and needs over the needs of the good of the general public.

Notes

1. Emile Durkheim, *The Division of Labor in Society* (New York: Free Press, 1933).
2. Talcott Parsons, "The Professions and Social Structure," *Social Forces* 17 (May 1939), pp. 457–467.
3. Ernest Greenwood, "Attributes of a Profession," *Social Work* 2, no. 3 (July 1957), pp. 44–55. For alternative lists of elements, see Pugh's list in Chapter 1 and the list by Edward Gross (*Work and Society* [New York: Thomas Y. Cromwell, 1958]): the unstandardized product, degree of personality involvement of the professional, wide knowledge of a specialized technique, sense of obligation [to one's art], sense of group identity, and significance of the occupational service to society.
4. Greenwood, p. 45.
5. Howard M. Vollmer and Donald L. Mills, *Professionalization* (Englewood Cliffs, NJ: Prentice-Hall, 1966), p. 2.
6. According to Theodore Caplow, the final step in the evolution of professionalization is the sanction of the community that provides monopolistic characteristics of powerful professions. See Caplow, *The Sociology of Work* (Minneapolis: University of Minnesota Press, 1954).
7. Greenwood, op. cit, p. 48.
8. Parsons, op. cit.
9. Greenwood, op. cit., p. 47.
10. Caplow, op. cit.
11. Caplow, ibid, p. 139.
12. Caplow, ibid.
13. Caplow, ibid, p. 140
14. Strong seniority systems are a modified form of tenure. In the public sector the presence of strong seniority considerations has meant that "true" merit was a key factor in initial hiring, whereas a modified form of professionalism has often been dominant thereafter.
15. See the next chapter for an extensive discussion of the range of organizations that exist.
16. Henry Mintzberg, *The Structuring of Organizations* (Englewood Cliffs, NJ: Prentice-Hall, 1979).
17. See for example, Howard M. Vollmer and Donald L. Mills, "Professionals and Complex Organizations," *Professionalism* (Englewood Cliffs, NJ: Prentice-Hall, 1966), pp. 264–294.
18. Mintzberg, op. cit. p. 349.

19. T.H. Marshall, "The Recent History of Professionalism in Relation to Social Structure and Social Policy," *Canadian Journal of Economics and Political Science* 5, no. 3 (August 1939), pp. 325–340.

20. Robert MacIver, "The Social Significance of Professional Ethics," *Annals of the American Academy of Political and Social Science* 297 (January 1955), pp. 118–124.

21. John A. Rohr, "The Problem of Professional Ethics," *Bureaucrat* (Spring 1991), p. 10.

22. R.A. Chapman, *The Higher Civil Service in Britain* (London: Constable, 1970); Richard Rose, "British Government: The Job at the Top," in *Bureaucrats and Policy Making: A Comparative Overview*, Ezra N. Suleiman, ed. (New York: Holmes & Meier, 1984), pp. 136–173; and Brian Smith, "The United Kingdom," in *Public Administration in Developed Democracies: A Comparative Study*, Donald C. Rowat, ed. (New York: Marcel Dekker, 1988), Chapter 4.

23. Alfred Diament, "The French Administrative System: The Republic Passes But the Administration Remains," in *Toward the Comparative Study of Public Administration*, William J. Siffin, ed. (Bloomington, IN: Department of Government, Indiana University, 1957), pp. 182–218; F. Ridley and J. Blondel, *Public Administration in France* (London: Routledge & Kegan, 1964); Ezra Suleiman, *Politics, Power, and Bureaucracy in France: The Administrative Elite* (Princeton: Princeton University Press, 1974); and Yves Meny, "France," in *Public Administration in Developed Democracies*, Donald C. Rowat, ed. (New York: Marcel Dekker, 1988), Chapter 17.

24. Frederick C. Mosher, *Democracy and the Public Service*, 2nd ed. (New York: Oxford University Press, 1982); Office of Personnel Management, *Civil Service Reform: A Report on the First Year* (Washington, DC: Government Printing Office, 1980); Cole Blease Graham, Jr., and Steven Hays, *Managing the Public Organization* (Washington, DC: Congressional Quarterly Press, 1986), especially pp. 127–130; Patricia W. Ingraham, James Thompson, and Elliot Eisenberg, "Political Management Strategies and Political/Career Relationships: Where Are We Now in the Federal Government?" *Public Administration Review* 55, no. 3 (May/June 1995), pp. 263–272; Patricia Wilson, "Power, Politics, and Other Reasons Why Senior Executives Leave the Federal Government," *Public Administration Review* 54, no. 1 (January/February 1994), pp. 12–19; and Barry Posner and Warren Schmidt, "An Updated Look at the Values and Expectations of Federal Government Executives," *Public Administration Review* 54, no. 1 (January/February 1994), pp. 20–24.

25. William D. Richardson and Lloyd G. Nigro, "Administrative Ethics and Founding Thought: Constitutional Corrections, Honor, and Education," *Public Administration Review* 47, no. 5 (September/October 1987), p. 374.

26. The statistics and quotations in this paragraph are drawn from Nicholas Henry, *Public Administration and Public Affairs*, 3rd ed. (Englewood Cliffs, NJ: Prentice Hall, 1986), p. 202.

27. Ibid.

28. Ibid.

29. Frederick C. Mosher, *Democracy and the Public Service*, 2nd ed. (New York: Oxford University Press, 1982) and "Professions in Public Service," *Public Administration Review* 38, no. 2 (March/April 1978).

30. Mintzberg, op. cit., p. 352.

31. Henry, op. cit., p. 204.

32. James Bowman, "Ethics in Government: A National Survey of Public Administrators," *Public Administration Review* 50, no. 3 (May/June 1990), pp. 345–353.

33. This is probably as true for the private sector as for the public sector.

34. David Osborne and Ted Gaebler, *Reinventing Government* (Reading, MA: Addison Wesley, 1992); Al Gore, *Creating a Government That Works Better and Costs Less: The Report of the National Performance Review* (New York: Plume, 1993).

35. For an excellent review of the strengths and weaknesses of professionalism in the public sector, see York Willbern, "Professionalism in the Public Service: Too Little or Too Much?" *Public Administration Review* 14 (Winter 1954), pp. 13–21.

36. James Stever, *The End of the Public Administration: Problems of the Profession in the Post-Progressive Era* (Dobbs Ferry, NY: Transactional Publishers, 1988).

37. Karen E. Watkins and Victoria J. Marsick, *Sculpting the Learning Organization: Lessons in the Art and Science of Systemic Change* (San Francisco: Jossey-Bass, 1993), p. 6.

38. Philip K. Howard, *The Death of Common Sense* (New York: Random House, 1994).

39. Henry, op. cit., p. 76.

40. Ibid.

41. Ibid.

42. Donald Kettl, "Managing on the Frontiers of Knowledge: The Learning Organization," in *New Paradigms for Government,* Patricia Ingraham and Barbara Romzek, eds. (San Francisco: Jossey-Bass, 1994), pp. 19–40.

43. Henry, op. cit.

CHAPTER 4

The Role of
Organizational Values*

Organizations may be perceived in many ways because of the mediating role the organizations play between individuals (both singly, and as groups of individuals, such as professionals) and large groups, such as systems and societies at large. Sorting the many possible perceptions should be somewhat facilitated by the division of Part II into five chapters. Chapter 2 looked specifically at the role of individuals in the public sector. Chapter 3 looked at the role of individuals as classes of professionals with their inherent rights and capabilities. Chapter 5 will focus on the political-legal system, and Chapter 6 on the societal or public interest perspective.

This chapter, the center of the five levels of analysis, focuses on the organization. Organizational values vary substantially in the organizational universe at any time, but the organizational universe does show coherent and consistent trends over time. This chapter looks at both the shift currently affecting public sector organizational values and the range of values exhibited among organizations. To help clarify the historical shift and contemporary range, the strengths and weaknesses of two competing sets of general organizational values are reviewed for their ability to provide congruence and integration in a world in which both the environment and the work of organizations are evolving rapidly.

The Organizational Values Environment

Some impressive analyses of organizational types have emerged in the last twenty years. For example, Henry Mintzberg's work on organizational

---

* This chapter was written with Bette DeGraw.

structure and design lays out five major types of organizations, which he matches with coordinating mechanisms, design parameters, functional characteristics, and contingency (environmental) factors.[1] An equally impressive but less prominent body of compatible work called the *competing values framework* will be used here, however, because it focuses on organizational types in reference to their value structures.

The competing values framework (also called the competing values approach or CVA) was first proposed by R.E. Quinn and J. Rohrbaugh in the early 1980s as an approach to conceptualizing organizational effectiveness.[2] The framework has its roots in theories of individual perception and information processing.[3] The competing values approach assumes that individuals and organizations make two fundamental distinctions about the information they receive: *environmental certainty or predictability* and a *necessity for action*. Environmental certainty or predictability depends on whether cues in the environment are recognizable. The degree of action necessary is a judgement of whether the level of competition is intense and variable or moderate and stable.[4]

Through physiological and social psychological development, organizations through their members become disposed toward particular responses to environmental cues. Those particular responses are styles of information processing, and they fall into four main catagories:

- *The rational style* (with an environment of immediate action but relatively high market certainty) analyzes patterns and selects the best strategy that it has used before. The rational style tends to value independent action and achievement.
- *The hierarchical style* (with an environment of high certainty and little need of immediate action) tries to maintain present behavior. It tends to value predictability and security.
- *The consensual style* (with an environment of low market certainty but only indirect competition) prefers to reduce uncertainty through interaction. It tends to value affiliation and mutual dependency.
- *The adaptive style* (with an environment of both high uncertainty and direct competition) plays the best hunch and uses a learn-and-adapt-as-you-go philosophy. It values flexibility and change.

The hierarchical style has been the clear and overwhelmingly dominant strategy in public sector organizations for most of this century, as well as in many of the United States' largest private sector organizations until the 1980s. It was, however, never as ubiquitous in the private sector as in the public, and it has now fallen completely out of favor in the private sector.[5]

The four quadrants form the basis for the competing values approach. The CVA model has been used to categorize cognitive values and metaphysical orientations,[6] leadership traits and behaviors, change strategies,[7] leadership styles,[8] organizational cultures,[9] environmental conditions,[10] reactions to change and transformation,[11] and management-education curricula.[12] This chapter first uses the model to analyze the conditions in the organizational environment.

Environmental Conditions

The environment influences the appropriateness of different effectiveness criteria and culture types, and ultimately elicits different leadership responses. A CVA analysis is an effective tool for sorting the different value sets characteristic of different organizations. The distinctions among various types of environmental conditions, resulting from a CVA analysis, are based on the primary perceptual differentiations already indicated. The vertical axis in Figure 4.1 represents the degree of environmental certainty (both in the type and amount of service or products needed by the market). The horizontal axis represents the degree of action perceived to be necessary, judging from the degree of threat or competition the individual or organization perceives in the environment.

Using those axes, the CVA distinguishes four basic environmental conditions, in this instance (starting with the bottom right quadrant and moving clockwise), *competitive, stable, interactive,* and *ambiguous.*

1. *The competitive environment* is characterized by the need for immediate action stemming from direct competition. The types of cues are relatively recognizable, meaning that the types of market demand are relatively well known. For example, three major organizations may compete in offering a service, but the type of service that each produces is relatively constant and changes relatively slowly. This kind of constant, slow change commonly existed in the private sector until the last decade.

2. *The stable environment* has indirect competition or a full monopoly, and service/product has high certainty because demand remains relatively constant over time. This has been, and

FIGURE 4.1

A Competing Values Framework of Environmental Conditions

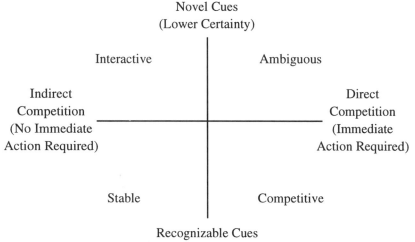

The vertical axis indicates the degree of change in the actual products or services in an industry. The horizontal axis indicates the degree of competition in an industry and the urgency caused by that competition. The four quadrants that result indicate the types of organizations that tend to be fostered by the differing environments.

Adapted from R.E. Quinn and J. Rohrbaugh, "A Competing Values Approach to Organizational Effectiveness," *Public Productivity Review* 5 (1981). Used with permission.

continues to be, a common environment for the public sector, but there is pressure to change this environment through tax revolts, the range of "privatization" efforts, different authorization structures, and different management philosophies.

3. *The interactive environment* is characterized by relatively indirect competition, which remains relatively constant, but is faced with a volatile market in which the service/product changes are frequent (low certainty).

4. *The ambiguous environment* is characterized by both direct (often intense) competition, which expands and contracts without much warning, and low certainty and novel cues in a market where services and products change frequently, either

because of frequent market improvements, changes in customer tastes, or demands for customization. Significant changes in an organization's environment result in significant changes in the approach to effective actions. The CVA model also enables an analysis of effectiveness criteria.

Effectiveness Criteria

In trying to determine the characteristics of effective organizations, Quinn and Rohrbaugh found little agreement on effectiveness criteria in the literature.[13] They therefore examined how researchers theorize about effectiveness and explored the assumptions underlying existing studies.

Using a panel of organizational researchers and factor analysis, they narrowed Campbell's 1977 list of 30 organizational effectiveness indicators to 16.[14] They then asked panel members to judge the similarity between every possible pairing of the remaining 16, and they analyzed the resulting data using multidimensional scaling. Based on that study, Quinn and Rohrbaugh proposed a theoretical framework of three competing value dimensions which, they argued, is implicitly shared by organizational theorists and researchers. They reasoned that effectiveness criteria used by researchers vary according to the value orientation of the individual researcher. The framework of competing values is a tool to help make implicit values explicit. The three competing value dimensions they identified relate to organizational structure, organizational focus, and time.[15] Figure 4.2 displays those value dimensions.

The vertical axis represents organizational structure; it contrasts an emphasis on stability and control with an emphasis on flexibility and change.[16] The horizontal axis represents organizational focus; it ranges from an internal focus—concern for the people and systems in the organization—to an external focus—concern for the organization, its task, and its environment.[17] The third dimension reflects time perspectives; it differentiates concern for means (process) from concern for ends (outcomes).[18]

The juxtaposition of the first two value dimensions creates four quadrants, which correspond to the four dominant models in organization theory. The lower-right quadrant represents the *rational goal model* of the organization; its emphasis is on planning and goal setting, and its focus is on the organization and its efficiency and productivity. It is sharply contrasted by the *human relations model* in the upper-left quadrant, which emphasizes cohesion and morale and focuses on human re-

FIGURE 4.2

A Summary of the Competing Value Sets and Effectiveness Models

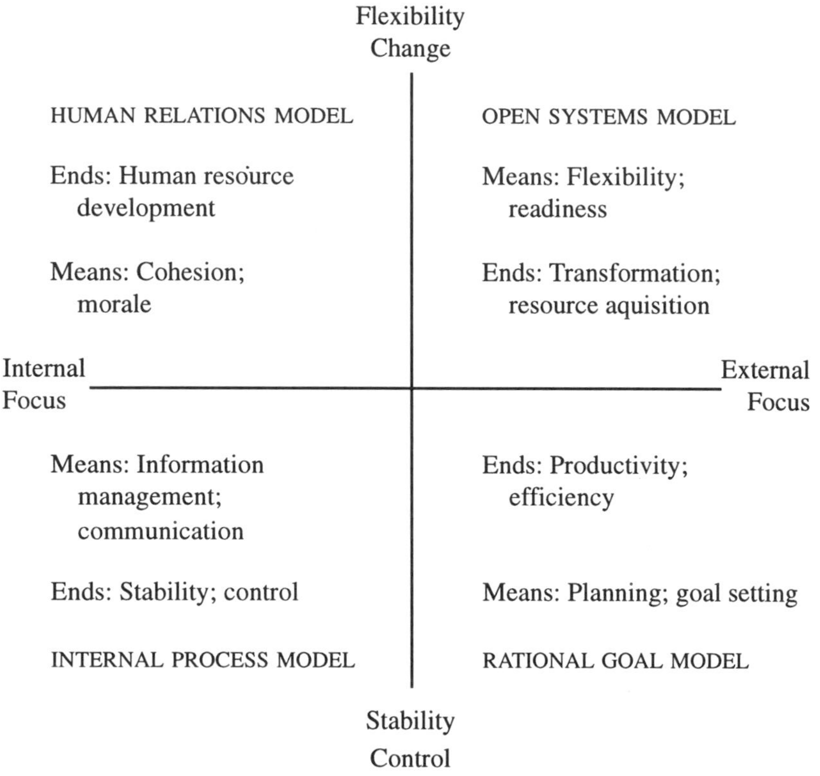

Flexibility
Change

HUMAN RELATIONS MODEL   OPEN SYSTEMS MODEL

Ends: Human resource   Means: Flexibility;
   development   readiness

Means: Cohesion;   Ends: Transformation;
   morale   resource aquisition

Internal   External
Focus   Focus

Means: Information   Ends: Productivity;
   management;   efficiency
   communication

Ends: Stability; control   Means: Planning; goal setting

INTERNAL PROCESS MODEL   RATIONAL GOAL MODEL

Stability
Control

The vertical axis indicates the degree of flexibility and change versus the degree of stability and control encouraged by an industry's environment. The horizontal axis indicates the organizational focus tends to be external or internal. The four quadrants that result indicate how organizations view effectiveness.

Adapted from R.E. Quinn and J. Rohrbaugh, "A Competing Values Approach to Organizational Effectiveness," *Public Productivity Review* 5 (1981). Used with permission.

source development. The *open systems model* in the top-right segment also reflects a preference for flexible organizational structure, but its focus is rapid transformation in order to acquire resources. And finally, the *internal process model* in the opposite lower-left corner reflects a preference for stability through careful information management and control of communications. The means and ends that are implicit and consistent with each model are displayed in each quadrant in a manner that portrays the opposing nature of the long-term (means) and short-term (ends) perspectives which they represent.

One of the strengths of the CVA is its comprehensiveness, due in large part to its ability to display concepts and values that seem to be contradictory or conflicting. The literature emphasizes that these oppositions are not mutually exclusive in organizational settings.[19] For example, a particular organization can be both cohesive and efficient as well as both stable and adaptable. Or an organization can engage in both planning and human resources development as well as focus on both growth and communication. There are two primary reasons for such paradoxical characteristics residing in the same organization. First, relatively few organizations are pure types, although some do exist.[20] Most, however, are "hybrids."[21] An organization might even be positioned almost perfectly on the intersection of the four models. It is important to note, however, that being positioned on the intersection does not necessarily make the organization either more "balanced" or more "schizophrenic." The proponents of CVA and Mintzberg's typology argue strongly that organizations are "healthy" based on their congruence with the environment and their own internal congruence. Different parts of an organization may have attractions to different values. In moderation, such seeming cross purposes can be both natural and healthy because of the different roles that parts of the organization play.[22] Organizations display such paradoxical characteristics, so the capacity of the CVA to portray those apparently contradictory values enhances the usefulness of the model. The literature also emphasizes the importance of assigning equal value to all the dimensions, opposites, and contradictions portrayed in the model and notes that each dimension has the capacity to be negatively defined if overemphasized.

Culture Types

Not only does the CVA assist in arraying narrowly restricted value sets such as information processing preferences or efficiency criteria, it also displays the universe of organizational cultures as well. Organizations develop collective worldviews and belief systems, just as individuals do. The collective views have been described as shared ways of processing information and generating meaning and as basic assumptions[23] about the nature of organizational transactions and exchange.[24]

The model distinguishes four types of organizational cultures (rational, hierarchical, group or team, and adaptive) and associated basic assumptions made by members of each culture. The model also identifies four related ideal organizational forms (market bureaucracy, hierarchical bureaucracy, team-based organizations, and project-based organizations). The characteristics of those organizational cultures are presented in Table 4.1.

Rational Cultures

Rational cultures focus on achievement, logic, and action. The orientation inside such an organization is toward functionality and structure. Formal processes are logical and objectives are clear. Although the general rule is important, sometimes rules can be broken if significant success results. Competence and experience are highly valued, as are timeliness and least-cost efficiency. Planning and productivity are stressed. Competition keeps decisionmaking decisive, and a lack of output or success will probably be punished. Market bureaucracies tend to flourish when competition is stable and when the environment and products change infrequently. A relatively few forceful people can direct large-scale activities with their superior insight and experience. High-performing, rational bureaucracies produce large amounts of services or products very efficiently, using decisive executive orders and technically expert implementation plans; low-performing rational cultures often suffer either by becoming too cautious and thus not decisive enough, or by becoming too bureaucratic and thus not producing efficiently enough. General Motors, up through the 1970s, exemplified a rational culture organization.

Hierarchical Cultures

Hierarchical cultures are characterized by security, stability, order, and routine. Factual and systematic analyses are important. Organizational rank is highly valued. Roles are formal and distinct; training, inputs, and processes are all carefully stipulated by technocrats. Rules and regulations are plentiful. Success is not a satisfactory excuse for breaking a rule. Control and accountability are emphasized since neither competition nor market change naturally curb organizational or individual self-interests over time. High-performing, hierarchical bureaucracies produce large amounts of services or products very efficiently, using authoritatively derived orders and technically expert implementation plans; low-performing, hierarchical bureaucracies often suffer by either becoming too stable

TABLE 4.1

Four Types of Organizational Cultures

	Rational Culture	Hierarchical Culture	Group or Team Culture	Adaptive Culture
Organizational Purpose	Pursue objectives	Execute regulations	Maintain group	Transformation, Flexibility
Performance Criteria	Productivity, Efficiency	Stability, Control	Cohesion, Morale	External support
Motivation	Achievement	Security	Attachment	Adaptation
Compliance	Contract, Rules	Regulations	Affiliation	Ideology
Decision making	Decisive	Factual	Participative	Intuitive
Locus of Authority	Boss, Rules	Regulations, Rank	Membership	Charisma, Environmental needs
Power Base	Competence	Technical knowledge	Informal status	Values, Adaptive skills
Evaluation of Members	Tangible output	Formal criteria	Quality of relationship	Intensity of effort
Organizational Form	Market bureaucracy	Hierarchical bureaucracy	Team-based organization	Project-based organization (Adhocracy)

Source: Used with permission from Quinn and Rohrbaugh, "A Competing Values Approach to Organizational Effectiveness," *Public Productivity Review* 5 (1981).

(rigid) and thus unresponsive, or by becoming too rule-bound and thus diminishing their efficiency, normally an inherent strength of this type.[25] While there can be little doubt that this is the most common cultural type in the public sector, what is open to great debate is the proportion of high- to low-performing organizations. This important distinction of high- to low-performing hierarchical bureaucracies is glossed over by some critics who use the terms *hierarchy* and *bureaucracy* in exclusively negative terms, thus short-circuiting the deeper debate. Indeed, it is quite possible in many cases that the best response to a low-performing hierarchical bureaucracy is to turn it into a high-performing one, rather than some other type altogether. In fact, those who understand both the virtues and the weaknesses of hierarchical bureaucracies are best able to change them and avoid the excesses inherent in any organizational type.

Group or Team Cultures

Group or team cultures focus on the feelings of individuals and groups. The primary perspective is a search for affiliation and harmony, generally through a lengthy process aimed at integrating conflicting views. Tradition, trust, and commitment to other members are valued and rewarded. Group cultures tend to flourish in environments in which change is complex and continuous, thereby incapacitating the ability of a few experts and executives to decide and plan all the responses. More people are brought into making the changes, which tend to be a bit slow, but the benefit is that knowledge is more broadly dispersed. High-performing team organizations adapt to large numbers of changes with minimal management oversight and direction but with some loss of mass production; low-performing team organizations tend to overuse time-consuming group processes and become highly inefficient, or to allow inferior group processes to result in mediocrity. Four waves encouraging group culture are finally making real strides in populating the landscape with this type:[26] the human relations movement of the 1960s and 1970s,[27] the organization-development movement of the 1970s and 1980s,[28] the Japanese emulation of the 1980s,[29] and the team-based reorientation of Total Quality Management.[30]

Adaptive Cultures

Adaptive cultures are characterized by creativity, risk, and flexibility. Adaptive cultures assume change and compromise, so they prize adaptation and intuition. The external environment is highly competitive as well, so external support and resources are sought. Intense, short-term commitment to the organization and its tasks is expected, but long-term commitment or security is not offered or even desired. Because of the dynamic environment, reorganization is the norm. The organizational form is sometimes called an adhocracy, implying an organization composed of temporary structures, or sometimes called a project-based organization, based on the rapid creation and dissolution of its work structures based on specific chunks of work. Although these types of organizations have existed for many years, especially in dynamic industries like advertising, the research and development side of the computer industry, and entertainment, they have been relatively rare.[31] However, they seem to be increasing in a more intense global market in which niche marketing is ever more pronounced, and they have been extravagantly praised by some management experts (such as Tom Peters) in recent years.[32] High performing adhocracies are "flat" organizations, highly responsive to customer needs, exciting and creative to work in, and instinctively self-organizing. They are also inherently the least stable form and can easily fall prey to their innate weaknesses, such as inefficiency (because they tend to reinvent everything), chaos (because they disdain rules and processes), and unrealistic production commitments (because they are generally poor at moving from single-batch to large-scale production).

Leadership Types

It only makes sense, in the CVA, that the four different environments, with their different effectiveness criteria and cultures, would have four different ideals for leadership styles.[33] They are called, for purposes of this discussion, *rational achievers* (rational culture), *empirical experts* (hierarchical culture), *team builders* (group culture), and *creative movers* (adaptive culture) (see Table 4.2).

- *The rational achiever* plays the producer and director roles. This leader feels most comfortable with short time frames and a high degree of environmental certainty. This leader tends to be structured, logical, action-oriented, and goal driven. Motivated by achievement and competence, the rational achiever is viewed as decisive, efficient, and productive.
- *The empirical expert* takes on the coordinator and internal roles in the organization. This leader is most comfortable in situations that permit lengthy time lines and offer a high degree of environmental certainty. The empirical expert, who is motivated by the need for security, order, and control, prefers the hierarchical organizational culture. Generating data and analyzing them are important to the more conservative and cautious empirical expert.
- *The team builder,* who best plays the group facilitator and mentor roles, is the conceptual opposite of the rational achiever. The

TABLE 4.2

Four Types of Organizational Leaders

	Rational Achiever	Empirical Expert	Team Builder	Creative Mover
Prime Function	Directing	Coordinating	Team building	Boundary spanning
Leader Roles	Director, producer	Monitor, coordinator	Mentor, group facilitator	Innovator, broker
Behaviors	Provides structure, initiates action	Provides information, maintains structure	Shows consideration, facilitates interaction	Envisions change, ·cquires resources
Leadership style	Directive, goal oriented	Conservative, cautious	Concerned, supportive	Risk oriented, inventive
Motive	Competence	Security	Attachment	Adaptation
Decision Style	Decisive	Hierarchic	Integrative	Flexible

Source: Adapted from R.E. Quinn and R.H. Hall, "Environments, Organizations, and Policy Makers: Toward an Integrative Framework," in *Organization Theory and Public Policy,* R.H. Hall and R.E. Quinn, eds. (Beverly Hills, CA: Sage, 1983). Used with permission.

team builder is most comfortable when time frames are long, even though the environment is uncertain. At home in a group culture, this leader relies on consensus building, interpersonal interaction, and trust to make decisions. Security, affiliation, and attachment motivate this leader, who is seen as concerned, supportive, and empathetic.

- *The creative mover* plays the roles of the innovator and broker in organizations and is most sharply contrasted with the empirical expert. Most comfortable when time frames are short and the environment is uncertain, the creative mover is at home in adaptive cultures. This leader relies heavily on intuition and creativity; motivation comes from the need for growth, learning, variety, and stimulation. An inventive risk taker, the creative mover is seen as flexible and future-oriented.

In studying Table 4.2, one should note that each type of leader shares affinities with the adjacent type of leader.[34] For example, the two leadership styles at the bottom of the CVA matrix, rational achievers and empirical experts, both tend toward authoritarian leadership. Both the rational leader and empirical expert exist in an environment where change in services and products can be directed by only a few people and where the bureaucratic structure and those in authority can command people to produce results in a certain way. The main difference is that the rational achiever focuses more on results and the empirical expert focuses more on process. The two leadership styles at the left-hand side, which include the hierarchical culture and the team culture, both have tendencies toward synergistic leadership because their environments are stable enough to harness long-term human interaction. Both the empirical expert and the team builder appreciate that work is accomplished through systems of people; however, the empirical expert sees classes of employees as reservoirs of expertise to be molded and called upon whereas the team player sees groups as active hubs of creativity. The leadership styles at the top of the CVA matrix in Figure 4.1 and 4.2, which are described as team builder and creative mover styles in Table 4.2, tend toward democratic leadership. Both see solutions to problems created by their rapidly changing service and product mixes in the efforts of persons working through group structures; however, the team builder has a long-term perspective on the life of groups, whereas the creative mover sees groups as temporary and sees accomplishments of those groups through individual contributions. Finally, the adaptive and the rational cultures share a tendency toward combative leadership since both are intensely aware of the competitive environment with numerous challengers either in, or poised to come into, the market. The difference between the two types of leaders is that the creative mover is in an environment with frequent service and product changes and must therefore rely heavily on many individuals and groups to respond, whereas the rational achiever is in a less dynamic market and can personally direct more of the responses to competitors.[35]

What Are Public Sector Organizational Values?

In examining the four organizational cultures arrayed in Table 4.1, it is easy to pick out the dominant public sector mode. In terms of organizational culture, public sector organizations overwhelmingly fall into a hierarchical culture.[36] Their purpose tends to be executing regulations. Their performance criteria are focused on stability and control. Security is a major organizational motivation. Compliance is largely through rules, as is the locus of authority. Decisionmaking is almost always based on facts. The strongest power base grows out of technical knowledge. Members are evaluated according to formal criteria. The hierarchical culture prefers repetitive technologies (it is excellent at mass production), the effectiveness model most applicable is an internal-process model, and the strategic orientation is generally defensive.

Evolution of the Hierarchical Culture in the Public Sector

Why has the hierarchical culture prevailed in the public sector? The answer lies in the environmental conditions of public sector organizations in the twentieth century. The conditions were quite different in the nineteenth century, and so were the organizations. As noted in Figure 4.1, hierarchical cultures flourish when the environment produces recognizable cues of higher certainty and the timeline for action is long-term. In other words, when mandates are changed only slowly and financial income is quite stable, a hierarchic culture emphasizing maintenance of present behavior, predictability, and security is nearly inevitable. Such an environment encourages an internal focus and an organizational structure emphasizing control.

Before elaborating on the dominance of the hierarchical and bureaucratic culture in the public sector, one needs to compare that dominance with the trends in the private sector. In fact, a similar environment has encouraged bureaucracies in both sectors since shortly after the turn of the twentieth century. The mechanization of agriculture increasingly fueled urban growth and allowed for the maturation of the mass production economy. The rise of the mass production economy in turn led to the large, relatively stable production needs within the country. Production of both consumables and durable goods could be predicted relatively easily. Large organizations had the upper hand throughout much of the twentieth century because the economies of scale far outweighed the need for rapid market change, to which smaller, more flexible and responsive organizations adapt better. Large bureaucracies are excellent at producing large quantities of similar goods by standardizing jobs, processes, and outputs.[37]

Because the environment changed slowly, only a few executives and engineers needed to monitor and respond to it for the entire organization. Others in the organization were best suited for highly specialized jobs, which they could do rapidly, repeatedly, and as mindlessly as possible. This trend began earlier in the private sector than in the public, but it was interrupted in its rapid pace during the Great Depression. In the public sector, the national income tax provided the means (and precedent) for funding a substantial growth in government size and scope, but the Great Depression catapulted the public sector into the service industry as a great provider against harm. The post–World War II boom, based largely on the destruction of all the other great economies in the world, assured U.S. business of enormous production opportunities for decades.[38] In its turn, government was able to play an ever greater role in providing service and monitoring and regulating an ever more complex economy and society.

The Movement Away from Bureaucratic Hierarchies

The private sector was also the first to feel the need for substantial change resulting in worldwide economic shifts. World production capacity in all areas had become enormous by the 1970s, and it only continued to grow in the 1980s and 1990s. The necessary factors for success in business (in common products) shifted from good prices for good quality, to great prices for great quality and for excellent terms such as rapid delivery of small batches. Many products needed to shift from occasional new products (and new generations of old products) to frequent new products (with the new generations of old products becoming extraordinarily compressed), especially in technological goods.[39] From the late 1970s, the tide turned against large, hierarchic bureaucracies, and even those leading commercially began to look at alternative organizational forms and cultures.[40] Perhaps the most telling feature of this trend has been the long-term propensity of large organizations to engage in wholesale downsizing, even when the company was seemingly quite healthy. Despite a healthy national and global economy, those monitoring this trend predict that it will continue for some time.

The public sector has been slower to feel this trend, but since the early 1990s, the pressure for significant cultural and organizational change has been building. The changes from tax revolts to government bashing have been recounted in many other sources and need not be rehearsed here. The effect has been to change the public sector environment radically.[41] The environment is no longer stable.[42] The work of the public sector is subject to enormous policy shifts at all levels concerning the involvement of government in society. Separately, public sector funding has been increasingly challenged. Whether as a (serious) cry for the dismantlement of large federal agencies or as a swelling sympathy for privatizing or contracting public service production, once-dependable financial streams have come under attack as they never were before in the history of the public sector. The very stability about which the public sector once boasted is now frequently derided by critics as excessively monopolistic, process-oriented, inflexible, and unresponsive.[43]

In a nut shell, public sector organizations are following their private sector counterparts in moving away from bureaucratic hierarchies. Yet a few features of the public sector environment will probably deter organizations from moving quite as far or as fast toward other cultural and structural forms. First, the stronger the outside control of an organization, especially detailed control of the direction and process, the more prone the organization is to bureaucratic structure (which is an appropriate response). Public sector organizations always have strong and relatively intrusive external legislative bodies that determine what and how business will be done.[44] In fact, state and local government must contend with layers of external influences. While some of the "excesses" of legislative micromanagement may be reduced thereby encouraging enhanced productivity, the legislative role will always be present and will always be a force for some bureaucratization.

Second, by its nature, the government is "owned" by the people and nearly everybody is its customer. Handling the scope of involvement necessarily requires some level of bureaucratization. Finally, constitutional biases toward due process and equity will always be strong forces in the public sector, even if they are somewhat abated in the next era. Again, these factors necessarily encourage a more bureaucratic response.[45] Thus, if organizational bureaucratization is arrayed on a spectrum, most government organizations have been almost "pure bred" bureaucracies. Even if the proponents of changing public sector organizations are wildly successful in the next few decades, it is unlikely that the bulk of them will ever become more than mixed forms built on sturdy bureaucratic architectures.[46]

Emerging Organizational Culture Values

As was identified in the competing values approach, at least four major organizational cultures and forms are possible. While the shift is away from one of the forms, hierarchical bureaucracies, it does not seem to be overwhelmingly toward any single alternative form. Even individual proponents of change such as Tom Peters, Peter Drucker, Warren Bennis, and Rosabeth Moss Kanter seem to urge multiple directions themselves, with the only common thread being that they are eschewing bureaucratic structures. B. Guy Peters, in a very perceptive essay about such trends in the public sector, noted that the forces of change seem to be for an increased customer focus, increased employee focus, and increased flexibility.[47] These three areas are roughly equivalent to the rational (market) culture, the group (team) culture, and the development (ad hoc) culture. These general trends are illustrated in Figure 4.3. A more detailed discussion of them follows.

Although these macrotrends are interesting heuristically, they do not identify the specific midlevel trends that are useful for practitioners and empiricists. Elsewhere I have identified 20 midlevel value trends that give more substance to the macrolevel trends already identified.[48] As Table 4.3 indicates, they are divided into traditional values and new values. The new values do not represent fully adopted values but rather those values competing for attention or even dominance vis-a-vis the traditional values.[49] No prescription is made here about new values being inherently superior, (because ultimately neither old nor new values are *inherently* superior), but an implicit assumption is adopted that values should be adjusted as the environment shifts. It is also assumed that substantial environmental shifts have and are occurring, creating a pressure on organizations to discover new patterns of internal and external congruence.

The 20 values are further divided into four sets: *macrolevel values* about the environment at large; *values about work* and the way it should be conducted and fostered; *values about structure* in organizations; and *values about employees.*

The four macrolevel values in Table 4.3 all reflect the heavy influence of an environment requiring more immediate action due to direct competition.[50] This is represented in the two right-hand quadrants of the competing values approach in Fig 4.1: the ambiguous environment (leading to adhoc-oriented configurations) and the competitive environment (leading to market-oriented bureaucracies).

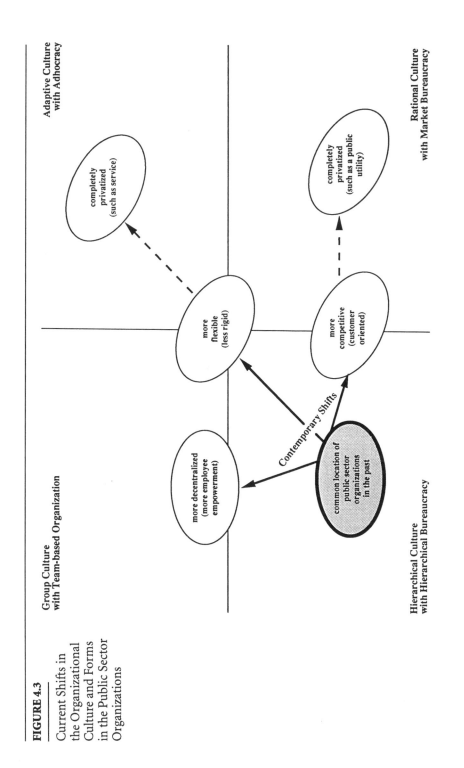

FIGURE 4.3

Current Shifts in the Organizational Culture and Forms in the Public Sector Organizations

Group Culture
with Team-based Organization

Adaptive Culture
with Adhocracy

completely privatized
(such as service)

more flexible
(less rigid)

more decentralized
(more employee empowerment)

Contemporary Shifts

common location of public sector organizations in the past

more competitive
(customer oriented)

completely privatized
(such as a public utility)

Hierarchical Culture
with Hierarchical Bureaucracy

Rational Culture
with Market Bureaucracy

Monopoly Versus Competition

Increasingly monopolistic elements of governmental organizations are being questioned in light of the size and scope of government. Just as large organizations in the private sector (for example, the telephone industry) have been broken up to induce better market performance, so, too, large public sector industries must, many believe, compete for better performance (education being an especially good example).[51] In this regard, past arguments about critical mass and economies of scale are not

---

TABLE 4.3

A Comparison of Traditional Public Sector Values and Those Now Competing for Emphasis

Traditional	New
	Macro-Level Values
Monopoly	Competition
Regulation	Market incentives
(organization for control)	(organization around mission)
Reduction v. growth	Continuous improvement/reengineering
Adding programs	Changing programs
	Values About Work
Expert focus	Customer focus
(internally driven)	(externally driven)
Focus on tradition	Focus on innovation
(status quo)	(change)
Problem analysis	Seeing possibilities
Measurement is feared	Measurement is an opportunity
Protective	Productive
Performance	Ability
Inspection and control	Prevention
	Values About Structure
Centralized	Decentralized
Supervisor as controller	Supervisor as helper
Nondemocratic	Participative
Individual work	Teamwork
Hierarchical organization	Flat organization
Simple jobs	Multidimensional jobs
Single service	Multiple versions of service
	Values About Employees
System indifference	Employee needs
Employees as expenses	Employees as assets
Manager focus	Employee focus
Appraisal/sanction/ranking	Development/learning/recognition

Source: Adapted from Montgomery Van Wart, "The First Step in the Reinvention Process: Assessment," *Public Administration Review* 55, no. 5 (September/October, 1995), pp. 429–438. Used with permission.

receiving as much support in an age of micro-niches, mass customization, and small-batch production. The new argument implies that if government is to remain as large as it has become, it must demonstrate that it can compete against higher standards, the private sector, and itself.[52]

Regulation Versus Market Incentives

Another concern is about the excessive reliance on control by regulation. Many types of control are possible.[53] The public sector has relied heavily on control by laws and rules. The new emphasis has been to explore opportunities to increase control through the market, that is, through the use of market incentives.[54] This tends to change the orientation of the mission from compliance to mission. An example of this is the move to housing vouchers and away from assigned housing units by the Department of Housing and Urban Development.

Growth and Adding Programs Versus Continuous Improvement and Changing Programs

The third and fourth trends in this area represent a fundamental reexamination of the notion of growth. Most public sector organizations came to assume that the ideal organizational development pattern was one of "growth," which implied increased revenues, personnel, and programs.[55] New programs could be offered only with new personnel and resources.[56] The new values assert that organizational development can be better thought of as improvement and adaptation to new customer and competitive demands. Thus, old programs should be continuously improved and scrupulously monitored for productivity. (From this mindset, trends such as reduction, downsizing/rightsizing, and privatization can be seen as healthy developmental patterns in organizational life). Unproductive programs should be proactively cut to free scarce resources. In the new mindset, new programs make old ones compete for resources, and growth is better thought of as renewal and vigor rather than increase in size.[57]

Expert Focus Versus Customer Focus

The next cluster of value dichotomies, values about work, also reflect a heavy influence of a more competitive environment, ranging from value trends that emphasize market-oriented bureaucracies (the most common traditional private form) to those that encourage more ad hoc–oriented configurations (strongly promoted in recent years and often called *project organizations*, indicating that all work is organized by projects).

The first of the seven trends noted here is a shift from an expert focus, a key feature of a hierarchical bureaucracy, to a customer focus. As Chrislip and Larson bluntly note, "Citizens no longer defer to elected leaders or experts."[58] This shift emphasizes an external focus, which is increasingly necessary in a dynamic and competitive environment, rather than an internal focus. When rules are the primary constraint, an internal focus follows; however, when resource acquisition is the primary constraint, an external competitive focus tends to emerge.

Status Quo Versus Change

A second work-value trend deemphasizes tradition and the status quo and emphasizes instead innovation and change.[59] Monopoly and rules tend to encourage a traditionalistic culture. As important is the long tenure of the hierarchic, bureaucratic model in the public sector. Any model can become inappropriate over a long time, even an ad hoc–oriented culture. Such a culture is highly changeable but may need to solidify its growth by bureaucratizing (or formalizing) some of its more stable production functions. This problem, of course, tends to be the opposite of that found in most public sector organizations, which have been resistant to change and strongly averse to risk. Yet due to tremendous and sometimes traumatic changes in the public sector environment, the reverence for tradition has been reduced.[60]

Problem Analysis Versus Seeing Possibilities

Under stable, rule-focused conditions, stress tends to be on the critical-analytic perspective. How should a defined task be organized, given specific resources? And does this program meet the required specifications? When the environment is unstable and unpredictable, and when flexibility (often called "responsiveness" in the public sector) is prized, then a narrow, problem-analysis mentality can be limiting.[61] A manager with a more functional perspective may instead be seeing possibilities, discovering opportunities, and linking resources and competencies hitherto unconnected.

Measurement Is Feared Versus Measurement Is an Opportunity

When bureaucratic hierarchies became excessively concerned about regulation, due process, and resource growth rather than about comparative worth in the market, their production is lowered. Low production in turn results in a suspicion of results-oriented measurements, no matter whether they are output, efficiency, or effectiveness measures.[62] However, when a switch is made to market incentives and-or rigorous comparisons, measurement becomes an opportunity because the organization values the hard data about how it is doing in order to see where it needs to improve.[63]

Protective Versus Productive

Hierarchies often become defensive when they feel threatened, thus becoming protective of their processes and resources. When work objectives or performance are called into question and when the attack is either weak or short-termed, bureaucratic hierarchies can often rationalize problems for themselves and their funding bodies. Because short-termed protective strategies become increasingly ineffective in a hostile, dynamic environment, many organizations move to a results-oriented definition of productivity. Those who do not look to new definitions and demonstrations of productivity often find defunding an increasing likelihood.[64]

Performance Versus Ability

Performance standards have become a widespread problem for public agencies. First, much of their performance is based on processes that do not lend themselves to measuring and quantifying. Second, the vast majority of employees often are categorized as superior, even when organizational productivity is inferior. As results become increasingly emphasized and organizational failure becomes an increasing likelihood through defunding and downsizing, performance standards reflect ideal performance abilities, rather than set categorical quotas, which are often insufficient in a competitive environment. New performance standards reflect the belief that not everyone is capable of superior performance and that many who are capable still do not achieve it.

Inspection and Control Versus Prevention

The final work value reviewed here is the deemphasis of inspection and control and the new emphasis on prevention. Inspection and control strategies assume that most or all work must be monitored and that a variety of checks is needed to curb internal abuse. Thus supervisors, accountants, and technocrats (such as personnel specialists, procurement officers, travel control, and so on) extensively review work of employees (including managers) to make sure not only that quality is adequate but that organizational workers comply with organizational rules and laws.

This after-the-fact approach can be time consuming and costly. For example, a recent General Accounting Office study of travel authorization procedures reported that an excessive inspection orientation costs the government over $1 billion each year.[65] The new approach is to monitor productivity patterns in order to fix systemic problems of quality control rather than monitor each individual case. Lack of compliance to internal rules is considered a rare problem that should be handled case by case with the offending party rather than by subjecting everyone to routine compliance checks.

Centralized Versus Decentralized

A third set of values are those affecting work and the employees who do it. These values have also shifted, but instead of the new values falling along the market bureaucracy/adhocracy continuum (at the left side of Figures 4.1 and 4.2), they fall into the group-adhocracy spectrum (at the top of the matrix). The value shifts are distinctly antibureaucratic (no matter whether hierarchical or market bureaucracies are considered).

Perhaps the single most profound rhetorical shift is the emphasis on decentralization. It parallels the shift from federal to state control in many areas.[66] It is important because it breaks the dominance of the "loop" theory of democracy, which strictly conforms to a chain of command for all decisionmaking, even at the political level. More tangibly, it means delegating authority for decisionmaking to those who are closest to the work. In the ideal situation, even the front-line worker has significant decisionmaking power and the supervisor becomes a source of support rather than a controller. Further, this shift should induce a more participative environment rather than the more authoritarian environment found in bureaucratic settings.

Individual Work Versus Teamwork

The "workers as replaceable parts" theory of bureaucratic assembly-line work was taken to its logical extreme in many large organizations in both the private and public sectors. Its appeal was strong in an era when mass production changes were relatively slow and could be engineered by experts and managers. However, in a market that requires frequent production shifts and a competitive arena that demands numerous accommodations to small batches or even individuals, production changes cannot be designed, implemented, and perfected by a small number of expensive experts and managers. The new values recognize that a fundamentally different model of production change is necessary to enhance rapid deployment capacities. It requires extensive employee input, generally through the use of teams. What individual team members may lack in overall expertise, they more than make up in collective experience and knowledge. Teams are increasingly used for design of new systems, implementation of systems, and the inevitable resolution of production problems. Managers' roles frequently are those of team facilitators and resources, not delegators.[67] Experts are more frequently used as resources for specialized projects.

Hierarchical Versus Flat Organizations

Decentralization and team structures open the way for an emphasis on flatter organizations. Many management functions, especially problem solving, are assumed by teams.[68] Thus the tendency is to increase the span of control to reflect reduced management responsibilities.[69] Further, many organizations have removed one or more layers of management altogether.[70] Whereas large organizations frequently had seven to nine layers of management, the new value is to have as few as five, even in the largest organizations.

Simple Versus Multidimensional Jobs

With the breakdown of the mass production model, the configuration of individual jobs has also changed significantly. Decentralization of responsibility, teamwork, extensive problem solving, and an enhanced process orientation (rather than task orientation) on the part of workers has led to job enlargement.[71] Job enlargement has the virtue of making work more interesting and fulfilling for workers. It also helps when fewer workers must do more types of tasks and can substitute for one another in different but related functions. It requires significantly higher levels of training and education of the workforce and tends to professionalize the labor pool.

Single Versus Multiple Versions of Service

In the past a unitary version of service was strongly valued in the public sector because of economies of scale and the apparent equity of one service for all. Economies of scale are less important today because of many technological breakthroughs (allowing for service to be provided by self-contained business units acting like "virtual corporations") and the increasing importance of factors other than cost (such as timeliness, appearance, and ease of use). Further, the equity of the one-service-fits-all approach is increasingly being questioned, and critics complain that in fact one service fits nobody. Of course multiple versions of service make customers more satisfied and help maintain market share. Also, multiple versions of service require a sophisticated workforce that can make adaptations at a lower organizational level, using internalized limits on the amount and nature of the service provided. Workers employing multiple versions of service are given more responsibility and are themselves evaluated in a more subjective system.[72]

System Indifference Versus Employee Needs

Most of the values about employees have leaned toward the group culture in recent years. Building on the traditional human relations approach of Argyris, Golembiewski, and Schön and others, the newest version has emphasized teams and new forms of corporate democracy in flatter, decentralized organizations. Four values shifts are identified here, the first of which is systems indifference versus employee needs.

In a hierarchical bureaucracy in which individual positions are as specialized and formalized as possible, employees are seen as replaceable and their needs are of little importance. This is true of market bureaucracy, in which employees must compete based on their current competence and output. However, as teams, flexibility, and decentralized decisionmaking have become more important, employee potential—that is, employee needs—has become more important too.[73]

Employees As Expenses Versus Employees As Assets

When employees are considered interchangeable and easily replaceable, any expenditures beyond their salary tend to be viewed as expenses. However, when employees are considered human investments in whom training has been devoted and experience has accrued, employees become increasingly viewed as assets. When there is an emphasis on the unique contributions of employees to contribute to the financial well-being of the organization, they actually become human capital.[74]

Manager Focus Versus Employee Focus

Heavy reliance on managers in a hierarchical system makes sense. Such reliance does not make sense in a participative and team-oriented environment. As Manz and Sims note, "Today's competitive environment demands intense improvement in productivity, quality, and response time.

Teams can deliver this improvement. Bosses can't."[75] They go on to assert that "almost every major U.S. corporation is seriously considering work teams." More ominously for managers, Tom Peters declares that "hierarchies are going, going, gone"[76] which has resulted in a "continuing middle management and senior professional blood bath."[77]

Appraisal/Sanction/Ranking Versus Development/Learning/ Recognition

Hierarchical bureaucracies spend as much time (and sometimes more) controlling their own employees as they do coping with outside forces. It is natural in such systems to appraise employees, to sanction those who are deficient or recalcitrant, and to recognize rank within the organization over accomplishment. In open systems that rely on human resources for survival, it is more natural to develop those human resources, to encourage learning and experimentation, and to recognize accomplishments at all levels within the organization.[78]

In summary, many value shifts are occurring at the organizational level. According to the competing values approach, none of these values is innately better than the others in a moral or absolute sense, as some writers suggest. In this vein, B. Guy Peters notes that "any choice of paradigm for administration is unlikely to be optimal, but we should be clear about what we receive and what we sacrifice when we make judgments about governance."[79] In fact, although hierarchical bureaucracies are under heavy attack by critics, they have a number of strengths *when* they are in congruence with environments characterized by stability, predictability, worker security, mass production efficiency, and strong executive and external control.

The organizational environment has changed however, so the relatively pure hierarchical bureaucracies that evolved in the late twentieth century are no longer seen *as* congruent. Different forms and cultures will be necessary in an environment that is less stable, in which worker security is purposely reduced, in which production capacities are reengineered, and in which exists a greater willingness to experiment with controls lacking strong rules and executive oversight.

Bureaucratic forms will not, and probably cannot, disappear as a significant part of the organizational landscape because of the democratic chain of command from the voters through elected officials to appointed officials and finally to the civil service. While a rebalancing of values in most public sector organizations seems inevitable, it seems nearly as inevitable that rebalancing will include elements of hierarchic cultures.

What Are the Potential Contributions of Organizational Values?

One important strength of organizational values is their midlevel focus. Organizational values need to reflect the environment in the long term, but they need not react to every external perturbation. Organizational values blend the interests of the systems, of which they are a part, and of the workers and leaders whom they employ. As mediating institutions, public sector organizations generally remain stable enough to protect the interests of the public and employees but still flexible enough to change if given time and good leadership. Public sector organizations have changed significantly in the past, and they will continue to change, even if they do not wish to do so.

A second important contribution of the organizational value set is that it recognizes that organizations are themselves a property, a tool, and an asset of the public interest. Healthy, balanced institutions take a long time to build. They are a joy to work in, and they tend quietly to produce large amounts of quality work. Although organizational interests should never be mistaken for ends in themselves, they are nonetheless the single, most powerful tools in the administrative repertoire and valuable as such. Organizational interests, *when not overweening,* are legitimate in the decisional context because their health and welfare is in the greater public interest.

Organizational values are important for a third reason—they can emphasize the unique needs of the system and environment of which they are a part. In the case of organizations in the public sector, there is a need for hierarchic elements because of democratic theory. Further, it is unlikely that the expertise, control, and stability that typify hierarchical bureaucracies will be entirely discarded in core governmental functions. Of course, some current governmental activities may be reclassified as being peripheral to the government's *core* functions, and consequently may be partially or wholly privatized. The agencies performing those functions are likely to see radical changes.

What Are the Potential Problems of Excessive Reliance on Organizational Values?

When the midlevel focus on organizational values is replaced by either excessively short-term or excessively long-term perspectives, departments may lose sight of their mission. A short-term focus may cause departments to become so involved in the functions they are performing and the crises they are addressing that they neglect to ensure that they are accomplishing their fundamental purposes. Many social service programs have been subjected to this critique. An excessively long-term focus can be harmful when agencies are unwilling to tackle substantial but transitory problems that do not specifically relate to their long-term goals. For example, it made sense for administrative purposes to close inner city schools as soon as possible after school, but these early closings did not make sense for the communities in which the schools are located.

A second problem of excessive emphasis on organizational values develops when the organization becomes reified as an end in itself. When this happens, organizations tend to become excessively concerned about tradition, prestige, and control; in a word, they become self-serving. Despite the excellent work that J. Edgar Hoover did in building up the Federal Bureau of Investigation, for example, he ultimately allowed it to become extraordinarily self-serving during his lifetime.[80]

A final problem is that in any organizational format, but particularly in a hierarchical bureaucracy, the power of the government is easily corrupted over time into innumerable bureaupathologies. Gerald Caiden listed over 150 such bureaupathologies.[81] Bureaucratic strengths (or any other organizational form) quickly become degraded if organizations are not vigilant in maintaining organizational interests in a healthy balance with other interests, especially those at the political-legal and public interest levels.

Notes

1. For his seminal book on the subject, see Henry Mintzberg, *The Structuring of Organizations* (Englewood Cliffs, NJ: Prentice-Hall, 1979); for updates and additional insights see *Mintzberg on Management: Inside Our Strange World of Organizations* (New York: Free Press, 1989), and *The Rise and Fall of Strategic Planning* (New York: Free Press, 1994), especially pp. 397–416.
2. R.E. Quinn and J. Rohrbaugh, "A Competing Values Approach to Organizational Effectiveness," *Public Productivity Review* 5 (1981), pp. 122–140; R.E. Quinn and R.H. Hall, "Environments, Organizations, and Policy Makers: Toward an Integrative Framework," in *Organization Theory and Public Policy,* R.H. Hall and R.E. Quinn, eds. (Beverly Hills, CA: Sage, 1983); R.E. Quinn and J. Rohrbaugh, "A Spatial Model of Effectiveness Criteria: Toward a Competing Values Approach to Organizational Analysis," *Management Science* 29, no. 3 (1983), pp. 363–377; J. Rohrbaugh, "The Competing Values Approach:

Innovation and Effectiveness in the Job Service," in *Organization Theory and Public Policy,* R.H. Hall and R.E. Quinn, eds. (Beverly Hills, CA: Sage, 1983).

3. M.J. Driver and A.J. Rowe, "Decision-Making Styles: A New Approach to Management Decision Making," in *Behavioral Problems in Organizations,* C. Cooper, ed. (Englewood Cliffs, NJ: Prentice-Hall, 1979); R. Forgus and B.H. Shulman, *Personality: A Cognitive View* (Englewood Cliffs, NJ: Prentice-Hall, 1979); C.G. Jung, *Psychological Types* (New York: Pantheon Books, 1923) and *Man and His Symbols* (New York: Doubleday, 1971); W. Taggart and D. Robey, "Minds and Managers: On the Dual Nature of Human Information Processing and Management," *Academy of Management Review* 6, no. 2 (1984), pp. 187–195.

4. Environments are only moderately competitive when organizations exist in monopolistic conditions or when the market is underserviced by the organizations operating in it.

5. This is *not* to suggest that it has also fallen out of practice.

6. Quinn and Hall, op. cit., 1983; R.E. Quinn and K.S. Cameron, "Organizational Life Cycles and Shifting Criteria of Effectiveness: Some Preliminary Evidence," *Management Science* 29 (1983), pp. 33–51.

7. R.E. Quinn, "Applying the Competing Values Approach to Leadership: Toward an Integrative Framework," in *Leaders and Managers: International Perspectives on Managerial Behavior and Leadership,* J.G. Hunt, D. Hosking, C. Schriesheim, and R. Stewart, eds. (Elmsford, NY: Pergamon Press, 1984).

8. Quinn and Hall, op. cit., 1983; R.E. Quinn and M.R. McGrath, "Transformation of Organization Cultures: A Competing Values Perspective," in *Organizational Culture,* P.J. Frost, L.F. Moore, M.R. Louis, C.C. Lundberg, and J. Martin, eds. (Beverly Hills, CA: Sage, 1985).

9. R.E. Quinn and J.R. Kimberly, eds., *New Futures: The Challenge of Managing Corporate Transitions* (Homewood, IL: Dow Jones-Irwin, 1984).

10. Quinn and McGrath, op. cit.

11. R.E. Quinn and K.S. Cameron, *Paradox and Transformation: Toward a Framework of Change in Organization and Management* (Cambridge, MA: Ballinger, 1988).

12. S.E. Faerman, R.E. Quinn, and M.P. Thompson, "Bridging Management Practice and Theory: New York State's Public Service Training Program," *Public Administration Review* 47, no. 4 (July/August 1987), pp. 310–319.

13. Quinn and Rohrbaugh, 1981 and 1983, op. cit.

14. J.P. Campbell, "On the Nature of Organization Effectiveness," in *New Perspectives on Organizational Effectiveness,* P. S. Goodman and J. M. Pennings, eds. (San Francisco: Jossey-Bass, 1977).

15. P.R. Lawrence and J.W. Lorsch, *Organization and Environment* (Homewood, IL: Richard D. Irwin, 1967) referred to these same three dimensions as structure, interpersonal orientation, and time and used them to explain differences in management behavior.

16. The first dimension, control versus flexibility, is explored best perhaps by Lawrence and Lorsch (ibid.) in their significant work on integration and differentiation. Recognizing these concepts as opposite sides of the same coin, they suggested that a balance between these competing approaches leads to the most effective organizational design.

17. The leadership and management literature identifies the second dimension—internal versus external focus—as the contrast between people and task

orientation. The debate in the organizational behavior literature between the classical school (task) and the human relations school (people) reinforces the contradictory nature of this dilemma. See J.D. Aram, *Dilemmas of Organizational Behavior* (Englewood Cliffs, NJ: Prentice-Hall, 1976); E.A. Fleishman, "The Description of Supervisory Behavior," *Journal of Applied Psychology* 37 (1953), pp. 1–6; and A.W. Gouldner, "Organizational Analysis," in *Sociology Today,* R.K. Merton, L. Broom, L.S. Cottrell, Jr., eds. (New York: Basic Books, 1959).

18. In addition to Lawrence and Lorsch (op. cit.), see D. Katz and R.L. Kahn, *The Social Psychology of Organizations,* rev. ed. (New York: John Wiley & Sons, 1978); and B. Georpoulos and A.S. Tannenbaum, "The Study of Organizational Effectiveness," *American Sociological Review* 22 (1957), pp. 435–440.

19. In addition to the CVA work already cited, see R.E. Quinn, *Beyond Rational Management* (San Francisco: Jossey-Bass, 1988).

20. Yet, ironically, I would hypothesize that a disproportionate number of "pure" organizations have existed in the public sector; specifically, the public sector has been relatively rife with those strongly leaning toward the internal process model described here.

21. For an excellent discussion of hybrid organizations see Mintzberg, op. cit., especially his pictorial representation of many hybrid types on pp. 470–471.

22. "There are forces that drive a great many organizations to favor one configuration overall. But within these organizations, there are always forces that favor different structures in different places. Each part of the organization strives for the structure that is most appropriate to its own particular needs, in the face of pressures to conform to the most appropriate structure for the overall organization, and it ends up with some sort of compromise" (Mintzberg, op. cit., p. 475).

23. Quinn and Kimberly, op. cit.; C. C. Lundberg, "Strategies for Organizational Transitioning," in *New Futures: The Challenge for Managing Corporate Transitions,* J.R. Kimberly and R.E. Quinn, eds. (Homewood, IL: Dow Jones-Irwin, 1984); and I. Mitroff and R.O. Mason, "Business Policy and Metaphysics: Some Philosophical Considerations," *Academy of Management Review* 7 (1982), pp. 361–370.

24. Quinn and Hall, 1983, op. cit.; and Quinn and McGrath, 1985, op. cit.

25. In addition to these organization-level critiques, there have been many individual-level critiques, the most famous of which is Karl Marx's about the deadening effect of mass production work. For a contemporary version of this argument in a public sector framework, see Richard T. Green, "Character Ethics and Public Administration," *International Journal of Public Administration* 17, no. 12, (1994), pp. 2137–2164. For a critique of the undemocratic elements of hierarchical bureaucracies, see Robert T. Golembiewski's work, such as *Men, Management, and Morality* (New York: McGraw-Hill, 1965) and *Humanizing Public Organizations* (Mt. Airy, MD: Lomond, 1985).

26. This style of organization has been the least natural to the American environment, with its stress on individualism as opposed to groups, and since it historically perfected modern market bureacratic organizations, which is the antithesis of a group culture

27. See, for example, the highly popular texts, Douglas McGregor, *The Human Side of Enterprise* (New York; McGraw-Hill, 1960) and Frederick Herzberg, *Work and the Nature of Man* (Cleveland: World Publishing, 1966). Of course, the

human relations school of thought can trace its roots back to the work of Mary Parker Follett and Roethlisberger and Dickson.

28. For example, Richard Beckhard, *Organizational Development: Strategies and Models* (Reading, MA: Addison-Wesley, 1969); Warren Bennis, *Organizational Development: Its Nature, Origins, and Prospects* (Reading, MA: Addison-Wesley, 1969); Wendell L. French and Cecil H. Bell, Jr., *Organization Development: Behavioral Science Interventions for Organization Improvement* (Englewood Cliffs, NJ: Prentice-Hall, 1973); and Robert Golembicwski, *Humanizing Public Organizations* (Mt. Airy, MD: Lomond, 1985). Of course Organizational Development's roots stem back at least to the 1940s, with the work of Kurt Lewin.

29. W.G. Ouchi, *Theory Z: How American Business Can Meet the Japanese Challenge* (Reading, MA: Addison-Wesley, 1981).

30. A few of the very good books on teams include J. Richard Hackman, ed., *Groups That Work (and Those That Don't)* (San Francisco: Jossey-Bass, 1990); Richard S. Wellins, William C. Byham, and Jeanne M. Wilson, *Empowered Teams: Creating Self-Directed Work Groups That Improve Quality, Productivity, and Participation* (San Francisco: Jossey-Bass, 1991); Charles C. Manz and Henry P. Sims, *Business Without Bosses* (New York: John Wiley & Sons, 1993); and, my personal favorite, Jon R. Katzenbach and Douglas K. Smith, *The Wisdom of Teams: Creating the High-Performance Organization* (Boston, MA: Harvard Business School Press, 1993).

31. Alvin Toffler is generally credited with the first use of the term *adhocracy* in *Future Shock* (New York: Bantam Books, 1970).

32. He says, "Organize everything into projects, and allow members to assign themselves to those projects. This is the congenital style of the professional service firm, and as giant firms like Arthur Anderson and EDS demonstrate, there's no limit to the size of a 'projectized' firm. More and more traditional organizations are getting the idea." In Tom Peters, *The Pursuit of WOW!: Every Person's Guide to Topsy-Turvey Times* (New York: Vintage, 1994). Project management is extensively discussed in *Liberation Management: Necessary Disorganization for the Nanosecond Nineties* (New York: Fawcett Columbine, 1992), especially Part 4, pp. 129–475.

33. It is popular for management consultants, and even for many academics, to propose one best leadership style. Such assertions must assume that their comments are relative only to the specific time period to which they speak and must generalize across organizations to such a degree that the exceptions are extensive.

34. Of course, this is also true for adjacent information processing strategies, environmental conditions, and cultures.

35. For a longer discussion of this point, see R.E. Quinn, "Applying the Competing Values Approach to Leadership: Toward an Integrative Framework," in *Leaders and Managers: International Perspectives on Managerial Behavior and Leadership,* J.G. Hunt, D. Hosking, C. Schriesheim, and R. Stewart, eds. (Elmsford, NY: Pergamon Press, 1984).

36. See the initial National Performance Review Report for an example of this belief, Al Gore, *Creating a Government That Works Better and Costs Less* (New York: Plume, 1993); for a discussion of why government organizations tend to be hierarchical bureaucracies, see the chapter on machine bureaucracies in Henry Mintzberg, *The Structuring of Organizations* (Englewood Cliffs, NJ: Prentice-Hall, 1979).

37. Mintzberg, op. cit.

38. This thesis was probably most powerfully argued by Paul Kennedy, *The Rise and Fall of Great Powers* (New York: Random House, 1987). Nicholas Imparato and Oren Harari make an argument that this shift is also the end of the modern age of organizations, which they trace to the beginning of the Industrial Revolution in their book *Jumping the Curve: Innovation and Strategic Choice in an Age of Transition* (San Francisco: Jossey-Bass, 1993).

39. As Tom Peters noted with characteristic verve: "To stay on top of this fermenting global brew will require people and companies to paddle like never before" in *In Pursuit of WOW!* op. cit., p. xii.

40. See for example, Michael Hammer and James Champy, *Reengineering the Corporation: A Manifesto for Business Revolution* (New York: HarperBusiness, 1993): "A set of principles laid down more than two centuries ago has shaped the structure, management, and performance of American businesses . . . we say that the time has come to retire those principles and adopt a new set." (p. 1)

41. For the federal example, see Montgomery Van Wart, "Reinvention in the Public Sector: The Critical Role of Value Restructuring," *Public Administration Quarterly* 19, no. 4 (Winter 1996), pp. 456–478.

42. Al Gore noted, "It is time to radically change the way the government operates," *Creating a Government,* op. cit., p. xxii.

43. See for example, Steven Cohen and William Eimicke, *The New Effective Public Manager: Achieving Success in a Changing Government* (San Francisco: Jossey-Bass, 1995).

44. "The administrative challenge is to fashion solutions to problems that are both managerially rational and politically feasible. This requires no small amount of cleverness and effort." Robert S. Kravchuk, "Liberalism and the American Administrative State," *Public Administration Review* 52, no. 4 (July/August 1992), p. 379.

45. As Kanter, Stein, and Jick have noted, "The sad fact is that, almost universally, organizations change as little as they must, rather than as much as they should," *The Challenge of Organizational Change* (New York: The Free Press, 1992), p. 2.

46. One of the problems for the public is the degree of control that it wishes to have. If it wants a high degree of control, which has been the tendency for the last half century, then bureaucracies are indeed the best organizational form, specializing in control as they do. While some of the excesses of the control orientation for public organizations is widely perceived, it is nonetheless difficult to shed the "there ought to be a law" mentality that spawns detailed and highly restrictive mandates that foster bureaucratization. Moving organizations or functions out of the public sector (partially or fully) is one way to avoid government's natural tendency toward bureaucratic structures. Of course, then the public has less or no control over those domains. Even when the government regulates a market, it is enhancing the bureaucratic elements in itself and the industry.

47. B. Guy Peters, "New Visions of Government and the Public Service," in *New Paradigms for Government: Issues for the Changing Public Service,* Patricia W. Ingraham and Barbara S. Romzek, eds. (San Francisco: Jossey-Bass, 1994), pp. 295–321.

48. Montgomery Van Wart, "The First Step in the Reinvention Process: Assessment," *Public Administration Review* 55, no. 5 (September/October 1995), pp. 429–438.

49. For example, one of the important management drives in the last decade, reengineering, "is the fundamental rethinking and radical redesign of business processes to achieve dramatic improvements in critical, contemporary measures of performance such as cost, quality, service, and speed" (p. 32). Further, "[r]eengineering rejects the assumptions inherent in Adam Smith's industrial paradigm—the division of labor, economies of scale, hierarchical control, and all the other appurtenances of an early-stage developing economy" (p. 49), Hammer and Champy, *Reengineering the Corporation,* op. cit. While I do not necessarily agree with Hammer and Champy's conclusions, especially as they relate to the public sector, much of their basic analysis is sound and widely held regarding the notion that the United States is in a new economic and organizational age.

50. In response to the overwhelming influence of competition to change organizations, Kanter notes, "The question most appropriate for the 1990s is not *what* the competitive world organization should look like but *how* to become one," in *The Challenge of Organizational Change,* op. cit., pp. 1–2.

51. Al Gore notes critically, "Many federal organizations are also monopolies, with few incentives to innovate or improve," in *Creating a Government,* op. cit., p. xxxiii.

52. For a good discussion of competition and market incentives in the public sector, see Michael Barzelay, *Breaking Through Bureaucracy: A New Vision for Managing in Government* (Berkeley, CA: University of California Press, 1992).

53. Montgomery Van Wart, "Trends in the Types of Control of Public Organizations," *Public Integrity Annual* (Lexington, KY: The Council of State Governments, 1996), pp. 83–97.

54. The renewed emphasis on market incentives actually began in the private sector. For example, Tom Peters and Robert Waterman in *In Search of Excellence* (New York: Warner Books, 1984 [1982]) make autonomy and entrepreneurship one of their eight basic principles. Of course, the use of market incentives in the public sector has some structural challenges, given the public sector's objectives and rationale in the twentieth century. Nonetheless, great progress has been made at introducing more competitive structures (as well as quasicompetitive features) and much flexibility to privatize is being built into most major governmental systems. Should governments at various levels run into serious financial shortfalls during the next decade, as economically seems inevitable, it seems likely enormous privatization initiatives will prevail.

55. Aaron Wildavsky, *The Politics of the Budgetary Process,* 2nd ed. (Boston: Little, Brown, 1974).

56. "[Government] knows how to add but not subtract," said Al Gore, referring to government programs (*Creating a Government,* op. cit., p. xxx).

57. "The most effective public managers are those who learn to adjust programs *rapidly* to reflect changed priorities" (Cohen and Eimicke, op. cit., p. 18).

58. David D. Chrislip and Carl E. Larson, *Collaborative Leadership: How Citizens and Civic Leaders Can Make a Difference* (San Francisco: Jossey-Bass, 1994).

59. This has been a trend that has been as important in the private sector as the public. James Champy recently stated that "nothing is simple any more. Nothing is stable. . . . Now we must not only manage change, we must create change—big change—and fast" (*Reengineering Management: The Mandate for New Leadership* [New York: HarperBusiness, 1995], p. 9).

60. For example, in a study by Martin Levin and Mary Bryna Sanger, they discovered a surprising amount of change occurring in the public sector currently. The successful leaders in their study tended to have the "qualities of management that emphasize risk taking, flexibility, and opportunism." *Making Government Work: How Entrepreneurial Executives Turn Bright Ideas into Real Results* (San Francisco: Jossey-Bass, 1994), p. 147.

61. Gary Hamel and C.K. Prahalad explain this perspective as a strategic intent. They explain that a strategic intent is different from the traditional view of a strategy. A strategy is an attempt to match resources with opportunities. The strategic intent tries to create a mismatch between resources and aspirations that will force the organization to stretch to reach its goal. The strategic intent rallies all of the company's resources around a common thrilling cause (*Competing for the Future* [Boston: Harvard Business School Press, 1994]).

62. This led Tom Peters to insist that the National Performance Review "make all agencies develop and use measurable performance objectives" (in the Preface of the Plume edition, in Al Gore, *Creating a Government*, p. xii.)

63. Yet there has been impressive improvement in this area. See, for example, Harry Hatry, et al., *Service Efforts and Accomplishments Reporting: Its Time Has Come* (Norwich, CT: Governmental Accounting Standards Board, 1990); Geert Bouchaert, "Measurement and Meaningful Management," *Public Productivity and Management Review* 17, no. 1 (Fall 1994), pp. 29–36; and Marc Holzer, *Public Productivity Handbook* (New York: Marcel Dekker, 1992).

64. Imparato and Harari suggest that "every business must continually prepare for obsolescence" in today's competitive environment. *Jumping the Curve: Innovation and Strategic Choice in an Age of Transition* (San Francisco: Jossey-Bass, 1993), p. 21.

65. Reported in the *Phoenix Gazette*, "Panel Urges Faster OKs for Travel," Saturday, March 9, 1996, p. B7. The study found that administrative costs range from $37 to $123 per trip voucher. The lowest is $17 over the best practices in the private sector. Some government trip voucher authorizations were found to take up to 60 steps.

66. As John Bryson and Barbara Crosby report, decentralization makes more sense in a shared-power world. *Leadership for the Common Good: Tackling Public Problems in a Shared-Power World* (San Francisco: Jossey-Bass, 1992).

67. "Teams may represent a whole new management paradigm. Perhaps they reflect a new business era as influential as the industrial revolution and are destined to revolutionize work for decades to come" (Charles Manz and Henry Sims, *Business Without Bosses* [New York: John Wiley, 1993], p. 14).

68. "Employees often rotate in and out of managerial responsibility as the occasion demands" (Hammer and Champy, *Reengineering the Corporation*, op. cit., p. 4).

69. "The interpersonal demands of the workplace used to be predominantly vertical. They are now much more horizontal, with peer influence and cooperation representing key skills. Not surprisingly, these interpersonal relationships are no easier to manage than authority-subordinate relationships of the past" (Karen E. Watkins and Victoria J. Marsick, *Sculpting the Learning Organization* [San Francisco: Jossey-Bass, 1993], p. 7).

70. "What we need now are flexible, flatter structures based on organizational relationships of partnerships, self-regulation, and interdependence" (Jill Janov, *The Inventive Organization* [San Francisco: Jossey-Bass, 1994], p. xii). See also

Morris A. Graham and Melvin J. LeBaron, *The Horizontal Revolution* (San Francisco: Jossey-Bass, 1994).

71. "Farewell to hyperspecialization of jobs and command-and-control management. Welcome multi-skilled employees and empowerment" (Tom Peters, in the preface to *Creating a Government,* op. cit., p. xiii).

72. See for example, Hammer and Champy, *Reengineering the Corporation,* op cit.

73. Golembiewski and other OD practitioners have long stressed the importance of employee needs in building productive organizations.

74. Manz and Sims support this notion by arraying the strategies by which employees can contribute real value, from suggestion systems to quality circles to self-managed teams.

75. Manz and Sims, *Business Without Bosses,* op. cit, p. 1.

76. Tom Peters, *In Pursuit of WOW!,* op. cit., p. 17.

77. Peters in *Creating a Government,* op. cit., p. xi.

78. This is particularly well covered by the learning organization literature. See Peter Senge, *The Fifth Discipline: The Art and Practice of the Learning Organization* (New York: Doubleday Currency, 1990); Chris Argyris, *Knowledge for Action: A Guide to Overcoming Barriers to Organizational Change* (San Francisco: Jossey-Bass, 1993); Donald F. Kettl, "Managing the Frontiers of Knowledge: The Learning Organization," in *New Paradigms for Government,* Ingraham and Romzek, eds. (San Francisco: Jossey-Bass, 1994).

79. B. Guy Peters, in *New Paradigms for Government,* Ingraham and Romzek, eds., op. cit., p. 318.

80. David K. Hart and David W. Hart, "George C. Marshall and J. Edgar Hoover: Noblesse Oblige and Self-Serving Power," in *Exemplary Public Administrators,* Terry L. Cooper and N. Dale Wright, eds. (San Francisco: Jossey-Bass, 1992).

81. Gerald E. Caiden, "What Really Is Public Maladministration?" *Public Administration Review* 51, no. 6 (November/December 1991), pp. 486–493.

CHAPTER 5

The Role of Legal Values

Societies must have an underlying organizing force, or else life would become—in the famous words of Thomas Hobbes—"solitary, poor, nasty, brutish, and short."[1] Yet the primary organizing force can vary: Some of the chief social constructs are: religious texts,[2] traditions,[3] ideological constructs of the perfect society,[4] or a social contract among individuals.[5] Individualistic cultures like those found in the United States and other Western countries prefer social contract states that set up constitutional-legal frameworks, through which authoritative values (supported by the potential for force) are expressed. Lawrence Kohlberg, for example, described the social contract orientation as "the official morality of the American government and Constitution."[6] In other words, legal values take on extreme importance in such cultures.

In American and other Western societies, the underlying social contract orientation does not just result in an idea of the law as an established process by which disputes can be resolved and social consensus can be built in a legitimate fashion. As John Rohr asserted, we have "law as a symbol of values."[7] That is, not only is there a tremendous social force supporting the fundamental political-legal *process* as unassailable, but there is an inclination to accept the *results* as moral by definition as well. This occasionally results in odd situations, as when a billionaire asserts his ingenious use of legal tax loopholes as a badge of virtue, or when politicians boast in their home districts of lavish spending implicitly understood to be at other districts' expense.[8] Generally, however, there is a good-will belief that public law is the public good and the "right" thing to do.

Of course, it is common and allowable to have complaints against the law by those who have a heartfelt value that is opposed—perceptions of excessive taxation, the immorality of abortion, the incursion of regulatory mandates, and so on. However, nothing brings wholesale social condemnation faster than extralegal actions by individuals such as tax evasion, the murder of abortion-clinic doctors, or the avoidance of regulatory requirements. In other words, although the legal system (the laws) becomes an allowable target for change through the legal system itself, nonlegal means of achieving personal goals or conducting social change are generally taboo.

There is also remarkably little debate about the underlying political-legal system itself, which, if anything, has gained stature in the post–Cold War era. However, the technical use of the law and even the strategic adjustment of the political system itself is a common and escalating point of dispute. (This point is examined in more depth late in this chapter.) As American society (as well as most other developed nations) casts about for new balances between individualism and society, between interest groups and the general interest, and between protection from harm provided by the state and individual responsibility, public administration values are significantly affected too. This chapter renews the discussion begun in Chapter 1 about the level of discretion appropriate for public administrators, a question that has been heightened by disputes about public administrators becoming more entrepreneurial, innovative, flexible, and responsive.[9]

Thus, the general agreement of the American public about the virtue of the legal system as an expression of social will continues largely unchallenged. However, the specific execution of the social will through public administration is very much debated, especially in terms of an ideal model balancing compliance and initiative. This debate is common in developed countries around the world.[10]

The Role of Legal Values in Public Administration

Two overarching legal principles apply to American society at large as well as to public administration specifically: (1) the law as the legitimate will of the people and (2) the importance not only of arriving at law through an authorized and orderly process but also of executing law in an explicit, predictable, and accountable fashion (often referred to as due process for the sake of simplicity).

Four Basic Assumptions About Legal Values

Flowing from these two great principles are four values specific to public administration: subordination of public administration to the law itself, subordination to legislative intent, subordination to the courts, and subordination to political bureaucrats (that is, elected and appointed officials). This chapter examines these four values and their connection to the ongoing debate about the nature of administrative involvement in law making and rule promulgation. The chapter concludes by alluding to, but largely deferring, the issue of administrative creativity and independence, which is covered in Chapter 6.

Subordination of Public Administration to the Law

The logic behind the subordination of public administration to the law has already been intimated. Public administration is just one of many areas controlled significantly by law for the public good. Industries as diverse as banking, telecommunications, and food preparation are also significantly affected by laws, but public administration differs from them in that its position is *controlled* by laws because, as executor of the law, it is given *public* power requiring more careful legal stipulation.[11] This follows from the use of public resources, partial or full monopolistic powers, and the authorized use of force. By its nature, public administration should be among the most regulated industries precisely because it is itself a frequent regulator and privileged service provider. Yet, because of the public administrator's role as executor of the law, there is a prohibition on public administration being a creator of law. Creating law, no matter whether through proposing law, enacting law, or rule promulgation, tends to beget a conglomeration of power and conflict of interest that is dangerous as a general principle. Public administrators do, of course, recommend law, sometimes have legislative functions, and frequently become highly involved in rule articulation as executors of the law. In theory at least, however, this aspect of their power is considerably mitigated by the next three legal values.

One publicly debated issue today regarding the subordination of public administration to the law, is the degree to which it is practical, or even desirable, to engineer administrative systems through elaborate legal edifices. At the extreme, Philip Howard insists that "we should stop looking to law to provide the final answer."[12] Such elaborately constructed systems either become Soviet-style centrally planned behemoths of rigidity, or they become susceptible to manipulation by those with special interests or resources. Yet even when agreement is widespread among experts that public administration needs more room to maneuver its management skills with new, more stringent requirements to produce results, the issue ultimately remains a legislative and legal one at its source.[13] In this regard, David Rosenbloom has noted that "in their zeal to promote visions of the public interest, American administration reformers sometimes seek to remake the political system to serve the needs of better management rather than to develop better management to serve the purposes of the political system."[14]

Subordination of Public Administration to Legislative Intent

A second important value in public administration is the subordination of public administration to legislative intent. Again, the basic logic is easy to grasp. Legislators are the authorized representatives of the people through elective processes, and their will is a surrogate for the people's will. Although legislators make their intent known through the law, their intent can never be perfectly communicated through the law alone because of the limitations of language and the inability of law to cover every contingency even when legislators are inclined toward great specificity. Thus, it is a generally acknowledged value that public administrators should try not only to comply with the letter of the law but with its spirit as well. Otherwise, gamesmanship and dangerous reconstruction would often prevail.

The difficulty of subordination to legislative intent is that defining it tends to become a legislative, judicial, or (political) executive function itself. For example, housing standards are carefully articulated by law for the public safety and to maintain satisfactory public standards. But such standards can seem highly dysfunctional when applied to constructing housing for homeless people or the very poor. Requiring an elevator in a retrofitted homeless shelter[15] or enforcing plumbing regulations beyond the reach of the very poor who are desperate for any housing at all[16] seems nonsensical. What then happens? It is certainly highly unlikely that administrators would return to legislators to ask their intent on such cases. Do public administrators who are aware of this problem use their discretion to make exceptions from the general (middle-class) standard that was probably the legislators' intent? Or do they propose additional regulations for legislators to approve? Not surprisingly, public administrators are often loath to go back to legislators because legal language was often a composite of numerous perspectives, sometimes warring factions, making subsequent explanation difficult. Often it is easier to make a best guess and await legislative comment in oversight hearings or wait for judicial challenge. All this simply shows that while following legislative intent is an important value in theory, it can be exceptionally difficult in practice.

Subordination of Public Administration to the Courts

The third legal value of public administrators is subordination to judicial interpretation and judicial mandates. The very difficulties described in determining legislative intent make judicial interpretation critical. Judges need to render the broad interpretation of laws for administrators because of imprecise language and varying historical circumstances. The Constitution, flexible in its broad sweep of principles, is made contemporary and vital by the Supreme Courts' annual review of hundreds of pertinent cases. Judges also clarify specific cases that create precedent. Finally, judicial actions directly review the legality of administrators' actions, as opposed to the content of administrative actions.[17]

The contemporary issue here is the type of compliance to which administrators should be held. If the legal system generally expects precise technical compliance to detailed statutes with numerous procedural specifications, then judicial review will tend to focus on administrative precision. If, however, the legal system generally expects general accomplishment of legislatively stipulated targets/goals and allows a latitude of procedural and technical means, then judicial review will tend to focus on broader administrative results.

Subordination of Public Administration to Elected and Appointed Officials

The fourth legal value of public administration is subordination of merit or civil service employees to elected and appointed political officials.[18] Elected officials have not only substantial executive functions but also legislative and judicial functions. Examples include the executive orders of presidents and governors, and the rule-making authority of many county supervisors and city councils who appoint their chief executive administrative officer. In the ideal, political bureaucrats are responsive to public sentiment, which is to have priority, while incorporating the professional expertise and legal tradition represented by career public service. This ideal is intended to avoid the dictatorship of expertise, no matter whether self-serving or simply overreaching in its decisionmaking.

For example, generals, because of their expertise and experience, may want the state of military preparedness upgraded, but political executives may refuse because the taxpaying public simply will not abide the additional expense. Professional opinion is valuable because of its focus, but conversely, it is also prone to myopic demands because of its narrowness. Of course, political bureaucrats are themselves highly limited by law, legislative intent, and the courts. Subordination of public administration to political bureaucrats is part of the generally accepted democratic chain of command.

Numerous issues are associated with this value. To what degree should political officials let administrators use their creativity? How deep in the organization should appointive bureaucrats be placed? Does administrative responsiveness to individual constituent needs short-change the political hierarchy?

What Is "Subordination," and How Much Is Enough?

General agreement on these four values—subordination of public administrators to the law, legislative intent, the courts, and political bureaucrats—is relatively easy and widespread. Disagreement emerges over the definition of subordination and judgments of the appropriate degree of subordination. This disagreement is heightened today as looser conceptualizations of subordination are competing with the long-term, New Deal trend for increasingly restrictive conceptualizations. Three major classes of cases pertain: exceptions to general rules, initiative in management issues, and initiative in policy issues.

Exceptions to General Rules

Public administrators execute millions of decisions every day, generally following identified legal values with little difficulty or reflection. However, among those millions of decisions, thousands of cases patently merit exceptions from laws as promulgated. Deciding who should make those exceptions, and how, is an act of power and governance of consequence. If public administrators are not measured by the strictness and accuracy of their responsiveness to "customers," what mechanisms can be used to ensure that specialized interests will not tyrannize the public interest at large? While looser definitions of discretion allow decisions to be made lower in the organization, closer to the facts of the case, more rapidly, and far less expensively, looser definitions of discretion require accountability and review of exceptions of a different nature.

Initiative in Management Issues

Public administrators are managers, and, according to many management experts, public managers should be allowed and encouraged to show more initiative in management issues.[19] Yet traditional notions of public management often specify management processes in great detail and discourage variation or experimentation not originated at executive levels. Consider, as a general example, whether a public manager should be given some discretion without legislative approval over the mix of full-time versus part-time employees, or salaried versus temporary employees. Many observers would answer yes, because contemporary use of competition and rigorous comparison is making management selection of personnel mixes increasingly likely. To continue our example in the area of correctional facilities, alternative management models are encouraging greater management variation. The traditional corrections model hired all personnel through centralized systems into regular state, county, or federal classifications. Some corrections managers now (1) provide oversight over facilities that are run completely privately with exclusively nongovernment employees, or (2) provide public managers the option of exercising more discretion in the use of temporary and part-time employees. Further, executives and senior managers are increasingly using alternative models within their systems as a source of dynamism and incentive. With increasing regularity threats of privatization are used to spur management improvements. The definition of public management as a strictly procedural or maintenance activity is increasingly giving way to the idea that public management is a creative activity with requirements for experimentation and modest risk. Managers in this model are judged more by the results that they achieve than by conformity to restrictions on personnel and program processes.

Initiative in Policy Issues

It is an easy step from increased management initiative in public organizations to encouraging public managers to take a more active and visible role in the policy process itself. As Chapter 1 discussed, the politics-administration dichotomy never existed in reality, but it had great force as an ideal. According to that ideal, public administrators, although they *do* affect policymaking at all stages in the policy process, *should* be highly subordinate in the system, emphasizing their roles as neutral technicians rather than as assessors and judges of policies. Public managers in the public administration dichotomy could not be held accountable for policy failures because those decisions were not theirs, but instead had been made by their legislative and executive masters. Many now suggest that policy entrepreneurship should be the ideal,[20] at least at a middle level.[21] If public managers must increasingly compete with private providers, should they not also have the discretion to direct significant policy efforts as well? For example, the California Franchise Tax Board (California's department of revenue) was faced with a crisis in its workforce. Simply put, its workforce did not have the skills necessary to fulfill the function legislatively assigned to it. Part of the skills gap was a result of a state requirement to give work preference to those receiving welfare payments; another followed from the quality of workers willing to accept the modest salaries paid by the board. As a matter of departmental policy, the Tax Board instituted a massive educational program including instruction in basic skills (reading, writing, basic math), general skills (facilitation and public speaking), and mechanical skills (typing and machine usage), as well as assistance in high school and college degrees. Agency personnel *did not* go back to the authorizing board for this permission; instead, they assumed it was an appropriate midlevel policy decision to be made by management implicit in existing legislative mandates.[22]

The Contributions of Legal Values in the Public Sector

The importance of legal values in public administration is so fundamental that sometimes their role is assumed. Actually, in both theory and practice, legal values are generally first among peer values. As Harold Gortner, John Rohr, and others have pointed out, practitioners generally make sure that legal compliance is attended to first, before turning their full attention to other value sets.[23] Legal values often frame the parameters of action, within which other value sets operate.

Legal values make three contributions that apply both to traditional (stricter) notions of legal compliance and to more contemporary (looser) notions. (Contemporary notions do not fundamentally challenge the basic role of legal values, only their specific definition and degree.)[24]

1. *Legal values give public administration an authoritative role in the governance of the state.* Modern democratic states generally rely on a social contract (constitution or legal covenant). The structure of the state articulated by the social contract in turn

relies on the law. It is public administration that executes the law. There is a wide range of opinion about the degree to which public administration is not referenced and therefore is a second-order component of the American governmental design[25] versus whether it is an implicit, first-order component of governance.[26] There is not, however, any significant debate about the fundamental, legally authoritative role of public administration. Further, although public administration legal values all imply subordination, in most modern governments the branches have checks and balances in terms of the power they wield. Because of the massive role of public administration, it is only appropriate that it should be subject to significant controls.

2. *Legal values provide a parameter of acceptable behavior through a legitimate and authoritative process.* Legal values ensure that public administrators have a system of accountability for their actions.[27] In particular, legal values ensure that general guidelines for public administrators are clarified and codified.[28]

3. *Legal values provide procedural protections against the misuse of public administration by any single constituency or powerful interest.*[29] Legal values provide the authoritative balance among individual, professional, organizational, and public interest values. One of the most important challenges for public administrators is fulfilling obligations despite the fact that various legal "masters" conflict. An infrequent but important conundrum for administrators arises when political masters request action that is (or appears to be) in conflict with the law. As challenging as this tension may be for the administrators, it can be healthy (in moderation) too. Political officials are quicker to overstep the law because of their shorter tenure, more ideological bent, and their orientation toward change. Administrators can help political bureaucrats find legal means to accomplish many of their ends while dissuading them from their extralegal ambitions altogether. Yet it is also true that public administrators are quicker to be excessively cautious and adverse to change because of long tenure, a technocratic orientation, and a tendency to avoid risk. Political bureaucrats can help public administrators explore the legal limits of new laws or legislatively replace old ones.[30] Although the four values of legal subordination cause tensions, confusion, and challenges for public administrators, they also provide a series of checks and balances critical to the long-term health of the public sector.

The Problems of the Legal Values of Public Administration

Legal values, like all value sets, present problems and challenges. The broadest and most fundamental one has already been cited as a sometimes virtue. The four values of subordination cause confusion because of the endless subtleties and conflicts that arise. A single legal value with clear and unambiguous precedence would make administration easier and more explicit. However, Green and Hubbell contend complex "decisions are usually mediated through subordinate public administration."[31] Administrators often have to begin implementing laws that are likely to be overturned by the courts. They also must make sense of conflicting mandates from political leaders and legislators and sift through the vagaries of the language of the law to determine the intent of legislators. These conflicts necessitate a level of judgment that defies the precise answers desired by those seeking an exact science.

Problems that arise from the stricter conceptualizations of legal values are loosely called legalism,[32] and they have become more prevalent in the last half century. Looser conceptualizations also have associated problems, but that discussion has been omitted here.[33]

1. *Legalism breeds inflexibility.*[34] This is less of a problem in stable situations. "Governance structures and strategies aimed at control, consistency, and predictability work well in stable, predictable environments," states Peter Block.[35] Yet these are not stable times as economic, technological, and cultural shifts accelerate. Legalism leads to situations in which it is impossible for any one person to even be aware of the full extent of the law. "Making law detailed, the theory goes, permits it to act as a clear guide. People will know exactly what is required. But modern law is unknowable. It is too detailed."[36] Legalism also retards change and reduces opportunities for learning. One reason is suggested by Walter Balk, who says that in government agencies "existing procedures are frequently punitive toward productivity innovators."[37] This explains why Vice President Gore noted that "many work hard to keep their innovations quiet."[38] Finally, excessive concern with administrative wrongdoing, a frequent outcome, inhibits right-doing and virtuous administrative behavior.

2. *Legalism breeds micromanagement by the legislature, political bureaucrats, and even the courts in areas better left to experts and*

managers.[39] Kenneth Mayer, for example, has outlined congressional micromanagement over the Department of Defense in terms of the number of line-item changes, the number of restrictions, conditions, and directions by Congress, and the amount of information Congress requires.[40] Political bureaucrats, trying to manage their organizations strictly, often overlook the fact that "laws and internal organizational policies can never be specific enough to cover all the situations and contingencies encountered by an administrator."[41] Yet Peter Block points out that "the belief, especially in the public service, is that we can legislate errors, loss, and embarrassment out of our institutions. Each act of control, inspection, and regulation reduces responsibility and ownership from those living under its rule."[42] A belief in thorough control has caused a legalistic trend at all levels, but especially at the federal level.[43] The newer trend toward reducing micromanagement while simultaneously demanding greater productivity gains means that significant shifts in accountability types are occurring (see Chapter 12).

3. *Legalism is cumbersome and expensive.* Extensive layers of control and inspection can mean that processes and services are slow and delayed. Yet as Philip Howard suggests, "Delay is equally an element of the lack of due process."[44] Fred Thompson has called the process of rule proliferation *encrustation:* "An abuse occurs, someone decides that 'there ought to be a law,' and a rule is promulgated to avoid the abuse in the future; but such rules often continue after the need for them has passed."[45] He argues persuasively that legalistic controls cause tremendous expense both to the organization and to its "customers" and should be created with care. The streamlining efforts spearheaded by the National Performance Review and similar efforts at state and local levels, as well as abroad, indicate that this antilegalistic initiative is being enthusiastically pursued.[46]

4. *Legalism squeezes out the more humane and interpersonal forms of consensus building and conflict resolution.*[47] Resolution of problems is seen as an adversarial situation that requires litigious action.[48] This has produced an impasse for government, which is called upon to do more than ever before but is challenged by excessive administrative protections. The modern trend has been to detail procedures more fully, rather than give broader

administrative discretion. This, however, results in ever more detailed rules, as the legal attacks become still more specific and lead to an endless spiral of legalism. Philip Howard summarizes the predicament this way:

An unworkable contradiction lies at the heart of the modern state. Process is a defensive device; the more procedures, the less government can do. We demand an activist government while also demanding elaborate procedural protections against government. We have our foot heavy on the accelerator, seeking government's help in areas like guarding the environment. Simultaneously, we have stomped hard on the break, refusing to allow any action except after nearly endless layers of procedure.[49]

Conclusion

The importance of legal values, and their frequent preeminence for public administration, flow from the nature of states with cultures that stress individualism and rely primarily on social contracts as the underlying organizing force. Law takes on a quasi-religious significance as the organizer and officiator of such societies. Social morality is ideally reflected in the law, in extreme cases the law drives morality. In such cases, the "good" is much less important than mindless obedience to the law. Public administration, which largely lives by the law, must be vigilant to this possibility.

As a social contract state, the United States views the law as the legitimate will of the people. Further, the law is seen as an authorized and orderly process achieved in an explicit, predictable, and accountable fashion. That is, the due process nature of the law is critical since the process by which law and decisions are reached affects outcomes enormously, by including and excluding parties to the process in different ways.

Public administration, in particular, has a special role with the law, since it is both a creature of the law and an executor for it. Thus, four important types of subordination typify public administration legal values: subordination of public administrators to the law (specific statutes and rules), to legislative intent, to the courts, and to political officials.

There are three strengths of these values for public administrators. First, legal values give public administration an authoritative role in the governance of the state. Second, legal values provide the parameters of acceptable behavior through a legitimate and authoritative process.

Third, legal values provide procedural protections against the misuse of public administration by any single constituency or powerful interest.

A general weakness of legal values is their contrariness to one another, since conflicts between and among the various types of subordination expected of public administrators are inevitable. However, four specific weaknesses are prevalent for contemporary legal values that tend toward excessive legalism. Legalism breeds inflexibility, micromanagement, excessive cost and waste of time, and discourages problem solving at a personal, nonlitigious level.

Although the excesses of legalism have already led to a substantial movement to reduce its detrimental effects, the fundamental importance of legal values in public administration—subordination to the legal process for which it authoritatively acts—is generally unquestioned.

Notes

1. Thomas Hobbes, *Leviathan,* Part 4, Chapter 13, 1651.
2. Modern examples include Iran and the Vatican.
3. Few true, tradition-based examples are left (e.g., Saudi Arabia and some of the other Arab sheikdoms). Aristocratic societies of old were largely tradition-oriented oligopolies. Great Britain and some of the other European monarchies still have traditional trappings (such as the House of Lords) but have largely converted to socialist or social contract states, or a combination of the two. Examples of the difference between religious-based and traditional based social orientations can be seen historically in the Puritan revolution in England, overthrowing James I and the monarchy for over a decade before the Cavalier restoration, and more recently, the overthrow of the Shah by Moslem religious fundamentalists in Iran.
4. Examples can range from societies built up from family and intergenerational obligations, such as are found in Confucianism, all the way to societies built down from large-scale social conceptions common in the forms of socialism and communism.
5. Of course most modern democratic states have at least modest social contract characteristics. Historically it has been common to have a single form dominate. It should also be noted that contemporary *civil* social contract states were preceded by *religious* covenants (generally for groups rather than countries). The Mayflower Covenant of 1620 would be a prime American example.
6. Lawrence Kohlberg, *The Philosophy of Moral Development: Moral Stages and the Idea of Justice* (San Francisco: Harper and Row, 1981), p. 19.
7. John A. Rohr, *Ethics for Bureaucrats: An Essay on Law and Values* (New York: Marcel Dekker, 1989), p. 5.
8. For example, Vincent Ostrom bemoans the substitution of legal rationality for broader standards of morality when he says, "A narrow reliance upon legal rationality with regard to penalties can lead to a perverse game of penalty-

avoidance by conforming to the letter of the law, searching for exceptions, and a response of trying to close loopholes and tighten prior rules with still more mandatory rules," in "The Challenge of the Quest for Excellence," *International Journal of Public Administration* 19, no. 2 (1996), p. 130.

9. For example, from this rapidly expanding literature see David Osborne and Ted Gaebler, *Reinventing Government* (Reading, MA: Addison-Wesley, 1992); Paul Aucoin, "Administrative Reform in Public Management," *Governance* 3 (April 1990), pp. 115–137; Charles Goodsell, "Reinventing Government or Rediscovering It?" *Public Administration Review* 53, no. 1, (January/February 1993), pp. 85–87; David Rosenbloom, *Public Administration: Understanding Management, Politics, and Law in the Public Sector* (New York: McGraw-Hill, 1993); and Larry Terry, "Leadership in the Administrative State: The Concept of Administrative Conservatorship," *Administration and Society* 23, no. 4 (February 1992), pp. 395–412.

10. See for example, Anthony B.L. Cheung, "Performance Pledges—Power to the Consumer or a Quagmire in Public Service Legitimation?" *International Journal of Public Administration* 19, no. 2 (1996), pp. 233–259; Arie Halachmi and Geert Bouchaert, eds., *The Enduring Challenges in Public Management: Surviving and Excelling in a Changing World* (San Francisco: Jossey-Bass, 1995).

11. For an extended discussion of the ramifications of recent Supreme Court decisions and general legal trends on public administration, see the symposium in the *International Journal of Public Administration* entitled "Legal Issues in Public Administration," edited by Thomas J. Hickey (19, no. 1, [1996], pp. 1–101).

12. Philip Howard, *The Death of Common Sense: How Law Is Suffocating America* (New York: Random House, 1994), p. 186. Thomas Barth makes an almost identical statement when he asserts "the false promise of technicism is that someone has 'the answer' to complex social problems like crime and poverty, so the public desperately flocks to the sound bites of the latest messiah." "Administering in the Public Interest: the Facilitative Role for Public Administrators," in *Refounding Democratic Public Administration,* Gary Wamsley and James Wolf, eds. (Thousand Oaks, CA: Sage, 1996), p. 175.

13. As Peters and Savoie note,

> A second constraint on the ability of agencies to become more autonomous is the law. Although it has been argued that some of the reforms of the past few years disregard the importance of law in controlling American government, in practice there is still a strong legal element shaping the organization and management of public programs. Every time an agency wants to issue a regulation, even if the intention actually is to deregulate, it must find a legal peg on which to hang that regulation. . . . In short, the system remains (for the most part, at least) one of 'laws, not of persons.'"

> B.Guy Peters and Donald J. Savoie, "Managing Incoherence: The Coordination and Empowerment Conundrum," *Public Administration Review* 56, no. 3 (May/June 1996), p. 286.

14. David Rosenbloom, "Have an Administrative Rx? Don't Forget the Politics!" *Public Administration Review* 53, no. 6 (November/December 1993), p. 506.

15. Howard, op. cit., p. 1–3.

16. Andrew Jack and David Kennedy (at the direction of Lewis Spence), *Building the Baltic,* Case Study from the Kennedy School of Government, Harvard University, 1989.

17. These challenges can be procedural, substantive, or constitutional. Peters and Savoie, op. cit., p. 286.

18. I use the terms *political official* and *political bureaucrat* interchangeably here.

19. Outstanding examples are Steven Cohen and William Eimicke, *The New Effective Public Manager: Achieving Success in a Changing Government* (San Francisco: Jossey-Bass, 1995); Steven Cohen and Ronald Brand, *Total Quality Management in Government* (San Francisco: Jossey-Bass, 1993); Martin A. Levin and Mary Bryna Sanger, *Making Government Work: How Entrepreneurial Executives Turn Bright Ideas Into Real Results* (San Francisco: Jossey-Bass, 1994).

20. This was probably most boldly and provocatively stated in *Reinventing Government* (op. cit.) in which the authors recommend that government become (among other things) more catalytic (Chapter 1), enterprising (Chapter 7), and anticipatory (Chapter 8). While the authors freely intermingle political bureaucrats (elective and appointive) with merit bureaucrats, they clearly imply that civil servants should be more than passive participants in the heightened public-sector-driven policy activism they view as necessary for the refurbishing of American government, including public administration.

21. In their book on policy entrepreneurship, Nancy Roberts and Paula King conjecture that generally radical change is "more likely to be initiated through legislative and judicial design rather than management design in organizations" (p. 230). As a corollary, they hypothesize that "to the extent ideas have a relative advantage, greater trialability and observability, and are more compatible with the existing system, they are more likely to be introduced by organization (bureau) or management design" (p. 230). Overall, their judgment is that "those inside the government and thus subject to greater oversight, such as bureaucratic entrepreneurs, are more likely to pursue incremental change" (p. 231). Nancy C. Roberts and Paula J. King, *Transforming Public Policy: Dynamics of Policy Entrepreneurship and Innovation* (San Francisco: Jossey-Bass, 1996).

22. Case prepared for the Kennedy School of Government Case Program at Harvard University by Michael Barzelay (Harvard University) and Catherine Moukheibir (Boston University) in 1993.

23. Harold Gortner, *Ethics for Public Managers* (New York: Praeger, 1991); John Rohr, op. cit.

24. This is not to underplay the very real and important differences of proponents on both sides.

25. This view is implied in most of the writings that emphasize the scientific, technical, or administrative aspects of public management. This view sees public administration as a neutral administrative instrument of the political system.

26. For proponents of this position, see John Rohr, *To Run a Constitution: The Legitimacy of the Administrative State* (Lawrence: University Press of Kansas, 1986); and Gary L. Wamsley and James L. Wolf who note, "the word *administration* most likely did not appear in the Constitution because the Founding Fathers assumed it to be so fundamental it needed no more mention than did oxygen." "Introduction: Can a High-Modern Project Find Happiness in a Postmodern Era?" in *Refounding Democratic Public Administration,* Wamsley and Wolf, eds. (Thousand Oaks, CA: Sage, 1996), p. 12.

27. As Dennis Thompson notes, elected officials and political appointees often share the public misconception that public administration standards are low and relatively loose. "Instead of finding lower standards of conduct in

government, they are shocked to find higher standards, or at least more restrictive ones." Dennis Thompson, "Paradoxes of Government Ethics," *Public Administration Review* 52, no. 3 (May/June 1992), p. 256.

28. Gary Brumback states that "government scandals notwithstanding, corruption is not the primary problem" when talking about the problems of ethical management. "Institutionalizing Ethics in Government," *Public Personnel Management* 20, no. 3 (Fall 1991), p. 362.

29. Richard T. Green and Lawrence Hubbell note, "Legal standards typically include a mix of substantive values and procedural guides. Rule by law, as a matter of prudence, attends as much to means as to ends. This is born of the centuries-old realization that results by any means may be more noxious to a political community than no results at all" (p. 48). After all, they note, "One person's 'red tape' may be another's 'due process of law'" (p. 59). "On Governance and Reinventing Government," in *Refounding Democratic Public Administration,* Wamsley and Wolf, eds. (Thousand Oaks, CA: Sage, 1996), pp. 38–67.

30. This heuristic stereotyping may become less of a typical phenomenon if entrepreneurial management trends make real inroads into public administration. Of course, as David Rosenbloom, Guy Peters, and numerous thoughtful management theorists remind us, different management paradigms may bring new opportunities in changed environments, but they inevitably result in trade-offs and new challenges as well. For example, increased entrepreneurialism raises serious concerns about procedural safeguards. See for example, R. Gurwitt, "Entrepreneurial Government: The Morning After," *Governing,* 1994, pp. 34–40; Ronald Moe, "The 'Reinventing Government' Exercise: Misinterpreting the Problem, Misjudging the Consequences," *Public Administration Review* 54, no. 2 (March/April 1994), pp. 111–122; James Fallows, "A Case for Reform," *Atlantic* 269, pp. 119–123; and Larry Hubbell, [Review of *Reinventing Government*], *American Review of Public Administration* 23, no. 4 (1993), pp. 419–421.

31. Green and Hubbell, op. cit., p. 45.

32. See Patrick Dobel, "Integrity in the Public Service," "*Public Administration Review* 50, no. 3 (May/June 1990), pp. 354–366.

33. For an excellent critique of the nonlegalist models of public administration, see Christopher Hood, "Beyond 'Progressivism': A New 'Global Paradigm' in Public Management?" *International Journal of Public Administration* 19, no. 2 (1996), pp. 151–177. Hood concludes that (1) the strict legalist model—what he calls progressivism—is "fading" somewhat in many countries recently, (2) it is unlikely that a single paradigm, market-driven or otherwise, will replace the legalist model, and (3) it is not even certain that the legalist model will not reemerge after a period of decline.

34. Vincent Ostrom states this boldly when he asserts: "A single, comprehensive, and uniform code of law is an *impossibility*" (op. cit., p. 131). Similarly, Hon S. Chan writes, "As the variety or complexity of activity increases in the policy environment, the administration must develop a comparable level of variety to adapt to the changes externally prescribed." "Scientizing Public Administration or Public Administration in Search for Quality Governance," *International Journal of Public Administration* 19, no. 2 (1996), p. 269.

35. Peter Block, *Stewardship: Choosing Service Over Self-Interest* (San Francisco: Berrett-Kohler, 1993), p. 26.

36. Philip Howard, op. cit., p. 30.

37. Walter L. Balk, "Productivity Improvement in Government Agencies," *Policy Studies Review* 4, no. 3 (1985), p. 482.

38. Al Gore, *Creating a Government That Works Better and Costs Less: The Report of the National Performance Review* (New York: Plume, 1993), p. xxxv.

39. Robert Behn, "The Big Questions in Public Management," *Public Administration Review* 55, no. 4 (July/August 1995), pp. 313–324.

40. Kenneth R. Mayer, "Policy Disputes As a Source of Administrative Controls: Congressional Micromanagement of the Department of Defense," *Public Administration Review* 53, no. 4 (July/August 1993), pp. 293–302.

41. Terry Cooper, *The Responsible Administrator* (San Francisco: Jossey-Bass, 1990), p. 167.

42. Peter Block, op. cit., p. 144.

43. See, for example, both reports by the National Performance Review, and scholars such as Robert Roberts and Marion Doss, "Public Service and Private Hospitality: A Study in Federal Conflict-of-Interest Reform," *Public Administration Review* 52, no. 3 (May/June 1992), pp. 260–269; and Elliot Richardson, "Ethical Principles for Public Servants," *Public Manager* 21 (Winter 1992–93), pp. 37–39. Private sector management experts have complained of parallel problems and have generally been on a campaign for reducing corporate legalism.

44. Philip Howard, op. cit., p. 108.

45. Fred Thompson, "Matching Responsibilities With Tactics: Administrative Controls and Modern Government," *Public Administration Review* 53, no. 4 (July/August 1993), p. 313.

46. Antilegalistic efforts are fairly universally supported by management experts. An example is Tom Peters: "Let's by all means make a Herculean effort to dent the stultifying impact of the hundreds and hundreds of thousands of pages [of regulations] that mindfully at the time, but cumulatively mindlessly, accreted over the decades." "Excellence in Government? I'm All For It! Maybe," *Bureaucrat* (Spring 1991), p. 6.

47. The role of public administrators as consensus builders, educators, facilitators, community builders, and conduits of trust is an explicit concern of the "Blacksburg Manifesto" group. See, for example, *Refounding Democratic Public Administration,* Gary Wamsley and James Wolf, eds. (Thousand Oaks, CA: Sage, 1996).

48. Vincent Ostrom (op. cit., p. 129) notes: "If public administration is viewed as a system of command and control in which the letter of the law and the threat of penal sanctions are the controlling criteria for administrative rationality, standards of judgment will inevitably clash about the meaning to be assigned to human actions. Standards of justice cannot be confined to legal rationality. Consensus and mutual trust are necessary in assessing the legitimacy of decisions and actions being taken."

49. Philip Howard, op. cit., p. 105.

CHAPTER 6

The Role of
Public Interest Values

Public interest values[1] are the broadest value cluster of the five considered in this text. The public interest includes what is good for society at large and balances the competing interests of different groups, including unborn generations. As a social construct,[2] public interest is the agreed-upon gestalt or totality of political, economic, and religious values of a particular society.

Because it is so broad, public interest is exceedingly difficult to define operationally.[3] One leading scholar, Glendon Schubert, largely abandoned the concept as being too vague.[4] More recently, scholars such as Charles Goodsell have resurrected the concept, despite its ambiguous nature, asserting that lacking a comprehensive notion of the public good, narrower concepts become the de facto definitions that inevitably are too parochial.[5] For example, defining the law as equivalent to the public interest (as is occasionally done) results in problems such as (1) what is legal is, ipso facto, ethical, and (2) asserting that the public interest can be perfectly captured in a political-legal process. It is intuitively understood, however, that laws are changed in the name of the public interest, not vice versa.

Yet despite the importance of maintaining a comprehensive ideal of the public good, the concept is invariably fraught with challenges because of the inevitable innumerable interpretations. Although all members of society may have ideas about what is in the public interest, public action becomes difficult or impossible when those ideas collide in substantial ways. In some societies, discussions about the public interest may be relatively undivisive, especially when survival and societal success are unchallenged or clearly defined. The United States experienced such a period during James Monroe's presidency that was known as the Era of Good Feeling because social consensus was high. Consensus also was high during World War II because of the social cohesion brought about by a widely agreed-upon enemy. Yet disputes about the public interest abound in those societies in which survival and societal success are not clearly defined. The disputes about what is in the public interest may lead to valid discussions and amicable disagreements, but such disputes can also lead to bitter ideological fights or even civil wars. Because "poll after poll has shown that Americans feel anxious and insecure to a degree unmatched since the Great Depression,"[6] it is little wonder that increasingly intense ideological feuds have become rampant. In American history, of course, rebellions and a civil war were animated by fundamentally different notions of the public interest.

Recent cries about the loss of traditional values, the breakdown of the family, the loss of trust in institutions, the viciousness of political discourse, and the disintegration of a coherent sense of community are all signs that a single notion of the public interest is in a period of turmoil and substantial transition. This is a worldwide phenomenon. It is also important, however, without discounting these profound and serious debates and the problems they raise, to emphasize the resilience of public interest values in mature and stable political countries such as the United States.[7] Although dynamic or heterogeneous countries such as the United States may experience times of intense discord and debate, such periods alternate with periods of relative consensus and agreement. Unfortunately some societies never seem to surmount their internal dissensions, which means that the bulk of the social energy is spent fighting one another, rather than striving to achieve a relatively unified set of social goals.

The Public Interest Values Environment

Because public interest values vary by society or country,[8] this text focuses on the values generally accepted in the United States. Further, the locus of this study is in public interest values in the political system, only indirectly including economic and religious values as they affect and are affected by ideals of governance. Six broad public interest values have stood the test of time in American society: systematic governance; a representational democracy; a division and separation of political power through federalism; protection and celebration of individualism; protection of religion as an individual right rather than as a universal way of life; and a relatively pure form of capitalism. These six values are in many ways mutually reinforcing. Capitalism, for example, thrives in stable, individualistic democracies. The six values also have inherent tensions, as ultimately do all value sets. Individualism, for example, will never have full vent whenever it is curbed by any form of systematic governance.

Systematic Governance

Systematic governance enables various issues to be brought into the public domain (or sent out of it) through an authorized process. This is generally a public interest axiom in large, modern societies. Only nomadic and anarchic societies do not endorse systematic governance at more than a clan or village level. Even cities have had a history of sophisticated systematic governance going back beyond the Greek city-states. However, modern states do vary significantly in what they deem appropriate to include in and exclude from the public domain. In the case of the United States, the public domain has generally increased in responsibilities, especially during the twentieth century. As a social consensus builds that the limits of state growth have been reached from the American perspective, policy debates increase about how to maintain or curb governmental growth (systematic governance). Should it be by shedding services, deregulation, privatization, reduced subsidies and redistribution, market devices such as fee for service or environmental credits, public-public competition, or other alternatives? Thus, although the basic assumption about systematic governance as fundamental to the public interest is unchallenged, the belief in the number of areas to be handled primarily as a part of the public domain is shifting considerably. The ramifications for public administration are enormous.

Representational Democracy

The second broad public interest value in American society is representational democracy, the belief that democratic political action and choice should be encouraged when possible, generally relying on a system of elected representatives to implement these choices.

It would be difficult to overstate the importance of choice to Americans. However, since direct democracy (such as the town meeting) is not viable in geographically large and populous entities, elected representatives are a means of considering the public's interest in a deliberative and fair way that is well established and popular in the U.S. system. Yet despite the success of representational democracy in the U.S. system, like many other countries there are a number of pressures to change. One contemporary issue for representational democracy is the increasing capability of providing direct democracy forums through technologies such as the Internet. While a major shift to direct democracy through frequent electronic plebiscites is unlikely, technology and information access have already created increased demands for responsiveness by both elected and nonelected officials. Another contemporary challenge for representational democracy is the increased cynicism about elected officials and government in general. With better information access, a more aggressive media, and a more competitive global economy, the public's trust of government officials has declined, ironically making bold, long-term leadership even more difficult. An issue that directly affects public administrators is their role in a representational system. What weight should nonelected officers have in the governance process? Election is only one of many ways to become an officer of the government.[9] Contemporary employee empowerment measures, as well as insertion of enhanced entrepreneurial behavior, are likely to significantly recast the traditional representational paradigm (see Chapter 8 for a detailed discussion of this point).

Division and Separation of Political Power Through Federalism

The principle of federalism divides power and encourages a variety of subaggregations of public interest through a federal system. Americans have always had a strong suspicion of governmental power.[10] John Adams urged "the only maxim of a free government ought to be to trust no man living with power to endanger the public liberty."[11] The answer the framers devised was a form of federalism that

1. separates the powers of the national government into three branches.
2. checks the power of any one branch by the other two.
3. divides the power of government between the national government and the states.

As John Rohr notes, "The very grammar of the name of our country—a *plural* noun modified by an adjective—mocks the idea of a comprehensive whole."[12] The design has been a brilliant answer to the quip about power corrupting and absolute power corrupting absolutely,[13] leading to much copying by other countries over the last two centuries. Of course, the current constitutional design was not the first. The ill-fated Articles of Confederation were essentially the first constitution, but they were found to give the federal government too little power to execute a coherent national policy. The limits of states' rights were forcefully checked in the Civil War, and for the last three decades there has been a broad concern that the national government has too much power. Typical of both popular and academic rhetoric is Theodore Lowi and Benjamin Ginsberg's complaint that "in 1789, 1889, and even in 1929, America's national government was limited in size, scope, and influence, while states provided most of the important functions of government."[14] Further, despite successive attempts at decentralization in recent forms of federalism, David Walker has found mixed results, and he is dubious that the current reinvention efforts will be more successful.[15] Emerging research lends credence to this hypothesis.[16] On the other hand, modern federalism has found the public interest to be too divided by the number of governmental units, the number of active and narrow special interests, and the loss of the civic sense of regionalism and nationalism. This has led to a concern that too many interests and governmental entities are "stealing" from the common good for narrow gain, and that there is too little sympathy for contribution to the national community. As early as 1960 President Kennedy was reminding Americans that they ought not to ask what their country could do for them, but what they could do for their country.[17] Despite the brilliance of American federalism, public administration is often seen as being part of the problem of excessive executive power[18] and as being another special interest. In general, federalism is unchallenged as a national basic assumption. The question that creates confusion is how to adjust federalism for contemporary circumstances to achieve better balance and avert exacerbating current excesses.

Protection and Celebration of Individualism

The principle of individualism protects the individual from an intrusive government or a tyrannic majority. Americans are among the most individualistic people in the world.[19] Two important political expressions of that individualism are the belief that individuals should be protected against the enormous power of government at large,[20] and the belief that minorities should be protected against majorities.

The most important protection of single individuals or small classes of them is written in the first ten amendments to the Constitution of the United States, the Bill of Rights. The following individual freedoms are protected there:

- Freedom of religion, speech, press, and assembly (Article 1)
- Freedom to bear arms (Article 2)
- Freedom from military billeting (Article 3)
- Freedom from unreasonable search and seizure (Article 4)
- Freedom from self-incrimination and double jeopardy (Article 5)
- Rights to due process, a speedy trial, and legal counsel (Article 6)
- Right to a trial by jury (Article 7)
- Freedom from excessive bail or unusual punishment (Article 8)
- General recognition that rights emanate from the people and are not granted by the government (Articles 9 and 10)

As a class, individual rights generally have been successfully guarded, and some areas such as due process and confidentiality have been expanded. In terms of the rights of minority groups, James Madison's concern about the "danger of factions" who are much too "disposed to vex and oppress each other than to cooperate for their common good"[21] has proven too true in American history.[22] Examples include the Alien and Sedition Acts of the late 1790s; the suppression of racial groups such as African and Chinese Americans; forcible internment of nationalities such as the Japanese Americans during World War II; and subtler forms of discrimination against women, people with disabilities, and other groups. As Lord Acton pithily observed, "The one pervading evil of democracy is the tyranny of the majority."[23] To protect against this evil, American governance seems to have expanded minority rights to nearly their logical limits.[24]

The concerns about excessive individualism in current society are frequently commented on. Members of both the Right and Left generally agree that "individualism run amok"[25] is a major problem. Two examples impinging on public administration may suffice. The first is the explosion of the number of individuals taking legal action rather than finding nonlitigious solutions.[26] A second troubling trend is the emphasis on citizen rights and customer-client expectations at the expense of broader civic responsibilities, which becomes a democratic concern for public administrators when their "empowered customers . . . make public policy without benefit of law!"[27] Ultimately, individualism is a source of great pride and celebration for Americans. However, the concerns about how to meld individuals' good into the common weal are shifting beliefs in this area as Americans attempt to find a new balance between individualism on the one hand and civic community on the other.

Protection of Religious Choice as an Individual Right

Separation of church and state ideally functions to protect the individual's freedom of religion without making religion a universal way of life. While Americans consider themselves a religious people on the whole, they express it politically by allowing individual expression of religious belief free from any interference by the state.[28] A number of the original colonies were founded upon specific religious convictions, among them Massachusetts, Connecticut, Rhode Island, Maryland, and Pennsylvania. Some of the later waves of immigrants came to this country to escape religious persecution. Because of this diversity of religious beliefs, religious tolerance became an increasing necessity for the republic. As Alexis de Tocqueville noted in the 1830s, "In the United States even the religion of most of the citizens is republican, since it submits the truths of the other world to private judgement."[29] Today the United States is still fairly thoroughgoing in its separation of church and state, with occasional lapses, as in favoring churches as charitable organizations for tax purposes and in the ironic placement of the motto In God We Trust on money. This basic assumption in American life—that church and state should be separate—has worked relatively well. However, until relatively recently, the United States has implicitly emphasized Christian, especially Protestant, values, tolerated Jews, and looked askance at the values of other religions as religious values percolated through the political process.[30] The contemporary pressures for change in this area arise from the perceived decline in the sense of community and sense of similar, shared ("traditional") values. Thus widespread calls for the reinvigoration of the great institutions target not only the family, local community, and nation, but also churches.[31] As with the other religious revivals in the United States, turbulent economic times and social-political excesses are likely to blend together to reshape views about welfare, education, birth control and abortion, drugs, parental responsibility, and a variety of other "social" issues.[32] Public administration will have to respond to changing social values. Consequently, while the basic assumption is that the United States separates church and state for the protection of both, beliefs about churches as builders of community and shared values are currently enhancing their relative position culturally (and thus politically).[33]

A Relatively Pure Form of Capitalism

Capitalism is valued as a means of encouraging classical liberal economics through governmental actions and appropriate inactions. Providing a stable society (but emphasizing individual protection and choices, dividing and controlling public power, and disavowing a state religion and morality) affords a fertile opportunity for capitalism.[34] That is, pure capitalism is both amoral and individualistic. Among the creeds of American capitalism is a belief in the least governmental intervention possible, following Thomas Jefferson's dictum that the government that governs least governs best. Preferably, governmental actions are severely limited to those that are necessitated by indivisible common goods such as the environment or the provision of military defense; activities that are inherently governmental, such as budget management,[35] or actions taken when the likelihood of harm to individuals is too significant and the individuals are too vulnerable to the variations or nature of the market (such as banking insurance).[36] Pure capitalism would carry these assumptions to their logical extreme, as it would not fund any social progams or corporate welfare. Most in society would consider this to be brutal, sharp edged, or extreme. Nonetheless, although American capitalism is far from "pure," it is still less "socialized" than most of its modern counterparts on the world stage. The general basic assumption in American life is that a modestly socialized form of capitalism is best, with economic and moral interventions by government (whether through taxes or prohibitions) into the lives of its citizens being appropriate only when community desire for them is particularly strong.

Despite widespread agreement on the necessity of the softening of capitalism for the collective good, few can agree *where* government intervention is appropriate and *to what degree.* Fiscal conservatives would like a better match of government expenditure to revenues, but even they disagree whether it should be accomplished through cutting military expenditures or social services or through an increase in taxes. Social conservatives generally want more intervention for the common good, but they disagree on the rationale for such intervention. Although many policy areas in which the government is deeply involved (in contravention to pure capitalist beliefs)—such as public education, social insurance, and environmental protection—are broadly supported, consensus breaks down in operationalizing the level of support.

The special conundrum for the American public, and for public administration more specifically, is that the current reality is beginning to (or has already, depending on your definitions) exceeded a modestly socialized capitalist state. Of course, it is commonly understood that individual citizens and groups are attached to their own social services and regulatory protections.[37] For example, public administrators are increasingly regulating various types of insurance, including retirement funds. Individual citizens believe that this is appropriate because a fundamental governmental function is to protect citizens from harm. Insurance companies view such regulations as pesky red tape that warps the market, and classical economists assert that passing losses back to consumers would make them more savvy and careful, thus ultimately strengthening true market forces.

Growth of government has accelerated since the New Deal ushered in an era of "positive government." For example, all government receipts in 1940 represented only 18 percent of the gross domestic product. In 1990, that figure had swollen to 37 percent. Similarly, government workers have increased as a percentage of the population from 4 percent to 7.7 percent in the same period. Since 1816 when the Census Bureau began keeping records, until 1990, the federal workforce, considered as a percentage of the population, increased twentyfold. Thus the common conception that government has gotten very large has a sound factual basis, but value decisions about how to address the reality are divisive.[38] Not only is the play of varying beliefs at work here; more than any of the other six values discussed, there has been a fundamental shift in the *basic assumption* in this century, which even a "return" to traditional (stricter) capitalist values is unlikely to fully correct.

In sum, then, Americans' basic values emphasize the stability of systematic governance despite their historic suspicions of government. They emphasize representative democracy (as opposed to alternatives such as monarchy, or theocracy), which is enhanced by a federal system that allows more electoral choices. The federal system also allows the people to control the power of government by dividing it, rather than adopting the more common unitary state model found in other countries. Individual choice is key to Americans, even in religion, which is separated from the state. The emphasis on a strong form of capitalism is somewhat softened by the contemporary needs and expectations of society, which has become accustomed to more active or positive government.

Public Administration and Public Interest Values

The general basic assumptions discussed earlier have substantial ramifications on the more narrow set of basic assumptions and beliefs of public administration. Of particular importance are Americans' suspicion of governmental power controlled through representation and their concern that government will usurp capitalist dynamism and individual initiative.

This section discusses four basic assumptions underlying public interest values for administrators. The first two are derived from their role as *implementors* of the governance; that role emphasizes neutral implementation and efficient and effective management. The third and fourth are derived from their role as *actors* in the governance process. That role emphasizes involvement in the governance process as executors or stewards, legal agents with joint responsibilities to the people and the law.[39]

Implementing Policy but Not Usurping the Process or Amassing Power

Public administrators should implement public policy but not usurp power. Despite ongoing disagreement about the specific role of public administrators in the system of American governance,[40] there is universal agreement that public administration is designed to implement public policy. There is also universal agreement that public administration should not usurp the policy process, either by its privileged position as implementor or by amassing power. Generally speaking, this is interpreted to mean that public administrators should be nonpartisan and nonideological in their professional capacities, and that they should not use their discretionary powers in an arbitrary way. It is also interpreted as a sensitivity to legal subordination, as discussed in the last chapter. Public administrators' basic assumption that they should implement but not usurp the policy process stems from the more general cultural assumptions of supporting systematic government, representative government, division and separation of powers, and protection of individualism. That is, public administrators become the primary tool of representative government's provision of systematic government; they do so in a system of divided governmental powers, in which the protection of individualism is generally one of the strongest values.

Scholars diverge in their views of administrative usurpation and power when operational issues such as degree and size are discussed. In the case of degree, one school of thought holds that the nonpartisan and nonideological character of public administrators should be strictly maintained because of a natural tendency to try to usurp power over time. Administrators must *strictly* avoid political preference (in their professional capacities) in the electoral process, must avoid showing policy preference during the legislative process, and must avoid using discretion during implementation.[41] This perspective is very concerned about the ease with which administrators can affect the political, policy, and implementation processes to reflect their own interests. The other school of thought stresses reasonableness over strictness. Administrators must *reasonably* avoid political preference, policy preference, and excessive discretion. They point out that the civil service plays a relatively small role in American politics, at least comparatively,[42] that administrators know more about most policies than anyone else because of their expertise,[43] and that discretion by professionals is actually necessary for coherent implementation.[44]

In the last fifty years, the size of government has itself become an issue. If an underlying basic assumption in American life is that a relatively pure form of capitalism is the ideal, at what point does government growth exceed that value? One school of thought holds not only that excessive size is possible but that it has long since occurred. From this perspective, government regulates too much (which causes economic inefficiencies) and provides too many services (which it does inefficiently). Government should make individuals more responsible for their own health, safety, and financial well-being and should not compete with the private sector for service provision. Government, by its very size, already dominates the policy process with its bureaucratic power and warps the market forces necessary for a long-term robust economy. This perspective points out that protection from too many economic and social ills in the short run can cause major economic disruptions in the long run, which in turn causes even greater pain and suffering.

A second (and contrary) perspective holds that government size is a function of societal complexity and social demand. A complex society makes it almost impossible for individuals to rationally protect themselves from all possible harms or to find the services necessary in the private sector with the level of security required. For example, those holding this perspective would point out that while a perfect market might make competition the best leveler in the ideal world, market imperfections abound in daily life. A heart-attack victim cannot shop around for the cheapest hospital, a taxi passenger finds bargaining difficult in new locations, and a Social Security recipient might find even occasional default by pension funds an unacceptably high risk.[45]

In sum, there is broad agreement that public administrators should not usurp the policy process or amass power. But how strictly should administrators observe dictates for non-partisan, nonideological, and nondiscretionary behavior? And to what degree is the size of government itself, significantly greater today than at any other time in its history, a form of usurpation and power dangerous to American ideals?

Being Efficient and Effective with the Public's Resources

The basic assumption that public administrators should be efficient and effective with the public's resources is borne out of the need to manage the resources of any organization well. Government organizations manage vast resources, over a third of the gross domestic product, and thus it is not an exaggeration to assert that "management processes are at the center of our system of governance."[46] Efficient and effective administrative practices are an expectation of all who are interested in the performance of government. This basic assumption of public administration is based on a balancing of two of the more general assumptions in our culture: Efficiency and effectiveness can simultaneously be seen as an appropriate outgrowth of systematic government and as the good management practices expected in capitalist organizations.

A clash of beliefs about efficiency and effectiveness arises, however, out of substantially different operational definitions. As James Q. Wilson has observed, it is "not hyperbole to say that constitutional order is animated by a desire to make government inefficient."[47] That is to say, governmental efficiency and effectiveness are not necessarily defined, as they often are in the private sector, as rapid decisionmaking, lowest cost, financial return, or risk avoidance. Examples are well known: public decisionmaking is often broader, slower, and more expensive but it is more democratic; public decisionmaking tends to emphasize long-term impacts over short-term results; least cost rarely equates with most appropriate level of quality; financial return is often a low priority in public processes such as social services; and risk acceptance is often defined as a public function in select areas because the private sector will not, or cannot, handle it. This debate over the proper definition of efficiency and effectiveness has had many variations and forms over the years. The major debate today pits a classic administrative model against a market model.[48]

The classic administrative model sees the public interest as best achieved by rational means. Voters make rational electoral choices; elected representatives make rational policy choices; and administrators should make rational implementation choices. This notion of democratic governance implies a relatively centralized administrative structure. It also typically implies strong executive oversight, clear hierarchical lines of authority, a limited span of control, separation of politics and administration, and other standard features of hierarchical bureaucracy. Although this notion of government has been powerful throughout American history, many aspects of it have also frequently been questioned. Jacksonian democracy, echoed during Ronald Reagan's presidency, emphasized responsiveness to elected representatives over political neutrality. In contrast, social egalitarians, such as the "New Public Administration" critics in the late 1960s and 1970s, argue that rational administrative structures underrepresent weaker constituencies and are prone to nondemocratic structures. The administrative model has even been criticized as being too subservient to elected officials and not institutionally powerful enough to embody long-term public interests through a large cadre of professionally devoted officials.[49]

The major challenge today, however, comes from the market model. To advocates of this model, voters, elected representatives, and administrators *all* distort the system because of their self-interests. Honesty can be restored to the system only by injecting competitive market forces wherever possible to ensure a self-correcting process. As one commentator observes, "competition is assumed to produce both more effective and more democratic public action. At its core, the market values choice and the mechanisms that make choice possible."[50] Market forces such as credits (tax incentives, pollution allowances, and so on), user fees, multiple service providers who must compete, governmental franchising, public corporations, and vouchers replace command-and-control mechanisms such as rules and regulations. Because of the competition it induces, this model encourages administrative vision, decentralization, multiple lines of authority, customer-client responsiveness, and greater risk and experimentation.

Clearly, no matter what its merits really turn out to be, the market model is gaining greater sway, both politically[51] and in practice. Yet this should not obscure the fact that what is in question, and what is currently shifting, is only the definition of the type of efficiency and effectiveness that administrators should observe. The larger assumption—that public administrators should be efficient and effective (once the definition is settled upon)—is unchallenged.

Supporting the Public's Right to Know

Public administration should support the public's right to know because three of the general cultural assumptions of American society—systematic governance, representational democracy, and protection of individualism—largely depend on the public having appropriate and accurate information on which to base their decisions. As Terry Cooper insists, "Communicating substantive information to the public is essential if self-government is to be even approximated."[52] Yet information is not enough for democracy to work well, with voters making informed choices and elected representatives making enlightened policy, if those with information do not also seek to assist citizens and representatives to understand the information. That is to say, public organizations, with their expertise and enormous data sets, must not only provide information, they must also seek to educate those with a need to know.

Beliefs begin to diverge when this informer-educator role is defined. Who is the public administrator's primary target for this information and education, and what is the responsibility of the target audience? Thomas Barth recapitulates this well-known issue in saying, "The classic question of who does the public administrator serve: the needs of elected officials (in the executive branch and Congress) or their appointees for whom they work in an organizational sense; or the needs of citizenry, which is ultimately sovereign?"[53]

The traditional and more technical perspective is that information and education by public administrators is aimed primarily at elected representatives, at least regarding policy formation, policy issues, and execution problems. All nontechnical and nonunique cases should be brought to the attention of at least appointed officials, and systematic problems should be addressed in some sort of legislative process. In practice, the key points of information and education take place during policy design, legislative review committees, the budget process, special reviews and audits, legislative constituent casework, and special reports to legislative masters and their appointed overseers. Information and education to the public at large, from this perspective, is a relatively passive and technical process. Although information is made available, education campaigns generally teach citizens what their responsibilities are so that they are able to comply with statutes and rules.

The more recent perspective is more activist. It emphasizes the public's right to knowledge and education as much as it emphasizes the elected representative's right. Citizen responsibility receives less emphasis and citizen rights and opportunities are underscored. Thus the key points of information and education are publicized performance results of agencies (such as, external evaluation or comparative surveys), ombudspersons, acccss to user-friendly information and forms, and education campaigns to teach citizens what their rights are. From this perspective, citizens should have as much evaluative information available to them as elected officials have (despite the expense and low utilization that might result). Also, public administrators should work hard to get the information out to individual users; individual users should not have to struggle to find information and then have to understand confusing legalese. Despite the intuitive appeal of this approach, which brings a fresh refocusing on the final "customer," it, too, has its challenges. Information dissemination is expensive. All but the most streamlined comparative data about agencies are far beyond the general public's ability to comprehend. And general information about the agency is more likely to be aimed at enhancing public relations than at genuinely informing the public about performance strengths *and* weaknesses.

No one questions the public's right to know. Yet it becomes less obvious when one is defining who the public is (which operationally becomes publics) and deciding on the means of delivering the information and education appropriate.

Supporting the Public's Right to Be Involved

Public administration should support the public's right to be involved. Informed and educated elected officials and citizens are necessary but not sufficient for a high-performing democracy—elected officials (and their appointed representatives) and citizens must act on their knowledge and beliefs as well. Public administrators have much of the information needed in policy design (or the ability to get it). They are ultimately the party responsible for implementation, and they actually handle the problems and exceptions that arise in policy execution. For all these reasons, they should facilitate the public's right to be involved. (They also can impede it.) Again, public administrators' basic assumption of supporting the public's right to be involved is based on their role in supporting systematic government, representational government, and protection of individualism, all of which depend on an involved citzenry.

The more traditional view of public involvement takes the perspective of the democratic electoral process, which emphasizes citizen voting, legislative open hearings, and communication with elected and appointed officials throughout the policy process. From this perspective, administrators must be careful not to be directly influenced by constituents, who have specialized interests that are largely beyond administrators' scope of legitimate power to decide. Facilitation with citizens is directed at obtaining accurate information from those affected in order to make assessments about what rights and services or what responsibilities and regulations apply. This perspective has the advantage of being a rational approach that is consistent with the classical, top-down notion of democracy.[54] Its disadvantages are that civic participation is not a phenomenon limited to the voting booth and that facilitating that participation is likely to significantly expand citizen involvement.

A second perspective sees a more active facilitative role of citizens at large, which is self-conscious and planned. As Terry Cooper observed: "Opportunities for participation must be carefully planned and systematically structured, using a variety of techniques to elicit the views of the public. The unstructured expression of public sentiment seldom gives direction to administrators."[55] Some commentators focus on public administrators' facilitative role in the design and implementation processes. These commentators see public administrators as balancing the often "polarized forces" that exist around policy discussions,[56] and as representing groups that are ignored because they are too poor or unorganized to become a part of the agenda.[57] A common criticism of this perspective is that it gives too great a role to public administrators in deciding how to balance discordant forces and which disaffected groups to assist and represent. A second group of commentators focus on the details of execution and the resolution of problems and exceptions after the policy process has been determined. These analysts use customer surveys, focus groups, advisory boards, and other input and facilitation techniques to ensure that execution is smooth and efficient. This perspective is represented in aspects of the reinventing movement, with its customer focus. The criticism of this approach, at least as it has been played out in the 1990s, is that important policy decisions often have already favored the more powerful interests in the policy process and that the remaining "customers" are already well represented.[58]

Many famous bureaupathologies—such as secretiveness, jargon, stonewalling, apathy, proceduralism, and so on[59]—point out ways administrators can obstruct authorized decisionmakers and prevent relevant constituents from being an integral part of organizational processes. It is clearly the role of public administrators to ensure that both authorized representatives and their appointed leaders, as well as the citizens they serve, are facilitated in appropriate interactions with public organizations. The challenge is determining what the appropriate balance and type of interaction should be among elected representatives, citizens, and the public administrators who serve both.

Contributions of Public Interest Values for Public Administrators

First and foremost, the public interest values of public administrators tend to enhance the American political state by reinforcing the dynamic tension of values typical of the constitutional design. No matter which particular school of thought does the analysis, public administration values carefully maintain a generally nonpolitical role that does not upset the balance and separation of powers which make American constitutionalism successful. Yet the values do allow enough flexibility for public administrators to be active in managing, educating, and facilitating the democratic processes of government. Further, this flexibility allows them to respond to different contexts[60] and different needs over time.[61] Despite the complexity of the tensions of these values, it is difficult to argue against the overall success of the public sector.[62] As Tom Peters observes, "American democracy and markets both work. Beware the champions of order who would clean them up."[63]

The second contribution of public interest values is that they are critical for creating a public service ethic. Legal values, on their own, tend to be mechanistic, hierarchical, and impersonal. Public servants are more than mere automatons of legal prescriptions; they contribute their intelligence, their commitment, and their passion for the public good. Public interest values capture not only the spirit of the law but the spirit of the democratic process, which balances individuals against groups and one center of power against another so that working consensus can be constantly reforged. While public administrators must be careful to carry out their roles as nonpolitical implementors, they enhance them by integrating their subtler roles as deferential actors in the governance process.

Potential Problems of Public Interest Values of Public Administrators

Public administrators are never directly mentioned in the Constitution, no matter how much their presence may be implied or assumed. Consequently, their public interest roles as participants in the constitutional governance process are by nature exceptionally vague. To what degree are public servants the stewards, conservators, and executors not only for all three branches of government but for the national public good itself? To what degree are public administrators the glue that holds the political-social process together? Such a view might raise strong concerns that current downsizing will lead to a "hollow" state. Or to what degree are such questions presumptuous in reference to a constitutional design that never anticipated this concentration of responsibilities, resources, and power by bureaucrats in a self-consciously capitalist state?

A second problem with public administrators espousing strong public interest values, as opposed to legal values, is that they provide much more opportunity, perhaps too much opportunity, for entanglement with their personal values as individuals or a corporate group. It is only human nature to project our own interests, biases, and conceptions onto those activities we control, even when we think we are being neutral. Thus public interest values are always vulnerable to the critique of self-aggrandizement and group bias.

Conclusion

Public interest values are at once the most important of the five value sets considered in this text and the most difficult to define and articulate. Public interest values capture the broadest level of social aspirations, within which individuals are encouraged to work cooperatively for the public good. Public interest values are so broad and abstract that some commentators have largely dismissed the concept as operationally meaningless. Yet others assert that public interest values represent the most critical values individuals have, and that denying them is akin to denying patriotism, love, or belief in God.

Six basic assumptions were described for the public interest values extant in American society. The first was a conviction in systematic governance; the second was in representational democracy. The third basic assumption was the principle of federalism, which divides and separates the powers of governance. The fourth was the tenet of individualism, which in the political sphere protects individuals from an intrusive government and oppressive majorities. The fifth principle is protection of religious choice by separating it from government. The sixth principle was a conviction for a strong form of capitalism, which would ensure relatively minimalist government so that markets could flourish without undue governmental intervention and so that individuals would have the responsibility for directing the bulk of their lives. The larger basic assumptions of society frame the narrower ones for public administrators. Public administrators are the primary purveyors of systematic governance, democratic processes, and the mechanics of federalism. They are the protectors of individualism, in a context that removes religion from a direct role in governance and that indirectly enhances capitalism.

Four specific public interest values were identified for public administrators. First, public administrators should implement public policy but not usurp the public policy process or amass inappropriate power. Second, public administrators should be as efficient and effective as possible with the public's resources. These two roles emphasize public administrators as relatively neutral implementors. The third and fourth roles emphasize these administrators' more activist role as actors in the governance process: public administrators should support the public's right to know, and they should support the public's right to be involved.

One major strength of these fundamental assumptions is that they reflect the tension found in the Constitution. Public administrators could usurp power easily, were it not for their strong principles about deference and conservation. Yet their role as executor does not allow public administrators to be mindless servants; they must creatively serve the public good within the many constraints placed on them. This leads at times to some frustration and confusion, as various values of the public good are pitted against one another. And of course, it is difficult to separate the public's good from one's own, and this is always a precarious risk for the exercise of administration discretion. Yet able administrators do master the subtleties of public interest values, and by working hard to transcend the operational tensions inherent in government, they are able to play an important role in the daily re-creation of democracy in action.

A Summary of the Five Sources and Part II

Part II has surveyed each of five sources or value clusters and examined the most elemental assumptions associated with each. It also explored 17

TABLE 6.1

The Five Value Sources and Seventeen Basic Assumptons Used in Decisionmaking in Public Administration

Individual Values	Professional Values	Organizational Values	Legal Values	Public Interest Values
Public administrators should . . .	*Public administrators should . . .*	*Public administrators should . . .*	*Public administrators should . . .*	*Public administrators should . . .*
have strong civic integrity supported by a belief in representative democracy and "universal" ethical principles such as honesty.	be well trained (managers and executives should have extensive professional education).	maintain organizational health by promoting organizational dynamism.	be subordinate to the law.	implement public policy but not usurp the policy process.
have access (themselves) to basic citizen and human rights.	be influenced by the expertise and wisdom of the professions via professional traditions, standards, and continuing-education requirements.	maintain appropriate organizational design parameters (varies significantly): —macrolevel values —structural values —values about work —values about employees	be subordinate to legislative intent. be subordinate to political bureaucrats. be sub-ordinate to judicial interpretations and judicial mandates.	be efficient and effective with the public's resources. support the public's right to know. support the public's right to be involved.
be capable of unique contributions and civic leadership.	encourage professional values in public organizations, such as independence in technical decision-making and a competitive income.	maintain an appropriate leadership style (varies significantly).		

basic assumptions used in decisionmaking in public administration. These are listed in Table 6.1.

These assumptions are not unidirectional or without tension. They frequently exist in tension with one another as counterbalances and thus must be reintereprered over time and for specific situations. While much of this burden of interpretation falls to policymakers, in the end it exceeds their capacity, both technically and quantitatively, and public administrators must play a role. The discussion and debate over the extent of the interpretative role will always be with us; and for the next few decades this discussion is likely to be high on the public's policy agenda.

Notes

1. Also known as *public good, common good,* or *civic values,* although each of these terms has slightly different connotations.
2. P.L. Berger and T. Luckmann, *The Social Construction of Reality: A Treatise in the Sociology of Knowledge* (Garden City, NY: Doubleday, 1966).
3. Charles Goodsell, "Public Administration and the Public Interest," in *Refounding Public Administration,* Gary Wamsley, et al., eds. (Newbury Park, CA: Sage, 1990), pp. 96–113.
4. Glendon A. Schubert, *The Public Interest: A Critique of the Theory of a Political Concept* (Glencoe, IL: Free Press, 1960).
5. Goodsell, op. cit.
6. Gary Wamsley and Lawrence Hubbell, "On Governance and Reinventing Government," in *Refounding Democratic Public Administration,* Wamsley and Wolf, eds. (Thousand Oaks, CA: Sage, 1996), p. 7.
7. Social cohesiveness is enhanced by many factors such as racial homogeneity, class coherence, and stable social traditions. In the United States, social cohesiveness is enhanced by a stable political tradition and a generally dynamic economy.
8. This assertion would be disputed by universalists on normative grounds but not on factual grounds. That is, those asserting a universal culture based on religion, ideology, or a single notion of the "good" would say that there *should* be a unitary notion of the public good around the world, but they would agree that there are in fact many different notions of the public interest (even if those notions are wrong).
9. John Rohr, *To Run a Constitution: The Legitimacy of the Administrative State* (Lawrence, KS: University Press of Kansas, 1986).
10. *The Federalist Papers* give an eloquent set of arguments about the nature of power and its dangers. See in particular James Madison's essay, *Federalist,* no. 10 (1787).
11. John Adams, *Notes for an Oration at Braintree,* 1772.
12. John A. Rohr, "What a Difference a State Makes: Reflections on Governance in France," in *Refounding Democratic Public Administration,* Wamsley and Wolf, eds. (Thousand Oaks, CA: Sage, 1996), p. 119.
13. Comment by Lord Acton in a letter in 1887.
14. Theodore J. Lowi and Benjamin Ginsberg, *American Government: Freedom and Power,* 3rd ed. (New York: Norton, 1994), p. 3.
15. David B. Walker, "The Advent of an Ambiguous Federalism and the Emergence of New Federalism III," *Public Administration Review* 56, no. 3 (May/June 1996), pp. 271–280.
16. In a study of the power of central agencies (the Office of Management and Budget, the Office of Personnel Management, and the General Services Administration) after the National Performance Review and the so-called REGO II, Peters and Savoie found as much central power as ever, despite the rhetoric to the contrary. B. Guy Peters and Donald J. Savoie, "Managing Incoherence: The Coordination and Empowerment Conundrum," *Public Administration Review* 56, no. 3 (May/June 1996), pp. 281–290. See also the next article in the symposium on reinvention for a similar finding, but focusing on the self-interested behaviors of central administrators: James R. Thompson

and Patricia W. Ingraham, "The Reinvention Game," *Public Administration Review* 56, no. 3 (May/June 1996), pp. 291–298.

17. John F. Kennedy's inaugural address, 1960.

18. Some scholars, such as John Rohr, give public administration a constitutional status apart from the executive branch and actually see public administration as an antidote for excessive executive power. For example, Richard Green and Lawrence Hubbell boldly state, "Program administrators must often choose sides in the battles among the branches, not only for their own good, but for the purpose of preserving or restoring a rough balance of powers among the branches." Richard Green and Lawrence Hubbell, "On Governance and Reinventing Government," in *Refounding Democratic Public Administration,* Wamsley and Wolf, eds. (Thousand Oaks, CA: Sage, 1996), pp. 45–46.

19. Citizens from other Anglo Saxon–settled countries with a recent frontier history, such as Canada, Australia, New Zealand, and South Africa, also pride themselves on their individualism.

20. Protection of majorities against tyrannic minorities is addressed through representative government. Elected and appointed representatives are supposed to protect society at large from small, powerful groups such as powerful capitalists. Antitrust legislation is an example of this protection in action because without it, areas of the market would be dominated by a few people who could coerce economic activities along paths they dictated.

21. James Madison, op. cit.

22. Justice John Marshall Harlan's famous dissenting opinion in 1896 gives testament to this ongoing concern, despite constitutional protections. "In view of the Constitution, in the eye of the law, there is in this country no superior, dominant, ruling class of citizens. There is no caste here. Our Constitution is color-blind, and neither knows nor tolerates classes among citizens. In respect of civil rights, all citizens are equal before the law. The humblest is the peer of the most powerful." Dissenting opinion, *Plessy v. Ferguson* 163 U.S. 537, 559.

23. Lord Acton, *The History of Freedom and Other Essays,* 1907.

24. Gay rights activists assert that they are the largest minority group currently excluded.

25. The expression is used by Gary Wamsley and James Wolf, "Intoduction," *Refounding Democratic Public Administration,* Wamsley and Wolf, eds. (Thousand Oaks, CA: Sage, 1996), p. 22, but is probably not original to them.

26. Walter K. Olson, *The Litigation Explosion* (New York: Penguin, 1991).

27. Green and Hubbell, op. cit., p. 58.

28. Ultimately this implies a structural edge of individualism over moral code, a disinclination to bring morality into public discourse, and a resistance against judging actions as good or evil, only the harmfulness of actions. Theodore Lowi, *End of the Republican Era* (Norman, OK: University of Oklahoma Press, 1996), p. 12.

29. Alexis de Tocqueville, *Democracy in America,* originally published in 1835.

30. Kenneth Wald, *Religion and Politics in the United States* (New York: St. Martin's Press, 1987) and George Thomas, *Revivalism and Cultural Change: Christianity, Nation Building and the Market in the Nineteenth-Century United States* (Chicago, University of Chicago Press, 1989).

31. See writers such as Amitai Etzioni, Robert Bellah, and William Bennett for related but contrasting perspectives on how family, community, and religious

values strengthen one another. The government is often seen as hostile to these institutions. For example, Etzioni states that "the anchoring of individuals in viable families, webs of friendships, communities of faith, and neighborhoods—in short, in communities—best sustains their ability to resist the pressures of the state." (*American Values: Opposing Viewpoints*, Charles Cozic, ed. (San Diego, CA: Greenhaven Press, 1995), p. 41.

32. See for example, Naomi Maya Stolzenberg, "He Drew a Circle That Shut Me Out: Assimilation, Indoctrination, and the Paradox of Liberal Education," *Harvard Law Review* 106 (January 1993), pp.581–667.

33. George Will, "Who Put Morality in Politics?" in *Piety and Politics: Evangelicals and Fundamentalists Confront the World,* Richard Neuhaus and Michael Cromartie, eds. (Boston: University Press of America, 1987). See also, Ralph Reed, *Active Faith: How Christians Are Changing the Soul of American Politics* (New York: Free Press, 1996).

34. Much of this discussion is based on Lowi, *End of the Republican Era,* op. cit.

35. For an excellent discussion of inherently governmental activities, see Larkin Dudley, "Fencing in the Inherently Governmental Debate," in *Refounding Democratic Public Administration,* Wamsley and Wolf, eds. (Thousand Oaks, CA, 1996), pp. 68–91. The classic text is Paul Appleby, *Government Is Different* (New York: Knopf, 1945).

36. Even here the call for shedding much social support has been so strong that the volunteer sector itself is showing great alarm. See Brian O'Connell, "A Major Transfer of Government Responsibility to Voluntary Organizations? Proceed with Caution," [Guest editorial] *Public Administration Review* 56, no. 3 (May/June 1996), pp. 222–225.

37. This leads Lowi to assert that "today there is a broad consensus favoring a large and active government," op. cit., p. 3.

38. Of course the issue is not just whether the government as a whole should shrink and which specific areas should shrink the most, it is also *how* services and regulation are provided. The reinventing government movement is primarily focused on changing management and organizational philosophies underlying service and regulation, e.g., more competitive public services and cooperative regulatory services.

39. Richard Green and Lawrence Hubbell (op. cit., p. 39) provide a useful list of public interest values for public administrators, which I will quote in full here. I have tried to incorporate their more widely accepted principles into four basic assumptions, and have tried to include their more disputed assertions in my discussion about the range of beliefs about those four basic assumptions.

> The facets include (a) the ability to sustain dialogue among competing interpretations of our regime values, and to balance their inherent tensions within and among diverse policy contexts; (b) stewardship or trusteeship, which includes notions of representation and standing in for the people on decisions of public interest; (c) conservatorship, which requires an articulate sense of institutional preservation and performance; (d) a restraining or tempering influence over public opinion for the sake of preserving long-term as well as short-term public interests; (e) protection of our fundamental rights, and maintenance of rule by law; (f) educators and nurturers of citizen roles in our governing process; and (g) constitutiveness, which involves presenting (or perhaps confronting) citizens with choices that will define their character as a common people.

Clearly Green and Hubbell, as well as others in the Blacksburg school, define a stronger role in the governance process for public administrators than is universally held.

40. "Public administration has never adequately come to grips with the problem of finding a legitimate place for itself in the American scheme of democratic government" (O.C. McSwite, "Postmodernism, Public Administration, and the Public Interest," in *Refounding Democratic Public Administration*, Wamsley and Wolf, eds. ([Thousand Oaks, CA: Sage, 1996], p. 198). Also, B.H. Craig and R.S. Gilmour, "The Constitution and Accountability for *Public* Functions," *Governance* 5 (1992), pp. 44–67.

41. This perspective is embodied in much of the classical public administration literature running from Woodrow Wilson's famous 1887 article, through Gulick and Urwick's *Papers on the Science of Administration* in 1937, to Herbert Simon's *Administrative Behavior* in 1947

42. American civil servants rarely seek elected positions, for example. This is much less true in some democracies in which civil service is a primary steppingstone to politics.

43. This observation, and the ensuing argument about the merits, goes back to Max Weber.

44. A strong advocate of this position is Philip Howard, who states: "Indeed, the main lesson of law without judgment is that law's original goal is lost" (p. 49). The answer, he asserts, is in "relaxing a little and letting regulators use their judgment" (p. 180). See *The Death of Common Sense: How Law Is Suffocating America* (New York: Random House, 1994).

45. These positions are held, broadly speaking, by contemporary Republicans and Democrats, but not without a good deal of ironic inconsistency.

46. Joy Clay, "Public-Institutional Processes and Democratic Governance," in *Refounding Democratic Public Administration,* Wamsley and Wolf, eds. (Thousand Oaks, CA: Sage, 1996), p. 94.

47. Quoted in Al Gore, *Creating a Government That Works Better and Costs Less: The Report of the National Performance Review* (New York: Plume, 1993), p. xx.

48. The historical antecedents of the administrative model were cited earlier. The historical antecedents for the market model include James Buchanan, Gordon Tullock, William Niskanen, Vince Ostrom, and Elinor Ostrom. For a fuller discussion of administrative paradigms, see Chapter 8, which discusses these two variants in detail and a third one as well (the strong administration paradigm).

49. This perspective is represented by those associated with the Blacksburg Manifesto, originally written in 1984 and updated in 1990, 1992, and 1996. Many of its proponents are cited in this chapter as authors in *Refounding Democratic Public Administration*. Others sympathetic to this school of thought include Larry Terry, Camilla Stivers, Philip Kronenberg, and Charles Goodsell.

50. James F. Wolf, "Moving Beyond Prescriptions: Making Sense of Public Administration Action Contexts," in *Refounding Democratic Public Administration,* Wamsley and Wolf, eds. (Thousand Oaks, CA: Sage, 1996), p. 150.

51. James D. Carroll and Dahlia Bradshaw Lynn come to this conclusion after examining both the positions of Republicans and Democrats in Congress. However, the current Republican position is much more traditionally

administrative, generally tending to favor hierarchical bureaucracy, after being significantly reduced by greater load shedding and privatization. Democrats, long the advocates of positive government, have adopted wholesale market reforms in government as a way to keep government active, if nonetheless using different underlying principles. Both parties' views are considerably more fluid than at any time since the Great Depression, and both are likely to be significantly affected by a change in party in either the White House or Congress. See Carroll and Bradshaw Lynn, "The Future of Federal Reinvention: Congressional Perspectives," *Public Administration Review* 56, no. 3 (May/June 1996), pp. 299–304.

52. Terry Cooper, *The Responsible Administrator* (San Francisco: Jossey-Bass, 1990), p. 54.

53. Thomas J. Barth, "Administering in the Public Interest: The Facilitative Role for Public Administrators," in *Refounding Democratic Public Administration,* Wamsley and Wolf, eds. (Thousand Oaks, CA: Sage, 1996), p. 176.

54. Gary Wamsley and James Wolf, "Introduction: Can a High Modern Project Find Happiness in a Postmodern Era?" in *Refounding Democratic Public Administration,* Wamsley and Wolf, eds. (Thousand Oaks, CA: Sage, 1996), p. 5.

55. Terry Cooper, op. cit., p. 179.

56. This perspective is emphasized by the Blacksburg group. See also James Carroll, "Introduction to the 'Reinventing' Public Administration Forum," *Public Administration Review* 56, no. 3 (May/June 1996), pp. 245–246; O.C. McSwite, op. cit.

57. This perspective was a major focus of the New Public Administration. See also Louis Gawthrop, "In the Service of Democracy," *International Journal of Public Administration* 17, no. 12 (1994), pp. 2231–2257; and Charles Goodsell, op. cit., p. 81.

58. See, for example, James Carroll, op. cit, p. 246; and George Frederickson, "Comparing the Reinventing Government Movement with the New Public Administration," *Public Administration Review* 56, no. 3 (May/June 1996), p. 263.

59. Gerald Caiden, "What Really Is Public Maladministration?" *Public Administration Review* 51, no. 6 (November/December 1991), pp. 486–493.

60. James F. Wolf, op. cit., pp. 141–167.

61. Montgomery Van Wart, "The First Step in the Reinvention Process: Assessment," *Public Administration Review* 55, no. 5 (September/October 1995), pp. 429–438.

62. Charles Goodsell, *The Case for Bureaucracy,* 3rd ed. (Chatham, NJ: Chatham House, 1994).

63. Tom Peters, *The Pursuit of WOW!* (New York: Vintage, 1994), p. 7.

PART III

Analyzing Values Using a Cultural Framework Perspective

The first two parts of the book examined values from an *individual administrator's* perspective, asking the question, How can values be divided so that we can understand how they affect different parts of administrators' lives—personal, professional, organizational, legal, and public interest? That perspective starts with specific public administration values and subsequently expands its scope to understand them more fully. It is particularly useful when assessing current norms—describing them, analyzing them in isolation or small groups, and/or prescribing them. The approach is weaker at identifying, describing, and predicting the relationships of the public administration values with society and social subsystems. For that reason, Part III presents a second perspective that is useful for analyzing values from a cultural perspective.

The *cultural framework* perspective starts with the culture within which public administration is set and then narrows the scope gradually to those values and decisionmaking processes that occur within cultural subsystems, in this case public organizations, and finally to individuals within those subsystems. Strengths of this perspective are that it is much broader, its examination is more analytic rather than descriptive or prescriptive, and it is particularly penetrating at identifying the deep structures occurring in decisionmaking and value prioritization. A deeper understanding of decisionmaking and value prioritization is always useful to administrators, but particularly so when significant change is afoot, as is currently the case. Otherwise administrators are likely to make changes based solely on intuition, hunches, and unrecognized biases.

The Cultural Framework and an Analysis of the Origins of Basic Assumptions in Public Administration*

Nothing is more important to human beings than their values, beliefs, and underlying assumptions. On a grand and profoundly important level, they determine our explanation for existence. They are the cultural glue of civilizations and the organizations within them, and the fundamental building blocks of culture. Whether national culture or organizational culture or subculture, values (beliefs and basic assumptions) drive the thoughts and actions of the people carrying the culture. Values form our broad, socially derived ethical standards for how the world should operate, and they blend together to make individuals and institutions unique. They even define the content of our individual characters. Yet on a humbler, more concrete, but nonetheless critical level, values are important because these beliefs and underlying assumptions ultimately drive our minute everyday actions. They provide the framework for our patterns of behavior and customs. Values even shape the physical world that societies, organizations, and individuals create, as well as the symbolic meanings given to material and linguistic artifacts.

Values are of profound importance to us all in every aspect of our existence because there is no such thing as a value-free decision. Nowhere is this more important than for public administrators, who hold the public trust and execute public power—that is, who make decisions in the public's stead—using both explicit and unconscious values. *It is therefore critical that public administration fully understand the values—and the cultural framework undergirding them—that they use in making these decisions.*[1]

---

* This chapter was written in collaboration with Bette DeGraw.

Speaking to this point, William G. Scott and David K. Hart state that "given the awesome power acquired by doing [such] significant jobs, why should it not be appropriate to have a heightened awareness of the implications of their metaphysical premises?"[2] At the more operational level, Mark Moore notes that public administrators "must explain which values are taking precedence, which are being subordinated, and why."[3] Yet many scholars, Terry Cooper and John Rohr among them, have noted that,[4] many—perhaps most—public administrators are only dimly aware of their values.[5] They are not necessarily critiquing the profession; they are instead asserting that the task of sorting out value contexts and articulating them in meaningful ways is remarkably difficult. Scholars in public administration have helped greatly through their work in such subfields as ethics, administrative law, organization behavior and theory, public administration history, and organization development. However, the field of public administration has rarely placed values in a broader cultural context in sustained treatments without shifting into perspectives dominated by political theory, management science, or administrative ethics. This part of the book aspires to use such an important perspective (borrowing heavily from sociology, anthropology, and philosophy), to produce a single, in-depth cultural framework.

The study of values within a cultural framework has special importance to the field of public administration today because of the unusual level of change under way in the political-administrative system. The system is currently experiencing policy shifts because of big cycle political and economic changes, as well as organizational adjustments stemming from those systemic shifts. These changes are exacerbated by a barrage of technological, demographic, and informational changes. Value changes can occur at several levels of degree. *Value shifts* are substantial changes in social systems that consequently affect subsystems such as public administration.[6] In stable societies, major shifts occur only every few generations.[7] In the United States, these shifts seem to form 50-year cycles; epochal changes occurred in the 1930s move to activist government, the 1880s progressivism, the 1830s Jacksonian patronage-responsiveness movement, and so on.[8] This infrequent level of substantial value changes is particularly important for public administrators now because the United States is in the midst of a substantial value shift.[9]

Value adjustments are the intermittent adaptations that institutional subsystems such as churches, civic organizations, and public organizations make in response to value shifts. Value adjustments may not occur in a direct linear relationship with value shifts because of internal traditions, priorities, rigidities, and critical mass issues. They are more like the pressure that builds up for earthquakes, sometimes producing a number of small earthquakes and at other times, a big earthquake with aftershocks. In the private sector, organizations that cannot make appropriate value adjustments usually go out of business. Many of their counterparts in the public sector are not allowed to die and are maintained in a state of suspended malaise for decades. Now, however, the increased use of options such as privatization, downsizing, and outsourcing, combined with the much expanded use of change strategies internally, are ensuring closer alignment between systemic value shifts and organizational value adjustments in the public sector.[10] In other words, the major shifts in the public administration environment have caused shifts in basic assumptions, which have in turn affected specific values. Public administrators are scrambling to make sense of these value shifts and to plan changes that bring greater congruence between the dynamic environment and their organizational existence.[11]

In public organizations, administrators help create a value-based framework for decisionmaking—for making complex choices among competing alternative strategies. This framework can be viewed as a set of appropriate values defining organizational purpose, which the administrator helps create and make explicit. In time, these values may become deeply held assumptions permeating the entire organization. In this sense, public administrators create or promote an organizational culture in which and through which the organization can produce, adapt, and survive.[12] Of course, the administrator is not a sole force in shaping a public organization and its culture; a complicated, shifting, evolving set of interdependent events, relationships, and individual interpretations interact to shape the forms and meanings called organizations. Managing and/or changing those organizations is both difficult and challenging. The public administrator is symbolic of the organization and therefore plays a special role in the organization's culture. From a cultural perspective, the public administrator does not just react to change, but rather should engage in the management of change through value-based decision-making.[13] This is the essence of the cultural framework and the basis for its importance for public administration.

The Four Levels of the Cultural Framework

Fundamental to this discussion is a definition and understanding of just what culture is. On the face of it, this is no easy task. By 1952, the cultural anthropologists Alfred Kroeber and Clyde Kluckhohn had identified 164 different definitions of culture.[14] In 1989, Steven Ott identified 73 words or phrases then used to define culture.[15] Some representative examples of how organizational culture has been defined include the following:

- Symbols, language, ideologies, rituals, and myths
- Guiding philosophy, patterns of interactions, values, and attitudes
- The way things are done
- A pattern of basic assumptions
- A system of values, symbols, and shared meaning
- Enactment of shared reality[16]

Working on the problem of defining *culture,* Roger Keesing in 1974 proposed a typology for the various schools of cultural anthropology based on two distinct worldviews: the adaptationist and the ideationalist.[17] The adaptationist view conceptualizes culture as those things that are observable about the members of a group, including patterns of behavior and artifacts. Within this school, culture is seen as serving instrumental functions that help communities adapt to their environments.[18] The ideationalist view focuses on culture as shared ideas, meanings, beliefs, and values. From this viewpoint, culture, in the form of shared patterns of meanings, is located in the minds of the group's members.[19] Y. Allaire and M.E. Firsirotu proposed that from the adaptationalist viewpoint, culture is integrated into the social system, and the two together are viewed as a sociocultural system, whereas from the ideationalist perspective, culture is distinct from the social system and may not always be in harmony with it.[20]

In tying these concepts to organization theory, L. Smircich attempted to crystallize them further, making the distinction that the ideationalist views culture as an organizational variable—something the organization "has," whereas the adaptationalist conceptualizes culture as a root metaphor—something the organization "is."[21] More recently, Edgar Schein and others have integrated these midlevel theories into a macrolevel theory that has been adapted for use in this text. According to this integrated theory, culture is made up of both tangible physical levels and values levels. The tangible elements are artifacts and actions and patterns of behavior, which the culture "has." The values levels include beliefs and basic assumptions, which the culture "is."

The Tangible Levels of Culture

The tangible levels deal with the most physical, visible, and immediate aspects of culture. The tangible levels generally can be seen, heard, smelled, tasted, or felt, and actions at those levels can ultimately be counted.

The Artifacts and Actions Level

The artifacts and actions level is the most basic level of culture. To catalog them, one asks, What are the material aspects (such as structures, consumables, and clothing)? The technology? The art and symbols? The language (including jargon)? Examples of public administration cultures from this level would include buildings, stationery, and uniforms; fire trucks, police cars, and special sirens; badges, insignia, and flags; and specialized language and nomenclature stemming from both authorizing legislation ("That's a Title I" or "That's a Section 6") and the professional nomenclature (such as biology for natural resource agencies). This level of culture also includes individual actions. (Chapter 10 uses this approach to examine a standard decisionmaking protocol that one individual might typically use in arriving at unique decisions.)

The Patterns of Behavior Level

The patterns of behavior level of culture includes the norms, rules, celebrations, rites, and rituals. What are the patterns of behavior and how do people learn them in the culture? Examples of public administration culture from this level would include rigorous procedural safeguards, equity of service, the standardization of pay; requirements for open examinations and competitive bidding and injunctions against nepotism; observance of anniversary dates of employment, and awards for attendance; training, mentoring, and coaching programs (formal or informal) for indoctrinating new members into the culture; and important indications of success (number of cases processed, an accuracy rate, ability to interact with powerful members in the organization) that lead to notice and promotions. (Chapter 9 reviews alternative types of rationality in order to sort out the modus operandi of different patterns of actions that occur at this level.)

The Values Levels of Culture

The values levels of culture deal with the less tangible, less visible, and less immediate aspects of culture. These levels are conceptual in nature, and meaning is therefore gleaned as much by consensus as by any concrete reality.[22]

The Beliefs Level

The beliefs level includes the explicit values about how the world (or system, or organization) does and should operate. It includes expressed principles and rationales, justifications, and codes. Examples from the beliefs level of public administration culture include the reasoning expressed in laws, rules, and operational procedures; perceptions about the appropriateness of standards and mandates (Are we doing the right thing?); perceptions about the actual performance levels (Is 90 percent a poor, good, or excellent level of performance?); and ideal statements and prescriptions of behavior. This level tends to be conceptual but still explicit, even though shared meanings may be in conflict, and notions of the ideal rarely match up with reality. At the organizational level, this is akin to Chris Argyris's notion of espoused theory. Values at this level are relatively discrete and focused in nature. (Chapter 8 looks at three competing paradigmatic outlooks of public administration as examples for the beliefs levels.)

The Basic Assumptions Level

The basic assumptions level is the most conceptual and least visible aspect of culture. Basic assumptions tend to shape broad patterns of values, just as beliefs shape patterns of behavior, and behaviors shape cultural artifacts and specific actions. The basic assumptions level deals with those aspects of culture that are so commonly accepted that members of the group are largely or wholly unconscious of their existence during times of relative stability. Only in times of change do basic assumptions tend to become more explicit, as pressure to adapt to a significantly changed environment causes deeper analysis and questioning.[23] Thus basic assumptions include the implicit understanding of how the world operates. This level is equivalent to an implicit worldview, and at the organizational level it includes what Argyris would term theories in use. Examples of basic assumptions include ideas about the nature of the universe, of human nature, and of political organization, which are discussed at length in the next section.

Figure 7.1 summarizes the four levels of the cultural framework that provides the theoretical foundation for subsequent discussion about values in the public sector. Although this discussion treats the four levels of

The Four Levels of the Cultural Framework

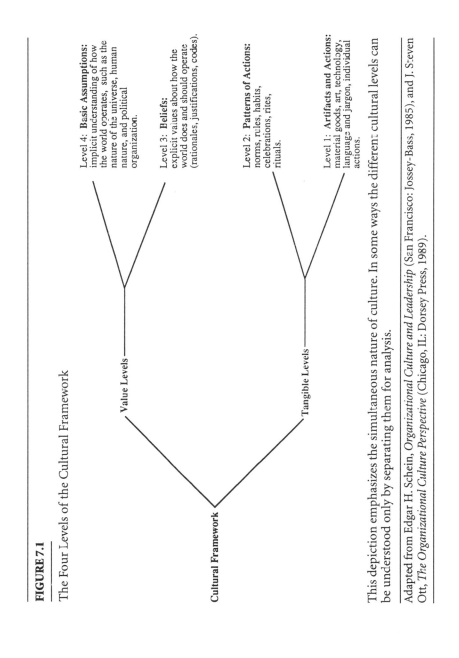

Cultural Framework

Value Levels

Level 4: **Basic Assumptions:** implicit understanding of how the world operates, such as the nature of the universe, human nature, and political organization.

Level 3: **Beliefs:** explicit values about how the world does and should operate (rationales, justifications, codes).

Tangible Levels

Level 2: **Patterns of Actions:** norms, rules, habits, celebrations, rites, rituals.

Level 1: **Artifacts and Actions:** material goods, art, technology, language and jargon, individual actions.

This depiction emphasizes the simultaneous nature of culture. In some ways the different cultural levels can be understood only by separating them for analysis.

Adapted from Edgar H. Schein, *Organizational Culture and Leadership* (San Francisco: Jossey-Bass, 1985), and Steven Ott, *The Organizational Culture Perspective* (Chicago, IL: Dorsey Press, 1989).

culture separately, they do not exist in isolation from one another. One of the challenges for researchers is to make sufficiently clear, meaningful distinctions to keep heuristic categories workable. The next section examines the interactions of the levels.

The Four Levels as Determinants of Actions

The selection of a social system is a long-term, largely unconscious, and culturally sweeping phenomenon that generally occurs over hundreds, sometimes thousands, of years. Members of social systems are rarely conscious of them, except when they explicitly compare them with other social systems. The most basic principles of the social system are its *basic assumptions*.

A society's basic assumptions shape the clusters of beliefs that individuals, groups, organizations, and subsystems have. *Beliefs* tend to be conceptual frameworks guiding action. Of course, the interaction and overlap between basic assumptions and beliefs is complex. For example, Chapters 2 through 6 identified 17 basic assumptions in the American public administration culture. (Chapter 6 has a summary of these assumptions.) These basic assumptions are extremely broad principles and enduring values that have changed little at their core during the Republic's history. Yet despite the broad, long-term agreement about these fundamental assumptions, consensus breaks down at the more operational (beliefs) level. For example, the basic assumption that public administration should be subordinate to political bureaucrats (elected and appointed) has been fundamentally unchallenged in the nation's history, but beliefs about how this basic assumption or principle should be operationalized have been widely discussed. Is it appropriate to have many layers of political bureaucracy controlling the civil service, or just a few? Should public administrators defer all decisions to political officials, or only substantial policy decisions? Should public administrators be highly insulated from political bureaucrats in terms of job selection and security or should political bureaucrats play a substantial role here? If so, what privileges and responsibilities should define that role? Despite their enduring nature, the 17 values identified at the basic assumptions level are all currently experiencing significant debate at the beliefs level. (Chapter 8 looks at the patterns of changes that might evolve and distills them into three paradigmatic alternatives.)

FIGURE 7.2

The Four Levels As Determinants of Actions

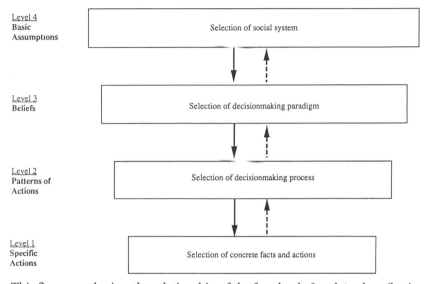

Level 4
Basic
Assumptions — Selection of social system

Level 3
Beliefs — Selection of decisionmaking paradigm

Level 2
Patterns of
Actions — Selection of decisionmaking process

Level 1
Specific
Actions — Selection of concrete facts and actions

This figure emphasizes the relationship of the four levels. Level 4 values (basic assumptions) largely drive Level 3 values (beliefs), which in turn drive Level 2 values (patterns of actions), which drive Level 1 values (specific actions). However, the accumulation of specific actions does affect patterns of action over time and so on up the chain of effect, even if this process is generally more subtle.

Specific beliefs drive the actual *patterns of action* that individuals follow. For example, if society generally believes in a strong division of church and state (a basic assumption), and that administrators should abstain from basing decisions on the exegesis of religious texts (a belief), then the pattern of actions for public administration should lack an explicit religious rationality. In another example, the deep American conviction in social contracts (a basic assumption) is exhibited in beliefs held by public administrators about a high respect for law and due process, and is, in turn, exhibited as patterns of actions demonstrating high levels of legal compliance, rule articulation, and procedural standardization.

Finally, patterns of actions drive *individual actions*. Some patterns of actions will leave almost no scope of discretion, others will leave considerable scope. Providing information to citizens about topics generally open to the public can vary from effusive, comprehensive explanations to very efficient, diffident responses. Yet providing information to citizens about topics under legal disclosure limitations, such as the status of municipal intent to purchase property, is highly circumscribed. In this latter case the concrete actions would tend to be highly consistent with written policies and ordinances.

So it is clear that cultural assumptions affect beliefs, which affect patterns of actions, which ultimately affect specific actions. However, the reverse is also true (even if not emphasized in this text). Over time, individual actions vary and thus change patterns. Patterns affect beliefs. And altered beliefs can reshape basic assumptions, but generally *only in the very long term*. Because in the short term the direction is overwhelmingly from basic assumptions to specific actions, that will constitute the basis for the presentation here. Figure 7.2 summarizes both of these relationships.

Basic Assumptions as a Determinant of Action

No basic assumptions are more important to a society than those in its political heritage. The political cultural values in U.S. public administration are more easily understood by viewing the larger contextual settings first, looking briefly at the levels of civilization (via general philosophy), nation (via political philosophy), and subsystem (via ethics).

Assumptions Flowing from General Philosophy

The first set of questions that Western philosophy considers are those relating to the nature of the human condition.[24] The questions can and have led to an almost infinite number of answers, among which three logical "ideal" types stand out. They are consistent with the *classical* versions of conservatism, socialism, and liberalism. Highly inconsistent contemporary use of these terms has confused their meanings, at times beyond understanding.[25] As used here, these terms refer to giving priority to one concept over two others. In their historic (if somewhat oversimplified) usage, *conservatives* give priority to tradition and religion; *socialists* give priority to society; and *liberals* give priority to individuals. While all three of these value systems have long traditions in which there are many examples of both honor and excess, the task here is not to judge but rather to sort out the traditions to determine which most closely resembles the U.S. framework.

What Is the Nature of the Universe?

1. One of the most ancient answers to this question[26] is that the universe was created by and continues to be organized by a god (or gods). God knows the meaning of the universe since he (or she) created it and it is god's right to expect those using his creation, and who themselves may have been created by him, to revere him. Without god's guidance, humans are as likely as not to guess the wrong meaning of the universe. Societies and individuals should be subordinate to religion.[27]

2. A second answer is to look at societies as being the major determinant of universal meaning. In other words, for all practical purposes, it is societies that define important meanings, including religious beliefs. Individuals can survive only in societies. The quality of society and social relationships is what defines the meaning of the universe. Religion and individuals should be subordinate to society.[28]

3. The third perspective emphasizes that the universe is ultimately experienced by individuals one at a time. God may or may not exist. Societies exist only because of individuals. It is the individual who is the ultimate master of determining the meaning of the universe in a private and unique fashion. Religion and society should be subordinate to individuals.[29]

What Is the Nature of Humanity?[30]

1. Humanity is innately weak or invariably tends to wickedness without guidance. Examples include humanity's original fall from grace, continual sinning, and fear of death without afterlife. God's help is needed to overcome weakness, discover meaning, and find goodness and rightness (usually called righteousness in this context). Societies should be formed around god's commandments; individuals should be subordinated to civil authority only if it has religious legitimacy.[31]

2. Humanity is basically good if individuals are properly socialized. Having good societies, is therefore, key in order not to warp individuals into fanatical or selfish extremes. Good societies encourage all individuals to contribute to the social welfare, and they also emphasize equality of distribution.[32]

3. Humanity is both good and wicked. The purpose of both religion and society is to help each individual discover goodness on his or her own terms. Wickedness is defined largely as obstructing others' pursuit of goodness. The "ideal" society institutionalizes individual rights to the greatest possible degree while still holding the social fabric intact. Religion is only one of many alternative avenues available to individuals in their quest to define and discover the good.[33]

Assumptions Flowing from Political Philosophy

The third question considered here concerns political philosophy, which is built on the metaphysical choices just discussed. How do assumptions about the universe and humanity steer Americans' choices in designing societies?

Given the Nature of the Universe and Humanity, How Should Humanity Be Organized Into a Society?

1. If god is the giver of meaning and humans are innately weak and inclined toward wickedness in the absence of strong guidance, the state should provide strong guidance through an administration dominated by the approved religious ideology.[34] In the extreme cases, which have become nearly extinct today, the leader becomes god or godlike. The religious head may also become the head of state. Contemporary examples of this ideal type are Iran, the Vatican, and formerly Tibet. Another possibility is to have the civil head become anointed or inspired by god. Kingdoms traditionally had strong religious ties in which the ruler also automatically became a religious leader. Thus, theocratic states and kingdoms tend to be the choice for highly conservative (religious) countries. Although classically conservative polities once dominated the West and indeed the world, they have waned tremendously in the last century. Nonetheless, even though the conservative political framework has waned, conservatives are actually undergoing a renaissance as a force in the classical liberal political framework.[35]

2. If society is, in practical terms, the great giver of meaning, and if goodness stems from social contribution and social equity, then society tends to be flattened so that goods and bounty are equally

served up to all its members. In the past, this ideology was confined largely to primitive societies in which the survival of the group depended on the full contribution of all members. The benefits of sharing were continued existence; because consumption was largely limited to basic needs, sharing was fundamental to survival. In the twentieth century, a number of variations have occurred, the most extreme versions of them in what was the communist world. In the Marxist ideal, the political apparatus of the state should wither away and eventually become similar to the primitive model just described, despite far-above normal subsistence levels and social complexity. In Leninist ideology, equality would be required. In practice, the USSR and other communist states completely failed in any attempt to reduce the state or give any genuine political role to the masses, and they had only partial success in achieving social equity. The more moderate versions of socialism in northern Europe have met with far greater success, in which high tax structures allow for strong collective goals and massive redistribution. Although communism is completely out of fashion, socialism is still a significant, albeit much less popular, ideology today.[36]

3. If the individual is the focus of social organization and there is an interest in maximizing individual expression and opportunity, and if strict equality is limited to areas of justice and political representation, not wealth, then laissez-faire capitalist democracies are the logical ideal state. Democratic forms of government are shared by both socialist and liberal states; however, socialist states concentrate on maximizing contribution and social distribution, whereas liberal states seek to minimize contribution and social redistribution (at least under state auspices). Although laissez-faire capitalism has economic origins, it is a political theory as well since it defines the state's interaction with the governed, which is essentially a minimalist strategy for democracies.[37] Since the fall of communism, liberal democracies have come to dominate the world stage. Further, most of the major developed democracies appear to be moving toward reducing governmental roles, which is a return to classical liberalism (paradoxically called conservatism today) from a more socialistic model.[38]

Assumptions Flowing from the Ethical Subsystem

The fourth and fifth questions have to do with how individuals should be expected to act within each of the political frameworks described in the previous section. Ethics is the branch of philosophy concerned with the morality of individual actions and individual accountability vis-à-vis society.

Given a Particular Society, How Should Ordinary Citizens Act?[39]

1. The first answer to this question is that if the state is based primarily on a religious model, then laws are largely civil support for divine knowledge and beliefs. Such knowledge tends to come from sacred texts, religious leaders, and traditions. Civil and religious laws should be nearly identical.[40]

2. If the state is based on a social model of absolute or near equality, individuals should be obedient to society for the good of all. Acting for the common good is the ideal drive. Laws should encourage social goodness and social equality.[41]

3. If the state is primarily based on a laissez-faire capitalist or liberal democratic model, then citizens act for their own satisfaction and personal fulfillment as long as it does not encroach upon others. Individual liberties are protected by a social contract, such as a constitution, which must be respected beyond all other institutions. Religion is an individual freedom protected by the state, but it is not part of the state. Personal satisfaction and personal fulfillment can be achieved by pursuing religious ideals, social virtues such as charity, or economic goals such as the acquisition of wealth. Economic goals are achieved by competition rather than by redistribution, as in the socialist model.[42]

Given a Particular Society, How Should Government Officials Act?

This is, of course, the question of most interest in this text, and the one with which most treatises on public sector ethics begin. This discussion, however, is limited to the broad cultural generalizations about ideal ethical behavior in each of the three mythical states:

1. If the political state is based on religion, and the civil and religious are inseparable in upholding a sacred text and sacred

leaders, then civil servants should act first out of a conviction of religious morality and obedience.[43]

2. If the political state is based on a social equity model, then civil servants' primary motivation should be civic virtue. Since the welfare of all citizens is the interest of the state and therefore of all citizens, civic virtue is doubly important for civil servants.[44]

3. If the political state is based on an individualist model and the social contract is the cement that holds diverse, private interests together, then it is the upholding of the social contract that has legitimacy. That is, legality becomes the primary ethical thrust of the civil servant. (This oversimplification will be addressed in the following chapters.) The irony in a (classically) liberal republic is that the diversity of pursuits allowed individual citizens (who can determine whether religious, social virtue, or economic values should take precedence, as long as they are within the law) are denied to civil servants who are the bearers of the law itself and must place the law first. Morality is determined first by the law, rather than by sacred text or individual social conscience.[45]

The focus of this section was to determine which of the three ideal frameworks most closely resembles the American case in terms of philosophical and political basic assumptions. Although exaggerated as ideal types, the third profile is clearly closest to the American framework. Table 7.1 summarizes the five questions raised in this section, and the cultural assumptions and customary fields associated with them.

Conclusion

The purpose of the first part of this chapter was to lay out the importance of understanding values, not only from a standard technical view but from a broader cultural perspective in order to reveal the deep relationships among them. Next, a four-level schematic (based on the work of Edgar Schein and Steven Ott) was discussed and amplified for use in a public administration context. Level 4 contained the basic assumptions of society, which change the most slowly and are, ironically, the most taken for granted. Level 3 contained the beliefs that are inherent in various parts of society and that conform to the basic assumptions and fur-

TABLE 7.1

Some Political and Ethical Considerations in Different Cultural Contexts

Questions Addressed	Customary Field	Different Cultural Assumptions
1. **What is the nature of the universe?**	Philosophy (metaphysics, especially cosmology and, indirectly, epistemology)	1. The universe is organized by a god or gods and given meaning by that god. 2. The universe is organized by societies and is given meaning by social relationships. 3. The universe is given meaning by each individual because a god (or gods) may not exist and societies exist because of individuals.
2. **What is the nature of the humanity?**	Philosophy (metaphysics, especially ontology); epistemology; moral philosophy	1. Humanity is innately weak and/or needs religious support and restraint. Individuals answer to a god through religious institutions. 2. Humanity is basically good if wholesome societies are supportive. Goodness for individuals is contributing to the social unity; wholesomeness for societies is equity of distribution. 3. Humanity is both good and evil. The purpose of societies is to encourage good and discourage evil.
3. **Given the nature of the universe and humanity, how should humanity be organized into a society?**	Political philosophy; rights theory	1. Theocratic states, kingdoms (ordained by a god) 2. Socialist (and communist) democracies 3. Laissez-faire capitalist democracies
4. **Given a particular society, how should ordinary citizens act?**	Moral philosophy (ethics); existentialism	1. By following the precepts of a god and tradition; laws are civil support for religiously divined knowledge. 2. By acting for the common good as one's primary drive; laws encourage social goodness and social equity. 3. By acting for one's own satisfaction and personal fulfillment as long as it does not encroach on the rights of others; laws protect individual rights and encourage fair competition.
5. **Given a particular society, how should government officials act?**	Moral philosophy (ethics); political philosophy	1. By placing morality first (derived from religion and tradition) 2. By placing individual virtue (for the social good) first 3. By placing legality (upholding the social contract and its laws) first, which in turn safeguards individual rights and fair competition.

ther articulate them. Level 2 contained the patterns of actions that steer most action, and Level 1 included the specific individual actions of the members of societies and its subsystems who instinctively follow cultural byways the vast majority of the time.

The second part of the chapter examined the basic assumption level (Level 4), using primarily a philosophical and macropolitical perspective. It reviewed five questions, identifying three possible responses to each. The first question was about the nature of the universe and its relationship (or lack of relationship) to a god figure. The second question was about the nature of humanity and assumptions about humanity's inherent goodness and wickedness. The third question was about the organization of society, into theocratic, socialist, or laissez-faire states. The fourth was about citizens' ideal actions, given the assumptions adopted in the earlier questions. The fifth and final question was about how government officials should act, again largely determined by the assumptions shaping society's notions of the universe, humanity, and the organization of society. The analysis outlined the typical responses in American society (captured in the third set of responses to each question in Table 7.1).

Chapter 8 will look at the beliefs level of public administration, crystallizing the current values competition into three paradigmatic alternatives.

Notes

1. This is a familiar and important point in both the decisionmaking and ethics literatures. In particular, John Rohr, Terry Cooper, Carol Lewis, and Harold Gortner explicitly make this point. Here I hope to support and broaden this perspective by merging it with the sociological and organizational culture literature in the context of contemporary value shifts.

2. William Scott and David K. Hart, "Administrative Crisis: The Neglect of Metaphysical Speculation," *Public Administration Review* 33, no. 5 (September/ October 1973), p. 415. Douglas T. Yates, Jr., made a similar point: "I cannot imagine anyone saying that the bureaucrat's role in value choice and balancing is a trivial feature of American government." "Hard Choices: Justifying Bureaucratic Decisions" in *Public Duties: The Moral Obligations of Government Officials,* Joel L. Fleishman, Lance Leibman, and Mark H. Moore, eds. (Cambridge, MA: Harvard University Press, 1981), p. 33. John Rohr adds an ominous note, "It is always dangerous when the powerful are unaware of their own power." *Ethics for Bureaucrats: An Essay on Law and Values,* 2nd ed. (New York: Marcel Dekker, 1989).

3. Mark H. Moore, "Realms of Obligations and Virtue," in *Public Duties: The Moral Obligations of Government Officials,* Joel L. Fleishman, Lance Leibman, and Mark H. Moore, eds. (Cambridge, MA: Harvard University Press, 1981), pp. 20–21. In a similar vein, Carol Lewis notes, "It is not selecting the right

values once and for all but selecting the right values for each situation we confront." *The Ethics Challenge in Public Service: A Problem-Solving Guide* (San Francisco: Jossey-Bass, 1991), p. 26.

4. Terry Cooper, *The Responsible Administrator* (San Francisco: Jossey-Bass, 1990); John Rohr, op. cit.

5. The problem, according to Fleishman, Liebman, and Moore, op. cit., is that "society has no habit of serious discourse" (p. ix). Dennis Thompson further asserts that "translating basic ethical principles and basic ethical character into ethical conduct in government does not come naturally to most people." "Paradoxes of Government Ethics," *Public Administration Review* 52, no. 3 (May/June 1992), p. 254.

6. Rosabeth Moss Kanter, Barry A. Stein, and Todd D. Jick, *The Challenge of Organizational Change* (New York: Free Press, 1992).

7. "There is a continuum from deep to variable conventions, and the location of particular conventions on it keeps changing" (John Kekes, *Moral Tradition and Individuality* (Princeton, NJ: Princeton University Press, 1989)], pp. 7–8.

8. Zhiyong Lan and David Rosenbloom, "Public Administration in Transition?" *Public Administration Review* 52, no. 6 (November/December 1992), pp. 535–537.

9. The change has been evident in the private sector for over a decade. See the work of Tom Peters and Robert Waterman (New York: Harper and Row, 1982) starting with *In Search of Excellence,* up to the more recent work of Gary Hamel and C.K. Prahalad, *Competing for the Future* (Boston: Harvard Business School Press, 1994). The sea change in values in the public sector has become evident and mainstream only in the 1990s, starting with works like David Osborne and Ted Gaebler's *Reinventing Government* (Reading, MA: Addison-Wesley, 1992); Patricia W. Ingraham and Barbara S. Romzek, eds., *New Paradigms for Government: Issues for the Changing Public Service* (San Francisco: Jossey-Bass, 1994); and Arie Halachmi and Geert Bouckaert, eds., *The Enduring Challenges in Public Management: Surviving and Excelling in a Changing World* (San Francisco: Jossey-Bass, 1995).

10. Keon S. Chi notes 10 forms of privatization: (1) contracting with public-private firms, for-profit or nonprofit, to provide goods or services, (2) vouchers allowing the public to purchase services from public/private firms available in the open market, (3) grants and subsidies, where the public sector makes monetary contributions to help other public-private organizations provide a service, (4) franchises where monopoly privileges are given, (5) asset sales, where the government sells or "cashes out," (6) deregulation to allow better competition with governmental operations, (7) volunteerism, where volunteers replace public services, (8) private donation, where private donations provide services formerly provided by public agencies, (9) public-private partnerships, and (10) service shedding, where the government drastically reduces the level of service that it provides. See "Privatization and Contracting for State Services: A Guide," in *Innovations* (Lexington, KY: Council of State Governments, 1988).

11. Scholars who have studied change in public organizations note that the political environment of public administration constrains change. In particular, Graham Allison, Robert Golembiewski, Terry Deal, Allan Kennedy, and Bob Denhardt make this point explicitly. The political context of public administration creates an atmosphere of conflicting values, ambiguous goals, and shifting coalitions; time frames for change are short and executive turnover frequent; and strong programmatic and professional subcultures complicate and

frustrate fragmented, diffused management hierarchies. Equity and responsiveness compete with efficiency; in short, public administrators have to juggle the distributive demands of politics and the integrative demands of management.

12. For further discussion of this perspective, see Warren Bennis, "Transformative Power and Leadership, " in *Leadership and Organizational Culture*, T.J. Sergiovanni and J.E. Corbally, eds. (Urbana, IL: University of Illinois Press, 1984); A. Bryman, *All Organizations Are Public: Bridging Public and Private Organizational Theories* (San Francisco: Jossey-Bass, 1987); Gareth Morgan, *Images of Organization* (Beverly Hills, CA: Sage, 1986); and Tom Peters and Robert Waterman, *In Search of Excellence* (New York: Harper and Row, 1982).

13. Edgar Schein makes this point powerfully in his excellent study of organizational culture, Edgar H. Schein, *Organizational Culture and Leadership* (San Francisco: Jossey-Bass, 1985).

14. Alfred Kroeber and Clyde Kluckhohn, *Culture: The Critical Review of Concepts and Definitions* New York: Vintage Books, 1952).

15. J. Steven Ott, *The Organizational Culture Perspective* (Chicago, IL: Dorsey Press, 1989), p. 51.

16. See A.M. Pettigraw, "On Studying Organizational Cultures," *Administrative Science Quarterly,* 24 (1979), pp. 570–571; William G. Ouchi, *Theory Z: How American Business Can Meet the Japanese Challenge* (Reading, MA: Addison-Wesley, 1981); Richard R. Blake and Jane S. Mouton, *Grid Organization Development* (Reading, MA: Addison-Wesley, 1969); T.E. Deal and A.A. Kennedy, *Corporate Cultures: The Rites and Rituals of Corporate Life* (Reading, MA: Addison-Wesley, 1982); Schein, op. cit.; C. Siehl and J. Martin, "The Role of Symbolic Management: How Can Managers Effectively Transmit Organizational Culture?" in *Leaders and Managers: International Perspectives on Managerial Behavior and Leadership,* J.G. Hunt, D.M. Hosking, C.A. Schrieskeim, and R. Stewart, eds. (New York: Pergamon Press, 1984); Gareth Morgan, *Images of Organization* (Beverly Hills, CA: Sage, 1986); L. Smircich, "Studying Organizations As Cultures," in *Beyond Method: Social Science Research Strategies,* G. Morgan, ed. (Beverly Hills: Sage, 1983); and K.E. Weick, *The Social Psychology of Organizing* (Reading, MA: Addison-Wesley, 1979).

17. Roger Keesing, "Theories of Culture," *Annual Review of Anthropology* 3, (1974), pp. 73–79.

18. This viewpoint is largely anchored in the more functional and material aspects of cultural anthropology. Proponents of this view have included Bronislaw Malinowski, *A Scientific Theory of Culture and Other Essays* (New York: Galaxy Books, 1944); A.R. Radcliffe-Brown, *Structure and Function in Primitive Society* (Cambridge, MA: Harvard University Press, 1952), Leslie White and Beth Dillingham, *The Concept of Culture* (Minneapolis: Burgers, 1973); and Marvin Harris, *Cultural Materialism: The Struggle for a Science of Culture* (New York: Random House, 1979).

19. This view is largely anchored in the more cognitive and symbolic aspects of cultural anthropology. Proponents of this view have included Ward Goodenough, *Culture, Language and Society* (Reading, MA: Addison-Wesley, 1971); Claude Levi-Strauss, *Anthropologie Structurale* (Paris: Librairie Plon, 1958); Anthony Wallace, *Culture and Personality,* (New York: Random House, 1970), Clifford Geertz, *The Interpretation of Cultures* (New York: Basic Books, 1973); and B. Schneider "Organizational Climates: An Essay," *Personnel Psychology* 28, (1975), pp. 447–479.

20. Y. Allaire and M.E. Firsirotu, "Theories of Organizational Culture," *Organization Studies* 5, no. 3. (1984), pp. 193–226.

21. Smircich, op. cit., reasoned that these perspectives emerged from the intersection of anthropology and organization theory and, in turn, led to the development of themes in organization and management literature. Viewing culture as a variable leads to research directed at causality, at ways to predict, and thereby control, the variables that help organizations accomplish goals. The themes emerging from this perspective are comparative management, focusing on the implications for effectiveness drawn from similarities and differences among cultures (e.g., Ouchi, op. cit.), and the study of corporate cultures, exploring how to mold, shape, and change culture to improve effectiveness (e.g., Peters and Waterman, *In Search of Excellence* [New York: Harper and Row, 1982]). Viewing culture as a root metaphor leads to research on how organization is made possible and what it means. Themes in the literature explore organizational learning and climate (e.g., Chris Argyris and Donald Schön, *Organizational Learning* [Reading, MA: Addison-Wesley, 1978]), organizational symbolism (e.g., S.P. Turner, "Studying Organization Through Levi-Stauss' Structuralism," in G. Morgan's anthology, *Beyond Method: Social Research Strategies* [Beverly Hills, CA: Sage, 1983]), and structural anthropology, trying to determine the unconscious underlying roots of persistent patterns in organizations (e.g., Ian Mitroff, *Stakeholders of the Organizational Mind* [San Francisco: Jossey-Bass, 1983]).

22. Steven Ott (op. cit.) makes this point well when talking about organizational culture:

> "The first step toward understanding the essence of *organizational culture* is to appreciate that it is a concept rather than a thing. This distinction is crucial. A thing can be discovered and truths established about it, for example, through empirical research. Unlike a thing, however, a concept is created in peoples' minds—that is, it must be conjured up, defined, and refined. Thus ultimate truths about organizational culture (a concept) cannot be found or discovered. There is no final authoritative source or experiment to settle disagreements about what is or what comprises it" (pp. 50–51).

23. Mitroff, op. cit., suggests that the fundamental role of executive leadership is to surface these underlying assumptions so that our organizations can deal with the complexities of modern life and society.

24. The branch of philosophy most concerned with first principles is metaphysics.

25. Theodore Lowi has been a major commentator on the confusion of the major "isms." See his *End of Liberalism* (New York: W.W. Norton, 1969); and more recently his excellent sequel volume, *The End of the Republican Era* (Norman, OK: University of Oklahoma Press, 1995).

26. The branch of philosophy most concerned with this question is cosmology.

27. The type of philosophy that supports this position most directly is theology. However, when nature is substituted for God, as it often is in the West, various types of scientism support this school of thought. In other words, when nature is a self-organizing force with which humankind must be in step, then humankind's meaning can be understood only as a part of the natural order. In turn, the natural order can be studied and, indeed, should be studied for ultimate meanings. Thus classical philosophers like Aristotle and modern

philosophers like Kant found it easy to support empiricism and religion simultaneously.

28. The major form of philosophy supporting this position are various types of humanism. Although elements of humanism were first introduced into Western civilization in classical Greece, the primary growth of humanism occurred during the Renaissance. Humanism is the philosophy that addresses itself exclusively to human as opposed to divine or supernatural concerns, often coupled with a belief that humankind is capable of reaching self-fulfillment without divine aid.

29. This is the most recent philosophical school, including various types of existentialism. Although existentialism did not mature until the twentieth century, it evolved from the empiricism and the ever more stringent limitations on philosophical knowledge begun by early modern philosophers like Descartes. It evolved largely through negation: first declaring that God is dead (Nietzsche) and later that society is dead too (Sartre). Today existentialism tends to center on the uniqueness and isolation of individual experience in a universe indifferent or even hostile to humankind, regarding human existence as unexplainable, and emphasizing freedom of choice and responsibility for the consequence of one's acts.

30. The branch of philosophy most concerned with this question is ontology.

31. The primary theological sources are the great religious texts, such as the Bible, Torah, Koran, Bhagavada, Gita and the Tripitaka.

32. Greatest-good utilitarianism is a prime example of a philosophy supporting this notion. This form of utilitarianism stresses the maximization of pleasure for the greatest number of people. In this form, one is obliged to create the maximum good for the greatest number of people in society, who in turn do the same for you. Eighteenth- and nineteenth-century utilitarians, such as Jeremy Bentham and John Stuart Mill, fall into this camp.

33. Least-harm utilitarianism is an example. This form of utilitarianism maintains that the greatest utility is not causing harm to others. The grounds for this more limited type of pursuit is that harm (pain) is relatively easy to detect and predict, whereas good (pleasure) is more difficult to detect and, ultimately, is a more personal decision and responsibility. Modern utilitarians, such as J.J.C. Smart and Anthony Quinton, are almost all of this variety.

34. As with all the ideological positions, this is a tremendous simplification of a diversity of the subpositions that make up conservatism. For example, conservatives can essentially substitute tradition (traditionalism) or special training through upbringing (elitism) or gifted leadership (e.g., Nietzschean superman) for religion, although these strains are often blended and intertwined.

35. Lowi (*The End of the Republican Era*) has pointed out that the United States has two "conservative" groups, an aristocracy of wealth and a religious right. Both seem to be growing stronger. Recent census data indicates that the wealth distribution is widening in the United States (as measured by the Gini Coefficient). That is, in the 1980s and 1990s, the "rich have gotten richer." A recent poll in Arizona found that 71 percent stated that they know a Creator exists and have no doubts, and another 16 percent said that they had doubts but still believed in a Creator. Only 2 percent denied a Creator altogether. In another question, 78 percent believed in an afterlife. However, formal church attendance was reported as declining, with half of the respondents stating that they attended church less than they had as children. Ben Winton, "Faith in the

Valley: Keeping the Faith: Most in the Valley Religious, Poll Says," *Arizona Republic,* April 7, 1996, pp. A–1 and A–18. No matter whether the rationale was primarily theological or tradition-based, numerous classical philosophers essentially endorsed conservative regimes. Aristotle endorsed the idea of a philosopher king; Hobbs endorsed a royal line to impose order on an unruly humanity; and Kant stressed the notion of duty to the hierarchical order.

36. These philosophies had their greatest impact on Europe, where they originated. Communal ideals have not found fertile ground in the United States, with most Western explicit communal sects (such as the Shakers) lasting barely a generation, and the "natural" communalism of Native American communities under constant pressure by the "dominant" culture. The most visible strain of community building in the United States is associationism, the tendency of Americans to join various voluntary civic, avocational, and vocational organizations. Alexis de Tocqueville found this peculiarly strong tendency in the American environment to be the healthy counterbalance to a strongly individualistic culture when he toured the United States in the early nineteenth century. Today, the strongest variety of socialism in the United States seems to be communitarianism, the best-known advocate of which is Amitai Etzioni. Among other precepts, communitarians hold that the health of individuals flows from the health of the community, which needs the active participation and consideration of its members. Communitarians are highly concerned about the "institutions" that contribute to the fabric of the community. Although many communitarians consider churches to be one of the best institutions to build community, theology is not their purpose, per se. Thinkers in this mode include Robert Bellah, who emphasizes religion in the building of community (*Habits of the Heart: Individualism and Commitment in American Life,* 1985; and *The Good Life,* 1994); Daniel Kemmis, who emphasizes citizen participation in government (*Community and the Politics of Place,* 1990; and *The Good City and the Good Life,* 1995); Benjamin Barber, who emphasizes education in democratic societies (*An Aristocracy of Everyone: The Politics of Education and the Future of America,* 1992; and *Jihad vs. McWorld,* 1995); and Scott Russell Sanders, who emphasizes family and neighbors in building community (*Staying Put: Making a Home in a Restless World,* 1993).

37. Similarly, socialism is an economic theory as well as a political theory since it deals with economic distribution and economic ideals.

38. Major proponents of this philosophy include Adam Smith, Edmund Burke, and Thomas Jefferson. Both of the contemporary parties in the United States fall into this general tradition, with the Democrats having traditionally believed in the modified form, in order to reduce the "hard edges of capitalism," and the Republicans believing in a purer form as expressed by George Will. Lowi (*The End of the Republican Era*) holds that *both* parties have traditionally been classical liberal parties (that is, stressing individualism through capitalist economic models) in all important matters, although the Democrats since the New Deal have been influenced by socialism and the Republicans have been influenced by conservatism. Yet he holds (and I agree) that to suggest that either party is not essentially a classically liberal party (stressing individualism and capitalism) is to believe the political propaganda that each party says about the other.

39. It is important to remember that the idea of morality is largely a theoretical construct of the role of the individual in a group setting. R. McKeon puts it succinctly:

> The idea of *moral* responsibility originated and developed in the context of the evolution of political and cultural responsibility. There was no moral responsibility until there were communities in which men were held accountable for their actions and in which actions were imputed to individual men. There were no moral individuals prior to the development and recognition of moral responsibility.

"The Development and the Significance of the Concept of Responsibility," *Revue Internationale de Philosophie* 11 (1957), p. 28.

40. Although modified for the American context, this idea is not without substantial support in the United States. Examples include the Christian models of William Bennett (*The Book of Virtues: A Treasury of Great Moral Stories,* and *The De-Valuing of America: The Fight for Our Culture and Our Children*), and at another extreme, Louis Farrahkan, who weaves aggressively traditionalistic ideals (e.g., the hierarchical role of men) and religious ideals together. While such ideas have always had a local appeal, conservative ideals have been nationalized (as have all ideologies) in the last few decades because of the federalization of much policymaking during the New Deal era and because of the nationalization of media outlets.

41. Intellectually, the dominant American mode here has been pragmatism as espoused by William James and John Dewey. William James once explained the test of pragmatism by stating that it was concerned with "What difference it would practically make to anyone if this notion rather than that notion were true?" *Pragmatism: A New Name for Some Old Ways of Thinking* (Cambridge, MA: Harvard University Press, [1907], 1975), p. 28. Pragmatism tends to be an applied cousin of utilitarianism. As mentioned in an earlier note, communitarianism is one of the lines of descent of pragmatism. Amitai Etzioni noted that "It is to the struggle between judgments and impulses that the moral voice of the community speaks." (*American Values: Opposing Viewpoints*, Charles P. Cozic, ed. [San Diego, CA: Greenhaven Press, 1995]), p. 39. On the Continent, utilitarianism has tended to give way to structuration theories, which focus on the way society shapes individuals through language and conceptual patterning.

42. Although not well represented as a philosophical school of thought in the United States, this ideology is represented by a pragmatism oriented toward harnessing individual talents, desires, and dreams, bolstered by strong microeconomic leanings and individualistic democratic notions. The strongest advocate of this position in the philosophical community may be Tibor Machan. A passage from his book captures this ideology well:

> Why would it be more appropriate to conceive of the human "essence" as the individuality of man? Mainly because what distinguishes human beings from other living beings is the form of consciousness—namely rational, conceptual consciousness—implies the capacity for original thought, for initiation of intellectual activity, for creativity, for volition. The human individual alone is capable of initiating original ideas—groups can only form the forum and fertilization for this. The mind of a human being is the mind of an individual. It does not operate alone, without props, without society, of course. I am not talking about the solipsistic mind. It does, however, perform creative acts, for which the individual brain is a necessary prerequisite.

Tibor Machan, *Individuals and Their Rights* (La Salle, IL: Open Court, 1989), pp. 21–22. [On the European continent, the dominant philosophy was existentialism for much of the twentieth century, which generally has a darker vision but nonetheless asserts that individuals must actively choose their fate, no matter how bleak their condition.]

43. In practice, this would lead to a form of traditionalism, that is, a strong respect for traditions, structures, and processes flowing from the past.

44. Different philosophies support this perspective. Egalitarianism is probably best expressed by John Rawls and his veil of ignorance. Postmodernists (e.g., Fox and Miller) emphasize the need for honest and clear speech in order to have genuine dialogue.

45. Of course, the laws or constitution do become kinds of sacred texts, especially the U.S. Constitution, which is hallowed in its own right today. Constitutionalism is as old a belief system as the Republic, when the idea of a social contract was given force by contemporary ideas such as those of Rousseau. However, the idea of a social contract was incipient in the American experience, from the Mayflower Covenant with its biblical antecedents, to the various state charters with their systemized rights dating back to the Magna Carta. Modern American Constitutionalism is probably best reflected in the opinions of Supreme Court justices such as John Marshall, Roger Taney, Oliver Wendell Holmes, Louis D. Brandeis, Benjamin Cardozo, Felix Frankfurter, and Thurgood Marshall.

Decisionmaking Paradigms for Public Administration: Valucs at Level 3

Different conceptualizations of the role of public administration in the United States precede the Constitution itself. Although they focused on political structures, Jefferson, Hamilton, Madison, and other designers of the Constitution clearly understood the implications of political structure for administrative practice. Their discussions and debates about the power of the federal government relative to that of the states and the people, and about the appropriate areas of governmental involvement still apply today. Out of these discussions, a paradigm of the rightful place and functions of public administration did emerge, a paradigm whose philosophy has certainly evolved with changing historical epochs. Since the Progressives and reformers placed their strong stamp on public administration at the end of the nineteenth century, the dominant paradigm has tended to emphasize the electoral decisionmaking process, the mandate of elected officials, and the subservience of hierarchically ordered administrators, all in a clean chain of command. Emmette Redford called this paradigm the overhead democracy model.[1] As Larry Lane explains, "The doctrine of overhead democracy asserts that democratic control runs from the elective representatives of the people down through a hierarchy of authority and command, reaching from the chief executive down through the units of government 'to the fingertips of administration.'"[2] However, that paradigm, perhaps best symbolized by Woodrow Wilson's famous 1887 essay on the division of politics and administration, is severely under attack—both in theory and in practice.[3]

Different perspectives or paradigms have life cycles, as Thomas Kuhn pointed out. For a time, a single paradigm may be dominant and all experience fits (or is made to fit) this perspective.[4] But over time, bits of experience are discovered that do not fit; they are anomalies. As anomalies increase, so does discomfort with the paradigm, and alternative paradigms are advanced which are thought to more adequately account for the anomalies.

Public administration is in a period of intense paradigmatic competition. A brief overview in this section will help orient the reader to the three major schools of thought. A fuller discussion follows in the next section. The paradigm of the overhead democracy model is now under attack. Comparativists call this paradigm a weak state model: that term is adapted here as a *weak administration paradigm*. (*Weak* applies primarily to the theoretical role in policy discussions and decisionmaking. It does not imply that administration cannot be large or that it cannot make more technical, "neutral" decisions.) The primary challenger has been the public choice model, which has enjoyed enormous influence since Osborne and Gaebler's book *Reinventing Government* was published in 1992.[5] This paradigm emphasizes a greater role in decisionmaking for public administrators (who become administrative entrepreneurs), but only after injecting enormous competitive (that is, market) forces into every possible aspect of administration. The paradigm implies that public administration will shrink in some areas and will get better in those in which it endures. Because of the blending of (private sector) market forces in public sector systems and agencies, I call it the *mixed administration paradigm*.

A third school of thought, although not as popular as the other two perspectives, has grown tremendously in theoretical rigor and is popular among a large number of renowned scholars. This paradigm is variously known as the Blacksburg school (because Blacksburg, Virginia, was and continues to be the capital of this movement) and the refounding project. I refer to it here as the *strong administration paradigm* because of the central role of public administration in both governance and decisionmaking. This perspective decries the excesses of top-down democracy,[6] implying "a radical revision of overhead democracy,"[7] as does the mixed administration paradigm. However, the rationale and desired outcome of this third paradigm is quite different because its adherents generally agree that "the obligations and competencies inherent to American governance make public administration a dramatically different endeavor from its private-sector counterpart."[8] While most proponents of the strong administration paradigm see some positive ideas in the reinventing revolution, they generally agree that the public administration that will evolve from such a perspective (which they consider to be naive at a minimum) will combine "the worst evils of laissez-faire corporate and the authoritarian state."[9]

The third perspective or paradigm was first formulated in the *Blacksburg Manifesto* in 1984. Of the subsequent versions and revisions, the edited volume entitled *Refounding Public Administration* (1990) was probably the best known and most influential. It is the recent volume of the Blacksburg school, called *Refounding Democratic Public Administration* (which is not a revision or new edition of the earlier volume) that will be the primary source for the remainder of this text. It does an excellent job of distinguishing itself from the better-known (at least in popular terms) entrepreneurial model here called the mixed administration model, as well as from the traditional weak administration model.[10]

What Do the Three Paradigms Look Like?

The classic administrative paradigm for public administration in the United States is called the *weak administration paradigm* because the independent institutional authority of the public organizations is minimized when possible (although the distinct "publicness" of organizations is maintained). This view encourages public administration, as much as possible, to leave policy choices and value decisions to elected officials and their appointed representatives, and it encourages public administrators to stick to their technical implementation issues. Woodrow Wilson's politics-administration dichotomy[11] and Herbert Simon's fact-value division[12] have been discarded as actual models of reality, in which administrators eschewed all politics all the time, or made decisions that were always "technical" and factual and passed all value decisions to political bureaucrats. Nonetheless, both were animating ideals to strive for. The classic administrative paradigm idealizes the technical expert. Externally, it typically casts the citizen as recipient because dialogue with citizens tends to be limited to technical issues related to service or regulation. It emphasizes the values of administrative neutrality, professional specialization, hierarchical bureaucracy, limited administrative discretion, and complete political subordination in all issues of governance.

The second administrative paradigm for public administration is called the *mixed administration model* because the distinctness of the public sector itself is reduced as much as possible. It does this by reducing the command and control functions of government, and encouraging instead independent institutional authority based primarily on fiscal success and on demonstrable management superiority of public organizations as much as on rule by law. This paradigm is also known as reinventing government, entrepreneurial government, and (to some degree) Total Quality Management, or the New Public Management. However it is labeled, this view encourages public administrators to (1) advise policymakers on ways to streamline complex policies, (2) deemphasize compliance modes and introduce market incentives where possible in regulatory functions, (3) actively seek citizen input on the qualities of the service received on an individual level (thus somewhat deemphasizing the social equity perspective), and (4) provide competition for service delivery systems where possible. This paradigm idealizes the entrepreneurial manager internally, and it typically casts the citizen as customer externally. It emphasizes the values of administrative commitment to competition, professional alignment to business and management science, nonhierarchical bureaucratic structures such as flexible adhocracies and team-based organizations, substantial administrative discretion based on microlevel customer input and macrolevel financial needs, and a legitimacy model based as much on the market as on the law. Jonathan West, a mainstream management expert, gives a clear sense of the impact of this paradigm in the introduction to his recent volume on local government management practices:

> Quality management (also referred to here as total quality management, or TQM) is a broad strategy that seeks to heighten citizen satisfaction and local government productivity through customer orientation, employee empowerment, benchmarking, and continuous improvement. According to a 1993 national survey of local government quality management efforts, about 11 percent of cities have a "substantial" (i.e., minimal and credible) commitment to quality management. V. Daniel Hunt estimates that by the year 2000, half of all federal, state, and local governments will be using quality management.[13]

The third administrative model (common to some democracies like France and Japan)[14] is called the *strong administration model* because the independent institutional authority of public organizations is enhanced, and public organizations are more frequently envisioned as the repositories of the "state" than are political institutions.[15] This view encourages career public administrators to (confidentially but strongly) advise elected officials about policy decisions and allows them relatively wide berth in implementation according to their professional dictates after legislative authorization. This paradigm idealizes the (extensively acculturated) "philosopher" administrators who dedicate themselves to a lifetime of career public service. It typically casts the citizen as client (whose lay input should be considered but who is expected to defer to professional wisdom). It emphasizes the values of administrative virtue and character, professional calling to the public service as one's discipline, professional bureaucracy in which professionals receive substantial deference and power, considerable administrative decisionmaking authority, and an administrative legitimacy equal to political branches. Although this paradigm does not currently enjoy popular favor in the United States, it is promoted within the American academic tradition by John Rohr and others, and it is a quietly held belief of many public administrators themselves. The three paradigms are partially illustrated in Figure 8.1.

These three paradigms, exaggerated here for clarity, interpret the basic assumptions of public administration so that they can seem quite different. For example, one of the basic assumptions already discussed is the subordination of public administration to elected officials. All three schools of thought agree on this overarching principle. The classic school of thought (the weak administration model) interprets this principle in a relatively technical and absolute sense. Public administrators should defer to policymakers fully and unquestioningly when policies are dictated, and policies should ideally be highly detailed, thereby limiting administrative discretion. The strong administration model interprets this principle in a general and relative sense. Public administrators should defer to policymakers ultimately, but only after discussing with them the appropriate options, and policies should leave policy implementation details to administrative expertise. The mixed administration model interprets this principle in a similar way, but balances it against the competing demands of customer needs and wants and market forces. Although public administrators should defer to elected officials, both the administrative and political spheres should seek to be better managers of public resources and power through market forces. Ultimately, this model sees the elective process as a powerful but very blunt-edged type of choice, rarely capable of detailed and rapid choices. The preferred method of choice is provided by competition and microeconomic incentives.

FIGURE 8.1

A Pictorial Representation of Three Paradigms of Public Administration

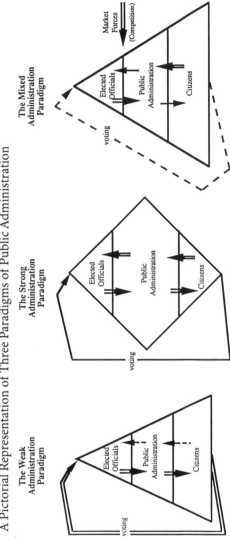

The Weak Administration Paradigm

This model emphasizes strict accountability to voters through a hierarchical chain of command. This model is simple (and elegant) but is also challenged by modern complexity and the vast size and scope of contemporary government.

The Strong Administration Paradigm

This model emphasizes public administration as the fulcrum of communication and decisionmaking. Although policymaking responsibility rests ultimately with elected leaders, it is necessarily shared with professional administrators.

The Mixed Administration Paradigm

This model emphasizes administrative responsiveness, not only to elected officials and citizens but also directly to market forces. While the model recognizes the complex, competitive reality already facing many administrators, it undoubtedly weakens the classic democratic chain of command.

Key

a double line (=) represents a strong force.
a single line (-) represents a moderate force
a dashed line (- -) represents a weak force

A Four-Point Comparison of the Paradigms

Although it is possible to compare the three models on innumerable points, this discussion limits comparison to four of the more common and integral themes found in *Refounding Democratic Public Administration:* achieving democracy through dialogue, ensuring social equity and fairness, valuing public agencies as social assets, and using professionalism and an enhanced sense of public service vocation to achieve the public good. The editors of *Refounding Democratic Public Administration,* Gary Wamsley and James Wolf, note that the stakes are high in the search for a new paradigm: "We have come to have serious doubts about America's ability to govern itself unless it develop[s] a new way of thinking about and conducting the activities called public administration."[16]

Achieving Democracy Through Dialogue

Like the other two paradigms, the strong administration paradigm is concerned about the tendency toward social deterioration "in a world marked by increasing fragmentation,"[17] in which "Americans are finding it increasingly difficult to discover common ground."[18] The weak administration paradigm tends to point to political or community solutions that do not involve public administration directly. The mixed administration paradigm asserts that cumbersome governmental systems and social solutions are part of the problem, and that individual initiative has been underutilized, and this analysis is currently gaining sway in an increasing number of policy areas such as welfare. But those in the refounding project point out that "by focusing on infusing competition, entrepreneurship, and decentralization, they [the reinventers] miss the equally fundamental importance of cooperation and working across organizations and sectors that is critical to success in the increasingly complex and interconnected world of American governance."[19] This school asserts a strong role for public administrators as primary facilitators and educators in the public dialogue, to articulating issues, discussing alternatives, and finding wholesome methods of consensus that do not rely excessively on elections and the market. A healthy civil society is based on more than hierarchically implemented election results and competitive regeneration; a healthy civil society needs trust, freely given social contributions, a sense of community and pride, and a dedication to the long-term good of the polity. A healthy, robust, and empowered civil service is necessary to achieve this type of society, according to the strong administration school.

Ensuring Social Equity and Fairness

Concern for social equity and fairness differs greatly among the three paradigms. The weak administration paradigm sees equity and fairness primarily in legal and procedural terms: What does the law require, and how is it implemented equitably? The mixed administration paradigm believes that government has sapped much individual initiative and social capacity (largely through excessive taxation). Lean and reduced government will enable individuals to participate directly in the economy, and government intervention will be more strategic and of shorter duration. Advocates of the strong administration school suggest that this adds fuel to the dangerous "radical individualism"[20] that is actually the source of much of America's current problems. They point out that the poor and the poorly represented are less equipped to compete in a highly entrepreneurial and competitive environment that is biased toward the rich, successful, and articulate.[21] Those not well represented need the strong advocacy of the public service to ensure that they are not bereft of voice and opportunity, which is for the overall good since society itself is weakened by a large and neglected lower class. In an excellent essay on inherently governmental functions, Larkin Dudley points out that while most functions can be privatized, the long-term social good may not be served if a strong sense of social responsibility is not also transferred.[22]

Valuing Public Agencies As Social Assets

The strong administration perspective also veers strongly from the other two in valuing the agency as an institution. For example, Gary Wamsley talks of "agencies as social assets."[23] Richard Green and Lawrence Hubbell say that "administering in a political context requires multifaceted 'agential leadership.'"[24] Joy Clay refers to the importance of the "public-institutional process" to resolve conflict, share understanding, and accommodate individual differences.[25] And James Wolf stresses the importance of the institutional (as well as networking and community building) functions relative to the excessive importance being given to market, bureaucratic, and organizational contexts.[26] These views vary significantly from the more technical role envisioned in the weak administration model, which is more acutely concerned about (overweening) agency power and ability to influence (or distort) policy. It also varies from the more enterprise-oriented idea inherent in the mixed-administration perspective, which leans toward the private sec-

tor, as noted earlier. When the strong administration school advocates
are the most explicit, they assert that public administration should be "a
legitimate partner in the governance process" itself[27] and "the constitutional center of gravity."[28] These ambitious assertions, at first almost
shocking out of context, are well reasoned and argued. (Of course,
many may appreciate the logic, but nonetheless disagree with the premises and outcome.) Advocates of the strong administration school argue this special and central agency role from their analysis of the constitutional founding (and thus their reference to "refounding") in which
public administration was understood to be the soul of the republic,
rather than the primary prop (and more recently whipping boy) of the
presidency. They plainly assert that the traditional idea of the field of
public administration, dating to 1887 during the Progressive Era
(which, much like today's reform movement also used a corporate
model) is a "misfounding" that leads to a "misgrounding" conceptu-
ally.[29] For those who believe that public administration can never play a
primary role in governance because democracy is founded on the electoral process, they are quick to point out that "there are 16 ways to become an officer of the government and election is only one of those
ways."[30]

Using Professionalism to Achieve the Public Good

The three attributes discussed so far—a greater role in facilitating
wholesome dialogue in society (including among the three branches of
government), retaining the public service's mantle as the steward of the
poor and disfranchised, and providing leadership in the resolution of
social and technical problems—place enormous responsibilities upon
public administration. To handle these responsibilities, the strong administration school emphasizes a fourth theme, professionalism, which
restores the concept "of the vocational quality of the public service."[31]
Professionalism in the weak administration model is a much more
technical affair, and in the mixed administration model it is highly
aligned with entrepreneurialism, opportunism, and rationalism. The
strong administration advocates assert that public administrators who do
not have a dedication to the common good, a sense of devotion to the
people they serve, and a commitment to gaining the skills to accomplish
tough or "wicked tasks" over a lifetime (traits not required or much encouraged in the other two perspectives), are unlikely to make the great
contributions that society needs.

Conclusion

Each of these models has strengths and weaknesses, which this text has tried to depict in a balanced light, leaving the reader, as much as possible, to select among them. For example, some of the strengths of the weak administration model are that it is the simplest to comprehend, it has worked relatively well in the past, and it is an excellent model for strong external control. Its weaknesses are due to the fact that in the current environment, simple, single models are giving way to multiple models. The weak administration model also has often given way to various forms of extreme "legalism," in which all values and actions must be micromanaged by law. And the external control exercised by elected officials has been questioned as electoral institutions have suffered a tremendous loss of trust.

The strengths of the strong administration model are that it is relatively simple to understand; it reduces the need for legalism and substitutes professional expertise and discretion; and professionals, who are imbued with additional power, are excellent at selecting the "right" models for different situations. Its weaknesses are that the strong administration model has never been tried on a large scale in the United States.[32] Moreover, it weakens external control and gives it to "unelected officials," a situation that strikes terror in American hearts even though those officials may be rigorously selected and qualified. Finally, because of the loss of credibility of (nearly all) professionals, many want alternative sources of control.

Although the mixed administration model is theoretically no better or worse than the other two, it does currently enjoy a historical edge. First, it might work well in the future if the many successes being reported are any indication. (However, the failures to improve through TQM, reengineering, teams, and other current approaches are also numerous, even according to advocates.) Second, it reduces the need for legalism and substitutes market forces and incentives. Third, it provides not one alternative model but at least three, depending on whether the employees, the work itself, or the competitive environment is the focus.[33] Fourth, the market is one of the few "institutions" that has gained credibility, probably far beyond reasonable expectations, whereas command-and-control models are out of fashion. The weaknesses, while not enough to stop a determined shift in this model's general direction, are significant. To begin with, reinventing government is incredibly complex and difficult to understand. It means everything to everyone, and thereby sometimes comes to mean nothing at all and leads to confusion and muddle-headedness. Also, it weakens external control, which causes fear in many who are nervous about eviscerating the political system even further than it already has been.

This brief summary of the three major paradigms gives a taste of the discussions that are only likely to increase in fervor in the next decade. Chapter 9 analyzes different types of rationality, which each of the three paradigms blends quite differently.

Notes

1. Emmette Redford, *Democracy in the Administrative State* (New York: Oxford University Press, 1969).
2. Larry Lane, "The Public Administration and the Problem of the Presidency," in *Refounding Democratic Public Administration,* Gary Wamsley and James Wolf, eds. (Thousand Oaks, CA: Sage, 1996), pp. 225–259.
3. Woodrow Wilson, "The Study of Administration," *Political Science Quarterly* 2 (June 1887), pp. 197–222.
4. Thomas Kuhn, *The Structure of Scientific Revolutions* (Chicago: University of Chicago Press, 1962).
5. David Osborne and Ted Gaebler, *Reinventing Government: How the Entrepreneurial Spirit Is Transforming the Public Sector* (Reading, MA: Addison-Wesley, 1992).
6. Gary Wamsley and James Wolf, "Introduction: Can a High-Modern Project Find Happiness in a Postmodern Era?" in *Refounding Democratic Public Administration,* Wamsley and Wolf, eds., p. 5.
7. Larry Lane, op. cit., p. 253.
8. Richard T. Green and Lawrence Hubbell, "On Governance and Reinventing Government," in *Refounding Democratic Public Administration,* Wamsley and Wolf, eds., p. 39.
9. O.C. McSwite, "Postmodernism, Public Administration, and the Public Interest," in *Refounding Democratic Public Administration,* Wamsley and Wolf, eds., p. 200.
10. I have already been made aware by peer reviewers that strong advocates of any of the three schools are unlikely to be entirely happy with my descriptions of their positions. Variations of beliefs within schools aside, it is difficult to perform a rigorous analysis of strengths and weaknesses and be perceived as fair to the spirit of a school of thought. Therefore I content myself that I have made proponents of the three schools equally unhappy, thereby being balanced among them, even if I fail to be fully fair to the loftier aspirations of any of them. I should also note that I have not designated the postmodern school of thought as a paradigm. While I believe that this school of thought certainly has that potential, the body of work and thought in this area is still too thin. It may overtake the strong administration model, or forcefully reshape it (as it already has in *Refounding Democratic Public Administration*), but this remains to be seen. The same is largely true of the new sciences approaches, including chaos theory, which does not yet have a comprehensive literature and perspective to formulate a new paradigm (even though it has already successfully challenged many old assumptions of the weak administration model).

11. Woodrow Wilson, op. cit., pp. 197–222.

12. Herbert A. Simon, *Administrative Behavior* (New York: Free Press, 1948).

13. Jonathan West, ed., *Quality Management Today: What Local Governments Need to Know* (Washington, DC: ICMA, 1995), p. xv.

14. See Ferrel Heady, *Public Administration: A Comparative Perspective*, 3rd ed. (New York: Marcel Dekker, 1991), especially pp. 193–205 on France and 238–250 on Japan.

15. To better appreciate this comparative perspective, see John Rohr's excellent essay on public administration in France, "What a Difference a State Makes: Reflections on Governance in France," in *Refounding Democratic Public Administration*, Wamsley and Wolf, eds., pp. 114–140.

16. Wamsley and Wolf, op. cit., p. 1.

17. Joy Clay, "Public-Institutional Processes and Democratic Governance," in *Refounding Democratic Public Administration*, Wamsley and Wolf, eds., p. 93.

18. Thomas Barth, "Administering in the Public Interest: The Facilitative Role for Public Administrators," in *Refounding Democratic Public Administration*, Wamsley and Wolf, eds., p. 171.

19. Ibid., p. 169.

20. Gary L. Wamsley, "A Public Philosophy and Ontological Disclosure As the Basis for Normatively Grounded Theorizing in Public Administration," in *Refounding Democratic Public Administration*, Wamsley and Wolf, eds., p. 378. Wamsley and Wolf also bemoan this tendency as "individualism run amok," op. cit., p. 22.

21. Green and Hubbell, op. cit., pp. 51 ff.

22. Larkin Dudley, "Fencing in the Inherently Governmental Debate," in *Refounding Democratic Public Administration*, Wamsley and Wolf, eds., pp. 68–91.

23. Wamsley, op. cit., p. 378.

24. Green and Hubbell, p. 39.

25. Clay, op. cit., pp. 92–113.

26. James F. Wolf, "Moving Beyond Prescriptions: Making Sense of Public Administration Action Contexts," in *Refounding Democratic Public Administration*, Wamsley and Wolf, eds., pp. 141–167.

27. Wamsley and Wolf, op. cit., p. 11.

28. Camilla Stivers, "Refusing to Get It Right: Citizenship, Difference, and the Refounding Project," in *Refounding Democratic Public Administration*, Wamsley and Wolf, eds., p. 260. Stivers is quoting Wamsley, et al. from *Refounding Public Administration*.

29. Wamsley, op. cit., p. 362.

30. See pages 5 and 177 in *Refounding Democratic Public Administration* for discussions of this point, both stemming from John Rohr's earlier research.

31. Wamsley and Wolf, op. cit., p. 11.

32. Some possible exceptions are perhaps to a modified degree in the Federalist and early New Deal periods at the federal level, in city manager systems, and in the judicial branch.

33. B. Guy Peters, "New Visions of Government and the Public Service," in *New Paradigms for Government: Issues for the Changing Public Service*, Patricia Ingraham and Barbara Romzek, eds., (San Francisco: Jossey-Bass, 1994).

CHAPTER 9

Selection of a Decisionmaking Process: Values at Level 2

Decisionmaking is inextricably linked to rationality. If there were but one form of rationality, then decisionmaking could take on a unitary, even monolithic, nature. However, as Max Weber noted long ago, there are different forms of rationality, hence decisionmaking.[1] This chapter looks at 12 different variations of rationality in order to better understand the sometimes subtle, other times profound, ways that decisionmaking is framed.[2]

Rationality itself has different definitions. One common meaning for the word is intellectual reasoning, probably because of the popularity of this type of rationality in Western culture. Here, however, *rationality* is used in its broader sociological meaning, which is *a consistency between the means used and the end that is to be achieved.* To use some homey examples, if the end were to marry for love (a human need), then basing a decision primarily on the financial worth of one suitor over another (a market approach) would not be rational. Or if a rapid, executive decision were needed to stave off sure disaster, using a democratic voting mechanism would not be rational. It would, however, be rational to use a cost-benefit analysis to decide which automobile price was the best buy, and it would be rational to use a voting technique to ensure popular participation and support for broad policies.

Rationality in this broader sense, then, takes into account the different types of ends that humans seek to achieve, and the means that customarily accompany those ends. Cognitively oriented approaches to rationality—market choice, reasoned choice, and nonlinear systems—use analytic perspectives to understand connections upon which to base decisions. Approaches that are not cognitively oriented—human needs, coercive, traditional, religious, and altruistic—use extralogical means as the basis for decisions. Political approaches to rationality—elite, democratic, legal, and anarchic—base decisions on governmental (or antigovernmental) strategies.

What types of ends do different cultures try to achieve? Market cultures strive to achieve efficiency, largely because it results in profits, and thus they tend to emphasize competition as a means. From this perspective, competition—Adam Smith's invisible hand—makes the wisest decision because it is perceived to be a natural product of a self-correcting law of supply and demand (rational choice). Bureaucratic cultures strive for effectiveness, a broader and more diffuse goal, and they tend to expect experts to use their judgment and experience to craft the best decisions. Experts know, for example, when not to use the cheapest possible materials because of the long-range risks they pose (reasoned choice). Change-oriented cultures emphasize vitality and mutability, and thus value dynamic evolution that sees spontaneous variation more as a source of creativity and growth (nonlinear systems) than as a source of error and deviation.

Types of rationality much older than these cognitively oriented ones do exist and will always be with us. Religious cultures believe that the most important end to achieve is coherence with God's will, and their primary means of decisionmaking is divine selection, whether through divine text or divine teachings. Traditionalistic cultures emphasize consistency with the past, and customs and habits are the basis of most of their decisions. Hedonistic cultures (a term with excessively pejorative connotations for our purpose here) emphasize satisfaction of human drives, and the decisionmaking is based on human needs and wants. Altruistic cultures (as are found in voluntary organizations) emphasize helping others, and thus decisionmaking is determined by others' needs. Finally, confrontational cultures bent on domination (or resistance to it), feature coercion and physical violence as means of deciding what should and will be done.

Elite cultures strive for the support of key groups who are revered for their position, wisdom, or special abilities; such cultures tend to emphasize aristocratic selection. In contrast, democratic cultures seek broad support among electorates and prefer popular (often majoritarian) methods of decisionmaking. Legalistic cultures are interested in procedural consistency, technical fairness, and social control, and they emphasize rules as a means of making decisions in the form of constitutions, laws, policies, regulations, ordinances, and the like. Anarchic cultures (at their extreme) allow complete freedom at almost any expense and are typified by both lack of rules and a fluid social structure.

It is important to remember that all cultures use all forms of rationality *to some degree*. However the degree of emphasis varies enormously. This is easy to perceive in more specialized organizations and extreme cultures. Rationality for businesses is biased toward selection based on competition, for bureaucracies toward expert choice, for research labs toward trial and error, for judges (without juries) toward aristocratic decisions, for political parties toward popular choice, for regulatory agencies toward rules, for churches toward divine dictates, for parents toward custom and habits, for avocational voluntary groups toward satisfaction of human needs for affiliation, for charities toward others' needs, in unanticipated calamities toward anarchy, and for law enforcement agencies toward the potential use of force. Kurt Baier, a noted philosopher, states that because of the different values inherent in different forms of rationality, "there is no appropriate supreme point of view from which to make the choice."[3] He, like others in the utilitarian-pragmatic tradition, emphasizes practical reasoning in determining the appropriate rationality, or rationalities, to use.

Public administration as a system clearly has its preferred modes of rationality, as does American culture in general. David Rosenbloom identified three particularly important approaches to public administration.[4] First, he identified public administration as a branch of management science. Bureaucracies, especially of the governmental variety, have always tended toward reasoned choice rationality, but rational choice rationality has never been absent and the recent movement toward market mechanisms has strongly tended toward the latter. Second, Rosenbloom points out the political approach to public management. For public administration this has elements of both democratic and elite forms of rationality. The overall political system is heavily based on democratic principles, and this affects public administration policies and implementation. However, public administrators must follow the dictates of the legislative branch and elected executives, who become anointed by the people and become an authoritative electoral elite. Finally, Rosenbloom, himself an eminent administrative law scholar, points out the crucial role of the legal approach in public administration, not only enforced by an external judiciary but also extensively internalized by public administration itself. As the following discussion will demonstrate, all forms of rationality do have some expression in public administration. However, the reasoned choice, rational choice, elite, democratic, legal, and coercive forms of rationality tend to be particularly influential.[5]

Twelve Types of Rationality and Decisionmaking Processes

Market (Rational Choice) Rationality[6]

A cutthroat marketplace puts a high price on efficiency because it helps maximize profits. Efficiency is achieved in the marketplace through competition forcing rapid, accurate responses to changing market conditions, new technologies, shifts in tastes, and altered financial factors. This type projects an economic man or woman who is a profit maximizer, egocentric, competitive, and driven by intellectual logic. At a minimum, decisionmaking in this type of rationality desires quantitative measurements of all elements being compared for choice. Preferably these quantitative elements have an economic equivalent, so that a single, comparable basis can be established among all alternatives. In its neoclassical form, all possible alternatives should be investigated thoroughly so that an absolutely best choice could be made without speculation.[7]

Herbert Simon's work on decision theory in the 1940s and 1950s, which ultimately won him the Nobel Memorial Prize in Economic Science, identified some of the limits of this type of rationality in its extreme form.[8] Simon showed that, in all but the most limited problems, all alternatives could never be known, that full information was too exhaustive and expensive, and that values could never be quantified. He pointed out that most decisionmakers who use this form resort to "satisficing," identifying a realistic number of plausible alternatives and undertaking a modest amount of research about those alternatives. Given the time, resources, and importance of the decision, the decisionmaker would expand the analysis toward the ideal, but could never achieve the ideal in complex problems because full knowledge was impossible to achieve and too expensive to strive for.[9] Yet the model has remained extraordinarily popular, serving as the underlying philosophy of many budget models such as the planning and program budgeting system (PPBS), computer applications able to accommodate staggering numbers of possible combinations, and aggressive scientific perspectives viewing all problems as conquerable given the resources and time. Indeed, in a market economy one would expect a rational choice type to remain popular, sometimes with almost a religious fervor. For example, one commentator explained that while "rational choice fails as a description of actual behavior; it remains unequaled as a theory."[10] This belief is not uncommon among economists and ardent capitalists, and it has increased in public appeal since the fall of communism and the expansion of the globalized, capitalistic economy.

The decisionmaking framework commonly based on the rational choice to rationality can be displayed as six phases:

- Opportunity identification
- Goals selection
- Alternatives generation
- Choice (based primarily on economic factors)
- Implementation
- Evaluation based on profitability

In brief, in the opportunity identification phase, a new situation is presented. Although potentially threatening, the situation should always be perceived as an opportunity to become more efficient. From this perspective, competition is merely the mechanism within the market that ensures at least commercial vigilance if not continual improvement. In the goals selection phase, the situation is analyzed so that the opportunity is framed in a similar fashion for all who are endeavoring to explore it. With a similar perspective, alternatives are generated and each is investigated. Ideally, each alternative is exhaustively studied so that the choice is made with near-perfect knowledge. The choice is made based on analytic understanding and fiscal maximization. Implementation is already outlined from the alternatives phase and is subsequently detailed and executed. The final phase is evaluation, using profitability as the ultimate criterion.

The rational choice approach to rationality is at its best in situations in which: the market and efficiency are the predominant factors; problems are relatively straightforward; social and environmental affects are minimal; the choice in (production or policy) decisionmaking is limited to one or a few people; prediction and control are desired; problems are easily divisible; and a "survival of the fittest" mentality is a wholesome antidote to human tendencies toward dissipation and regression over time. It tends to be a poor approach in situations in which: complex and full knowledge is far beyond reach; economic factors are a small part of the decisionmaking calculus; large numbers of individuals must be involved in decisionmaking; involvement, conviction, or other feelings are more relevant than prediction and control; or values other than economic ones are significant.[11]

Reasoned Choice Rationality

A cousin of rational choice, a reasoned choice type focuses not on efficiency as the most important end to achieve, but on effectiveness, which has a broader, and less econometric focus. Although it uses a similar decisionmaking framework, it allows other—most importantly, noneconomic—factors to be considered.[12]

Relaxing economic and numeric factors has the advantage of allowing a much broader choice of means in the types of problems people confront most of the time. For example, buying a house is not just an economic problem; it involves taste and past habit. Public administrators generally have important noneconomic values to factor into decisions such as safety, beauty, durability, tradition, legality, popular approval and even use of force, among others.

The problem raised by the reasoned choice type of rationality is how to incorporate multiple values into a single decision stream. Who decides which values to incorporate (and which to omit) and what weight to give them in making the choice? Larger problems are rarely as technical or value-neutral as they seem after they are studied carefully. For example, for many decades the transportation issues raised by downtown employment and suburban living seemed straightforward: Build freeways from the core cities to the suburbs, often "improved" by the inclusion of trees and landscaping, enhancing the driving experience but further expanding their width (essentially variations of rational choice). It was not fully recognized until much later the toll this was taking on the inner cities, whose neighborhoods and business districts were artificially divided by rivers of noisy, unattractive traffic (needing a more balanced reasoned choice solution). In other words, a reasoned choice form not only includes many types of values, it tries to weigh numerous competing values in which economic factors may not even be central. Because such problems have many technical aspects and take careful study in order to propose balanced, effective proposals, a broad array of experts is often required. The designing of a highway today is rarely solely the decision of an engineer tasked with the least-cost solution. Dozens of other types of planners and community actors must be involved.

The reasoned choice form uses the following type of framework:

- Problem identification
- Goals selection
- Alternatives generation
- Choice (based on multiple values)
- Implementation
- Evaluation based on overall effectiveness of solution

In the reasoned choice form, the perspective is generally a problem-solving rather than opportunity-enhancing one. Value clarification becomes a primary function of goal identification, and it becomes exceedingly difficult in complex and "wicked" problems. Alternatives tend to array different value options (in which cost is often secondary) rather than different economic solutions (in which noneconomic values are secondary). Choice in the reasoned choice form becomes more subjective, whereas it is perceived to be more objective in the rational choice type.[13]

The reasoned choice form is much used by, and often well-suited to, public bureaucracies because they are inherently repositories of expertise.[14] A strength of the public sector is its ability to consider in depth many perspectives, and generally to deliberate more fully than lone individuals or commercial interests would, for the public good. The use of the reasoned choice form by public bureaucracies has incurred many problems as well, only a few of which will be mentioned here. First, expertise in the public sector tends to be divided into separate agencies and departments, which often communicate and collaborate poorly. Second, public sector experts often have a difficult time genuinely incorporating the public in the planning process. Experts have a tendency to feel they "know best," so that even public comment meetings can become superficial events, affecting the planning process only marginally. Third, the more values that are pursued and the more people whose values are considered, the more difficult it is to find a workable solution achieving broad agreement. This crucible of values can lead to poor solutions in many ways: Experts short-change numerous groups to expedite planning; everyone gets something, but the final solution is neither cohesive nor "owned" by anyone; or, frequently, no solution at all is acted upon because of an inability to reach consensus.[15]

Nonlinear Systems Rationality

Both the rational choice and reasoned choice types of rationality emphasize systems that are linear and in which opportunities or problems can best be understood by analyzing that component of the system in an increasingly narrower scope. Both tend to seek to understand the system fully, so that they predict and ultimately control it. The new sciences such as chaos theory (nonlinear dynamics) and quantum theory tend to repudiate these assumptions.[16] Nonlinear dynamics (as opposed to the more radical quantum theory) is used as the exemplar here partially because it is still clearly within the systems family of rationality and partially because it has had the most management applications of the new science approaches.

A nonlinear systems approach to rationality stresses that the natural or best state of a system is not necessarily equilibrium, as traditional rational approaches assume. Disequilibrium is as important and natural as is equilibrium. Nonlinear theorists point out, for example, that accidents often lead to inventions and that market failures (such as recessions) often lead to healthy market restructurings. They stress that some disequilibrium must be present in a "healthy" system or else the system will become rigid and ultimately collapse completely (rather than adapt and evolve). Nonlinear systems analysts also stress that systems are much more complex than we often admit and that the interaction of systems is also much less predictable and controllable. Nowhere is this complexity more apparent than when dealing with social systems, in which thousands or millions of human actors organized into hundreds of collectivities interact and react, which causes the amplification of unintended consequences in complex systems (called the *butterfly effect* in chaos theory). Under such conditions, prediction and control is a myth. This means that rather than trying to fully understand all possible outcomes in advance, one must often act, learn from the reactions, and adapt. The emphasis becomes adapting to change as much as engineering change, which tends to be the mindset of the rational and reasonable choice approaches.

Nonlinear approaches to rationality also point out that randomness is as fundamental to the universe as is order. In this conception, order will sometimes give way to disorder, and order will eventually emerge out of disorder. From this extremely broad view of systems comes the idea that systems are as much self-organizing as they are consciously organized. This insight becomes particularly important during times of change. People naturally cling to the old established ways that have worked well under stable conditions and that have been largely perfected (which, ironically, contributes to the change process). They resist new forms of organization that can emerge from new environments and may distrust "natural" configurations using new assumptions. Yet in times of change, nonlinear theorists suggest, this is exactly what is needed.

A nonlinear type of decisionmaking for public administration might look something like this:

- Identify a need for more order or for more disorder (such as innovation).
- Explore the large patterns and look for the complex relationships.
- Generate multiple responses, minimizing the role of concentrated power, hierarchy, and notions of control, but increasing the role of democratic inclusion, shared risk, commitment, and flexible planning.
- Allow for multiple local responses to the greatest degree possible.
- Encourage evolution of response(s).

The strength of the nonlinear approach to rationality is that it contradicts the "overblown utility or applicability of the rational model"[17] and counteracts the "wildly incomplete"[18] picture of an orderly, machinelike universe in which operation is fully understandable and predictable if only one could study the parts carefully enough. Rather, it brings back into respectability the other half of the universe—that is, chaos, randomness, and complexity. Even some fairly mainstream analysis is asserting that "the new paradigm is that of the nonlinear system."[19] Used properly, these ideas are not excuses to abandon attempts to understand; rather, they are tools to relax excessive microanalytic assumptions so that public administrators can appreciate the larger systems. Public administrators have tended to see their role as reducing conflict, creating order, and superimposing coherence on chaos.[20] Nonlinear theory emphasizes the roles of facilitating diversity, allowing the chaos that accompanies evolution during significant change, and relaxing assumptions about one's ability to understand and control. Nonetheless, past rational models "have proven adequate for many purposes and remain not only adequate but also the most appropriate for certain situations in the social world."[21] Rational and reasoned choice types are rarely wrong per se; they simply are overused and often misapplied in situations needing a broader perspective that embraces, rather than reduces, complexity.

Human Needs Rationality

The end for a human needs rationality is satisfaction, and that is achieved by fulfilling perceived needs. Maslow's hierarchy of needs[22] indicates that human needs are not simple, but indeed are multiple, complex, and overlapping. He suggested at least five successive types of needs, each demanding satisfaction before "higher" needs can become dominant. His categories are physiological needs, safety needs, belongingness and basic social needs, esteem needs (including advanced social needs), and self-actualization needs. Knowledge is gained by instincts at the basic levels of human needs and by complex drives at the more advanced levels.

Although cognitive forms of rationality have been very popular in the age of reason, it is wise to remember the power of human needs, which tend to emphasize the physical and emotional side of us all.[23] Hunger, lust, patriotism, accomplishment, and art are all examples of human needs that have their own powerful logic of fulfillment. The question of which takes precedence is often raised with regard to cognitive rationality versus human needs rationality. Are humans creatures capable of harnessing the power of needs in a cognitive framework (a rational person with needs) or is reason a "slave of passions" as David Hume suggested,[24] so that people are best described as needy creatures capable of rationalizing?

Because of the nature of modern life, satisfaction of needs is more indirect and difficult to discern but is nonetheless clearly present. Loss of job may be far more terrifying for some than its cognitive assessment would merit. The drive for more airline and medical safety may have far exceeded rational choice logic of cost-benefit analysis. Arguing with people with whom we disagree may be foolish from a cognitive basis, but we may be driven to do it nevertheless. The drive to accomplish may lead young adults into careers that have little financial or logical rationality except that they feel compelled to fulfill themselves in a certain way. Thus human needs are neither simple nor easily dominated by other forms of rationality.

Human needs logic follows approximately this path:

- Realization of an impulse, human need, or complex drive
- Choice among competing needs and desires
- Satisfaction or fulfillment of most pressing need or complex drive

Choice in this form is based not on an intellectual assessment of choice but on an intuitive assessment of what feels most important.

The virtues of human needs rationality should not be overlooked, as they sometimes are. Instincts and drives are the "built-in" or innate parameters that largely determine our values, which in turn determine the choices we make. Feelings are the glue of families, communities, and nations. Physical needs shape the landscape of our homes and neighborhoods. Higher drives, such as achievement and social belongingness, have general respect and often lead to accomplishments that reason would scoff at as impossible. The important new communitarian movement,[25] which emphasizes cultivating the best in human nature for the social good, ultimately stands on a human needs logic.[26] Actually, most broad-based motivational and practical political systems are built on human needs theories. Although the framers of the Republic may have been unsure of the ultimate nature of woman or man, they were convinced of the importance of the human needs rationality, as when they insisted on the individual's personal decision about the "pursuit of happiness." It is also true that human needs at their worst can be unattractive: greed, gluttony, lechery, fear, megalomania, and all other human needs in excess can be ugly and destructive. Many would argue that Western culture has become too materialistic and hedonistic, with satisfaction of immediate wants becoming far too excessive. The concern is that the postmodern era is fraught with insatiable desires of lower-level human need fulfillment, to the detriment of both higher-level drives and other forms of rationality. This relates to an age-old issue: Either the baser part of human nature must be firmly contained by other types of rationality, or the better part of human nature must be encouraged and allowed to evolve with the gentle support of other types of rationality. But no matter whether the nature of humankind is perceived to be predominately wicked, good, or mixed, human needs alone tend to emphasize individually oriented rationality, largely ignoring social perspectives and even other nonrational modes.

Coercive Rationality

Domination (or resistance to domination) is the end of coercive rationality. The means are types of physical confrontation. This might take the form of two equally matched individuals fighting with one another, or parents using corporal punishment with their children, or a mugger using overwhelming force against an unarmed victim, or a group of vigilantes wreaking vengeance. From a governmental perspective, the means could be legal sanctions against citizens or a war against another country.

Yet it can also take the form of individuals committing acts of terrorism or guerilla warfare against the government in power. Knowledge, in this type of rationality, is attained by force.[27]

The logic of coercion is relatively simple:

- An opportunity for or threat of confrontation
- An assessment of the utility of coercion and of the types and levels of force
- Choice (such as fight or flight)
- Use of force (to dominate or resist domination)

Of course, coercion is often implied rather than executed. The bully may rarely actually fight with others, parents may infrequently use their prerogative, and government sanctions are enacted with the hope that they will seldom need to be enforced.

Of particular note is the wholesale appropriation of the use of force by the modern government, especially in lethal forms such as capital punishment. Although often thought of as a primitive form of rationality, capital punishment as a state function creates an unusually important role for public administrators. Various types of police and corrections officials (municipal, county, federal) enforce laws, and the various military branches generally use force in foreign situations. Yet even noncoercive agencies have the legitimacy instilled by the indirect use of force, through civil and ultimately criminal proceedings, which can result in force. Public power can mean the use (or potential use) of irresistible force.

Developmental psychologists remind us that force is generally a part of childhood, and some social thinkers believe it is a social phase or level that is never entirely outgrown.[28] In any case, unless humankind has entirely escaped the animal kingdom, force is a part of nature that is undeniable. Certainly force is a common mode used by humans against other species. The potential use of force is important for protection against aggression. Also, the imposition of sanctions against unauthorized social acts (criminal behavior) is an unfortunate but necessary evil that the state must perform. The weaknesses of force as a form of rationality are well known. It often results in multiple losers. It subverts the cognitive and political forms of rationality that our society endorses. It is expensive to maintain defenses against criminality and aggression. It instills fear among those who are likely victims.

Traditional Rationality

Traditional rationality is a powerful factor in human society as well as in public administration. It emphasizes the importance of consistency with the past, social stability, physical continuity, and psychological order, and it ultimately places a high premium on community. In its more basic forms it is expressed as habits and routines for individuals; in a group context, it is expressed as customs and rituals. In its more advanced forms it is expressed as apprenticeships, training, and education of individuals; or it is expressed as elaborate socialization protocols for groups. It was much studied and appreciated by early sociologists like Weber and Durkheim,[29] and by early psychologists such as B.F. Skinner.[30] Without habits and traditions, individuals could not exist and societies would collapse. Habits perfect individual practice. Customs coordinate groups. Wisdom is passed on through mentoring and/or education. Respect for the past ensures that age-old knowledge and experiences are not lost or foolishly brushed aside. As one philosopher noted, customs' "generality, their public availability, and their widespread employment and revision, generation after generation, gives them a high likelihood that more errors have been eliminated than any single individual among us could eliminate by his own efforts and therefore are normally our best bet."[31]

Even in the age of reason, traditional rationality has had relatively high respectability until a consistent assault diminished its appeal starting in the 1950s. Sociologists, political scientists, and business experts increasingly emphasized change, rapid evolution, and industrialization spurred by mass production and leading to mass culture.[32] "Developed" nations and successful businesses became the model to emulate. Such organizations and cultures, it was thought, could reasonably and rationally rebuild their traditions to engineer predictable results. Unsuccessful organizations and cultures were thought to be resistant to change or bound by tradition. Even the traditionalism of the United States and other "advanced" Western countries was increasingly questioned in the global economic revolution of the 1980s.[33] On the behavioral side, advanced forms of traditionalism—training and education—themselves increasingly used as change agents rather than agents of continuity, are currently seeing an escalation. Also becoming more prominent is a call for traditional values, which generally stands for support of traditional family structures, Christian and Judaic monotheism, a strong work ethic, civicism, and volunteerism.[34]

The logic of traditionalism is approximately as follows:

- Awareness of the need to act or decide
- Identification of the relevant past tradition
- Following past practices

In practice, even in a change-oriented age, most actions are routinely based on past tradition and most new problems are interpreted with an eye to following the past, rather than finding genuinely new solutions.

One strength of traditionalism is its generally good fit with religious and elite forms of rationality. It also encourages a respect for elders (for example, in Confucianism) and an appreciation for past social practice. This leads to a social continuity within society, providing a stability that is appealing to many people. Finally, socialization is relatively easy in traditional societies because changes are introduced slowly and carefully, and people have a lifetime to learn and perfect their roles, about which there is little confusion. In contrast, people in nontraditional societies are often unclear about their roles as social custom is diminished. The weaknesses of traditionalism are all too apparent in modern society. Traditionalism is, to varying degrees, antithetical to cognitive rationalities, especially market or entrepreneurial rationalities, which have little respect for custom per se. It also tends to be intolerant of change and also of diversity, which threatens to fragment tradition within the culture. Finally, traditionalism promotes the status quo; although this is a disguised blessing for elites, it can be oppressive for nonelites.

Public administration has strong traditionalistic tendencies promoted by an ethic of following laws as authoritative traditions; powerful institutional cultures; and leanings toward hierarchism and risk avoidance. Because of society's tendency toward reducing legalism and hierarchism and increasing cultural change and risk, traditionalism is declining substantially in public administration in the 1990s.

Religious Rationality

The end of religious rationality is coherence with god's will. The means of this rationality is divine selection of the good or the right thing to do. Knowledge is gained through divine teachings and/or through holy scriptures and texts. Because proof or verifiability in scientific terms is impossible, knowledge is often based on a leap of faith.[35] Whereas most types of rationality focus on the present and near-term, religious rationality spends a great deal of time explaining first causes and original creation and the afterlife.[36]

Religious rationality generally uses a transcendental logic that is supported by faith, prayer, and meditation. Religious rationality tends to mesh best with elite rationality when that system is based at least in part on religious doctrine (for example, the divine right of kings or the eminence of religious leaders among the elite in society); quasi-legal rationality; traditionalism, when the society is of a single religious persuasion; altruism in some cases (for example, Franciscan Catholicism); and use of force in others (conquistador Catholicism). It can conflict with systems, especially rational choice rationality because of the different explanation of cause (a machinelike universe or a self-powered evolutionary process) as well as democratic rationality. It is not accidental that, despite their piety, the framers of the Constitution kept religion out of the governmental sphere so that market and individual drives could have full expression. This omission was as much for the protection of government as it was for the religious freedom. The reemergence of religious states in the Middle East and in Asia has again illustrated the fundamental contrast of this type of rationality.

The religious rationality type uses the following type of framework:

- Belief in a particular faith
- Choice of relevant divine text or teaching
- Application of divine teachings as models of living

This form has the advantage of providing a framework that surpasses the immediate and temporal world. When the scientific explanations of systems rationality describe the beginnings of the world, species, and human life, they tend to dwarf individuals' significance. Religious rationality gives believers a secure place for eternity, even if a divinity, rather than they, is the center of that eternal place. The limits of religious rationality in its more moderate forms are its lack of scientific proof, its lack of coherence in multireligion states, its awkwardness and sometimes brittleness in addressing the needs of technological and complex societies (such as the debate about the exact beginning of life), and its ability to become antidemocratic[37] and legalistic (like almost all successful organizations and systems). In its more militant forms, religious rationality is fundamentally at odds with the types of systems and political rationality that have come to dominate the world. Such a contest of rationalities can contribute forcefully to the types of conflict that have erupted not only in places like Algeria, Iran, Ceylon, and Afghanistan, but also in the former Yugoslav states and Northern Ireland.

Altruistic Rationality

Since the end of altruism is helping others, the means are perceptions of others' needs and efforts to fulfill those needs. Knowledge is gained by compassion for others' plights and empathy given the hardships that all humans ultimately face. At a simple level, altruism assumes that human comfort could be immeasurably increased if everyone could simply act toward others as they want to be treated. Elements and variations of altruism can be found in many types of rationality and philosophy. A strong altruistic theme is found in many of the great religions; in pure Marxism, with its notion of the withering away of the state because of the beneficence of individuals in society toward one another; in de Tocqueville's characterization of a mutually helping civic and volunteer America, despite its mercantile passion; and in the enlightened king and the duty-bound compassionate autocrat celebrated by various philosophers, from Aristotle to Kant. Altruism is also a major theme in communitarianism, which blends it (in various forms) with traditionalism, religion, and democracy.[38]

Altruism is important in the modern "welfare" state because many of the altruist functions generally carried out at the family and community levels have been assumed by the state. Part of the reason may have been for greater uniformity of support of the poor, the sick, and the needy; another part of the reason may have been the less cohesive nature of families and communities. Altruism has become almost hopelessly involved with arguments over big government, so that many critics of government blame misplaced altruism as a primary source of financial woes. Popular targets are foreign aid and welfare. Yet in reality, foreign aid is largely a tool for foreign policy, and welfare is not large by comparable measures. More difficult to discern is when altruism and responsible social planning are mixed, as is the case with Social Security and Medicare. Is it fair to give a larger payment to a rich widow who never worked than to a poorer woman who did? Is it responsible to pay for the medical expenses of millionaires eligible for Medicare? Here the arguments of altruism and various notions of fairness collide as long-term public debt promises to escalate to wartime levels.

The logic of altruism is:

- Awareness of others' needs
- Assessment of greatest need (putting aside one's own needs)
- Choice of need to fulfill
- Charitable action

It should be noted that altruism is far from the market or rational choice type, which sees individuals at their best when they are meticulously and aggressively achieving their own purposes.[39] It is also relatively antithetical to the coercive type of rationality, which does not acknowledge common good or compassion as significant.

The virtue of altruism is its purity of spirit and its seeming crystallization of the best in humanity. It captures the maternal instinct, the fraternal bond, the communal drive, the we-can-all-succeed-together spirit that is generally much respected. Despite its much touted pedigree, however, altruism is rarely the dominant form of rationality in Western society, which is individualist and capitalist at heart. In fact, it seems that the enormous trends toward state altruism since World War II are going to be fundamentally curbed throughout the Western world. Critics of altruism complain that it is often abused by those who administer it as well as by those who receive it. More important, it can lead to a cycle of dependence. Why farm or work when assistance will be forthcoming anyway? This captures the debate but oversimplifies the complex issues involving safety nets, calamities, level of risk assumed by individuals versus societies, and so on. It remains to be seen how much of the altruistic rationality that has pervaded the public sector can be reintegrated into communities and families, and how much of it will require individuals to assume more risks and hardships on their own.

Elite Rationality

The elite form of rationality is the first of four politically oriented approaches to rationality examined in this chapter. The elite and democratic forms often compete with one another as opposite ends of a spectrum; legal rationality is a companion form for either of them. Anarchic rationality is more concerned with unfettered individual freedom than with the social cohesion and control that characterize the other forms of political rationality.

Elite rationality assumes that small groups of individuals are better qualified to make decisions because of their special birth status (class or race), powerful role or position (elite), education and training, extraordinary talents, or unusual assets.[40] The end of elite rationality is to gain the support of these leading constituents. In historic times, elite rationality tended to be based on hereditary status and position (royal or aristocratic title) and highly restricted education (special tutors or select schools and universities) combined with substantial hereditary land and financial assets. People with these advantages were generally viewed as having been groomed from birth for power, decisionmaking, and leadership. Relative leadership positions might shift within a class based on special talents, but such shifts would be highly restricted. Examples of elite systems include royal families, aristocracies, oligopolies based on long-term (especially property) wealth, class systems (for example, the Indian caste system), racial systems (slavery), and, to a lesser degree, gender-based systems (systems that exclude women from most classes of important decisions, such as voting and holding office). Inherent in all elite systems is the belief that some people are better equipped to make decisions for the general good. Proponents of various elite systems include Aristotle, Hobbes, Kant, and Nietzsche. Like all forms of rationality, elite decisionmaking in the past has produced examples of general admiration (leading to great art, great monuments, great ancient systems, and so on) as well as examples that are today generally despised (contrasts of unearned opulence and hereditary poverty, an excessive elite-orientation, and excessive subjugation of nonelites).

Although the more blatant trappings of elitism are markedly less than in the past, especially in Western democracies, it would be foolish not to recognize modern forms of elitism and to recognize that elites (with their special decisionmaking power) will always be with us in some form. Modern elites tend to be established based on wealth, special position, and special talents.[41] Capitalist societies revere wealth, and even democratic states give great advantages to those with wealth. Those with special positions—corporate leaders, university presidents, elected officials, religious leaders, and appointed officials such as cabinet secretaries—are accorded unique decisionmaking authority. Individuals with special talents, especially those related to entertainment and the media, are also accorded special authority in the modern world; it is not uncommon for news personalities, actors, and athletes to become political giants (as did Ronald Reagan and Bill Bradley), financial giants (as did Oprah Winphrey and Merv Griffin), and nonprofit leaders (as have innumerable actors, serving as national chairpersons of volunteer organizations). Nor is it unusual for those modern elites to become involved in decision-making outside their normal professional orbit.

It is also important to recognize that many elite structures still exist within the American political-administrative system. Elected representatives (members of Congress, state legislatures, county supervisors, city councilors, board and commission members and others) become elites the day they take office, exercising decisionmaking authority far beyond that of the average citizen. Elected executives (presidents, governors, other state officeholders, county row officers, mayors) similarly have decisionmaking far beyond the norm. Other elites are judges, department heads, and senior career officers. Modern political elites are *ideally* different from past political elites in that they are more systematically and directly accountable for their actions and performance through elections, open hiring processes, institutional removal procedures (such as impeachment or recall options), and legal accountability mechanisms (lawsuits based on fraud, criminal negligence, abuse of power, and so on).

The elite form uses the following type of framework:

- Problem identification limited to elite leaders
- Alternatives discussed and debated among elite
- Choice dictated by wisdom of elite leader(s)
- Action overseen by elite

This form has the advantage of confining decisionmaking to a realistic number of people, which is important when universal consensus would be unrealistic. The modern addition of numerous accountability mechanisms tempers widespread abuse of power bestowed on elites. Modern Western elites tend to demonstrate a commitment to work hard and be highly involved. At their best, elites take the time to consider difficult and complex issues in depth (which is onerous for the average citizen) and for the long term. But elites frequently do not function at their best, and they are still commonly accused of being self-serving. As serious a problem, however, is that accountability mechanisms often encourage short-range or narrow actions more than the inherent wisdom elites are supposed to possess. It may behoove an elected official seeking reelection to bow to special interests and to short-term popular whims rather than to do a better job at promoting the commonwealth and good of future generations.

Democratic Rationality

If elite rationality emphasizes the support of a narrow base of people qualified by their special status as the appropriate end, democratic rationality emphasizes the support of a broad base of support, with consensus often being the ideal, though rarely achieved. If elite rationality emphasizes means that limit and narrow the decisionmaking process, democratic rationality emphasizes means that expand the process as broadly as possible. Whereas knowledge for elite rationality is ultimately founded upon the special endowments of a few, knowledge for democratic rationality is founded upon the opinion of the majority.[42]

Democratic rationality has been widespread only in the last few centuries, although it has ancient roots both in various civilizations and in the culture of various nomadic peoples. To take part in public decisionmaking (democratic rationality) at a substantial level, individuals need time, understanding (education), means of getting information where they live in a timely fashion, and the ability to participate. Many factors have contributed to this trend in the last 150 years: mass production, widespread public education, rapid transportation and communication, the broadening of the voting franchise, and the broadening of individual liberties. Although the idyllic democratic equality achieved in the small, homogenous New England town hall is unlikely to be achieved in most situations, even with unlimited electronic capability, the expansion of democratic rationality has been impressive and looks likely to continue to increase in the upcoming decades.

The democratic form uses the following type of framework:

- The need for *group* action (this step also assumes that individual actions are screened out).
- Selection of the democratic procedures and their order (such as discussion, debate, voting, and selection by representatives).
- Authoritative choice (maybe a direct form such as plebescite or an indirect form such as choice by representatives).
- Implementation by government.
- Accountability mechanism for reporting and review by others (such as public, media, hierarchical superiors, elected officials, judicial review, and so on).

This type of rationality has the advantage of gaining wide support for specific decisions, providing for broad input, encouraging compromise, enhancing fairness, and establishing a widely accepted legitimacy for public decisionmaking. Yet democratic rationality is not without its substantial limitations. It is primarily a *public* decisionmaking form; it functions poorly as a mechanism for individual decisionmaking. For example, legislating the type and color of car that everyone will drive is both democratic and efficient, but is hardly a use of democratic rationality that most Westerners would accept.[43] Taken to its extreme, democratic rationality quashes rational choice types. Because so many are involved in democratically determined decisions, decisionmaking tends to be slow, and some situations necessitate haste. Complex issues are difficult for the public at large to understand because of the intricate nature of issues and the time needed to master them. Democratic compromise can lead to an important balancing of power and inclusion of divergent interests; however, it can also lead to an inferior decision that is a less effective, and perhaps even a contradictory solution. In its representative form and with its vastly heightened sense of immediate accountability, democratic rationality makes it difficult to retain a commitment to the long-term future in many instances. For example, voters (and stockholders) are often relatively inattentive to long-term investments and savings; this can result in raids on pension funds, deferred infrastructure maintenance, and savings depletion. This may be democratically endorsed, but it is poor policy indeed. While broadly constituted publics generally have a healthy conservatism, they can nonetheless be guilty of a mob mentality (especially in times of national crisis), giving way to behavior later viewed as unethical and intrusive. The internment of Japanese American citizens during World War II was a democratically endorsed decision, but it was later recognized as a terrible breach of constitutional liberties.

Legal Rationality

The raison d'être of legal rationality is primarily procedural consistency, and secondarily, fairness and control. It harmonizes well with either elite or democratic rationality in an instrumental capacity. It is generally characteristic of most large, complex, and/or powerful organizations or systems. If the end of legal rationality is procedural consistency, then rules—whether constitutional principles to ordinances or general policies to detailed specifications—are the means. Knowledge is based on mastery of rules.[44]

Legal rationality is generally the means by which superordinate public-oriented decisionmaking types are perpetuated. Not only is legal rationality typical of a democratic state such as the United States, as well as an elite state such as China, it is also extremely common in states and organizations that are religious and traditionalistic. In religious organizations, the sacred text becomes the "constitution" and religious edicts and pronouncements become the laws enforced by the priests. In traditional societies, customs become canonized and systematized, having the same force and effect as case law. In modern history this often has led to proscribed customary behaviors becoming technically legal. In extreme cases, the customary reason is forgotten while the legal status remains. Yet in all cases, legal rationality places a premium on social control.

In American public administration, there can be little doubt that legal rationality is an important approach. According to David Rosenbloom, there are three primary sources for this rationality.[45] First, the tradition of administrative law, which generally holds "that part of the law which fixes the organizations and determines law as the competence of authorities which executes the law."[46] The second source is the judicialization of public administration, which concentrates on the "establishment of procedures designed to safeguard individual rights."[47] The third source is constitutional law, which since the 1950s has expanded "procedural, equal protection, and substantive rights and liberties *vis-à-vis* public administrators."[48] Not surprisingly, Rosenbloom notes that the values that legal rationality brings to public administration are due process, individual substantive rights such as those found in the Bill of Rights, and equity. He also notes that the legal approach has resulted in a downgrading of the cost-benefit reasoning that largely dominated and stemmed from the management approach to public administration.[49]

The legal rationality form uses the following type of framework:

- Adoption of rules by a legitimate authority that establishes the legal system
- Detection of a possible violation of a rule
- Selection of a legal process
- Choice of appropriate action
- Implementation by a use of force and/or hierarchical system as appropriate

This type has the important advantage of providing social stability. Control, fairness, and predictability all are generally enhanced by legal rationality. However, legal rationality has tremendous limitations, as do all other types of rationality. It is singularly uncreative, since its main goal is consistency. It has a tendency to grow ever more complex and cumbersome over time, so that it becomes more expensive and obscure. Legal rationality is a poor primary social mover. Sometimes the fact that law is an instrumentality is forgotten (which is roughly equivalent to the law for the law's sake). This leads to the small but important class of cases where people may follow "immoral" laws without compunction, or where abiding by the law is satisfactory evidence of good decisionmaking (whereas it may in fact only mean nonconviction due to lack of conclusive evidence, or noncriminal but socially destructive behavior).

Anarchic Rationality

If the desired end is complete freedom from social control, then the desired means are a lack of rules or defined social structure. It is likely that this type of rationality flourished with prehistoric humankind, along with coercive rationality. Elements of anarchism also flourish in a frontier situation, such as existed in America for centuries. Daniel Boone is an American folk hero famous for his strident anarchist beliefs. Certainly many situations still lend themselves to anarchic rationality, even in the contemporary world, in which crowding often makes anarchy a bit of a problem. Many social gatherings are fun only to the degree that they are anarchic and relatively unstructured: cocktail parties, picnics, family gatherings, and "chat" rooms on the World Wide Web are common examples. Some organizations, especially those constructed as networks, feature anarchic features that discourage hierarchy, structure, or defined leadership (even long-term democratic leadership): examples include user groups, problem-solving and improvement teams, and Quaker meetings, where only the time is predetermined. However, few larger organizations and political structures are organized on fundamentally anarchic principles today. One of the closest examples in the last century is the hundreds of attempts at communal living with anarchic principles (no leadership or spontaneous leadership), which tended not to be implemented as planned or did not flourish or have not stood the test of time.[50] As a political system, "anarchist societies have not come about anywhere and with the demise of the Soviet Union, even the hope for a classless society in which the state has withered away seems to have withered away, too."[51]

In one sense, anarchists can be seen as supreme individualists. In fact, many contemporary social critics argue that today's tendencies toward radical individualism lead to anarchy and social disintegration. Yet from another point of view, anarchists simply want leadership to be as local, modest, accountable, and revolving as possible. In this view, anarchists disdain central government, large hierarchical governmental organizations, broad governmental scope of functions, and professional leaders. From this perspective (a less extreme one than that in general usage), there are strong anarchist strains in the American tradition, with its more than 80,000 governments, strong balance of power between the states and federal government, philosophy of deference to the private sector, and tradition of the citizen legislator. Anarchic rationality, in this sense, is relatively compatible with either rational choice or nonlinear systems rationality.

A major concern with anarchic rationality is that disputes among individuals and groups have no clear process of resolution and no social mechanism for mediation and enforcement of solutions. This means that in truly anarchic situations, where passions and stakes are high, there is a great likelihood of sinking into a coercive rationality mode, as often occurs in times of revolution or civil unrest. However, in the long view, some would hold that even this is not necessarily a bad thing. Thomas Jefferson is well known for his comment (in a letter to James Madison in 1787) that "a little rebellion, now and then, is a good thing, and as necessary in the political world as storms in the physical."

The logic of anarchy is very simple:

- Need for individual action
- Choice of action based on individual preference without significant social input

Although the term *anarchy* often has taken on a derisive meaning, it is a mistake to think that anarchic rationality does not still exist in each person's life to a greater or lesser degree—in social urges for spontaneity and freedom, in market capitalism, and in Americans' fear of overweening government and organizations, even thoroughly democratic ones.

Conclusion

This chapter began by asserting that there are many forms of rationality. Part of being ethical is selecting the right decisionmaking process for the right situation. When aggregated, the systems that coordinate the usage of various types of rationality determine social and administrative paradigms, which in turn make up broad societal assumptions. The operational definition of rationality was a consistency of the means with the desired end. Some ends, such as efficiency and effectiveness, lend themselves to analytic means in trying to increase rationality. An organizational manager seeking efficiency because of the competition in her organizational environment would tend to study and analyze the ways in which she could achieve the maximal productivity. Many other types of rationality are nonanalytic. A police officer who, with a judge's warrant, is about to break down the door of a suspected criminal would have domination as the immediate goal and physical confrontation as a likely means in subduing an armed suspect. Or, in an example of political rationality, even though democratic rationality is often premised on the notion of the sum of individuals' analytic choices, in reality their purposes (ends) are so diverse, and their reasoning (means) so different and often nonanalytic, that democratic rationality is usually merely a means of imposing a workable compromise, rather than being analytic per se.

Using the broader definition of rationality, then, 12 forms were briefly discussed, and they were placed into three broad families. A summary of the twelve forms can be found in Table 9.1. The cognitively oriented forms of rationality are market (or rational choice), reasoned choice, or nonlinear systems. Despite the differences in their conceptualization of the good—in the first case a competitive marketplace, in the second a reasonable organization or community, and in the third a dynamic and evolving milieu—they all end up using analytic means to achieve these desired states. The market can be studied, the reasonable organization can be analyzed, and evolutionary environments, while they may not be controllable, are amendable to better adaptation and understanding through scrutiny and intellectual appreciation.

Rationalities that are not cognitively oriented have an even greater range of desired ends. At least two look toward ends outside the individual. Religious rationality places the end in a supreme being whose knowledge and power created humanity and thus rightfully defines our purpose or end. Altruistic rationality looks closer to home for its end, at the needs of others. Yet other forms of noncognitively oriented rationalities look to individuals for their ends. Human needs rationality uses the satisfaction of humanity's "built in" needs as the desired end to achieve— no matter whether those needs are "lower" basic instincts for survival and procreation or "higher" drives for fulfillment and achievement. Tradi-

TABLE 9.1

Types of Rationality: Their Means and Ends and Associated Sources of Knowledge

Category	Rationality	Means	Ends	Knowledge
Cognitively Oriented	•Market or rational choice	Competition	Efficiency	Market action
	•Reasoned choice	Expertise	Effectiveness	Varied experience and study
	•Nonlinear systems	Variation (both patterned and random)	Dynamic evolution	Disequilibrium and chaos
Non-cognitively Oriented	•Human needs	Perceived needs	Satisfaction	Instinct/advanced drive
	•Use of force	Physical confrontation	Domination (or resistance to it)	Coercion
	•Traditional	Customs	Consistency with past	Socialization
	•Religious	Divine guidance	God's will	Divine teaching and scripture
	•Altruistic	Perceptions of others' needs	Helping others	Compassion, empathy
Politically Oriented	•Elite	Aristocratic	Key group support	Special endowments
	•Democratic	Popular	Broad agreement among electorate	Consensus
	•Legal	Rules	Procedural consistency	Mastery of rules
	•Anarchic	Lack of rules or social structure	Complete freedom	Being unencumbered

tionalism uses an individual's or society's own past wisdom as the best guide to present actions. Coercive rationality uses an individual's (or group's) ability to impose its will as the critical end state to achieve in certain situations.

Finally, politically oriented rationalities all look to social models of decisionmaking, which involve authoritative governmental structures. Elite rationality stresses the decisionmaking superiority of a select group, based on their assets, wisdom, skills, position, or innate superiority. At the opposite end of the spectrum, anarchic rationality stresses the superiority of individual decisionmaking to the greatest degree possible, and in its less severe forms encourages extremely limited government and prefers highly decentralized government to those that are centralized. Democratic rationality falls between elite and anarchic rationality and can be viewed as having elements of one or the other in different situations. Democratic rationality has broad agreement among individuals in the electorate as its end, so that it focuses on the individual's choices, but is more willing to impose social coercion through law than is the anarchic point of view. But democratic rationality ends up relying on elite means because of representative forms of governance (with the representatives becoming an elite themselves) and hierarchical executives who drive policies or run large governmental organizations. Finally, there is legal rationality, which generally professes to be the servant of either democratic or elite rationality, but which over time often becomes the overall framework itself. For example, when those with elitist preferences and those with democratic preferences can agree on nothing else, they often resort to a fundamental assertion of the Constitution, which is, at heart, a legal rationality perspective.

It cannot be stressed enough that all types of rationality exist in American culture and in public administration more specifically. However, it is also true that there are preferences for the use of some rationalities more generally and in more situations. Here I will give my assessment of the prioritization of the 12 rationalities for public administration, not because it is authoritative, for it is not, but because it is an example of the thought process necessary for administrators and commentators alike who are making decisions or giving normative or prescriptive advice. I suggest not my preferences, but my assessment of the current biases actually used in public administration thinking and decisionmaking.

In the first tier of decisionmaking influences I would place democratic, legal, and reasoned choice rationalities. Democratic and legal rationalities are part of the larger political framework of which public administration is merely a part. The democratic ethos pervades as a spirit but in practice administrators actually live by, for, and through the law. Administrators rarely forget that they work for the people. But they also never forget that this is a nation of laws and that they are the nation's and the laws' principal agents. In addition, in practice most administrators dwell in organizations that are concentrations of expertise, based on professional education, technical training, and actual experience. Administrators are adept at bringing expert opinions to bear to inform the democratic state about options, to help formulate the actual policies to be legitimated, and to aid specific operational implementation. Their expertise helps them blend the legal and technical, without violating the overarching democratic spirit underlying our government.

In the second tier I would place rational choice, elite, and coercive rationalities. Rational choice has always played an important role because of the capitalist system that the public sector supports, to a greater or lesser degree. Prior to this century the implicit rational choice was for government's scope and scale to be relatively small. In this century, with the relative growth of government, rational choice has become an increasing force within government operations, first in practices such as competitive bidding, and later in efforts at competitive public services and privatization. Despite the public's complaints about elite rationality, as exhibited by the hostility toward legislators, elected executives, judges, and bureaucrats, only the most overt and egregious excesses of elitism are likely to decline. Campaign finance, true judicial review, and limitation of bureaucratic discretion are difficult to attain. Further, it is unclear that a certain amount of elitism is not both good and commonly desired. Statesmanship is often thought of as the ability to ignore current popular passions for the long-term good; insulation of judges does indeed reduce politicization and "popularity contest" reviews; and sometimes bureaucratic leadership requires more, not less, discretion. You want the best and brightest at the helm and you want them to have the power they need, but you do not want to dictate or impose their will—not always an easy or clear balance. And, finally, coercive rationality is a specialty of the state and of public administration as the state's executors. No matter whether the coercive rationality is regulatory and indirect, or physical and direct, the state has a near monopoly on legitimate coercion. It is rare for public administrators not to have thought through the "what if" scenarios: What if a citizen does not willingly comply with a rule? What if a citizen continues to violate a rule or cheat on it? What if the violation reaches criminal levels? In fact, it is common for public administrators to have a progressive coercive protocol for those who do not comply. While it may be rarely used, coercion is available.

In the third tier I would place nonlinear, traditional, human needs, altruistic, and anarchic rationalities. Formerly traditional rationality ("We have always done it that way") was quite strong, but it has probably dropped a tier in the last decade because of the tremendous pressures for systems changes. Likewise, nonlinear and anarchic rationalities have probably increased in importance because of these same pressures. Nonlinear rationality requires administrators to be more flexible and more creative, to draw innovations into their orbits from more diverse fields, and to accept change as a healthy force rather than a destructive one. Anarchic rationality, itself somewhat antithetical to the public sector mindset, will increasingly be integrated as responsiveness to multiple stakeholders (and their competing interests), responsiveness to private sector practices while maintaining public sector sensibilities about the common good, and responsiveness to the diminution of government it-self. The public sector has always been sensitive to the human needs of its clients and employees but has been careful to put these needs in other frameworks first (such as a legal mandate). Much of the public sector has had an altruistic spirit, but again, this has been constrained by other frameworks and is likely to decline as the welfare state is reconstructed into some other form.

In the final tier, religious rationality has a special status altogether. It is simultaneously elevated outside government in the Constitution by keeping government out of its domain, and it is demoted within government by specifically disallowing it legitimacy as an explicit decisionmaking influence. To act specifically as Episcopalians or Muslims or Jews or Catholics is expressly forbidden in public sector decisionmaking. Of course, the indirect cultural influence of religion on society in general and on individual administrators in particular is important and is not likely to be disputed by many.

Although these 12 forms of rationality were presented as a means of understanding patterns of actions at the second level of culture, that is, a level of culture rather close to the individual, it should be clear that these forms of rationality can also be thought of as analytic tools to understand beliefs and basic assumptions levels as well, where complexes of rationalities merge into unique cultural configurations. Chapter 10 will examine the first level of culture in Schein and Ott's model, the specific actions level in which concrete decisions are actually made.

Notes

1. Max Weber, "Basic Sociological Terms," in *Economy and Society,* vol. 1, Guenther Roth and Claus Wittich, eds. (Berkeley: University of California Press, 1947), pp. 3–62.

2. I have arbitrarily selected the words *type* and *form* to speak of variations of rationality in this chapter. I use the word *model* in the next chapter to refer to variations within one type of rationality.

3. Kurt Baier, *The Rational and the Moral Order: The Social Roots of Reason and Morality* (Chicago, IL: Open Court, 1995), p. 5.

4. David Rosenbloom, "Public Administration Theory and the Separation of Powers," in *Classics of Public Administration,* 3rd ed., Jay Shafritz and Albert Hyde, eds. (Pacific Grove, CA: Brooks/Cole, 1992).

5. See the conclusion for an extended discussion of my sense of the hierarchy of importance for public administration of the different types of rationality.

6. Variants of rational choice theory are expected-utility theory, transaction cost analysis, and agency theory.

7. See, for example, Jay Barney and William Ouchi, *Organizational Economics* (San Francisco: Jossey-Bass 1986); Oliver Williamson, *Markets and Hierarchies: Analysis and Antitrust Implications* (New York: Free Press, 1975), and Jon Ulster, *Ulysses and the Sirens: Studies in Rationality and Irrationality* (Cambridge: Cambridge University Press, 1979).

8. Herbert A. Simon, *Administrative Behavior,* 2nd ed. (New York: Macmillan, 1957).

9. A few other well-known critiques include Graham T. Allison, *Essence of Decision: Explaining the Cuban Missile Crisis* (Boston: Little, Brown, 1971); Charles E. Lindblom, "The 'Science' of Muddling Through," in *Public Administration Review* 19, no. 2 (1959), pp. 79–88, D. Braybrooke and Charles Lindblom, *A Strategy of Decision: Policy Evaluation As a Social Process,* 3rd ed. (New York: Free Press, 1969); Michael Cohen, James March, and Johan Olsen, "A Garbage Can Model of Organizational Choice," *Administrative Science Quarterly* 17, (March 1972), pp. 1–25; and Herbert Kaufman, *The Forest Ranger* (Baltimore: Johns Hopkins Press, 1960).

10. Richard Herstein, "Rational Choice Theory: Necessary but Not Sufficient," *American Psychologist* 45 (March 1991), pp. 356–367.

11. An excellent comprehensive critique of rational choice is presented in an edited volume by Mary Zey, *Decisionmaking: Alternatives to Rational Choice Models* (Newbury Park: Sage, 1992).

12. Rational choice and reasoned choice are not generally presented as two distinct and separate forms. However, I believe the differences warrant two forms, which certainly seems supported by the degree of interest generated by the topic. Most critics cited in the previous section are advocates of a form of reasoned choice.

13. David Collingridge, *Critical Decision Making: A New Theory of Social Choice* (London: Frances Pinter, 1982).

14. Max Weber, *Essays in Sociology,* H.H. Gerth and C. Wright Mills, eds. (New York: Oxford University Press, 1946).

15. Because of the long and relatively unchallenged reign of reasoned choice in the public sector since World War II, its weaknesses and excesses have had ample time to be exhibited. For example, these critiques are found in the literature on organizational change, total quality management, and reengineering.

16. A few of the general works are James Gleick, *Chaos* (New York: Viking, 1978); Erich Jantsch, *The Self-Organizing Universe: Scientific and Human Implications of the Emerging Paradigm of Evolution* (Oxford: Pergamon, 1979); John Briggs and David Peat, *The Looking Glass Universe: The Emerging Science of Wholeness* (New York: Cornerstone, 1984); David Bohm, *Science, Order, and Creativity* (New York: Bantam, 1987); Margaret Wheatley, *Leadership and the New Science: Learning About Organizations From an Orderly Universe* (San Francisco: Berrett-Koehler, 1992); Ilya Prigogine and Isabelle Stengers, *Order Out of Chaos* (New York: Bantam Books, 1984); Danah Zohar and Ian Marshall, *The Quantum Society: Mind, Physics, and a New Science Vision* (New York: William Morrow, 1994). A few of the works that specifically look at the implications for public administration are L. Douglas Kiel, *Managing Chaos and Complexity in Government: A New Paradigm for Managing* (San Francisco: Jossey-Bass, 1994); Gregory Daneke, *The Agathon Agenda: Non-Linear Dynamics and Practical Policy* (London: Oxford University Press, 1994); Theodore Becker, *Quantum Politics: Applying Quantum Theory to Political Phenomena* (New York: Praeger,

1991). The postmodern literature also implicitly accepts many nonlinear and quantum assumptions. See Charles Fox and Hugh Miller, *Postmodern Public Administration: Toward Discourse* (Thousand Oaks, CA: Sage, 1995).

17. Ulf Zimmer, "Beyond Rational Choice," *Public Administration Review* 56, no. 2 (March/April 1996), pp. 214–215.

18. E. Sam Overman, "The New Sciences of Administration: Chaos and Quantum Theory," *Public Administration Review* 56, no. 5 (September/October 1996), p. 487.

19. Francis X. Neumann, Jr., "What Makes Public Administration a Science? or, Are Its 'Big Questions' Really Big?" *Public Administration Review* 56, no. 5 (September/October 1996), p. 412.

20. Linda F. Dennard, "The New Paradigm in Science and Public Administration," *Public Administration Review* 56, no. 2 (March/April 1996), p. 495.

21. Karen G. Evans, "Chaos As Opportunity: Grounding a Positive Vision of Management and Society in the New Physics," *Public Administration Review* 56, no. 5 (September/October 1996), p. 491.

22. Abraham Maslow, *Motivations and Personality* (New York: Harper & Row, 1954). Some well-known related theories and studies are proposed by C.P. Alderfer, *Existence, Relatedness, and Growth* (New York: Free Press, 1972); Frederick Herzberg, et al., *Job Attitudes: Review of Research and Opinion* (Pittsburgh: Psychological Service of Pittsburgh, 1957), and Frederick Herzberg, "One More Time: How Do You Motivate Employees?" *Harvard Business Review,* 46 (1968), pp. 36–44; Anthony Downs, *Inside Bureaucracy* (Boston: Little, Brown, 1967); W.A. Niskanen, *Bureaucracy and Representative Government* (Chicago: Aldine, 1971); and David McClelland, *The Achieving Society,* (Princeton: Van Nostrand, 1961).

23. See for example, Helena Flam, "The Emotional Man and The Problem of Collective Action," *International Sociology* 5, no. 1 (1990), pp. 39–56.

24. David Hume, *A Treatise of Human Nature,* 2nd ed., L.A. Selby-Bigge and P.H. Nidditch, eds. (Oxford: Oxford University Press, 1978), p. 415.

25. Also called *civism* (by Fox and Miller), and *civil religion* when it is elevated to the sacred. See Will Herberg, *Protestant, Catholic, Jew* (Garden City, NJ: Doubleday, 1960); Robert Bellah and Philip Hammond, *Varieties of Civil Religion* (San Francisco: Harper and Row, 1980); and Robert Bellah, *The Broken Covenant: American Civil Religion in Time of Trial,* 2nd ed. (Chicago: University of Chicago Press, 1992).

26. See for example, Amitai Etzioni, *The Active Society* (New York: Free Press, 1968) and *The Spirit of the Community: Rights, Responsibilities, and the Communitarian Agenda* (New York: Crown Publishers, 1993); Robert Bellah, et al., *The Good Society* (New York: Knopf, 1991); David Norton, *Democracy and Moral Development* (Berkeley: University of California Press, 1991); Terry L. Cooper, *An Ethic of Citizenship for Public Administration* (Englewood Cliffs, NJ: Prentice-Hall, 1991); Alasdair MacIntyre, *After Virtue,* 2nd ed. (Notre Dame, IN: University of Notre Dame Press, 1984); Alasdair MacIntyre, *Whose Justice? Which Rationality?* (Notre Dame, IN: University of Notre Dame, 1988). Charles Fox and Hugh Miller (op. cit., p. 33) place public administrationists like Ralph Chandler, Terry Cooper, George Fredrickson, Louis Gawthrop, and Camilla Stivers in this school of thought.

27. The literature on force and coercion is found mainly in sociology, in various discussions of social conflict at the group and societal levels, and deviance and control at the individual level. Some of the classic writings in this area are

Lewis Croser, *The Functions of Social Conflict* (New York: Free Press, 1956); Ralf Dahrendorf, *Class and Class Conflict in Industrial Society* (Stanford, CA: Stanford University Press, 1958); Randall Collins, *Conflict Sociology: Toward an Explanatory Science* (New York: Academic Press, 1974); and Stephen Schafer, *The Political Criminal: The Problem of Morality and Crime* (New York: Free Press, 1974). Of course, Karl Marx was the original conflict political theorist; more modern critical thinkers in this school would include Theda Skocpal, Immanuel Wallerstein, and Charles Tilly.

28. Lawrence Kohlberg, *The Philosophy of Moral Development: Moral Stages and the Idea of Justice* (San Francisco: Harper and Row, 1981).

29. For a comprehensive review of Durkheim and Weber on this topic, see Charles Camic, "The Matter of Habit," in *Decisionmaking,* Mary Zey, ed. (Newbury Park, CA: Sage, 1992), pp. 185–232.

30. B.F. Skinner, *Science and Human Behavior* (New York: Free Press, 1953); *Beyond Freedom and Dignity* (New York: Knopf, 1971); and *About Behaviorism* (New York: Knopf, 1974).

31. Baier, op. cit., p. 51.

32. Examples of schools of thought that were unfavorable or even disparaging of traditionalism included neoevolutionism (eg., Talcott Parsons, Gerhard Lenski), modernism (e.g., Samuel Huntington, Myron Weiner, Arthur Lewis, Gabriel Almond, S.N. Eisenstadt, Edward Shils, Fred Riggs, Lucian Pye, W.W. Rostow), and, to some degree, organizational development (e.g., Kurt Lewin, Chris Argyris, Robert Blake, Rensis Likert). Although these schools of thought added tremendously to the base of knowledge, some of them were themselves attacked in the 1970s and 1980s as being normatively biased toward a specific set of values while asserting that their theories were value neutral.

33. Critiques of modernism and developmentalism included those of Mark Kesselman, Susan Bodenheimer, Fernando Cardoso, and Andre Gunder Frank.

34. William Bennett's work is an excellent example from the mainstream, as is the work flowing from the Christian Coalition and similar movements.

35. This probably overstates the case for clarity. For example, Thomas Aquinas, in *Summa Theologica* uses Aristotelian logic to prove the existence of God. Other exceptions are not hard to find in the world's great religions.

36. Some classic studies of religion include Max Weber, *The Protestant Work Ethic and the Spirit of Capitalism,* translated by Talcott Parsons, trans. (New York: Scribner's, 1904/1958); Emile Durkheim, *The Elementary Forms of Religious Life,* Joseph Swain, trans. (New York: Free Press, 1912/1947); Peter Berger, *The Sacred Canopy: Elements of a Sociological Theory of Religion* (Garden City, NJ: Doubleday, 1967); Charles Glock and Robert Bellah, eds, *The New Religious Consciousness* (Berkeley, CA: University of California Press, 1976); John Wilson, *Religion in American Society: The Effective Presence* (Englewood Cliffs, NJ: Prentice-Hall, 1978); A. James Reichley, *Religion in American Public Life* (Washington, DC: Brookings Institution, 1985); and Allen Hertzke, *Echoes of Discontent: Jesse Jackson, Pat Robertson, and the Resurgence of Populism* (Washington, DC: Congressional Quarterly Press, 1993).

37. Such as Marx's famous critique of religion as the opiate of the people. Karl Marx, "Contribution to the Critique of Hegel's Philosophy of Right," in *On Religion,* Karl Marx and Friedrich Engels (New York: Schocken, 1844/1964), p. 42.

38. Some examples of the literature on altruism and otherness that are not primarily associated with religion are Robert Axelrod, *The Evolution of*

Cooperation (New York: Basic Books, 1984); Lawrence Blum, *Friendship, Altruism, and Morality* (Boston: Routledge & Kegan Paul, 1980); David Collard, *Altruism and Economy: A Study in Non-Selfish Economics* (Oxford: Martin Robinson, 1978); Rosabeth Moss Kanter, *Commitment and Community: Communes and Utopias in Sociological Perspective* (Cambridge, MA: Harvard University Press, 1972); Jane Mansbridge, ed., *Beyond Self-Interest* (Chicago: University of Chicago Press, 1990); and John Rawls, *A Theory of Justice* (Cambridge, MA: Harvard University Press, 1971). See also the literature on communitarianism cited in an earlier note.

39. Although there is a contention in the rational choice literature which asserts that altruism is merely a subtle form of self-interest, here I put aside that argument for a simpler analysis.

40. See for example, the classic works of Vilfredo Pareto, Gaetano Mosca, and Robert Michels, who investigate the inevitable control of systems, parties, and organizations by small groups, ultimately for relatively self-serving purposes. Michels called this the "iron law of oligopoly."

41. General references about elitism, including some critical of elite systems, include C. Wright Mills, *The Power Elite* (New York: Oxford University Press, 1956); Martin N. Manger, *Elites and Masses* (New York: Van Nostrand, 1981); William Welsh, *Leaders and Elites* (New York: Holt, Rinehart and Winston, 1979); Samuel Huntington, *Political Order in Changing Societies* (New Haven, CT: Yale University Press, 1968); P. Bachrach, *The Theory of Democratic Elitism* (Boston: Little, Brown, 1967); Peter B. Evans, Dietrich Rueschemeyer, and Theda Skocpol, eds., *Bringing the State Back In* (Cambridge: Cambridge University Press, 1985); [elites among countries] Immanuel Wallerstein, *The Modern World-System*, vols. 1 and 2 (New York: Academic Press, 1974, 1980).

42. Of the thousands of excellent references on this topic, one can give only a few favorites: *The Federalist Papers;* Alexis de Tocqueville, *Democracy in America* (New York: Vintage, 1831/1945); E.E. Schattschneider, *The Semisovereign People: A Realist's View of Democracy in America* (New York: Holt, Rinehart, and Winston, 1960); Robert Dahl, *Who Governs?* (New Haven, CT: Yale University Press, 1961) and *Dilemmas of Pluralist Democracy: Autonomy vs. Control* (New Haven, CT: Yale University Press, 1982); B. Barber, *Strong Democracy: Participatory Politics for a New Age* (Berkeley: University of California Press, 1984); Theodore Lowi, *The End of the Republican Era* (Norman, OK: University of Oklahoma, 1995). Just two of many writers who do a good job of relating public administration to democratic theory are John Rohr, *To Run a Constitution* (Lawrence: University Press of Kansas, 1986) and Charles Goodsell, *The Case for Bureaucracy,* 3rd ed. (Chatham, NJ: Chatham, 1994).

43. In the United States this ambivalence about democratic rationality is sometimes ironic. On one hand, the merits of democratic decisionmaking are touted enthusiastically. Yet when public decisionmaking is perceived to intrude upon those areas considered essential private domains (right to property, right to bear arms, right to choose employment and place to live, etc.), it is generally labeled socialism and viewed in extraordinarily negative terms.

44. Some major sources on the U.S. law tradition are Oliver Wendell Holmes, Jr., "The Path of Law," *Harvard Law Review* 61 (1897); Benjamin Cardozo, *The Growth of Law* (New Haven, CT: Yale University Press, 1924); H.L.A. Hart, *The Concept of Law* (London: Oxford University Press, 1961); Lawrence Tribe, "Structural Due Process," *Harvard Civil Rights-Civil Liberties Law Review* 10 (1975), pp. 269–321; William Evan, ed., *The Sociology of Law* (New York: Free

Press, 1980); and Philip Howard, *The Death of Common Sense* (New York: Warner Books, 1994). A few references relating law to public administration are John DiIulio, Jr., *Deregulating the Public Service* (Washington, DC: Brookings Institution, 1994); Robert Kaufman, *Red Tape: Its Origins, Uses, and Abuses* (Washington, DC: Brookings Institution, 1977); Robert Kravchuk, "Public Administration and the Rule of Law," *International Journal of Public Administration* 14 (1991), pp. 265–301; and David Rosenbloom and James Carroll, *Toward Constitutional Competence* (Englewood Cliffs, NJ: Prentice-Hall, 1990).

45. David H. Rosenbloom, "Public Administrative Theory and the Separation of Powers," in *Classics of Public Administration*, 3rd ed., Jay M. Shafritz and Albert C. Hyde, eds. (Pacific Grove, CA: Brooks/Cole Publishing, 1992), pp. 510–522.

46. Frank Goodenow, quoted in ibid., p. 514.

47. Ibid., p. 515.

48. Ibid., p. 514.

49. Ibid., p. 516.

50. Of course Marx's prognostication of a withering away of the state ended up being turned on its head in reality.

51. Baier, op. cit., p. 287.

CHAPTER 10

Using a Decisionmaking Process: Reasoned Choice Models (Level 1)

So far the discussion has focused on cultural values—basic assumptions (Level 4 values) and beliefs (Level 3 values)—and selection of decision processes (Level 2 values). This chapter examines the values actually used in specific decisions (Level 1 values) and the type of rationality most common to public administration—reasoned choice. Just as cultural values emphasize the role and needs of the larger group over the long term, decisions emphasize the role and needs of the individual or specific group at a single moment. And just as cultural values emphasize long-term group survival, decisions tend to emphasize short-term success of individuals and specific groups within a culture. Thus the abstract and largely internalized sensibility established through cultural values (basic assumptions and beliefs) must be made concrete and external through the choices (patterns of behavior and individual actions) actually made in the decisionmaking process. In other words, individual decisions (always made in concrete contexts) tend to reflect the value conflicts and competition of daily life.

The key word in this discussion, *decision,* actually has two meanings. First, a decision is a judgment or conclusion reached or given. This definition emphasizes the *choice,* the selection of a single option based on a variety of factors. Logically, if there are no options, there is no decisionmaking. Further, once there are a number of options, the values inherent in the options will influence the decisionmaker's selection. The more the options vary, the greater will be the role of those values. While most decisions involve values within the appropriate (norm-approved) cultural frameworks, decisions can also include violating cultural norms. Stealing is not culturally approved, but it occurs because some decisionmakers' choices emphasize personal gain even at the cost of possible social opprobrium. In fact, some of the most difficult decisions involve alternatives that, from the decisionmaker's perspective, all violate at least one major cultural norm. Public administrators are frequently expected to obey laws that they consider good in general but that have unfair consequences on a few, or to obey laws that they consider unfair or immoral in general. Thus the particularly important value of following the law comes in conflict with personal assessments of the public interest or private notions of morality.

The second definition of a *decision* is that it is the act of making up one's mind. This definition emphasizes that decisionmaking is a process. While discussions of decisionmaking often focus on one element, the choice, it actually has many elements. The model examined later in this chapter breaks decisionmaking into six steps. Values affect each of the six steps in the decisionmaking process, not just the choice itself.

Characteristics of Values in Practical Decisions

Values in practical decisionmaking—individual actions and patterns of behavior—tend to emphasize those *values that can lead to a satisfying or successful conclusion*, given the values that are competing.[1] For example, a police officer is taking part in a drug bust and must decide whether to fire his gun in a highly dangerous situation. He must consider (in just a fraction of a second in this decisionmaking scenario) such factors as level of threat, accuracy of visual perception (since part of the scene may be obscured), danger to self, danger to others, options other than firing (such as taking cover), where to fire, how long to wait to fire, and so on. Through extensive peace officer training, the values in this scene should have been carefully rehearsed so that almost instantaneous decisionmaking can occur. In this situation, with criminal apprehension as the goal, the emphasized values would probably include maximizing officer safety, least possible use of deadly force, and due process rights. However, a value important in other settings, such as courtesy, might be deemphasized as not furthering the technical objective.

Values in practical decisionmaking also tend to emphasize the *range of allowable values in the cultural values framework*. In the drug-bust scenario, the officer may know that the suspects are armed and suspected of a crime in which other officers were killed. Although he may personally prefer to enter the scene shooting, he will be intensely aware that this is not an appropriate law enforcement action since it violates the technical application of the value of least possible use of deadly force. His decisionmaking will therefore, tend to focus on what is culturally allowable.

Values in practical decisionmaking have a third emphasis: the *consequences of deemphasizing or violating certain cultural values* (such as basic assumptions) *in order to emphasize other values* (such as beliefs reflecting personal preferences). This tendency is especially strong when the violated values are strongly supported by a culture and interpreted as ethical minimums. Although individuals (and groups) decide to violate ethical norms all the time for all types of reasons, cultural sanctions (and rewards) ensure that cultural or higher-level values have at least been considered. For example, the officer in the drug bust may have known one of the officers who was killed and decide to violate the value of using the least possible deadly force. In this case he is aware of the possible sanctions for exceeding a highly restrictive technical standard representing a constitutional value, but he may for personal reasons decide to take the risk of detection and censure.[2]

Strengths and Weaknesses of Values in Practical Decisionmaking

An assessment of the values in practical decisionmaking is a useful analytic exercise but must be considered a highly relative one. One of the key strengths of values in practical decisionmaking is that they tend to be focused and sensible. The values considered are only those that pertain to the specific case. If all cultural values had to be consciously considered in every decision, then few decisions would ever be made. Another strength of the values in decisionmaking, which ultimately blend higher-level values with more immediate lower-level values, is that they are tested and tempered by the reality of the situation rather than by vague prescriptions propagated in cultural values. While cultural values have the wisdom of time and long experience, practical decision values have the prudence of concrete circumstances and immediacy. If decisionmaking processes consistently contradict cultural values over a significant period of time, the cultural values themselves are likely to be transformed.

Values in practical decisionmaking have a number of common weaknesses; three are particularly important for this discussion:

1. Important values are often obscured or overlooked during decisionmaking. The reason may be lack of attention to the importance of the decision, lack of time to consider the values fully, lack of clarity about the values that apply (perhaps due to lack of training or education), a change in the value priority of the culture, emotional attachment to certain value clusters, and so on.

2. Because the values in practical decisionmaking are focused on a specific application, values may lose cohesion with those in other decisions. A series of decisions can become disjointed or even contradictory because, over time, the cultural values have been stretched excessively in different directions for different situations. Predictability, control, and integrity can all suffer as a consequence.

3. Different decisionmaking models incorporate values in divergent ways, allowing for subtle but highly significant value differences.

An Example of Decisionmaking and Values in the Public Sector

An example of how decisionmaking and values filter into even the most straightforward public sector task is a useful prelude to considering decisionmaking models in one type of rationality.

The public sector has been responsible for the building and maintenance of tens of thousands of bridges. Almost all bridges are built with public funds, using public authority, and based on public trust. Each time a bridge is built, technical experts in public administration recommend plans based on a variety of criteria. These plans are approved by other public administrators. Not infrequently, the bridges have received prior legislative approval as a part of a larger transportation system or as a part of a legislative decision package that gave few details other than cost. Thus, other public administrators often select the final bridge plan that is executed. In other words, other than the "build/do not build" decision, all other decisionmaking is left up to public administrators.

What are some of the decisions that are made and whom might they affect? One decision might be to construct sidewalks and bike paths. This will affect local residents and bikers, and also general taxpayers, who will have to cover the increased cost. Other decisions will focus on structure and design. For example, a single-span bridge without supports provides greater safety for drivers using arterial underpasses, but at what expense to taxpayers? Whether the bridge is built to stand for 50 years or 500 years affects future generations. To what degree should beauty be considered? For example, when is an angular, steel-girdered bridge sufficient, and when is an elegant, stone-faced bridge appropriate? Sometimes beauty doesn't involve cost at all, but is simply a matter of taste. Should the bridge use a classic, traditional, or avant garde style? Should it be painted gray or brown? As those who maintain San Francisco's Golden Gate Bridge can attest, even the color of a bridge can be of great importance to many people.

Implicit in these questions is that most substantial decisions involve a variety of types of important subdecisions, each with a variety of value assumptions. Various layers of administrative recommendations and approval of those recommendations may make the authoritative policy selection a mere formality in all but rare cases. Illusions of anesthetic technical selection based on efficiency and effectiveness break down under scrutiny because even these classic administrative values are open to wide interpretation. If safer bridge construction can save an estimated one or two lives over 20 years at a cost of $5000, is it worth it? The decision will probably be yes. What if the extra cost is $1 million? Probably not, but where is the cutoff point? Who decides how much local residents or communities should be appeased in incorporating upgrades when a much broader tax base is paying the bill? What value should be given to future generations, and what value be given to poorly represented groups (such as pedestrians)? Should bridge aesthetics be a factor; and if so, how much and when? Who decides and how do they decide which of the innumerable technical decisions will be highlighted for policymakers who are often overwhelmed by macrolevel decisions alone?[3]

Decisionmaking Models

In practice, decisions are made using different assumptions about how to make choices. Therefore, a single decisionmaking model does not apply equally well to all situations. In reality, one of the most common decisions a public administrator makes is which decisionmaking model to apply to which decision.[4] The following discussion identifies three such models—instinctive, simple, and (rigorous) reasoned choice—and then addresses some of the additional factors significant in group and national decisionmaking situations.

The less sophisticated decisionmaking models (instinctive and simple) share an absence of critical analysis, which would be of little use because most of the decisions made with the help of these models are simple or routine. In these elementary cases, administrators cannot analyze each routine afresh each time they act. However, most problems and new issues involve complexities that make unsophisticated approaches highly vulnerable to error and personal bias. Rational decisionmaking models do take more time and resources to practice, but they are usually worth the effort for decisions about nontrivial problems or issues.

Instinctive Models

An instinctive model assumes that the correct decision is obvious or that the decisionmaker has already informally processed the information and analysis is unnecessary. Reordering supplies and following applicable laws and organizational rules generally do not need critical analysis because the choice is so clearly known at the outset and the values affecting the decisionmaking are clear, aligned, and stable. Most ethical contexts actually use an instinctive model. Employees rarely need to consider whether or not to lie, steal, or break laws. When employees say that they, "simply know right from wrong," generally implying a moral upbringing or long-time organizational indoctrination, they are asserting an instinctive model. The benefit of using an instinctive model is that it is efficient and easy, and it relies on the instinctive competence of experienced employees. Ultimately, instinctive models allow scarce time and resources to be directed at problems and more complex issues.

But sometimes instinctive decisionmaking is used when a more rigorous model would be more appropriate. If the correct choice is not widely accepted as an operational given, or the values to be used in making the decision are not clear, aligned, or stable, a more rigorous decisionmaking model is needed. For example, when an office buys a new set of personal computers and the manager decides to buy a certain brand simply because he uses that brand at home (it is the only one he is familiar with and "it works just fine"), the manager is using an instinctive approach to decisionmaking. It is inappropriate because the manager did not clarify and prioritize the values of the various users (including his own) and did not identify the alternatives prior to making a significant choice.

Simple Models

Simple models generally apply a few tests in the decisionmaking process. Like instinctive models, simple models work in decisionmaking environments in which the values are clear, aligned, and stable. Simple models usually work best when a class of decisions has been identified and analyzed in the past and found to have only a few key differentiating factors. Bureaucratic decisionmaking often uses simple models and sometimes reduces complex decisions to a series of simple decisions, as in the following:

- Provide administrative allowances based on rank.
- Use a set hiring protocol (a complex process with a series of simple decisions) except under emergency conditions in which a condensed protocol may be used.
- A warning or a citation (and fine) may be selected by an inspector within a given range of violation, based on the inspector's sense of the violator's intent and past practice.

Even some relatively complex problems use simple decisionmaking models. Many ethical situations function satisfactorily using a simple decisionmaking model. Minor conflicts of interest might routinely lead to disclosure and/or recusal, depending on circumstances. Employee peccadilloes might be handled by convenient rules of thumb.

Simple decisionmaking models generally do not work well when the values environment is not clear, aligned, and stable, or the decisionmaking choices have changed. Perhaps, for example, a new product has come out on the market; or an organization's hiring practices are suboptimal and not identifying the best candidates; or inspectors' common practices appear arbitrary and capricious to regulatory recipients; or a medical protocol has come under attack so that doctors and patients need to weigh alternatives and consider the values and uncertainties more rigorously.

When public administrators say that they imagine how a decision would look in tomorrow's paper, they may be asserting a simple decision making model using appearance and disclosure as the key tests. As handy as these two criteria are in resolving many ethical dilemmas, there are certainly cases in which neither of these principles can be given priority.[5] Consider the workers in child protection services who frequently handle cases that require confidentiality and that are so complex as to be easily (and frequently) misunderstood by the media. These workers must have the courage to act in ways that are legally and ethically appropriate, despite how they suspect their actions will look in the next day's paper. In such cases, public administrators may recommend that decisionmakers be prepared for extreme scrutiny, but this concern for appearances will be only one criterion for decisions. The rigorous reasoned choice decisionmaking model (described below) is actually implied in this and similar instances.

Reasoned Choice Decisionmaking Models

The classic reasoned choice decisionmaking model has six stages: problem or issue identification, goal identification, generation of alternatives, choice, implementation, and evaluation. A fully rational model requires comprehensive analysis of each stage to achieve certainty that all relevant information has been gathered, analyzed, and prioritized. Desirable as a fully rational model might seem at first blush, it can be very time consuming and expensive, and it is often impossible to attain. For example, when a fully rational model is applied to vague problems, such as recidivism, no action is possible. The problem and goal identification stages would never be completed due not only to a lack of complete information about the rates and circumstances of relapses and the types of offenders but also to a lack of social consensus about the goals to be achieved. Similarly, if a new process, such as a new performance appraisal system, is being implemented, comprehensive generation of alternatives might mean surveying tens of thousands of organizations to identify all possible alternatives and their strengths and weaknesses. In practice, a limited or bounded rationality is generally used.[6] Bounded rationality means that, although the full decisionmaking process is used, complete information or absolute consensus is not necessary. The decisionmakers must then decide what constitutes sufficient information and consensus on a case-by-case basis.

Problem or Issue Identification

This first stage in the reasoned choice model is represented in terms of yes/no, critical/not critical, or investigate/don't investigate dichotomies. When an issue is relatively simple or technical, this stage can be relatively straightforward. Something needs to be done because the equipment is broken, a position has become vacant, or the child protective services system has been notified of the death of a child in foster care.

A seemingly simple case may illustrate the complexity of problem identification for the public manager. A park manager realizes that at any given time there is a significant amount of litter in the park she maintains. She has received numerous complaints about its unsightliness, despite the resources already devoted to litter abatement. First, she must decide whether she even perceives this to be a significant problem. She may rely on her experience and use an informal mental calculus of obvious factors. Or she may seek the advice of a group of park rangers on whether the litter is excessive and should be considered a problem. Or she may have a professional assessment of the level of litter and a comprehensive ranking of the litter level of the park she manages relative to others. No matter what technical assistance she receives, however, ultimately she must decide what value she places on aesthetics, cost, customer complaints, and other concerns. She must make the decision about whether litter is truly a "problem" relative to her resources and other problems, which may include funding cuts, high employee turnover, park expansion, facilities overload, and physical plant deterioration.

Goal Identification

Goal identification can also be fairly straightforward, as when the goal is either fixing or replacing a broken tool, filling a vacant position or distributing its work, or following a routine investigation protocol or supplementing it. Although goal identification can be seen as a refinement of problem identification by defining purpose, it can also be seen as a preparation for the generation of alternatives by narrowing the purpose.

In the case of the park manager, she must identify the goal of her litter abatement initiative after she has decided that it is a significant problem to address. Is her goal technology improvement, punishment, education, or a combination of these? That is, how does she consider the problem? As a dearth of litter collectors roaming the park? An insufficient number of receptacles? A lax public, whose slovenliness needs to be reprimanded (negative behavior modification)? Or an uninformed public that needs to be educated (positive behavior modification)? These are dramatically different goals, and they will generate different alternatives.

Goal identification becomes more critical as resources become more constrained, thus limiting the number of alternatives that will be chosen. Research is often useful for goal identification. Are the receptacles sparsely placed, often full, or inaccessible? Do youngsters blithely throw litter out of cars in defiance of posted rules? To what degree can the public become part of the positive solution (through education) rather than the problem? If goal identification is unrealistic, the park manager may frustrate park patrons by encouraging them to use overflowing trash containers, or she may increase the number of receptacles and their collection schedule but find that more containers remain empty while the public's penchant for littering remains constant.

Generating Alternatives

Goal identification sharpens the focus of where to look, but generating alternative solutions fans out the range of possible solutions. Should the broken tool be replaced with an identical product or with a substitute with different features and costs? Should antilittering education be through park signs, TV advertising, or notices on the backs of park tickets and information handouts?

Choice

The selection of one or more alternatives is the heart of the decision-making process. Here the decisionmaker's values play an especially important role in choice. In a hiring decision, for example, the chosen candidate is likely to be a combination of the value the decisionmaker places on technical education, technical experience, professional demeanor, and cost considerations. Does the organization want a less expensive candidate, whom it will groom and train, or a more experienced but also more costly professional? Does the park manager want to attempt a regional educational campaign with other park managers, using TV advertising, or to conduct a campaign limited to her own park, using billboards and signs? Is the problem important enough to justify multiple goals and strategies?

Implementation

The quality of implementation can be as important as the choice itself. Choice generally leads to numerous technical subdecisions. The success of the job candidate can have as much to do with his or her subsequent training and support as with the individual's original qualifications. Careful selection is unlikely to overcome poor organizational indoctrination and weak institutional support systems. In the public sector, many macrolevel choices are stipulated by the policy level, and many midlevel implementation choices are similarly noted in the authorizing legislation. Nonetheless, values of the implementing administrators can either foster and improve the legislation or mitigate and partially ignore it.

Evaluation

Whether evaluation occurs at all is a value. Furthermore, how evaluation is done represents numerous, usually silent, values. Is the evaluation on-going or occasional, full or partial, sensitive or insensitive to feedback from front-line workers, inclusive or exclusive of the actual program recipients, likely or unlikely to cause change if the evaluation provides recommendations? Ideally, evaluation provides an opportunity to assess the value decisions made in all the other stages and provide course corrections, identify errors, clarify inconsistencies, and so on. For example, if the park manager discovers that the level of litter has dropped significantly in the annual park-litter benchmark comparison, she probably will be satisfied that her decisions were effective.

A Contingency Approach

A fully rational decisionmaking model like the one just described is clearly the most rigorous. But whether a full or bounded rational model is used, or even a simple or intuitive model, is based largely on the situation or contingency. Organizations frequently use inappropriate models. A fully rational model may be ridiculous for a mundane operational decision. In highly bureaucratic public agencies, a minor purchase can need interminable justification, and minor actions may be subjected to a rigorous decisionmaking matrix and be comprehensively analyzed beyond their worth. Yet such organizational dysfunctionalism may also occur because employees rely excessively on intuitive or simple decisionmaking models when more comprehensive rational models are actually called for, but bureaucratic procedures do not require them. The quality management movement, which preaches organizational decentralization and procedural streamlining while stressing the teaching of decisionmaking skills and analytic techniques to front-line workers and supervisors is keenly aware of the problem of devolving responsibility with adequate decisionmaking training. Simply decentralizing decisionmaking is as likely as not to lower the quality of the decisions if training does not occur. Finally, it should be noted that even the more comprehensive reasoned choice decisionmaking strategies pay little attention to the learning that inevitably occurs during large projects. As Robert Dahl points out, even limited rationality models should make use of feedback and should consider experimentation or "small-scale tryouts."[7] Decisionmaking, in many cases, is better conceived as an iterative, rather than a linear, process.

Reasoned Choice Decisionmaking at Other Levels

Groups and nations, as well as individuals, make reasoned choice decisions as aggregations of individuals. Decisionmaking becomes more complex as it becomes more embedded in group process.

At the Agency Level

Agency decisionmaking in the public sector has long been noted for its incrementalist[8] and status quo bias.[9]

Incrementalism is a bias toward small increases in funding and resources, all other factors being equal. It was especially prevalent during the 35 years following World War II, when incrementalist expectations permeated all aspects of American life. This bias suggests that agencies ultimately want more resources (pay, facilities, and so on) to do the current job, as well as more resources to do additional jobs (mission creep). Bureaucratic self-interests fit nicely with politicians' preference to promise more, according to this critique.[10] Yet with the pressures that government began to experience in the early 1980s and that have been expanding in the 1990s, incrementalism seems to be less of a problem. Rather, public agencies' bias for the status quo seems to have become a more central issue for contemporary critiques and remedies.

The second bias—status quo bias—often results from overidentification with the program and its goals, bureaucratic self-interests and ownership, cooption by interest groups, and a diminished capacity to envision alternative use of resources. At its worst, a status quo bias is the result of values displacement; the more general public interest values have been replaced by local and particular values so that the original goal attainment has become secondary to bureaucratic and client interests. This can best be seen when an agency has successfully achieved its short-term mission but its staff and clients fight vigorously to retain their jobs and benefits. In times of great rescissions, those who can maintain the status quo are often perceived to be the "winners." However, at its best a status quo bias can also represent a disincentive to make hasty or radical choices, especially with the public welfare at stake. This latter perspective is not without merit. During periods of radical policy shifts and economic downsizing, such as the one now in effect, the status quo bias will be substantially deemphasized.

At the Policy Level

Decisionmaking at the policy level is more complex still, incorporating at different times all the models discussed, from instinctive (nonanalytic) to full rationality models, as well as incrementalist and status quo tendencies. Yet at this level, decisionmaking is liable to further distortions since the stakes in Lasswell's famous dictum describing politics—who gets what, where, and how—become so intense. In the phenomenon known as special interest group pluralism, those whose interests are at stake put extreme pressure on the weakest elements in the legislative process to achieve their particular wants. This means that needs and wants of subsets of the population can take precedence over the common or future good. Thus, if the public at large is easily manipulated, a special interest group might use advertising to stimulate constituent pressure on legislators. If the interest base is too small to use advertising as an effective method, the relevant committee chairperson might be the target of pressure and manipulation. At its best, special interests cancel one another out and form the basis for a dynamic competitive legislative system. At its worst, interest group pluralism can lead to all powerful players winning major concessions at the public expense, with weak players and the long-term common good being squeezed out. For example, because rampant special interest pluralism can lead to reduced public abilities to foster savings and investment, the long-term ramifications can be serious.

Values are critical in reasoned choice decisionmaking at the agency and policy levels. For example, at the agency level, the interests of executives, employees, and operations are legitimate values, but they are also factors that easily become overweening and subsequently illegitimate. At the policy level, values *are* the central issue—so much so that the values in decisions are sometimes made on almost entirely emotional and subjective appeals. Because values are ultimately subjective and nonrational, emotional appeals are *not,* of themselves, necessarily inappropriate. However, emotional appeals are often used with logical manipulation and even distortion. In other words, politicians (and others) sometimes campaign for legislation for a select group as if it were in their behalf, when the substance of the legislation actually reduces or regulates the interests of that group. This "I'm-doing-it-for-your-own-good" approach can be both purposely confusing and disingenuous to the values debate.[11]

In sum, cultural values tend to provide sets of broad generic responses across classes of cases. However, the specific values are actually decided one case at a time through various decisionmaking processes. The decisionmaking process analyzed here was reasoned choice, broken out as a number of models and variants. When instinctive and simple decisionmaking models are used, generic norms are usually being efficiently followed. When a fully rational decisionmaking model is used, it allows a greater opportunity for value identification and conscious prioritization. Ultimately, decisionmaking models cannot be evaluated except as a function of their circumstances and the purpose to be achieved. Public bureaucracies in the last half century have been characterized by the status quo bias and the incrementalist bias, which add complexity to reasoned choice decisionmaking. Of course, multitudes of specific cases in turn establish patterns and beliefs and, ultimately, even shape the basic assumptions underlying cultures. See Figure 10.1 for a representation of the role of reasoned choice decisionmaking in the overall cultural framework and for a synopsis of the discussions in Part III.

The Special Nature of Decisionmaking in American Public Administration

American public administration has had special concerns about the nature of decisionmaking that trace back to the founding of the field. As noted earlier in this text, Woodrow Wilson in 1887 presented one ideal model of administrative decisionmaking, which subsequently came to be called the politics-administration dichotomy. As an ideal model it holds that policy decisions should be reserved exclusively for elected politicians and their elected appointees (political bureaucrats). Policy decisions are those initiating significant action and in which social value choices need to be made. Administrators are limited to "value-free" decisions, that is, those issues involving only technical aspects such as efficiency and effectiveness. Putting the accuracy of the model aside, it captures the idea that the American political system idealizes comprehensive political control over its policy process.[12] Compared with stystems in some other nations, there is a good deal of truth to this. A federal state allowed the political system to handle decisions at various levels, sublocal (as in special districts) through the national. Unlike parliamentary systems in which the party in power both initiates and executes policy, the American system generally divides the legislative and executive functions more fully. Therefore, as an ideal, nonpolitical career administrators would make no substantive policy decisions.

As an exact description of reality, however, the politics-administration dichotomy has long since been discarded as inaccurate and naive.[13] Administrators affect the policymaking process at every decisionmaking stage, often deciding which issues to consider, what goals to pursue,

FIGURE 10.1

The Four Levels as Determinants of Action in Public Administration:
A Synopsis of the Four Levels of Values Discussed in Part II

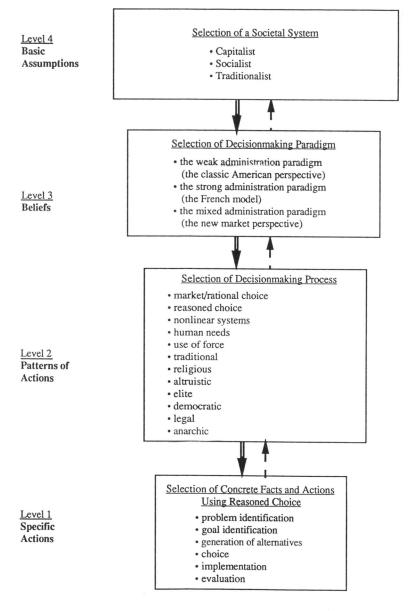

Level 4
**Basic
Assumptions**

Selection of a Societal System

• Capitalist
• Socialist
• Traditionalist

Level 3
Beliefs

Selection of Decisionmaking Paradigm

• the weak administration paradigm
  (the classic American perspective)
• the strong administration paradigm
  (the French model)
• the mixed administration paradigm
  (the new market perspective)

Level 2
**Patterns of
Actions**

Selection of Decisionmaking Process

• market/rational choice
• reasoned choice
• nonlinear systems
• human needs
• use of force
• traditional
• religious
• altruistic
• elite
• democratic
• legal
• anarchic

Level 1
**Specific
Actions**

Selection of Concrete Facts and Actions
Using Reasoned Choice

• problem identification
• goal identification
• generation of alternatives
• choice
• implementation
• evaluation

which alternatives to recommend, and which choice to select. They also have traditional discretion relating to implementation and evaluation. In reality, public administrators make many important choices either because the macrolevel policy is so broad that midlevel administrative decisions are actually policies themselves, or difficult policy choices are delegated to administrators under the guise of technical expertise.[14]

Two technical issues have complicated the simplistic politics-administration dichotomy. First, how are policy decisions differentiated from technical decisions? At the extremes, policy and technical decisions are easy to segregate into neat categories. The decisions that a county will purchase a building and will refurbish it for county use are policy decisions; the actual plans for the refitting are technical and administrative. The board of supervisors generally has the right to review the plans but in reality will probably only scrutinize the price tag. Yet it is not uncommon for a strong county manager to place only one serious option before the board. In turn, the county manager may be influenced largely by a strong planning or operational department in charge of the project. In other words, powerful administrative actors often influence important decisions.

A second technical complication with the politics-administration dichotomy is the notion of a "neutral" value motivating "technical" decisions. In an earlier period, some values, such as efficiency, were considered relatively neutral, but even they are now displaced from that ideal category. Efficiency frequently competes with other important values (which are notoriously inefficient) such as due process, safety, customization, and aesthetic appeal. Even the subcomponent values of efficiency (as it is commonly construed)—least cost and rapid competent service—can compete with the more general value. To return to the bridge example mentioned earlier in this chapter, is it most "efficient" to build extra traffic lanes that will not really be needed for another 20 years, when the state budget is tight now? Is it most efficient to restrict pedestrians to one side, making them cross the street for the 80-year life of the bridge? Is it most efficient to steer the contract to the most reputable local builder or to open the bidding as widely as possible, knowing that the least-cost bid will probably go to an out-of-state contractor who will not have the same level of professional integrity? Efficiency, like all other guides for action, is rich with values, no matter how it is defined.[15] As noted repeatedly in this text, *the challenge for administrators is not to reach "value-free" decisions but to reach decisions with the values explicitly identified and analyzed.*[16]

Currently the politics-administration debate has found new life, although the arguments have shifted to a prescriptive, rather than a descriptive, mode. Three major positions can be identified: those who believe there is excessive administrative discretion; those who argue that there is insufficient discretion; and those who contend that current levels of administrative discretion are appropriate.

Excessive Discretion

Those who argue that there is currently an excess of administrative discretion (or at least a threat of it) tend to focus on the political systems level similar to the original politics-administration dichotomy ideal. One of the best-known proponents of this position is Theodore Lowi who claims that legislation since the New Deal has increasingly become overly ambitious and vague.[17] Such legislation has three deleterious effects:

- It allows special interests to burrow into the policy process without requisite countervailing forces.
- It has a propensity to fail because of unclear and legalistic goals.
- It invites public administrators to be key actors (inappropriately) and to become politicized.

In other words, excessive administrative discretion is as much a symptom of a poorly functioning political system as it is a problem in its own right. Although Lowi's position is more extreme than that of most practitioners and academicians, the classic school of thought generally preaches administrative restraint and careful political deference, even when political expediency seems contrary to administrative wisdom.

Insufficient Discretion

At the other end of the spectrum are those who believe that administrative discretion is too limited. This perspective tends to focus on organizational architecture (rather than systems architecture). A popular proponent of this position is Philip Howard, who argues a case opposite that of Lowi.[18] Howard asserts that current legislation is far too detailed and that it not only reduces administrative discretion but also seriously limits administrative flexibility, creativity, customization, and, ultimately, thinking. From his perspective, administrators are locked into tight, rule-bound regimens that often produce idiotic results.[19] His arguments are sympathetic with those advocating quality management systems, which emphasize procedural simplification and decision-making devolution. An even more extreme position is implied by the administrative entrepreneurial school, which advocates modest policy activism for administrators, usually along with radically different controls on administrative discretion.

Moderate Discretion

Most practitioners and academicians take a moderate position. Rather than focusing on unwieldy legislative agendas and overarching administrative reforms, moderates tend to focus on the successes achieved with current levels of administrative discretion. Charles Goodsell's comments typify this moderate position:

> Have we noticed that the Social Security Administration conducts the largest income redistribution system the world has ever seen, and very efficiently at that? Or that the National Institutes of Health is the most important health research enterprise and sponsor in the world? Have we noticed that our air and water are appreciably cleaner than a few decades ago, that our highways are much safer than they used to be, and that over the past quarter century the federal government's productivity has gone up 30 percent? Do we remember how smoothly Desert Storm was conducted, or how brilliantly the Hubble Telescope was fixed (its wobble having been caused by private enterprise), or how sensitively the Oklahoma City bombing victims were treated?[20]

This school of thought also asserts that senior managers and careerists have a larger role due to their experience and position.[21]

In sum, as administrative discretion expands, so, too, do the opportunities for the values that administrators prefer, for good and ill. While a perfect separation between policy decisions and technical administrative discretion has long since been discredited as a descriptive reality, the debate about the appropriate degree of administrative discretion continues, recently with renewed enthusiasm and more polarized positions. This debate encompasses divergent notions about public administrators as members of various communities of values. That is, the long-term resolution of this debate about administrative discretion will likely reshape public administrators' cultural values as members of a political-legal system, operational managers of organizations, technical experts, virtue- and happiness-seeking individuals, and even as especially well-informed members of the public (interest).

Conclusion

I conclude by reintegrating our two values perspectives: cultural values and operational decisionmaking values. Cultural values are distinguished by being relatively stable and long-term and by setting numerous fundamental priorities that affect the good of larger collectivities. Public administration cultural values draw from many other cultures that coexist in society: the American political legal culture, the various organizational cultures, diverse professional communities from which public administration draws (such as lawyers) and which it fosters (such as peace officers), the specific cultural heritage of individual members of the public sector, and the national community that defines the public interest of which we are all part. Public administration cultural values are an overlapping blend of these value sets.

Yet cultures are exhibited through practical decisions that are discrete, timely, and biased toward the values of individuals and smaller collectivities. Thus if cultural values reinforce long-term social needs, practical decisional values emphasize equally important shorter-term individual and group needs. Individuals will generally strive to achieve cultural expectations because of a variety of sanctions and rewards built into systems of behavior. If the sanctions and rewards wane, or new sanctions and rewards emerge over time, the culture, too, will change, but not quickly.[22]

Further, public administration decisionmaking has a special schizophrenic perspective on decisionmaking. In the classic articulation it seems to assert that public administrators should be seen but not make decisions, while it is generally acknowledged that public administrators do make numerous operational and substantive decisions, and even affect major policy decisions in important ways. The debate continues to rage about the best role or even the best value priorities for public administrators.

I also conclude where I began: by noting the unusual amount of macrolevel change transpiring. Public administration is at the end of one era and the beginning of a new one. Its contributing culture is undergoing epochal changes as the New Deal and post–New Deal (the Great Society) eras give way to new values. The new policy environment, the radical management changes, the public groping for a new national consensus and identity, the expansion of professionalism, and the millions of individuals desperately redefining their pursuit of happiness are all part of the metamorphosis. This study of values has an especially important purpose today. Without an understanding of the broad cultural values that serve as a stable framework of both beliefs and actions, as well as the significance of the decisions that animate daily actions, public administrators cannot claim to be truly masters of their trade in this or any age.

Notes

1. James Bowman notes that: "the quest for 'right' and 'good' bases for decisions is a conscious attempt to reconcile the claims of competing values," in *Quality Management Today,* Jonathan West, ed. (Washington, DC: ICMA, 1995), p. 68.

2. For a discussion of ethics and practical decisionmaking, see Mary Guy, *Ethical Decisionmaking in the Workplace* (Westport, CT: Quorum, 1990).

3. Although administrative discretion has been endlessly discussed, I particularly like John Rohr's description of it: "Thus by 'administrative discretion' I mean the discretionary activity of bureaucrats in which they advise, report, respond, initiate, inform, question, caution, complain, encourage, rebuke, promote, retard, and mediate in a way that has an impact on what eventually emerges as 'agency policy.'" *To Run a Constitution: The Legitimacy of the Administrative State* (Lawrence: University of Kansas Press, 1986), p. 36. See also Donald P. Warwick on an excellent discussion of types of administrative discretion: "The Ethics of Administrative Discretion" in *Public Duties: The Moral Duties of Government Officials,* Joel Fleishman, Lance Liebman, and Mark Moore, eds. (Cambridge, MA: Harvard University Press, 1981).

4. Although this contingency perspective is not as satisfying to rationalists or those desirous of simple answers, it more accurately describes the real world of decisionmaking than does a single model. In another sense, the popular notion of a bounded rationality model—that decisionmakers will use rationality only to the degree that they have the resources to do so—can be seen as expansive (or retractable) as resources and interests allow. Although bounded rationality in this usage gains in simple elegance and parallels the perspective used here, its descriptive power for most routine reflexive and automatic decisionmaking is both weak and slightly biased (implying that instinctive and simple decisionmaking is necessarily inferior).

5. As a single test, I believe the "imagine-this-in-the-newspaper" analysis is one of the best because disclosure is one of the most powerful curbs on inappropriate behavior. However, I cringe when it is offered as the ethical golden rule for all situations, because frequently it does not apply at all, or it gives short shrift to other values more important than disclosure and appearances. For a case in point, see the example in the text.

6. Herbert A. Simon, *Administrative Behavior: A Study of Decision-Making Processes in Administrative Organizations,* 3rd ed. (New York: Free Press, 1976).

7. Robert A. Dahl, *Modern Political Analysis,* 5th ed. (Englewood Cliffs, NJ: Prentice-Hall, 1991), pp. 140–42.

8. Charles E. Lindblom, "The Science of Muddling Through," *Public Administration Review* 19 (Spring 1959), pp. 79–88.

9. James G. March and Herbert A. Simon, *Organizations* (New York: John Wiley, 1958), p. 38; Michael Crozier, *The Bureaucratic Phenomenon* (Chicago: University of Chicago Press, 1964), pp. 220–224.

10. W. A. Niskanen, *Bureaucracy and Representative Government* (Chicago: Aldine, 1971).

11. Disingenuous public dialogue is one of the most important points of the postmodern school. Fox and Miller's text, *Postmodern Public Administration: Toward Discourse,* extensively discusses the growing gap between words and deeds (see their Chapter 3) and the need for authentic discourse (see their Chapters 5 and 6).

12. For a discussion about how elected and appointed officials feel about this concept, see Donald Warwick, *Theory of Public Bureaucracy* (Cambridge, MA: Harvard University Press, 1975).

13. For a particularly good and balanced discussion, see Dwight Waldo, "Public Administration in a Time of Revolution," *Public Administration Review* 28, no. 4 (July/August 1968).

14. Donald Warwick (op. cit., p. 93) noted some time ago that "recent empirical studies show that far from being cogs in an administrative machine, public officials exercise vast discretion in formulating and implementing public policies." A more recent commentator noted, "Career executives are more than mere executors of public policies formulated by elected officials; they participate actively in both formulating and implementing public policy." Larry Terry, *Leadership of Public Bureaucracies: The Administrator As Conservator* (Thousand Oaks, CA: Sage, 1995), p. 12.

15. Louis Gawthrop notes that "many public administrators have sought to link their commitment of service to the amoral pretense of detached objectivity, neutral competence, and dispassionate rationality". See "In the Service of Democracy," *International Journal of Public Administration* 17, no. 12 (1994), p. 2221.

16. In a similar vein, Kathryn Denhardt notes, "Public administration is a value-laden enterprise demanding of its members the exercise of moral judgment." "Character Ethics and the Transformation of Governance," *International Journal of Public Administration* 19, no. 12 (1994), p. 2169.

17. See Theodore Lowi, *The End of the Liberalism* (1969 and revised in 1979) and *The End of the Republican Era* (1995).

18. Philip Howard, *The Death of Common Sense* (New York: Random House, 1994).

19. A few of Howard's (ibid.) more acerbic comments will give the flavor of his critique: "Modern law tells us our duty is only to comply, not to accomplish" (p. 174); "Understanding of the situation has been replaced by legal absolutism" (p. 174); and "Modern law has changed its role from useful tool to brainless tyrant" (p. 175).

20. Charles Goodsell, "Public Administration As Republican Ally," *Public Administration Review* 55, no. 5 (September/October 1995), p. 480.

21. For example, Mark Lilla reflects this position: "As he moves higher in the administrative or Congressional bureaucracies, the public official must be more statesman than mere functionary." "Ethos, 'Ethics,' and Public Service," *Public Interest* 63 (Spring 1981), p. 16.

22. Due to the length of the chapter, I omitted an interesting discussion about decisions affecting culture. They do, of course, as suggested here in the text. Most of the time discrete actions do not have a *significant* impact on culture because there are millions and millions of decisions being made and the effect of any one decision is trivial. However, it is possible for important single decisions to affect a culture. The most interesting case for the political-administrative world is probably the decisions of the Supreme Court. For example, landmark decisions, while reflecting a national mood, have profoundly shaped race relations to a significant degree in this country. However, the resiliency of cultural values is normally more than a match for single decisions, much to the chagrin of impatient executives who sometimes expect their mandates and plans to change a national or organizational culture. In the United States the Constitution has a profound effect on national culture and public administration culture. Changes in the constitution rarely have the same effect in other countries (in terms of value changes). For example, France has had four republics and two empires since Napoleon set up the powerful French administrative state. Those seemingly radical changes have had relatively little impact on French bureaucracy, whose culture is almost impervious to these national political reorganizations.

PART IV

Shaping and Managing Values to Ensure Coherence and Legitimacy

As important as understanding the values underlying decisions is, understanding alone is not enough for public administrators who, as implementors, are actors. Decisions about selecting the "best" values must be made within specific contexts, and these values must be encouraged by organizations and their leaders so that they are either widely maintained or adopted. Chapter 11 looks at the problems of selecting values, finding consensus, and educating about legitimate values. Although Chapter 11 looks at the use of incentives and disincentives in supporting value systems, Chapter 12 takes up the issue more forcefully in monitoring and controlling values. If monitors and controls are not actively used in value systems, they will quickly disintegrate. However, as Chapter 12 points out, not all controls are external ones, such as laws, rules, and public opinion. Some, such as personal virtue and professional norms, are internal. Market controls such as competition and comparison have also become extremely popular recently.

Chapters 11 and 12 do not assume a preference for one administrative paradigm over another—weak administration, strong administration, or mixed administration, as discussed in Chapter 8. They do assume that values will change (or have been changing) in most organizations because of time, government-wide policy shifts, economic pressures on government, technology infusion, and so on. In other words, even though a government system or agency may generally maintain a paradigm such as the weak administration model, significant value changes are likely in the future. For those shifting their paradigm, the shift is likely to result in massive value changes.

CHAPTER 11

Encouraging the "Right" Values

"Doing the right thing" requires that the right values are generally *agreed upon,* that the individual is *informed* of what the right values are and knows how to use them, and that the individual *wants* to use those values. The first three parts of this text presented analytic frameworks that can be used to understand the values environment as it exists in and outside the organization and from an individual perspective and an organizational one. It was noted, however, that two major considerations can make acting on values extraordinarily difficult. First, decisionmakers often have to pit important values against one another in unique circumstances. Second, the value priorities of cultures shift over time, especially in transitional periods such as the current period, leaving individual decisionmakers confused about what values are applicable and how. In other words, understanding values alone does not mean that any of the three requisites for a functional and ethical environment—"doing the right thing"—will necessarily occur. Understanding, although a critical prior step, is by itself insufficient in providing the practical and ethical leadership required of today's public sector employees in these times of value change.

A contemporary example may illustrate. A hypothetical federal agency finds that the policy environment has shifted and that much of its support in Congress has eroded to the extent that some members of Congress actually recommend dismantling the agency. Simultaneously, the political leaders in the executive branch decide that the federal government spends too much time and too many resources on "marginal" regulatory compliance and too little on service excellence. They there-

fore encourage the agency to emphasize service and education and to use
a more targeted approach in compliance, focusing more time on habitual
violators rather than comprehensive strategies. The agency also under-
goes a massive consolidation of programs, some program elimination,
staff reductions, and process streamlining. In such an environment, individual decisionmakers are likely to be confused and frustrated. First, a
change in executive policy does not necessarily engender agreement on or
support for that policy. The agency may simultaneously use both the
"old" and the "new" values until the new values have been systematically
supported for a long time. Second, the individual decisionmaker may not
know about the changes or, more likely, may not understand them. An
employee whose function was wholly oriented toward compliance for 20
years will not easily understand the need to become oriented instead toward education and support, and that employee undoubtedly will lack
the appropriate skills for the new focus. Third, individuals may not want
to change to the new mindset because they believe it is unnecessary, silly,
too much work, or simply wrong.

This chapter, then, looks at the issues of consensus on values, education about values, and incentives and disincentives for realizing coherent
value systems.[1]

Consensus About Values

Correctly or not, consensus on values was generally assumed in most
public organizations from World War II to the early 1990s. Values
changed little and the changes occurred slowly, so it is not surprising that
most organizations were relatively unconscious of change. Even in times
of slow change, an awareness of values is important to the life of organizations and societies. John Gardner reminded us of the importance when
he stated, "Values always decay over time. Societies that keep their values
alive do so not by escaping the processes of decay but by powerful processes of regeneration."[2] Studies of values in the late 1980s and early
1990s (even before the wholesale changes in government began to take
effect) showed, however, that *effective* values consensus in public organizations was sometimes overstated. A study by James Bowman in 1989 indicated that a group of senior managers found no consistent ethical approach in almost 70 percent of the organizations they represented, and
another 22 percent had a reactive and blame-oriented approach. In the
mid-1990s, Barry Posner and Warren Schmidt found that more than 50

percent of the federal executives they surveyed felt pessimistic about the general trends.[3]

To understand what an effective consensus on values means, it is useful to refer to the cultural framework identified in Chapter 7. The cultural framework has four levels: the visible cultural artifact level, including language; the visible patterns of behavior, including rules; beliefs, including values about how things *should* occur; and basic assumptions, including the underlying "values" *actually* driving systemic patterns of behavior. According to this model, all levels in the cultural framework are necessary for a full understanding of culture, but the more visible the level of culture, the less likely it is to have broad explanatory power. But two additional aspects of these levels of values are critical for an understanding of an effective values consensus from the broad standpoint of cultural anthropology.

First, the beliefs level is not always consistent with actual behaviors or the basic assumptions driving them. We may say collectively that merit is the primary factor an organization uses in promotions, but it may nevertheless be true that in reality most promotions are highly affected by organizational politics or gender or minority status. This inconsistency between beliefs and basic assumptions has been commented on extensively by writers such as Argyris, Schön, Senge, Schein, Ott, and others.[4]

Second, even if the two value levels are consistent with each other and the more visible decisionmaking levels (the artifact and behavior levels), that does not assume congruence with the external environment.[5] This is most apparent when a radical shift in the environment has occurred, such as is produced by a massive, long-term financial shortfall. While all organizations have some incongruence between their beliefs and basic assumptions, or between their values (either beliefs and/or basic assumptions) and the external environment, a great deal of incongruence generally means there is a great deal of organizational dysfunction. A key function of organizational leaders is to be aware of organizational incongruence at either of these levels and seek to reduce it over time. This is a very difficult and complex task.[6]

An effective consensus on values, then, does not mean a uniform belief in a set of values. First, it means instead an acceptable *range* of beliefs that are generally *consistent with the basic assumptions* actually affecting decisionmaking and implementation. Second, it means an acceptable alignment with the external environment. The single most important element of leadership today is achieving a viable value consensus in order to create a cohesive organizational culture that is aligned with new public sector realities.[7] Doig and Hargrove noted that rhetorical leadership (using evocative symbols and language) and coalition-building skills have become particularly important for administrative leaders.[8] The articulation of values, as an interactive process, is now critical in public as well as in private organizations.[9] Since the values currently practiced in organizations are often poorly understood, the first step is frequently to assess what those values are.[10]

Determining the Environment of Current Values

Seven different strategies can be used to ascertain current values and desired future values.[11] They are ethics assessments; reviews of mission, vision, values, and planning statements; customer and citizen assessments; employee assessments; performance assessments; benchmarking; and quality assessments. Each strategy has its strengths and weaknesses, which organizational managers and leaders must judge in relation to their own circumstances.

Ethics Assessments

Ethics assessments, also sometimes called *ethics audits*,[12] may determine what the stated legal norms are and/or probe the gap between the stated legal values and the actual performance of the organization. The former is best done by an ethics audit structural assessment and the latter by an ethics audit perceptual assessment.

An *ethics audit structural assessment* may be conducted by one or a few people. The researchers determine, through document review, interviews, and expert analysis, what ethics controls exist (such as rules on conflict of interest), how operational areas that commonly lead to breaches of ethics are controlled (such as in travel), and what types of support for ethical norms exist (such as through training).

An *ethics audit perceptual assessment* focuses on what employees perceive rather than the controls and stated policies themselves. Such an audit is important because some organizations have few ethics policies but are nonetheless perceived to be highly ethical, whereas other organizations have many rules but are considered unethical. Perceptual assessments may survey overall ethical issues, specific operational issues, and types of support and inspiration. Perceptual assessments should either survey a large sample or the entire agency. Although responses must be anonymous, responses can be color coded by division for better followup. (See page 261 for an example of an ethics audit perceptual assessment.)

EXHIBIT 11.1

Perceptual Assessment of Ethical Conduct

I. Explicit Ethical Issues:

1. How well do you think the individuals in your agency (as a whole) do in complying with the letter and the spirit of ethics legislation, ethics policies, and informal standards of conduct expected of the public sector?

    Conflict of interest
    Competitive bidding
    Disclosure of confidential information
    Discrimination (hiring/promotion)
    Employment of relatives
    Gifts, favors, or extra compensation
    Political activity by employees
    Conducting meetings open to public
    Public records access
    Use of public equip., personnel, or facilities for personal use
    Safeguards of whistleblowers

2. (a) How good and clear are ethics legislation and ethics policies?
  (b) How well are the informal standards explained through handbooks, training, and administrative explanation?

II. Operational Ethics Issues:

3. How well do you think the individuals in your agency (as a whole) do in complying with the standards of conduct expected of the public sector in the following categories?

    Financial allocation and expenditure
    Procurement
    Equipment
    Personnel
    Travel

4. Do you have an inspector general, designated ethics ombudsman, ethics hotline, or ethics office? (Yes, No, Don't know)
If yes, do they seem to make a difference? (No, Some, or Big)

III. Personal Ethics Issues:

5. Is there an organizational credo which promotes aspirational values? That is, is there a statement or part of a statement that talks about ideal or model behavior for employees? (Yes or No)

If yes, do you think that it provides a useful ideal for you? (Yes or No)

Where is it located and in what format is it? (open ended question)

6. Rate the professional ethics of employees at-large in your organization in each of the five areas below:

  (a) Service to the public is considered beyond service to oneself.
  (b) There is respect, support, and understanding of the Constitution and laws of the land.
  (c) The highest standards of personal integrity are demonstrated at all times.
  (d) Strengthening organizational capacity to operate efficiently and effectively is a goal.
  (e) There is an effort to strengthen individual capacities and to encourage professional development.

Respondents were asked to reply to each item of each question by assigning it a number on a 5-point scale ranging from 1, "very poorly," to 5, "very well."

Adapted from Montgomery Van Wart, "The First Step in the Reinvention Process: Assessment," *Public Administration Review* 55, no. 5 (September/October 1995), p. 432. Used with permission.

    Ethical norms form part of the bedrock of an organization and egregious or common breaches of ethical standards must usually be corrected before adjustments to organizational values can be made; for example, if petty theft, disclosure of insider information, or vehicle use for private purposes are common, they will create an environment of cynicism, distrust, and anger. However, if ethical controls are already tight and commonly internalized, executives may decide to place assessment resources elsewhere.

Mission, Vision, Values, and Planning Statements

Organizations generally have formal statements of what they do, what they value, and how they plan to achieve their goals. Organizational value adjustments usually begin with a review of those statements. In the public sector, this area is deceptively complex because, as Levin and Sanger note, "public organizations have diverse and multiple goals, defined for them by external elements; private firms have far fewer and can define their goals themselves."[13]

Mission statements represent the global purpose of an organization or system. Organizational missions generally change slowly, although they should occasionally be reviewed for clarity and currency, even in stable times. In the public sector, mission statements can be found in the authorizing legislation. Mission statements are also found in published documents as a part of the budget process, for public education, and for internal training purposes. Many of the current changes in organizational values in the public sector are so profound that some organizations are seeking or experiencing in their authorizing legislation changes that fundamentally change their purpose.[14]

Values statements express the principles that organizations expect their members to honor. Such statements used to be uncommon because values changed little for such a long time. They have become much more common in the last decade. Traditional values are largely implicit and may be best explored by comparing them to values now being adopted by many contemporary organizations. Generation of a values statement has been widely hailed as a highly useful tool for those organizations changing their values.

Planning statements are nearly as common as mission statements. They are efforts to define planned achievements. Planning and vision statements form a part of strategic plans, the budget process, and public relations materials. The planning elements have traditionally included goals and objectives in highly rational blueprints. Because of this, strategic plans have received great criticism as being sterile planning rites that led to large tomes that sat on shelves. This may have been due partially to the tedious and mechanical quality they often assumed. Those plans may have also been susceptible to exaggerated assertions based on excessively optimistic assumptions. Vision statements also focus on the future but tend to be more universal, less detailed, more inspiring, and more realistic about the challenges that organizations inevitably face. Contemporary planning has tended to deemphasize and reduce inflexible, long-term strategic planning and to integrate popularly held vision elements. For example, planning models are increasingly allowing for learning and change as a natural part of the project cycle.[15]

Customer and Citizen Assessments

An explosion of interest in values related to customer and citizen preferences has led to an immense expansion in such assessments in the public sector. The previous tendency to rely on experts to analyze and recommend has recently given way to the tendency to solicit direct input from customers and citizens, and to use this input in problem selection and decisionmaking processes. Many consider customer assessments to be the single most powerful tool in assisting government organizations in making value adjustments. There are five types of customer/citizen assessments:

1. *Customer identification* (similar to what was formerly called stakeholder analysis) is a popular tool in quality-improvement initiatives. The assumption is that many organizations and units have become so process-oriented and legalistic, and so captured by self-interests and territoriality, that they have forgotten who their customers (stakeholders) are. Customer analyses can be powerful tools for discussion and for focusing more sophisticated assessment strategies that succeed them.

2. *Citizen surveys* are generally more expensive but reliable ways to tap into contemporary citizen values. They are more common in local government; one recent report stated that 74 percent of all local governments implementing quality improvement initiatives also promoted some sort of customer-satisfaction survey.[16] They can serve two functions—rating perceptions of past services, and ranking perceptions of future expenditures. See page 264.

3. *Customer focus groups* are a less expensive and ambitious assessment, but are nonetheless time consuming if conducted properly. Focus groups can be selected at random but are more often selected from experience. Such groups may range from 3 to 50, but 5 to 15 is generally recommended for manageability.

4. *Customer complaint resolution* in the public sector has been generally handled by relatively legalistic dispute systems (administrative law). Several new trends are emerging. One is a trend to track complaints by type over time. Such tracking provides valuable information about systemic problems that are handled more

EXHIBIT 11.2

Citizen Assessment of Services (by Telephone) with Ratings of Current and Future Preferences

Questions 9–62: As you know, the City of Phoenix provides various services to the community ranging from fire protection to street maintenance. On a scale of one to ten where one means you think the city is doing a poor job and where ten means you think the city is doing an excellent job, how would you rate each of the following?

Questions 63–89: Now let's go through the list again quickly, but this time for each service tell if it is one on which the city should be spending more money, less money, or about what it spends today.

Rating	Service	More	Same	Less	OK
6.8	Police protection in your area	54%	43%	2%	1%
8.1	Fire protection in your area	27	71	1	2
6.5	Endorsement of traffic laws	40	53	6	1
4.6	Juvenile crime prevention and youth programs	82	14	1	4
7.7	Garbage collection	15	81	2	2
5.6	Frequency of uncontainerized trash collection	47	49	1	3
5.3	Controlling and cleaning up illegal dumping	61	34	1	4
5.6	Protecting our water supply from pollution	73	24	1	3
6.1	Helping citizens understand how to conserve water	49	47	3	1
5.6	Street repair and maintenance	44	50	6	1
5.8	New street construction	37	52	9	2
6.2	Providing bus services for the handicapped and elderly	54	37	1	7

Rating	Service	More	Same	Less	OK
6.3	Providing regular scheduled bus service in your area	40%	55%	1%	4%
6.0	Preventing street flooding during rains in your area	41	54	4	2
6.8	Providing adequate parks in your area	30	65	4	1
6.0	Providing adequate recreation programs in your area	44	49	3	4
5.1	Providing housing for the elderly	66	25	1	8
4.2	Providing housing for the poor	71	21	3	5
4.0	Caring for the homeless	74	19	3	4
7.3	Library services in your area	20	74	4	2
5.6	Attracting new employers to the community	57	34	5	4
5.2	Helping existing employers to grow	60	33	3	4
5.6	Requiring homeowners to maintain their properties to minimum standards	49	44	5	2
8.0	Ambulance and paramedic service	25	72	1	2
5.9	Preserving the character of residential neighborhoods	44	49	4	2
5.0	Providing facilities for recycling	64	31	3	2
6.1	Providing art and cultural events	31	57	10	3

90. Would you say that you are very satisfied, somewhat satisfied, somewhat dissatisfied, or very dissatisfied with the overall performance of the city in providing services to Phoenix residents?

Very sat.	Somewhat sat.	Somewhat dissat.	Very dissat.	Not sure/OK
15%	64%	16%	5%	0%

Adapted from Montgomery Van Wart, "The First Step in the Reinvention Process: Assessment," *Public Administration Review* 55, no. 5 (September/October 1995), p. 432. Used with permission.

efficiently as process changes or improvements than as individual problems to be resolved. Another trend is to be more aggressive in getting point-of-service evaluations, which assist in tracking complaints. Sometimes those evaluations consist of cards placed on service counters. In other cases, evaluation cards are sent periodically to every nth customer. Many police departments have begun sending every twentieth speeding ticket "customer" an evaluation form asking about the officer's courtesy, informativeness, and accuracy.

5. *Community visioning* encourages citizens to offer suggestions about ideal futures for their locality. By envisioning an ideal future and unifying behind it, community members contribute ideas, direction, and enthusiasm to the political process, which normally tends to be rather divisive in today's environment. Such a process simultaneously reflects and molds community values as citizens envision objectives. Instead of focusing solely on problems to solve and conventional implementation issues, citizens look to the future. The challenge is to relate their visions to realistic adjustments in organizational values.

Employee Assessments

Assessments of employee opinions and values have become much more common and more important in helping organizations make value adjustments. A long-time emphasis (and many would now assert an imbalanced one) placed on the issues and values of management has recently veered toward a focus on employee input and values as organizations become flatter and many management issues are decentralized to self-managing employee teams. Due to these trends, employee assessments are becoming more important. The three main types are: employee opinion surveys, employee focus groups, and employee value sorts.

Employee opinion surveys can be administered internally. An external consultant, whose experience and neutrality may improve confidence in the results, can also be used. Employee opinion surveys tend to focus on the factors and levels of job satisfaction, as well as on evaluations of organizational effectiveness in various areas. Although a strict sense of confidentiality must be maintained, results can be identified by division so that feedback can be more specific and follow-up action can be more targeted. As with other survey data, it is useful to see results compared longitudinally. (See Figure 11.1.)

FIGURE 11.1

Assessment Results from an Employee Survey

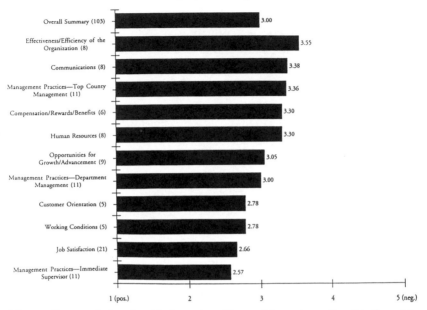

Mean ratings on 1–5 scale with 1 most positive and 5 most negative. 3 is the midpoint. Numbers in parantheses indicate number of factors composing category.

Employee focus groups are relatively easy to assemble. They are usually used either to identify the details of an already articulated problem (such as a general problem identified in an employee opinion survey), to brainstorm alternative strategies, or to critique a revised process. Employee focus groups bring not only employee values to bear but employee creativity as well.

One important use of *employee value sorts* is to gather employee perceptions of organizational values. Such a profile can be useful when new values are being considered for the organization. High-performing organizations tend to have similar organization values, so a wide range of perceptions in values should lead to sustained employee discussions about organizational value adjustments in order to enhance loose consensus.[17] Employee value sorts can also be used to identify specific employee values about their preferred work environment.[18]

Performance Assessments

Every organization and unit has its own performance standards. In the public sector, performance standards traditionally have suffered from at least six problems:

- Weak comparability with other similar units
- Lack of unit costs
- Lack of rewards for efficiency
- Inability to measure true effectiveness
- Inability to measure team and system performance
- Deficiency in identifying and correcting systemic errors

Because of the tremendous importance of performance standards in a competitive environment, there has been much work in this area in the last decade,[19] but the results are still rudimentary. Without improvement in performance assessment that remedies traditional weaknesses, organizations will have difficulty in tying their value adjustments to concrete goals.

Traditional performance standards include those that focus on individuals, organizational divisions, and the overall organization. For example, individuals have workload requirements such as the amount of work that must be produced, the size of the budget to be managed, the number of employees to supervise, error rates, timeliness, customer relations, service and product appearance, expertise, ease of use, accessibility, and problem-solving ability.

Evaluation and audit performance measures are internal mechanisms that monitor performance. In the past, most of the attention was devoted to stopping poor or illegal practices after they had occurred, which resulted in a legalistic inspection approach to evaluation. There has been some value adjustment in many organizations with more interest in preventive and educational approaches in regulatory areas and a search for market-based incentives to replace legal mandates in service-providing areas. Finally, a great deal of attention has recently focused on improving the measurement of efficiency, both by expanding cost accounting and by calculating unit costs and on measuring effectiveness by targeting results as much as production.

While some of the newer trends in performance measurement have been intimated, there are others worthy of mention because they are likely to complement major value adjustments. Measures of team performance are still nearly nonexistent, but there is a tremendous interest in bringing them into individual performance evaluations. Additional progress will be needed as self-managed teams become more commonplace in the public sector. Continuous learning and continuous improvement are almost entirely unmeasured in most public sector organizations. Continuous learning and improvement must be captured quantitatively much as Japanese companies routinely record thousands of improvements by thousands of workers. Measures of reengineering[20] or massive systems redesign[21] tend to be conjectural or nonexistent. Organizations need also to ensure that routine failure associated with experimentation is not penalized in traditional microanalytic performance assessments as individuals and units systematically search for better ways of doing things.[22]

Benchmarking

Bogan and English define benchmarking as seeking out superior performance through systematically searching for and using the best practices.[23] These include searching for innovative ideas, effective operating procedures, and successful strategies. Although the term is usually used in its most sophisticated form—the analysis and use of practices adapted from world-class leaders—Bogan and English identify a seven-level hierarchy of benchmarking. The seven levels are learning from past internal successes, borrowing good ideas regardless of their origins in the organization, developing internal best practices, matching average or standard practices, establishing leadership through industry best practices, targeting national best practices without regard for industry, and matching or exceeding world-class practices. Because it focuses on changing practices, processes, and procedures, benchmarking frequently requires appropriately adjusting values.

Benchmarking has been hampered in the public sector by lack of data, especially in unit costs for citizen and regulatory services; lack of comparable services, due to varying local conditions (such as the different weather conditions affecting road maintenance); and fear of public misuse of comparison data. The only benchmarking in the public sector has ironically tended to be by auditing organizations, which have used benchmarking data to judge and critique agencies. Such an after-the-fact and critical use helps little in fostering a desire to improve and learn. However, benchmarking may receive a far better reception as a proactive organizational assessment strategy in the future because of other value adjustments toward measurement, continuous improvement, and reengineering.

Quality Assessments

The numerous types of quality assessments that exist today share a number of features. All are relatively comprehensive, emphasizing—far more than had been common—such areas as customer satisfaction, employee involvement and development, continuous learning and improvement, prevention over inspection, and supplier partnerships. Taken seriously, quality assessments inevitably cause numerous substantial adjustments in values because the principles they promote diverge from the operational values of most current organizations.

The most renowned quality award system is the Malcolm Baldrige National Quality Award. The Malcolm Baldrige Awards, given annually to two or three organizations, recognize excellence in seven formal categories of assessment: senior executive leadership, information and analysis, strategic quality planning, human resource development and management, management of process quality, quality and operational results, and customer focus and satisfaction.[24] The different categories receive different weights, with customer focus and satisfaction being emphasized substantially more than the other categories. The awards do not insist on a particular assessment strategy, but they do suggest that routine assessment is the foundation of management by fact. The types of assessment discussed in earlier sections of this chapter therefore are consistent with Malcolm Baldrige Award criteria and implicitly expected of world-class organizations. Some of the outstanding strengths of this award system are the comprehensiveness and the rigor of the criteria.

The Malcolm Baldrige Awards, for all of their virtues, do have a number of weaknesses, which are relevant for organizations undergoing change and searching for assessment criteria. First, for the organization new to quality management, the comprehensiveness of the award criteria can easily lead to confusion and conceptual overload. If many areas need work, which ones should an organization start with? Some organizations attempting ambitious change agendas have failed to make any lasting changes at all. Second, the rigor of the award system and the technical nature of the language of the award criteria can be daunting to those new to quality improvement initiatives. Third, the awards currently are intended for and limited to the private sector, and some of the criteria occasionally show a strong orientation toward such private sector characteristics as market-based competition and the drive for market share and profits. Those criteria apply weakly or not at all to most of the public sector, which tends to be oriented toward publicly derived mandates, due process, and social equity. For example, despite its comprehensiveness for the private sector, the Malcolm Baldrige Awards have no equivalent for the ethics assessments that were discussed earlier in this chapter and that take into account the legal compliance and norms critical in the operational mechanisms of a constitutional democracy.

The Malcolm Baldrige Awards are not the only relatively comprehensive system of quality assessment. Others, although not dominant, are noteworthy. Since 1988, the federal government has bestowed the President's Award for Quality and the Quality Improvement Prototype Awards (QIP). The awards programs currently use the same criteria, with the highest-scoring applicant receiving the Presidential Award and the runners-up receiving the QIP Award. The award criteria have always been modeled on the Malcolm Baldrige Awards, but their language is more accessible to the quality initiates and more consistent with usage in the public sector. There are plans to integrate those federal awards with the Malcolm Baldrige system in the next few years.[25] In addition to the federal awards, many states have initiated quality awards programs for state government agencies. Numerous states have adopted the Senate Productivity Award, which allows local government applications. Of course, the prototype for quality awards, the Deming Award, was created in Japan. Europeans use a system called ISO 9000, which is a quality assurance system rather than a quality awards system.

This section has reviewed seven assessment strategies that can help organizations identify current values, gaps between stated and actual values, or values worthy of adoption.[26] Such strategies may help reveal either of two logical possibilities: that a relatively good values consensus exists, or that a good values consensus does not exist. The next two sections examine those possibilities.

Supporting a Consensus on Values When It Exists

Sometimes a relatively good consensus on values already exists.[27] That is, not only do most people agree about the general value priorities in decisionmaking, but those priorities remain appropriate for the political and economic environment. Maintaining and enhancing a values consensus may be easier than making major shifts of values (such as changing the culture of the organization), but doing so nonetheless takes diligence.

Discussing the values in issues is both important[28] and time consuming, so such a discussion should take place when time allows contemplation. That time might be in a staff meeting or during a retreat, when particularly difficult issues can be analyzed. For example, a general agreement may exist among seasoned staff on the appropriate regulatory perspective and values, but occasional discussions about how those values should be implemented in specific cases can refine consensus. As a test of consensus, identical cases could be given to veteran employees for independent resolution, and the group could then compare results and discuss interrater reliability.

Teaching values to new employees is also important because demographic trends indicate that employees will represent increasingly diverse backgrounds. New employees need to understand both the values of the profession and the values that apply to a specific department. Law enforcement agencies, for example, frequently schedule additional training periods specific to their agencies (such as state highway patrol) after long and relatively comprehensive certified peace officer training programs.

Establishing a Consensus on Values
When Significant Disagreement Exists

Levin and Sanger have noted that "altering the values and behavior of individuals is one of the most challenging activities an executive undertakes."[29] Crosby similarly stated that "changing mindsets is the hardest of management jobs."[30] Public administrators face this difficult task in two situations that can cause significant values disagreement in organizations. First, even though the general environment may have changed little, organizational values may have become blurred. Second, the environment itself may have changed, requiring a cultural shift in the organization.

Values may blur in an unchanged environment for a number of reasons. One is growth: When agencies grow, they add new members and new systems. Large agencies always find it a challenge to maintain a relatively consistent culture. Another reason is diversity: Public organizations are often blends of many types of professionals trained to emphasize different values and of many individuals who represent diverse cultural backgrounds. Finally, values may diverge over time as a consequence of the mixed missions common to many public departments, including the balancing of service and regulation.

A more fundamental cause of values discrepancies is that the environment itself has changed. As economic and political environments evolve, public administration must change too. To date, the largest example of a radical effort to change in public administration is the federal government's change initiative, headed by Vice President Gore. The commission overseeing that change is the National Performance Review. Gore stated: "The National Performance Review is about change—historic change—in the way the government works."[31] Numerous examples from state and local government, smaller in scale but no less ambitions, have been amassing in the 1990s.[32]

Finding consensus in either situation, on common ground or altogether new territory, requires change. Two strategies for accomplishing that change are presented here. One, discussed in the text, is derived from Levin and Sanger, who urge administrators to take a more activist and entrepreneurial attitude in public administration. The other, which is placed in Table 11.1, is from the foremost expert on change, Rosabeth Moss Kanter, and her colleagues.

According to Levin and Sanger, diagnosing the culture is a necessary preliminary step for developing a strategy for implementation. (Diagnosing was extensively discussed earlier in this chapter.) The next step is communicating the new mission in such a way that a new, viable culture is established. The message then needs to be reinforced again

---

TABLE 11.1

Commandments for Change

1. Analyze the organization and its need for change.
2. Create a shared vision and common direction.
3. Separate from the past.
4. Create a sense of urgency.
5. Support a strong leader role.
6. Line up political sponsorship.
7. Craft an implementation plan.
8. Develop enabling structures.
9. Communicate, involve people, and be honest.
10. Reinforce and institutionalize change.

Reprinted with the permission of The Free Press, a Division of Simon & Schuster from *The Challenges of Organizational Change: How Companies Experience It and Leaders Guide It* by Rosabeth Moss Kanter, Barry A. Stein, Todd D. Jick. Copyright © 1992 by Rosabeth Moss Kanter, Barry A. Stein, Todd D. Jick.

and again, both in words and in deeds, and credibility has to be established through concrete results. Levin and Sanger warn that it is not enough to have commitment only from the top of the organization: The leaders must "reach down into the organization to build allegiance and commitment," and they must be willing and able to "use and manage multiple cultures" because of multiple missions, audiences, and employee diversity.[33]

Education About Values

Communication is often lauded as a necessary ingredient in consensus building and change strategies, and as such it is an aspect of encouraging the "right" values. The most powerful approach to communication is education and training because of the thoroughness and depth of understanding they produce.

A Prerequisite for Consensus: Knowledge and Awareness

Kohlberg observed that "virtue is knowledge of the good. . . . He who knows the good chooses the good."[34] Although Kohlberg's statement may be more optimistic than many would agree to, the reverse is certainly an even stronger statement: *If people do not know what the right thing is, they are highly unlikely to do it.* The problem of "knowing" then has several elements.

Many individuals lack training in decisionmaking and values clarification. As noted previously, instinctive and simple decisionmaking models may suffice for routine and simple issues, but a more rigorous rational model is necessary when decisions are exceptional and complex. The classic rational decisionmaking model involves six stages: problem or issue identification, goal identification, generation of alternatives, choice, implementation, and evaluation. Without training in using these more rigorous strategies, individuals will have problems arriving at more difficult decisions.

A second problem is that, even when decisionmakers have a satisfactory model for decisionmaking available, they may be unaware that a values problem exists and therefore never engage the explicit decisionmaking model. Joel Fleishman, Lance Liebman, and Mark Moore have bemoaned the fact that "society has no habit of serious ethical discourse."[35] In colonial days, there was a tradition of sending the "best and brightest to William and Mary [and similar institutions] for an improvement of morals and faculties,"[36] but today many lack that philosophical training. This means that administrators are frequently unaware of issues about values. And, as Kathryn Denhardt has stressed, "Being able to perceive the existence of a moral problem is central to moral agency."[37]

Third, there is the problem of articulating which principles are involved even if a problem is identified and a decisionmaking model is used. As Terry Cooper noted about his workshops on decisionmaking: "Many have difficulty in articulating which values and principles are at stake,"[38] so goals and alternatives are not clearly linked to specific stated values. Choices become the result of habit or ideology rather than a product of reflection and comparison.

The solution is to provide education and training about *both* the decisionmaking processes and the values used in decisionmaking. Education about values expands consensus by providing information about the organizational culture and the ways values are typically used in routine decisions. Education can result from training of different sorts, such as orientations, supervisory and management development, quality management training, and ethics training. Education may also result from many organizational activities, such as retreats, award ceremonies, and publishing newsletters.

Education is facilitated when information about traditional and new values is consolidated. Some of the more effective techniques are handbooks, codes, mission statements, values statements, and other official documents. As Terry Cooper has noted, "We must undertake a multifaceted, systemic approach" if we are to "produce a responsible public administration."[39]

A Simple Model for Evaluating Consciousness of Values

Public sector values can be viewed as levels or stages, as Kohlberg viewed moral development more generally.[40] Doing so produces a three-stage model, in which the domains are not mutually exclusive but rather are heuristic points in a hierarchy. Thus the degree of individual or organizational values consciousness can be divided into unconsciousness, elementary consciousness, and advanced consciousness (see Table 11.2). At Level 1, Values Unconsciousness, administrators fail to understand or to be cognizant of their agency's core values, mission, rules, and authorizing legislation, or they willfully take illegal or bla-

TABLE 11.2

Consciousness of Values Among Public Administrators

Level 1: Values Unconsciousness

1. Is unaware of agency's overall mission, grants of authority, or sources of administrative control

2. Is unaware of the basic laws, codes, or rules about legal or ethical behavior

3. Takes illegal or blatantly inappropriate actions because of lack of knowledge or willful disregard

Level 2: Values Consciousness: Elementary

1. Generally understands agency's mission, grants of authority, types of discretion, and sources of administrative control

2. Is aware of basic laws, codes, and rules about legal and ethical beavior

3. Focuses on following administrative standards, legal prohibitions and clear-cut ethical norms

Level 3: Values Consciousness: Advanced

1. Deeply understands the agency's mission, grants of authority, types of discretion, and sources of administrative control

2. Understands and appreciates the dynamics of competing values and can discern the underlying conflicts involved in difficult or subtle ethical conundrums

3. Identifies issues for analysis and uses a logical decisionmaking framework; regularly uses ethical perspective as a management skill

4. Expands ethical perspective to embrace vigorous notions of public service including ideals such as excellence, consistency, equity, leadership, courage, and commitment to the public good

tantly inappropriate actions. At Level 2, Elementary Values Consciousness, administrators demonstrate a general understanding of the agency's mission, basic laws, and regulations; they focus on following administrative standards and avoid illegality and clearly inappropriate actions. At Level 3, Advanced Values Consciousness, administrators demonstrate a deep understanding of their agency's mission, authority, and the dynamics of competing values. They make decisions consistently, using an expansive perspective that embraces challenging ideals such as excellence, consistency, equity, courage, and a commitment to the public good.

Although public administrators generally move from an unconscious to an elementary level with the passage of time and the exposure to the job, this is generally an insufficient strategy without education for two reasons. First, the time will be too long and the new individuals will experience high levels of confusion and doubt. Second, without values education, gaps of knowledge are almost inevitable, and incorrect assumptions cannot be corrected. Education is as important as experience in moving people from the elementary level to the advanced level as the emphasis shifts from what is illegal to do to what is ideal to do as public administrators.

Two questions emerge from the discussion of education and levels of values consciousness: Where should attention be focused? and, How should attention be implemented as education?

Where Should Attention Be Focused?

The first question is one of common sense because attention needs to be focused on all levels of values consciousness. Level 1, Values Unconsciousness, is a completely unacceptable state for public administrators. To move individuals from that level and into the elementary level of consciousness, attention must be directed toward basic information and inculcation of basic values. Otherwise, individuals will engage in inappropriate, unethical, and even illegal acts. Much attention must also be paid to the Level 3, Advanced Values Consciousness. Advanced training, retreats, newsletters, task forces, management meetings and handbooks provide opportunities to promote this level. Sophisticated understanding and behavior based on competing values take both organizational concern and individual interest. Experience alone rarely suffices to produce sophisticated values consciousness.

How Should Attention Be Implemented As Education?

The second question is substantially more difficult: In what form should attention to the various stages be implemented? Many have lamented that much basic training focuses primarily on moving individuals to the elementary level, at least in terms of ethics training.[41] Certainly when basic training is the only training, a problem does indeed exist, but it is also true that workers new to positions want specific guidance on what to do and what not to do. In fact, individuals *first* learning about new procedures and practices want, and indeed learn best, when the do's and don'ts are explicitly—even simplistically—spelled out. When the first round of learning includes tremendous amounts of new technical information, the intensive training period may last many weeks or even months before actual placement. Periods of apprenticeships, probation, or intensive supervision may augment and elaborate formal training in inculcating techniques and values in new employees.[42]

Kohlberg asserted from his research that most Americans were in a stage akin to the elementary level of values consciousness.[43] Because of public administration's necessary emphasis on legal baselines and because some believe that activist values are not the province of public administrators,[44] there has been some tendency to hold all values to a more elementary level, yet all schools of thought have their advanced levels of consciousness in the ideal.

Others have also noted, however, a marked trend recently to spend more attention on more sophisticated issues and on a more complex understanding of problems in values.[45] Moving to the advanced level of consciousness is probably no less difficult than moving from an unconscious to an elementary level;[46] however, the methodologies and approach must shift because those who are learning are taught to ask the right questions rather than to recite the correct answers.[47] In his considerations about this important shift, John Rohr states,

> It should be clear that a bureaucrat's reflection on American values will not and should not lead to a dogmatic assertion that "the following are the values of the American people and this is what they must mean for all bureaucrats." Our concern is not to persuade bureaucrats that they should act in a certain way in the light of certain values. On the contrary, it is to provide them with a *method* for discovering these values themselves and putting them into practice as they see fit.[48]

In sum, distinguishing between legal and illegal acts on one hand, and the various competing values in complex administrative decisions on the other, requires completely different levels of sophistication, just as the teaching of legal baselines versus complex decisions requires different educational approaches.

Use of Incentives and Disincentives in Value Systems

Education is necessary for consensus on values in today's turbulent environment, but education does not suffice. Incentives and disincentives are also necessary.

Goals of Incentive Plans for Values

Incentive plans accomplish three goals, which have successively higher aims.

Establishing Appropriate Minimum Values

Incentives need to support the establishment of appropriate minimum values. In today's environment this often means incentives are used to reestablish a baseline in the face of new realities. Otherwise, organizational inertia may continue to support values that have outlived their usefulness. For example, many public sector organizations are finding that they have unacceptably high levels of specialization, which have been locked in by employee expectations and union rules. Excessive specialization can make job enlargement, cradle-to-grave delivery, one-stop customer centers, core-process reengineering, and similar initiatives difficult or impossible. When extreme specialization prevents new organizational structures and the concomitant values from emerging, incentives for organization renewal of values become critical; otherwise, the logical policy choice may be some form of contracting out or of privatizing services.

Discouraging Deviation From Established Values

When appropriate values have been established or reestablished, disincentives for violators or for excessive deviation should be instituted simultaneously. If laws and appropriately derived organizational rules are disregarded or disobeyed, and if there is no disincentive for such actions, confusion quickly develops. As Sheldon Steinberg and David Austern note, "The ethical behavior of government employees requires . . . the establishment and maintenance of systematic management practices to support its preventive and proactive elements and substantially reduce the reactive mode."[49] Ironically, in today's changing workplace, that may actually mean punishing behaviors resulting from obsolete values that some organizational members still regard as legitimate. For example, it was common practice in government agencies to allow or even encourage a slow pace in many request and requisition processes. Slowness was implicitly related to deliberateness, and speediness was not highly valued. Rapid processing in government has now become a high priority, and managers and workers who cannot find ways to deliver it are far more likely to be pressured, punished, or removed.

Promoting Development of New Expectations and Aspirations

There must be incentives to promote development of values beyond minimal levels. As Wayne Leys long ago pointed out, "We cannot expect administrators to act wisely if their only guides are statements of what they must *not* do."[50] Avoiding illegality and unethical behavior is a low threshold indeed, as is maintaining minimal standards and norms. It is quite another matter to set high expectations and aspirations, which may eventually lift minimal standards and norms. As public systems change their goals and as public organizations shift their values, minimum thresholds change, and so do aspirations. Without incentives, new aspirations will wither under the attack of old certainties. Organizational retreats, widescale involvement in strategic planning and divisional goal setting, and departmental problem-solving programs are examples of ways of developing values beyond the minimal level. The creation of statements of values, vision, and mission is another excellent means. Of course, new aspirational standards and values must be praised and rewarded, both by managers on a daily basis as well as in public forums, such as award ceremonies and newsletters. Incentives should include material rewards as well as psychological ones.

It is useful at this point to review the methods by which organizational cultures are transmitted. Incentives and disincentives must consistently support these methods if organizational congruence is to be attained.

Transmittal of Organizational Culture

Steven Ott has identified six factors that perpetuate culture and that need to be considered if organizational change is desired.[51]

- *Preselection and Hiring of Members.* (Merton[52] called this *anticipatory socialization.*) Careful organizations ensure that those they hire will fit an appropriate psychological profile.

- *Socialization of Members.* Through these processes, members learn the "cultural values, norms, beliefs, assumptions, and required behaviors that permit them to participate as effective members of an organization."[53]

- *Removal of Members Who Deviate from the Culture.* Not only do organizations cause deviants to leave the organizational fold, they often celebrate these departures.

- *Behavior.* Behaviors become ingrained in people's very physio-psychological makeup. Even when beliefs and assumptions change, actual behaviors are extinguished slowly.[54] Those desiring organizational change must allow organizational members numerous opportunities to practice new behaviors.

- *Justifications of Behavior: Beliefs.* It is quite possible to have beliefs that are contrary to actual behaviors and actual basic assumptions. Changing espoused or rhetorical beliefs should never be mistaken as the only or even the key means of accomplishing cultural congruence or as a change strategy, but neither should it be omitted.

- *Cultural Communications.* Communicating cultural values is more effectively done in an organization's myths, stories, heroes, ceremonies, metaphors, and rituals. "Information transmitted through these implicit forms of communication is heard more clearly and remembered longer."[55]

Incentives and disincentives included in any general system of values must keep these six important pillars of culture transmission in mind.

Common Elements of Incentive Plans for Values

The minimum values need to be established and written. They are usually represented in the laws, rules (both promulgated and operational), and codes of the organization which have incentives and disincentives embedded in them. Most, but not all organizations, have many written standards representing values. Collecting and rationalizing (streamlining) minimum standards is the next step. Although it is possible to have too few written standards, that is generally not the problem for most organizations today.[56] Most organizations today have problems either with standards being scattered in many sources, or standards being inconsistent with themselves and the current reality, or both. Collected values, whether statutory, operational, or ethical do little good if they are not widely disseminated. Dissemination, then, is the next step. The final step is to make sure that all are aware of the standards and that education and training occur for new employees and veteran employees alike. Because major restructuring of values is becoming increasingly common, it means that all the steps noted here must be reexamined and largely redone after a philosophical renovation of the organization.

The organization must also have written disincentives for violating minimum values. Punishments must be suitable to the transgression, must be enforceable, and must be enforced. Organizations undergoing change may find this a challenging task. Some organizations, for example, still have high penalties for failure—at any level and of any kind—at the microlevel of day-to-day operations. At the macrolevel, however, they state that they want to stimulate innovation and creativity to deal with a new environment. Intrapreneurs within such organizations may be willing to try small-scale experiments to test alternative methods, but they will be dissuaded by organizational practices that regard any experimental failure as an individual failure rather than as a natural part of trial-and-error learning. The disincentives are too high in such organizatins. At the other end of the spectrum, some organizations, including many public sector agencies, are finding that disincentives for team failure are generally too low. Many agencies are heavily invested in team-based strategies, in which teams carry on much of the organizational workload. Disincentives for poor performance are frequently maintained at the individual level, but individuals are not held accountable for team performance. Individuals may therefore allow team projects or processes to fail because failures are of little real consequence to them. In such cases, new accountability mechanisms must be instituted if teams are to do more than sporadic or marginal work in the organization. The private sector organizations that are most strongly oriented toward project management are generally aggressive in both their rewards and their punishments of teams. Members of unsuccessful teams may even find their jobs discontinued because no new projects are given to them.

Written descriptions of aspirational values are found in many places: mission, vision, and value statements; codes; public relations materials; and miscellaneous internal documents. They, too, may need revision. Several questions can help in this assessment. Do the aspirational values reflect current realities, and are they agreed upon (definition and consensus)? Many federal agencies are currently retooling their aspirations in light of the major policy shifts that have affected the role and size of government. Next, are such values truly aspirational? Legal and ethical values focus on containing and balancing the self-centeredness of individual, professional, and organizational interests, with an emphasis on legal interests. However, with aspirational values, public interest values transcend legal interests. After all, firefighters and police do not lay their lives on the line because of the law; social workers do not exercise compassion because of a rule; and teachers do not touch students' hearts because they are mandated to do so. Public workers make such contributions because they feel they are the "right thing to do" and because they are committed to helping the public interest, one person at a time, regardless of themselves or their organizations. Aspirational values generally see compliance with the law as a given, but they look to the possibilities of working within the law for the good of society and its members.

There is a final question to be asked about aspirational values: Are they realistic? Having aspirational values permeate an organization in a consistent operational fashion takes extremely hard work and requires strong leadership. It has become common for organizations to assert their desire to be national or international leaders in their areas when in reality they might more realistically strive for mediocrity. Ultimately, defining and agreeing upon aspirational values that are realistic is an even more difficult task than is defining legal and ethical baselines.

Because of the difficulty in articulating reasonable aspirational goals in written form, rewarding them with any consistency is difficult. Formal recognition can include raises and promotions, awards, written commendations, and laudatory evaluations. Informal recognition can include praise of the individual in staff meetings and in discussions about models of excellence. While rewards for excellence and aspirational values may not have to be as consistent or rigorous as disincentives for violating legal and ethical baselines, a lack of incentives for surpassing expectations and setting higher standards is sure to create a lackluster organization. Aspirational values help organizations "abandon thoughts of corporate discipline, and focus on corporate spirit."[57]

Conclusion

This chapter focused on the challenges organizations encounter when encouraging the "right" values. First there is the problem of identifying the values and agreeing upon them. In times of shifts in values, identifying and agreeing on right values present special difficulties. Second, there is the challenge of informing all members of the organization of just what the right values are. In the case of new employees, informing them may simply entail adequate training and mentoring as they learn technical information and absorb organizational values. With veteran employees, it may mean sharpening values consensus and refining and strengthening aspirational values. Finally, it is critical that the "right" values are supported through judicious incentives and disincentives. Inappropriate behavior that goes unpunished will likely spread; and excellence and personal sacrifice will fade if they are not often recognized and rewarded.

Notes

1. This chapter takes a more prescriptive approach than others in the book. While I want to be forceful in my encouragement about engaging in constructive values debates in public agencies and to provide specific guidance for doing so on one hand (in this chapter), I also want to be as balanced as I can in presenting those debates on the other.

2. John W. Gardner, *On Leadership* (New York: Free Press, 1990), p. 13.

3. James S. Bowman, "Ethics in Government: A National Survey of Public Administration," *Public Administration Review* 50, no. 3 (May/June 1990), p. 347. A survey in 1996 by James Bowman and Russell Williams indicates a slight improvement in consistency of ethical approach but also a slight increase in the percentage of organizations using a blame-oriented approach. See also, Barry Z. Posner and Warren Schmidt, "An Updated Look at the Values and Expectations of Federal Government Executives," *Public Administration Review* 54, no. 1 (January/February 1994), p. 23.

4. Chris Argyris and Donald Schön, *Theory in Practice* (San Francisco: Jossey-Bass, 1974) and *Organizational Learning: A Theory of Action Perspective* (Reading, MA: Addison-Wesley, 1978); Peter Senge, *The Fifth Discipline* (New York: Doubleday/Currency, 1990); Edgar Schein, "Coming to a New Awareness of Organizational Culture," *Sloan Management Review* 25 (1984), pp. 3–16; J. Steven Ott, *The Organizational Culture Perspective* (Chicago: Dorsey Press, 1989).

5. See Rosabeth Moss Kanter, Barry A. Stein, and Todd D. Jick, *The Challenge of Organizational Change* (New York: Free Press, 1992).

6. Schein, op. cit.

7. "The only thing of real importance that leaders do is to create and manage culture and . . . the unique talent of leaders is their ability to work with culture," Edgar H. Schein, *Organizational Culture and Leadership: A Dynamic View* (San Francisco: Jossey-Bass, 1985), p. 2.

8. Jameson W. Doig and Erwin C. Hargrove, *Leadership and Innovation: A Biographical Perspective on Entrepreneurs in Government* (Baltimore: Johns Hopkins University Press, 1987), pp. 15–18.

9. The importance of values articulation is frequently commented upon. For example, "Leaders must be able to articulate good reasons for undertaking the effort if people are to be mobilized and inspired to pursue collective action for the common good," John M. Bryson and Barbara C. Crosby, *Leadership for the Common Good* (San Francisco: Jossey-Bass, 1992), p. 352; "It also requires leaders to reach out to their followers and articulate, in ways appropriate to today's context, the values that give meaning to their lives," James L. Perry, "Revitalizing Employee Ties With Public Organizations," in *New Paradigms for Government,* Ingraham and Romzek, eds. (San Francisco: Jossey-Bass, 1994); and the chapter entitled "The Newest Responsibility of Leadership: To Explain What's Going on. To Everyone," James Champy, *Reengineering Management: The Mandate for New Leadership* (New York: HarperBusiness, 1995), p. 39).

10. Montgomery Van Wart, "The First Step in Reinvention: Assessment," *Public Administration Review* 55, no. 5 (September/October, 1995), pp. 429–438.

11. I do not discuss in the text the general sources or determinants of organizational culture. Researchers in this area have identified three primary sources. *The broad cultural context* in which an organization exists, *the nature of the organization's business* (the professional groupings, the nature of the work itself, and the degree of risk and the speed of feedback on performance); and *the impact of the founder or,* in the case of many public sector organizations, *the original authorizing legislation and the first influential leader.* See Ott, op. cit.; see also S.M. Davis, *Managing Corporate Culture* (Cambridge, MA: Ballinger, 1984); T.E. Deal and A.A. Kennedy, *Corporate Cultures: The Rites and Rituals of Corporate Life* (Reading, MA: Addison-Wesley, 1982); V. Sathe, *Culture and Related Corporate Realities* (Homewood, IL: Irwin, 1985); and Schein, op. cit.

12. Carol W. Lewis, *The Ethics Challenge in Public Service: A Problem-Solving Guide* (San Francisco: Jossey-Bass, 1991).

13. Martin A. Levin and Mary Bryna Sanger, *Making Government Work: How Entrepreneurial Executives Turn Bright Ideas Into Real Results* (San Francisco: Jossey-Bass, 1994), p. 69.

14. Of course, missions can change without changes in the authorizing legislation as well.

15. Gary Hamel and C.K. Prahalad, *Competing for the Future* (Boston: Harvard Business School Press, 1994); Tom Peters, *Liberation Management* (New York: Fawcett Columbine, 1992); and Tom Peters, *The Pursuit of WOW!* (New York: Vintage, 1994).

16. Jonathan West, Evan Berman, and Anita Cava, "Ethics in the Municipal Workplace," *Municipal Yearbook 1993* (Washington, DC: ICMA, 1993), pp. 3–16.

17. Jon R. Katzenbach and Douglas K. Smith, *The Wisdom of Teams: Creating the High-Performance Organization* (Boston: Harvard Business School Press, 1993); Peter Drucker, *Managing for the Future: The 1990s and Beyond* (New York: Plume, 1992).

18. Because employees rank aspects of work differently, a profile of values can assist management in meeting needs better as well as in enhancing employee understanding of alternative priorities. For example, those in a research unit may place a high value on a creative work environment, freedom, and support. However, the administrative and clerical elements of that same unit may place a low value on those elements and instead select structure, security, and financial rewards as the most important values. Preferred work environment value sorts should not be used to try to change personal preferences, but they

can be used to enhance mutual respect of alternative priorities. For a review on research on public employee values, see Linda deLeon, "The Professional Values of Public Managers, Policy Analysts, and Politicians," *Public Personnel Management* 23, no. 1, (1991) pp. 135–142.

19. Harry P. Hatry, et al., *Service Efforts and Accomplishments Reporting: Its Time Has Come* (Norwalk, CT: Governmental Accounting Standards Board, 1990); Geert Bouchaert, "Measurement and Meaningful Management," *Public Productivity and Management Review* 17, no. 1 (Fall 1994), pp. 29–36; Marc Holzer, *Public Productivity Handbook* (New York: Marcel Dekker, 1992).

20. Michael Hammer and James Champy, *Reengineering the Corporation: A Manifesto for Business Revolution* (New York: HarperCollins, 1993); James Champy, *Reengineering Management: The Mandate for New Leadership* (New York: HarperBusiness, 1995); Michael Hammer and Steven A. Stanton, *The Reengineering Revolution: A Handbook* (New York: HarperBusiness, 1995); Jerry Mechling, "Reengineering Government: Is There a 'There' There?" *Public Productivity and Management Review* 18, no. 2 (Winter 1994), pp. 189–198.

21. Joseph Fiorelli and Richard Feller, "Re-engineering TQM and Work Redesign: An Integrative Approach to Continuous Organizational Excellence," *Public Administration Quarterly* 18, no. 1 (Spring 1994), pp. 54–63.

22. Paul C. Light, "Creating Government That Encourages Innovation," in *New Paradigms for Government: Issues for the Changing Public Service,* Patricia W. Ingraham and Barbara S. Romzek, eds. (San Francisco: Jossey-Bass, 1994); Walter L. Balk, "Managing Innovation and Reform," in *The Enduring Challenges in Public Management,* Arie Halachmi and Geert Bouchaert, eds. (San Francisco: Jossey-Bass, 1995); Rosabeth Moss Kanter, *The Change Masters: Innovation and Entrepreneurship in the American Corporation* (New York: Simon & Schuster, 1983).

23. Christopher E. Bogan and Michael J. English, *Benchmarking for Best Practices* (New York: McGraw-Hill, 1994).

24. Malcolm Baldrige National Quality Award, 1994 Award Criteria.

25. Office of Personnel Management, "President's Quality Award Will Move to Baldrige," *Federal Quality News* 2, no. 6 (April 1994), pp. 1 and 9.

26. For a more expansive discussion of these seven strategies and of the strengths and weaknesses of them, see Van Wart, "The First Step in Reinvention: Assessment," op. cit.

27. Assuming a value consensus because of a lack of explicit discord is unwise. Sometimes major value cleavages exist (which are really dysfunctional from an organizational perspective and seem schizophrenic from an outside perspective), but employees have simply learned to coexist. Therefore, some assessment is warranted even where a values consensus seems to exist.

28. "There are many ways a local government can encourage and nurture ethical values. A commitment to communicate with employees in defining the organizational values is an important first step." Stephen Bonczek, "Ethical Decision Making: Challenges of the 1990s—A Practical Approach for Local Governments," *Public Personnel Management* 21, no. 1 (Spring 1992), pp. 77–88.

29. Levin and Sanger, op. cit., p. 172.

30. Philip B. Crosby, *Quality Is Free* (New York: Mentor Books, 1980), p. 24.

31. Al Gore, *Creating a Government That Works Better and Costs Less: The Report of the National Performance Review* (New York: Plume, 1993), p. xxii. Note,

however, that some areas of the federal government had been engaged in major change prior to the National Performance Review. For example, the military departments had all undergone significant efforts at cultural transformation leading to a good deal of recognition in the federal quality awards programs.

32. See for example, Michael Barzelay, *Breaking Through Bureaucracy: A New Vision for Managing in Government* (Berkeley: University of California Press, 1992) for the Minnesota experience; David Osborne and Ted Gaebler, *Reinventing Government* (New York: Plume, 1993); and various award programs such as those of the Ford Foundation (administered by Harvard) and the National Productivity Center (administered by Rutgers).

33. Levin and Sanger, op. cit., pp. 204–206.

34. Lawrence Kohlberg, *The Philosophy of Moral Development: Moral Stages and the Idea of Justice* (San Francisco: Harper and Row, 1981).

35. Joel L. Fleishman, Lance Liebman, and Mark Moore, *Public Duties: The Moral Obligations of Government Officials* (Cambridge, MA: Harvard University, 1981), p. ix.

36. William Richardson and Lloyd Nigro, "Administrative Ethics and Founding Thought: Constitutional Correctives, Honor, and Education," *Public Administration Review* 46, no. 5 (September/October 1987), pp. 367–377.

37. Kathryn G. Denhardt, "Character Ethics and The Transformation of Governance," *International Journal of Public Administration* 17, no. 12 (1994), p. 2171.

38. Terry L. Cooper, *The Responsible Administrator* (San Francisco: Jossey-Bass, 1990), p. 19.

39. Ibid., p. 185.

40. Kohlberg's six stages (orientations) are (1) punishment and obedience, (2) instrumental relativist, (3) interpersonal, (4) law and order, (5) social contract, and (6) a universal ethical principle. His framework is examined in more detail in Chapter 2 of this text. Lawrence Kohlberg, *The Philosophy of Moral Development: Moral Stages and the Idea of Justice,* vol. 1 (New York: HarperCollins, 1981).

41. Elliott Richardson provides an example: "Ethics training should be broadened beyond the current briefings on laws, regulations, and rules. Training sessions should include case studies utilizing the practical precepts. Continuous training is required to keep the core ethical values alive and relevant within a government agency" ("Ethical Principles for Public Servants," *Public Manager* 21, no. 4 (Winter 1992–1993), p. 39. See also David K. Hart, "To Love the Republic: The Patriotism of Benevolence and Its Rhetorical Obligation," *International Journal of Public Administration* 17, no. 12 (1994), p. 2240; Rohr, op. cit.

42. Montgomery Van Wart, N. Joseph Cayer, and Steve Cook, *Handbook of Training and Development for the Public Sector* (San Francisco: Jossey-Bass, 1993).

43. "Most adults in American society reason not at the principled but at the conventional stages, Stages 3 and 4" (Kohlberg, op. cit., p. xxxiii).

44. See the section in Chapter 10 entitled, "The Special Nature of Decisionmaking in American Public Administration."

45. West, Berman, and Cava, op. cit. pp. 3–16.

46. For example, Dennis Thompson notes, "Translating basic ethical principles and basic ethical character into ethical conduct in government does not come

naturally to most people." "Paradoxes of Government Ethics," *Public Administration Review* 52, no. 3 (May/June 1992), p. 257.

47. For example, Kohlberg strongly recommended the Socratic method: "The teaching of virtue is the asking of questions and the pointing of the way, not the giving of answers" (op. cit., p. xxix, and Chapter 2 of this text).

48. Rohr, op. cit., p. 74.

49. Sheldon Steinberg and David Austern, *Government, Ethics, and Managers: A Guide to Solving Ethical Dilemmas in the Public Sector* (New York: Praeger, 1990).

50. Wayne A.R. Leys, "Ethics and Administrative Discretion," *Public Administration Review*, 3 (Winter 1943), pp. 10–23.

51. Ott, op. cit., pp. 87–97.

52. R.K. Merton, *Social Theory and Social Structure* (Glencoe, IL: Free Press, 1957).

53. Ott, op. cit., p. 89.

54. This idea is rooted in the work of B. F. Skinner, *Science and Behavior* (New York: Macmillan, 1953).

55. Ott, op. cit., p. 97.

56. Exceptions include small organizations or rapidly growing organizations.

57. James Champy, op. cit., p. 29.

Identifying the "Right" Controls to Monitor and Limit Administrative Discretion*

As enormous pressures for change cause substantial and widespread re-design of public organizations, overarching constitutional and cultural values may not shift significantly, but almost all other values are on the table for reconsideration. Organizational redesigners—whether they be executives, managers, or front-line workers—are confronted with three sequential questions. The first question—What are the right values to have?—was examined in depth in Part II. As that discussion noted, the more common value shifts being encouraged, not without significant difficulties, include moving from an emphasis on individual performance to teamwork, from an emphasis on stability to an emphasis on change and innovation, and from steep hierarchical organizations to significantly flattened organizations with more decentralized authority.

The second question—How are these values disseminated and inculcated?—was examined in Chapter 11. Psychologists tell us that changing nonaddictive habits usually takes at least seven repetitions of the new behavior before the new routine can be successfully established. New values and new formations of values probably take many more repetitions through some combination of discussions about new needs (or impending crises), reading, probing questions, training, inspirational messages, and incentives for changed values. The third question—How are these values monitored and controlled?—is the focus of this chapter. It looks at the functions of controls, the seven types and sources of control, and the current trends in the use and emphasis of the seven types of control.

---

* This chapter is adapted from Montgomery Van Wart, "Trends in the Types of Control of Public Organizations," in *Public Integrity Annual,* James S. Bowman, ed. (Lexington, KY: The Council of State Governments, 1996), pp. 83–97.

The Functions of Controls
of Public Organizations

Controls serve many necessary and useful functions. On one end of the spectrum, controls provide a baseline for minimum performance and behavior. Even the best of us, being human, has a tendency to excess in the absence of limits.[1] Individuals need to know exactly what the limits are as well as the associated punishments for those whose performance is substandard or who exceed established limits. A powerful reason for monitoring as a control, often used in conjunction with "sunshine law" requirements, is that the "most important procedures in fighting corruption are those that ensure that an official's acts will be reviewed by others."[2] This is true for administrators at any level whose unmonitored actions are more susceptible to poor performance and wrong behavior.

On the other end of the spectrum, controls can be part of management systems supporting the highest standards and performance. Monitors and controls have the benefit of improving consistency and predictability.[3] Equity and equal treatment are inherently important factors in public sector service and regulation. Controls help organizations ensure that treatment of citizens and customer groups is consistent and fair. As controls become a part of the goal-setting systems, measurement practices, benchmarking procedures, and training of standards of excellence, they become powerful management tools for all employees to achieve high levels of excellence. Thus, controls not only discourage wrongdoing and poor performance, properly constructed, they can also focus on "rightdoing" and excellence. For example, the National Assessment of Educational Progress (widely known as the Nation's Education Report Card) has broken with the former practice of a single "passing" score, which indicated very limited competence in basic skill areas, in favor of three standards.[4] The new "basic" standard is roughly equivalent to the old, very low passing standard; the "proficient" standard reflects educators' beliefs about the progress most students should have achieved; the "advanced" standard indicates excellence. Simply getting students to conform to minimal standards is no longer considered adequate by the public at large.

Much of the current debate about controls reflects different perspectives on the proper blend of controls as minimum standards (with their associated punishments) and as inducements for achieving increasingly high standards. Since the New Deal, controls of administrative discretion have tended to focus more on minimum legal and organizational practices, thus concentrating on controls as inputs, procedural safeguards, legal liability avoidance, and technocratically designed, mass-production systems. Traditional use of controls in the public sector has run into at least four problems.

1. Controls have tended to monitor only inputs and processes, rarely outputs.[5] In the private sector, the financial bottom line constitutes a powerful curb to prevent procedural controls from deterring results; in the public sector the lack of a profit-and-loss statement can allow undue attention to procedural controls without a clear understanding of their effect on overall productivity.

2. A mistaken belief has sometimes existed that errors, loss, and embarrassment can be legislated out of our organizations.[6] One observer noted, for example, that "during the last four decades, the number and types of controls on the conduct of federal officials have multiplied at a frenetic pace."[7] Laws and rules help set general parameters of behavior, but it is foolish to think that every eventuality can be regulated. In fact, in times of rapid change, such as the current one, more flexibility is often needed in order to adapt.

3. The expense of legalistic regulation has often been underestimated.[8] In many cases, legislative bodies (as well as the administering agencies themselves) have been unwilling to look carefully at both the external and internal costs associated with detailed regulations.

4. Demotivation of employees and stifling of initiative have been well-known results of excessively rule-oriented controls.[9]

These four problems have led to increasingly shrill critiques of more negatively oriented control systems and the rule-making process that spawns them. Payne summarizes many of the problems with traditional control emphases when he states:

> More laws and rules, more hierarchy, more bureaucratization, may indeed reduce corruption, but how much money and organizational effort is this goal worth: What are the costs in democratic values, in organizational morale, and in character, of pursuing these anticorruption strategies more vigorously?[10]

To understand traditional emphases and the newer emphases that are evolving, it is necessary to examine the different types of control of administrative discretion, which is the topic of the next section.[11]

TABLE 12.1

Seven Types and Sources of Control of Public Organizations

Laws	Rules	Public Opinion	Virtue	Norms	Competition	Comparison
Legislative and judicial actions	Organizational actions and philosophies	Civic sentiments and political processes	The character and values of individuals	Professional standards	Public choice	Financial and management contrasts

The Types and Sources of Control

Public organizations use seven types of control, each with a correspond-ing source or locus. As Table 12.1 indicates, these seven types (and their corresponding sources) are laws (legislative and judicial actions), rules (organizational actions and philosophies); public opinion (civic senti-ments and political processes); virtue (the character and values of indi-viduals); norms (professional standards); competition (public choice); and comparison (financial and management contrasts).

All seven types of control of public organizations and administrative discretion have existed since the beginning of the Republic. However, cer-tain types have dominated, and others have been little emphasized or used. Broadly speaking, the public sector has relied most heavily on laws, rules, and public opinion; to a lesser degree on virtue and norms; and relatively little on competition and comparison. The lack of emphasis on competi-tion and comparison has been both hailed as a distinctive asset and decried as an insidious invitation to abuse.[12] Yet competition and comparison have always been present, albeit implicitly, in such decisions as whether it was best for the young Republic to establish a national postal service and na-tional bank or provide these services through private hands. The "reinven-tion of the public sector" has certainly meant a reexamination of these his-toric emphases.[13] After a brief description and examples of the seven types of control, the discussion returns to this topic and to other current trends that are reshaping the use of controls in the public sector.

Examples of the Seven Types of Control

Because of limited space, the more traditional types of control (the first five—laws, rules, public opinion, virtue, and norms) will be described

TABLE 12.2

Examples of the Seven Types of Control Over Administration

Laws	Rules	Public Opinion	Virtue	Norms	Competition	Comparison
Ethics legislation	Supervisory control	Complaints	Concept of public service:	Ethic of education & expertise	Public-public	Comparative unit costing
Conflict of interest	Financial allocation	Direct through legal representatives	Trustworthiness	Credos:	Public-private	Public review of comparable data
Financial disclosure	Budget preparation	Litigation	Self-restraint	statements about the ideal values and actions of public administrators	Contracting out	Better evaluation of systems and products (outcome assessments)
Discrimination	Internal comptroller	Citizen (customer) input	Belief in dignity of citizens		Establishing a public corporation	
Sexual harassment	Internal audit	Citizen review boards	Concept of Individual Contribution:		Privatization (not a true control)	
Nepotism	Procurement/purchasing control	Policy boards	Diligence			
Future employment	Executive approval	Public comment meetings	Competence			
Gifts and favors	Personnel procedures	Interest group analysis	Belief in excellence			
Supplemental compensation	Hiring and promotion	Citizen surveys	Commitment and optimism			
Use of public resources for private gain	Firing and salary	Voting /recalls				
Information legislation	Grievance policies	Press				
Access confidentiality	Affirmative action	Coverage of scandals				
Employee political activity	Outside employment	Investigation of waste and abuse				
Open meetings	Seniority protection					
Competitive bidding and procurement	Change of appointed employees					
Whistleblowing	Facilities/equipment					
Budget authorization	Inventory control					
Legislative oversight and audits	Vehicle control					
Judicial review of individuals	Travel authorization					
Agencies' authorizing legislation	Special controls					
	Inspector generals					
	Ethics ombudsperson					
	Ethics hotlines					
	Advisory boards					
	Agency codes					

very briefly here with only select examples. They do not need substantial discussion since they are well known and understood. Table 12.2 provides a more comprehensive listing of examples of each of the types. The last two types (competition and comparison) will be discussed at more length because of their relative lack of use in the past and their new-found popularity. Note that the categories, like many classifications in a complex and fluid world, are not entirely mutually exclusive. For example, laws and rules tend to overlap, as do competition and comparison (along with, to some degree, public opinion). Nonetheless, the distinctiveness of the categories provides sufficient usefulness in description and analysis to make them worthwhile.

Control by Laws

Many types of legislative and judicial controls monitor and limit behavior through laws, legal proceedings, and legal oversight. So-called ethics legislation is just one category that seeks to prohibit personal gain, situations in which personal gain would be difficult to discern, and undue use of power for personal ends. Legislative controls both constrain and protect public employees. Laws often restrict the access to and guarantee confidentiality of information about private individuals, regulate the freedom of access to public-agency transactions, restrain political activity by public employees, require public meetings or outside expert review before regulatory approval, order strict bidding guidelines for government contracts and purchases, and protect those who uncover wrongdoing.

Some legislative controls are broader and control the organization at large, rather than the individuals in the organizations. The budget-authorization process is probably the most important and public form of control, but legislators also exercise legislative oversight in committee and occasionally as a body. Constituent service by individual legislators reviews individual administrative decisions in a somewhat random fashion. Legislative audits can critique either agency financial management or performance.

Although judicial controls are applied less frequently, their imposition can substantially affect a public administrator's career or an agency's policy. Individual administrators can be subject to judicial review of their actions in civil and criminal proceedings. Administrative practices rarely go to the Supreme Court as constitutional issues to be resolved, but when they do, they can massively reshape national administrative policy. Some landmark administrative cases are *Miranda v. Arizona* which affirmed the need for police to inform individuals of their rights when they are arrested, and *Brown v. Topeka Board of Education,* which clarified policies on school desegregation. In subsequent cases where desegregation did not occur in a timely or appropriate fashion, courts have even assumed administrative control to execute judicial orders directly. Although somewhat rare, levels of government or other agencies in the same system can also exercise judicial-like proceedings and impose fines or penalties on agencies, such as withholding federal block grants when certain conditions are unmet.

Control by Rules

A second major source of administrative discretion occurs at the level of the executive branch, which imposes rules and policies on itself. (The term *rules* here is used in a generic sense so that it may apply to organizational settings; it is not meant to take on the more technical meaning of the articulation of laws through rule promulgation.) Executive controls are those that result from hierarchy, special units, or organizational mechanisms.

The most ubiquitous control is exercised by a public employee's supervisor. This control is both direct (instructions and counseling) and indirect (reviewing a subordinate's work and actions). Employees' actions are usually subject to many organizational controls. There is invariably rigorous control over administrative decisions in finance and procurement. Financial expenditure is generally tightly regulated and closely monitored in both the planning and expenditure phases through extensive budget-approval processes, internal comptroller functions, and internal audits. Procurement is generally tightly controlled by a special department. Most expenditures of any size require numerous signature controls.

Personnel decisions are also highly controlled in terms of hiring, promotion, reprimand and firing, and salary. Examples of other controls over a manager's personnel decisions include grievance procedures, affirmative action requirements, and seniority and tenure protection systems. Facilities and equipment (after construction or purchase) are monitored by inventory and vehicle control. Travel is also usually monitored with special care, and larger agencies generally have an office that approves travel requests and expenditures, in addition to the approval by several levels of supervisors and a program accountant.

Finally, there are an increasing number of ethics-related offices in executive agencies. In 1990, the federal government had over 7,000 designated ethics officers on a part-time basis and 178 on a full-time basis.[14] Much of their time is allocated to education and the supervision of ethics legislation issues. Almost all the major federal agencies have well-staffed inspector general offices that maintain ethics hotlines. Many larger state and city agencies are following suit. Some agencies have ethics ombudspersons instead of ethics officers, and many smaller jurisdictions have ethics advisory boards, often staffed with ordinary employees who review cases. An increasing number of agencies have codes that consolidate legal and organizational rule restrictions as well as augment prohibitions not covered elsewhere.

Control by Public Opinion

Controls by the public at large—the citizens and their nonelected media representatives—have occasionally been characterized as insignificant against "the faceless bureaucratic monster" sometimes called the fourth branch of government. However, the control by citizens over administration is actually quite substantial, and it occurs in a number of ways.

First, citizens can complain directly to the relevant administrative organization. In many matters, the citizen may be able to complain first to a street-level bureaucrat, then to a supervisor, and finally to an ombudsperson of some type. Many agencies dispensing benefits have an administrative review process for citizen-applicant appeals. Often the power of citizen appeals is not direct but indirect: The frustrated citizen may resort to getting assistance from an elected official or may take the matter into litigation. Groups of citizens can form powerful citizen groups, which can affect either the content of policies or administrative processes.

Second, citizens are being put on more citizen-review boards and policy boards, placing nonelected citizens in the policy process. Public comment meetings are expected prior to both planning and implementation. Special interest groups continue to play a significant role affecting administrative action through direct pressure on administration as well as through the media, judiciary, and legislature. One area of enormous recent increase is that of citizen and "customer" surveys of all types.[15] Surveys tell administrators about citizens' perceptions of problems and unnecessary expenses and about areas of excellence and special areas where citizens would be willing to see greater resources devoted.

Third, citizens can voice their opinions of the operation of government through routine voting cycles, referenda, recalls, initiatives, and the like. Voting and recalls are indirect means of controlling government bureaucracy, and referenda and initiatives are an attempt to model direct democracy at the policy level. In recent years, however, more and more politicians have run with a plank in their platforms about decreasing administrative expense, size, pay, and benefits while increasing speed, responsiveness, efficiency, and effectiveness. Administrative reform is now a routine political pledge of all parties and is more often an exception in its absence than in its presence.[16]

Finally there is the press itself, which has the time and clout to pursue administrative issues and individual administrators with substantial efficacy. Press coverage of administrative problems and scandals seems to be deeper and more critical than ever before. More dramatic is the recent rise of popular news features that *routinely* depict an administrative problem. One national television network calls this weekly feature "It's Your Money."

Control by Virtue

Not all controls are external: individual values and character, often broadly called virtue, also serve as a control. As one observer noted, "Laws and internal organizational policies can never be specific enough to cover all the situations and contingencies encountered by an administrator."[17] Without the ability to rely on individual values and character, external controls do not work satisfactorily in democratic systems.[18] Only two aspects of control by virtue will be discussed here: the concept of public service and the concept of individual contribution.

The concept of public service is widely debated by practitioners and academics but is poorly defined. Generally, it refers to high standards of honesty, trustworthiness, honor, and self-restraint. The private sector also supports honesty, trustworthiness, and honor, but these standards take on an aspect of sanctity when public resources and power are used.[19] James Bowman concluded after an empirical study that "ASPA members do endorse a double standard, one for industry and a much higher (and more publicized) one for government."[20]

The two sectors differ even more in the emphasis placed on the value of self-restraint. In the private sector, with its competitive, capitalist-model underpinning, self-restraint is a value frequently relegated to secondary or tertiary status in relation to such other values as initiative, boldness, and financial success. In the public sector, however, the value of self-restraint is discussed in nearly hallowed overtones, in a context in which "sacrifice" is demanded.[21] Consider Bonczek's statement: "Ethics involves sacrifices and

selflessness and becomes the principal criterion of integrity in public officials. This results in the acknowledgment that personal career aspirations
must take second place to furthering the public interest."[22]

The concept of public service overlays individuals' sense of proper
contribution. Related values are diligence, competence, and belief in excellence. As mentioned earlier, those values are having a renaissance in organizations of all types through quality initiatives. The idea of excellence
in government may be the value most affected. For those values to remain
vital in the long run, as Stephen Bailey and others have also pointed out,
an individual must value optimism because the challenges are sometimes
great and "success" may be far off.[23] Another related value is commitment,
because without commitment, successes are likely to be humble.

As with the concept of the public service, the concept of individual
contribution in the private sector is often discussed with an expectation of
exceptionally high standards. However, the application frequently differs.
For example, Bailey lists courage as a core virtue for public servants. In the
private sector, courage tends to mean taking risks for later private gain. This
differs from the courage to do the right thing for the public good even if
personal sacrifice is involved, as is often the case in the public sector.

Control by Norms

Although norms can stem from numerous sources, the term *norm* is used
here in a narrow sense to mean control of administrative discretion
through professional standards. The power of professional norms varies
greatly, depending on the profession or trade and the extent to which it
has historically played a key role in organizational matters.[24] For example,
high prestige professionals such as doctors often pay as much attention to
the standards set by their discipline as they do to standards imposed by
the organizations in which they are employed. Professions typically control their members by: restricting entry to the field, tightly regulating
high educational standards required *before* employment is allowed, requiring continuing-education standards, and providing sanctions for
those who transgress professionally promoted standards.

The ethic of education and expertise has increased in the public sector, as it has among many loosely defined occupational groups that have
adopted professional traits. The number of administrative experts and
subject-matter experts has dramatically increased in the public sector,
with the result that in hiring and promotion, lack of educational creden-
tials is increasingly frowned upon.[25]

Nevertheless, professional restrictions, codes, and sanctions do not at this time play the determining role in the practice of public administration that they play in the most highly regulated professions such as medicine and teaching. Although this appears to be changing in some areas of training, such as law enforcement, where statewide standards for certified peace officer training and statewide sanctions have become very common, many of these new training restrictions are legally required rather than propagated by a strong professional organization per se. Codes for such organizations as the American Society for Public Administration (ASPA), the International City/County Management Association (ICMA), and the International Personnel Management Association (IPMA) are really more like credos, aspirational statements of ideal practice. Although disciplinary actions are taken on occasion by ICMA and are now possible in ASPA, discipline by the professional organization does not significantly affect the field. A strong case can be made that professional behavior in the public sector is already so overregulated with disciplinary measures that members need to be reminded about the inspirational aspects of the occupation. From this perspective, a primary responsibility of professional organizations and scholars is to help define public service and individual virtues worthy of the public servant.

Control by Competition

Market competition uses rival organizations or units to induce high performance. In a public setting, at least five types of competition are possible: public-public, public-private, contracting out, government corporations (quasi-privatized), and privatization. Although isolated examples of competition can be found from the earliest days of the American republic, the relatively small size and scope of government did not make competition a significant factor. The modest exception is in the area of contracting out, especially in services and goods that had never been under the government aegis (such as military supplies and armament).

Public-public competition places one public organization against another. School districts may compete for students without regard to school boundaries, as when magnet schools compete with "regular" schools for talented and bright students. The armed forces have undergone significant, long-term restructuring that has included incremental and organizational downsizing. Several of the services have announced that at the end of a set time period, inefficient supply depots and other facilities will be closed. This has spurred tremendous improvements and has led to the domination by the military of the Presidents' Award for Quality since its inception.

Public-private competition places public organizations in rival positions with private companies. Many cities solicit bids for such services as garbage collection and vehicle maintenance, and city departments must compete with private companies for the fees generated. The new wave of school voucher initiatives across the country is allowing students to carry a larger percentage of their proportional funding to charter and private schools. In Arizona, in the first year that charter schools were allowed to receive public funding, the number and enrollment far outstripped almost everyone's expectations. The federal government has also eliminated the monopoly of the Government Printing Office by making it compete through a bidding process.[26]

The third type of competition—*contracting out*—often occurs when policymakers or executives decide that the public sector is not appropriate as a producer-provider or not truly competitive, and that it has a public trustee role to play. Contracting out enables public control and monitoring of the process but private implementation of the work. As mentioned earlier, the government has a long history of contracting for services and goods. When these services and goods are common or relatively small, the government can normally participate in an ongoing market. Such contracting out includes everything from enormous amounts of routine supplies to equipment, research, construction, and services. However, when the goods are uncommon and large (as is a B-2 bomber), contracting out actually creates a wholly dependent market that can have monopolistic characteristics because of the few providers available and their interdependent status.

Setting up a *government corporation* is meant to create a surrogate competitive environment by breaking the links connecting the budget, the personnel system, and other traditional bureaucratic mechanisms to the more rigid governmental procedures. Quasi-control and quasi-responsibility are generally maintained, as is the case with the Tennessee Valley Authority. The U.S. Postal Service provides an example of an original central federal function (the bulk of all federal workers in the first half of the nineteenth century were postal employees) being quasi-privatized in order to increase efficiency and reintegrate a service into a newly competitive environment.

Privatization is the most severe reaction. The government activity is "sold off" and no control or responsibility is maintained. The best examples are from countries other than the United States. For example, the newly independent states of the former Soviet Union have privatized many of their national holdings, including industries, land, and facilities. Privatization is not a true control; rather, it is often seen as a response to new financial conditions (for example, the financial exigency of the government) or market environment (a government monopoly no longer provides a strategic or unique role) or as a punishment for poor public productivity.

Control by Comparison

Financial and management comparison create an approximation of a market situation. Detrimental comparisons may lead to punishment or lack of rewards; complimentary comparisons should lead to increased discretion and rewards. The use of comparison, like the use of competition, is hardly new. Comparison of past performance with current and projected performance is an old and much-relied-upon method of control, especially during the organizational budget and individual evaluation processes. Reliance on past performance as the sole tool of comparison has proven insufficient in the past, however, because it omits industry and "best practices" comparisons, often relies on data that are presented in an arcane manner, provides little stimulus to achieve necessary changes or innovations, and is frequently unable to move beyond a reliance on inputs and process measures to output and outcome measures. Impressive advances in management science (such as the expanded use of comparative unit costing, public review of comparative data, and better evaluation of systems' end products), along with a public demand for increased accountability, have led to a huge surge in this type of control.

Comparative unit costing creates standard methods of accounting for individual products, services, or functions. This is often difficult because personnel and other major costs are not linked to discrete service or regulatory costs. Enhanced comparability measures stimulate higher performance. How much does it cost to provide a public-supported ambulance on a single average call? To provide a special education to a child? To produce a Social Security check? To provide welfare? When such measures are determined in identical ways, they yield comparable data. Then offices, divisions, and systems of government can compare performance to determine which variances are due to special local conditions and which are due to lower or higher productivity. Such comparisons are powerful incentives to executives and policymakers interested in maintaining pressure for productivity improvements. Significant strides have been made in this area with the service efforts and accomplishments research and other performance-based initiatives.[27]

Increased *public review of comparable data* also creates inducements for improvement. Such review may be of more traditional aggregate data types or comparison of the activity-based costing types mentioned earlier. The growing trend to publish studies that compare the 50 states on a variety of measures from child protection to quality of life discourages policy or administrative complacency. *Financial World,* for example, compares financial and management capabilities and publishes an annual review and ranking of the 50 states and the top 30 cities.[28] The British central government has one of the most extensive and successful efforts in this regard. The British Audit Commission (an independent watchdog over local government and police expenditure) began to require local authorities to publish details of their performance, in 1994. In 1995, it required them to publish *comparisons* of their performance, using standard performance indicators. "The Commission's 1995 reports drew widespread media coverage but were generally well received."[29] A more policy-oriented initiative, but one with clear administrative ramifications, is the well-known *Oregon Benchmarks,* which is a compilation of long-term, statewide policy objectives. A likely trend will be the publication of comparisons of laypersons' perceptions of public services and productivity. This will add to the more traditional comparisons of financial analyses and management expert assessments.

Finally, *better evaluation of systems' end products* (or an outcome assessment) is becoming more important in an era of scarce resources. Does the program or agency produce what it is supposed to and can it *prove* it? Countless agencies and programs are currently under attack as being of marginal effectiveness. Many budgets will be cut; some will disappear. For example, administrators can prove that welfare rolls have increased, that benefits have increased, that new fraud techniques are constantly being instituted, and that administrative costs are reasonable. Yet there is a growing consensus, even by traditional supporters of the program, that it has been largely unsuccessful at achieving the underlying goal of assisting families to become self-supporting. As the inevitable cuts ensue, those welfare administrative units that can demonstrate higher effectiveness at achieving recipient family self-sufficiency are more likely to fare better. Another example is from New Zealand, where an emphasis on output-oriented performance has resulted in local authorities being given the freedom to organize service delivery as they see fit, including privatization of services and joint ventures with the private sector.[30] A final example comes from the state of Texas, in which statewide annual testing of students and rigorous *in-class* comparisons of districts by economic category has led to significant changes, forcing rich school districts to use only themselves as benchmarks and encouraging poor districts by acknowledging the top performers among them.[31]

In sum, each of the seven types of control of administrative discretion has its strengths as well as its weaknesses. Some controls logically align with others, as rules align with laws, and comparison aligns with competition. Other controls naturally conflict with one another, as laws and rules conflict with virtue, at least when the controls are implemented to their logical extreme. The next section examines current long-cycle change in controls.

Current Shifts in Emphasis

Historically, different organizational needs have resulted in significant shifts in control of public sector organizations. For example, Federalist administrators emphasized *virtue* in a genteel era, Jacksonian era administrators emphasized political responsiveness and *public opinion,* Progressives focused on merit through professional standards or *norms,* and New Dealers emphasized *laws* and *rules* as government expanded at a rapid rate. It is not surprising, given the current size and scope of government, that *competition* and *comparison* are now being emphasized enthusiastically in an economically competitive era. Some of the other controls are experiencing modest expansion as well. Public opinion is driving much of the reinvention change, and virtue is again a popular concept as an answer to other antibureaucratic trends. Professional norms are experiencing countervailing trends. However, the areas of biggest decline are in laws and rules, which have been important since the founding of the Republic but have taken on overwhelming importance since the New Deal. Table 12.3 gives an overview of the shifts of the seven types of control.

Laws and Rules

Fred Thompson noted, "Detailed rules result from encrustation: An abuse occurs, someone decides that 'there ought to be a law,' and a rule is promulgated to avoid the abuse in the future; but such rules often con-

TABLE 12.3

Current Shifts in the Emphasis of the Seven Types of Control

Type	Overall Trend	Recent Historic Shifts	Rationale by Proponents of Shift
Laws	→	• Privatization and decreased funding stabilizes or decreases size of many public sector domains • Deregulation and streamlining reduce or simplify legal restrictions • Program consolidation reduces legal specification and detail	Government needs to be smaller, less intrusive, and more rational.
Rules	→	• Administrative accountability for cost containment and results rather than process • Use of broader administrative guidelines rather than strict, detailed rules • New emphasis on rule flexibility for innovation and experimentation • Decreased emphasis on proceduralism that is costly or excessively time consuming	Government needs to emphasize productivity over excessive due process and proceduralism and to be more *entrepreneurial*.
Public Opinion	←	• Surge in direct citizen input through better complaint mechanisms, citizen surveys, citizen review boards, public comment meetings, and so on • Increased press activism in investigating administrative waste • Continuing strong role of special interest research and lobbying • Increased citizen anger causing political leaders to change administrative structures	Government needs to emphasize responsiveness to the citizens and needs to subject government to the same restructuring that the private sector has experienced.
Virtue	⇄	• Emphasis on administrative discretion "to do the right thing" legally • Emphasis on administrative discretion "to do the right thing" practically • Emphasis on administrative discretion "to do the right thing" ethically	Public servants should be trusted more in order to reduce legal and rule controls, which have become excessively costly, cumbersome, and dehumanizing to both those regulated and those regulating.
Norms	←	• Increased emphasis on education, training, and remaining current professionally • Decreased capacity to master all skills necessary as jobs enlarge, responsibilities expand, and resources diminish	Although the training and education of government workers has never been more appreciated, the resources to encourage professionalism have never been more constrained and stretched.
Competition	←	• Increased pressure to reduce the size and scope of government • Increased private sector competition leading to pressures for competition in public sector	Without public choice, government processes and programs become decadent (self-serving, bloated, inefficient, entitlement-oriented, and so on).
Comparison	←	• Increased use of comparative data for administrative management and policy choices • Increased use of comparative data as public information • Increased use of comparative data for evaluation of systems	While competition may not always be possible in government organizations, it is possible to measure and compare productivity far better than has been done in the past.

tinue after the need for them has passed."[32] Even impartial analysts note that "compulsion by law is the most expensive way to make people behave."[33] Few would argue that any of the legislative and judicial controls over administrative agencies are inappropriate, but many do argue that they are overused, badly used, and even abused, thereby making the work of administration more tedious, overly cautious, and expensive. Three trends are particularly noticeable:

1. Privatization and decreased funding have stabilized or decreased the size of many public sector systems. Thus, areas of responsibility are taken out of the public sector and the laws that govern it. This is occurring around the world, both in highly developed countries such as Canada, Great Britain, and France and in others such as Russia and the newly independent states, where both industries and residential holdings are being sold off.

2. Extensive deregulation and streamlining are reducing or simplifying legal restrictions. President Clinton and Vice President Gore ridiculed both the federal personnel rules (which were over 10,000 pages) and the procurement rules, and have since simplified both procedural systems enormously.[34]

3. Program consolidation reduces legal specification and detail. For example, the U.S. Department of Housing and Urban Development is combining 65 separate programs into 3 and is abandoning most of its former strict regulations.

Although trends to decrease size, streamline, and consolidate legal regulations ultimately must be legislatively approved, and in fact are often policy driven, agencies themselves usually are responsible for devising plans for the redesign and implementation. Of course there are select exceptions in which control by law is increasing; however, these cases pale in comparison to the widespread interest in making government smaller and less intrusive.

Organizational rules have self-evident strengths, which will not be detailed here because their perceived over-use is driving the current trend to reduce reliance on rules. The problems with executive controls (rules) are substantial, and they are being scrutinized by many governments. Like all controls, executive controls are largely reactive. So much energy must be exercised in controlling wrongdoing, mistakes, and administrative decisions, that creativity, initiative, and trust may wane. Avoiding risk then becomes more important than task completion. In many areas, executive controls are extremely expensive, so much so that the control of mistakes or problems becomes more important than its cost-benefit. An audit of one overmanaged state agency revealed that 22 signatures were necessary to approve the purchase of a laser printer, which consumes six months from the time of the request to delivery.[35] In extreme cases, the routine cost of control exceeds the cost of potential abuse, even if the abuse occurred in every instance. Delays also show up in hiring. Filling an opening for a new, full-time employee typically takes four to eight months in public agencies, and senior positions can take longer. Managers may find they spend most of their time justifying and approving rather than planning and directing, because accountability for the public trust seems to require more control than for the private sector. Streamlining and rationalizing some of the excessively onerous and overlapping systems are occurring through traditional process-simplification and restructuring under the guise of Total Quality Management, reengineering,[36] and more conventional organizational reviews. Overall, the critics of government driving the current trend argue that government needs to emphasize productivity over excessive proceduralism and needs to be more entrepreneurial.

Public Opinion

Perhaps one of the underlying causes for the significant sea-change in public sector values and controls is public opinion, which has registered extreme levels of dissatisfaction with past legislative policies and administrative practices. Increased citizen anger is clearly causing political leaders to change administrative structures and procedures. Citizen input has undergone a profound change; its increase can be attributed to better complaint mechanisms, citizen surveys, citizen review boards, and public comment meetings, among other popular techniques. Citizen surveys, a rarity only a decade ago, are now commonplace. Even when they were conducted in the past, their purpose was often analytical rather than practical. Those who want to implement new customer-oriented strategies now often strengthen their proposals by presenting citizen survey information to the appropriate legislative bodies, at least at the local level.

Increased citizen anger has also resulted in a more activist press, which is conducting more investigative work on administrative matters than in the past. While the accuracy and balance of press coverage of public administrative exposés is often quite suspect, there can be little doubt that it is part of a larger trend to subject formerly dull administrative practices to increasingly shrill public review. The major public sentiment seems to be that government needs to emphasize responsiveness to its citizens and needs to be subjected to the same type of restructuring that the private sector has experienced.

Virtue

The increase in virtue as a control is the convergence of a number of trends. The advocates of related initiatives such as quality management, entrepreneurial government, and employee empowerment support virtue for both practical and humanitarian reasons. They generally believe that government work will be done more cheaply and better with less red tape and more self-direction; simultaneously it is better (more moral) to expect greater responsibility from government workers at all levels than to provide expensive and dehumanizing layers of authority. While the thrust began in the private sector with writers such as Deming,[37] Juran,[38] and Crosby,[39] this perspective is widespread in the public sector management literature today.[40]

Closely aligned with this school of thought are those who think that the legalistic and proceduralist approach to control has become outlandish. For example, Philip K. Howard begins his popular book, *The Death of Common Sense: How Law Is Suffocating America,* by describing how Mother Teresa abandoned a homeless shelter project in New York City because the mindless red tape was too much for her. His book, which is a litany of such cases, advocates allowing managers and bureaucrats to use more discretion.[41]

A final trend has academic sources. Academics such as Terry Cooper and N. Dale Wright,[42] David K. Hart,[43] and Kathryn Denhardt[44] point out that rules apply only to egregious wrongdoing and that administrators have an obligation to seek out the exemplary. Civic-minded administrative heroes often need courage to do the right thing when it is uncertain what that right thing is. Furthermore, they often make personal sacrifice as a matter of course. This school of thought seems to suggest that years of education and dedicated service give public servants a powerful moral gyroscope that could be trusted more than it currently is.

Overall, these trends share a common direction. They suggest a need to trust public servants more in order to reduce legal and rule controls, which have become excessively costly, cumbersome, and dehumanizing both to those who are regulating and to those who are regulated.

Norms

Trends to decentralize decisionmaking, increase flexible responses to problems by administrators at all levels, and vastly reduce rules logically give norms a far greater role in control. Rather than requiring standardized procedures or outputs, norms require a standardized *approach*, which can come from professional education or organizational training. Members of the organization internalize certain values and principles, so that there is a similar response to different issues, even though there are not specific rules. The use of norms can provide the benefits of consistent but flexible solutions that allow for customization and esprit d'corps among workers as a professional class. Thus both the public sector environment in which citizens are demanding more flexible responses in their initial encounters and the employees themselves encourage the rise of professionalism through education and training.

But education and training are expensive, and organizations are experiencing unprecedented cuts in their budgets and personnel just as they are motivated to enhance the use of norms. The enormously time-consuming and costly elements of norms become apparent when organizations perceive that the training for each employee undergoing an organizational change amounts to hundreds of hours. For example, the current popularity of teams has masked the liabilities and challenges of using teams (especially the potential inefficiency, diffused accountability, and endless meeting schedules) *unless* teams are carefully trained and coached. Organizations that decide that employees will learn on their own are often unwittingly encouraging employees to learn dysfunctional practices and then rehearse them. Use of norms as controls is mixed. Although the training and education of government workers has never been more appreciated, the resources to encourage professionalism have never been more restricted.

Competition and Comparison

When government was small proportionate to the population or economy, competition and comparison could easily be deemphasized as control factors. For example, in 1816 federal workers were only .06 percent of the population, but by 1990 this figure had grown to 1.25 percent—a more than two-thousandfold increase. The federal budget was only 5 percent of the gross domestic product as late as 1869, but it had grown by a factor of four by 1990. State and local government growth has been nearly as profound. For example, between 1930 and 1990, state and local employment increased from 2.1 percent of the population to 6.1 percent. While these numbers may still be low using comparative international figures, these proportionate increases are large indeed by American experience and tastes. There seems to be a growing sentiment that if government is going to play such an enormous role in the economy (37 percent of the gross domestic product in 1990 was government receipts), then it must more often play by rules similar to those used by the private sector.[45] The increased pressure to reduce the size and scope of government, a debate that will dominate the policy arena for decades because of long-term structural problems such as the deficit and entitlements, will profoundly affect administrative design as well. This clearly means a historic shift in the control mechanisms. Agencies will need to demonstrate both efficiency and effectiveness in market conditions whenever possible. In other words, critics argue, without public choice through market competition, government processes and programs often become decadent—self-serving, bloated, inefficient, entitlement-oriented, and so forth. Of course, issues like equity and fairness, important features of government, are less well served in competitive environments.

Even where marketlike conditions cannot be established, better comparability is clearly possible. Policymakers want better comparative data for their decision processes. The public itself wants better data to compare the performance of government programs and processes. Administrators need comparative data in evaluating and improving their own performance and standards. Poor comparability measures occurred in the public sector in the past because of a lack of motivation to overcome parochial measurement interests, a concern for misunderstanding or intentional manipulation of comparative data, and poor internal measurement systems. Today, however, the growth of measurement is one of the most rapidly expanding areas of management technology. While competition may not always be possible in government organizations, it is possible to measure and compare productivity far better than has been done in the past.

Conclusion

When the need for organizational and systemic change arises, the question of proper controls is among the first needing consideration. Immediately after the decision on what the "right" values are for a given set of conditions (as well as how to disseminate those values), the question of the right balance of controls becomes critical. Controls do not just serve their more commonly observed function of providing a minimum baseline of behavior; controls also can serve as benchmarks for excellence. In this less commonly perceived role, controls are mechanisms for management and (self-management) to achieve high performance. That is, they act not only as disincentives but as incentives in well-designed systems. Systems that exclusively use controls as disincentives are indeed gloomy and oppressive. Some types of controls are better at setting and maintaining minimum standards such as laws, rules, and public opinion. Other types of controls, such as virtue, norms, competition, and comparison, are better at motivating high performance. All types are useful, and a combination is necessary given the complex systems that exist in the public sector. The issue becomes, for the organizational designer, one of achieving the proper balance.

Currently, values are changing dramatically in public sector systems. Just two examples of values being emphasized are entrepreneurialism and decentralization of authority. For these to become truly achieved values, the use of controls as disincentives must be deemphasized. This means that laws and rules are unlikely to receive the same emphasis as in the past. Furthermore, in high-performance organizations, controls that act more as incentives will have to be increased. Because of the complex interrelationship of controls in organizational design and the amount of such design now under way, more attention will need to be given to shifting values and the concomitant shifts in the use of controls.

Notes

1. Gerald E. Caiden, "What Really Is Public Maladministration?" *Public Administration Review* 51, no. 6 (November/December 1991), pp. 486–493.
2. Bruce L. Payne, "Devices and Desires: Corruption and Ethical Seriousness," in *Public Duties: The Moral Obligations of Government Officials,* Joel L. Fleishman, Lance Liebman, and Mark H. Moore, eds. (Cambridge, MA: Harvard University Press, 1981).
3. Peter Block, *Stewardship: Choosing Service Over Self-Interest* (San Francisco: Berrett-Koehler Publishers, 1993), p. 2.
4. Sandy Kress, "Accountability in Public Education," a talk delivered at the conference *Managing for Results: Advancing the Art of Performance Measurement,* in Austin, Texas, November 1, 1995.
5. Dalton S. Lee and Susan C. Paddock, "Improving the Effectiveness of Teaching Public Administration Ethics," *Public Productivity & Management Review* 15, no. 4 (Summer 1992), pp. 487–500.

6. Peter Block, op. cit., p. 144.

7. Robert N. Roberts and Marion T. Doss, "Public Service and Private Hospitality: A Case Study in Federal Conflict-of-Interest Reform," *Public Administration Review* 52, no. 3 (May/June 1992), p. 260.

8. Fred Thompson, "Matching Responsibilities With Tactics: Administrative Controls and Modern Government," *Public Administration Review* 53, no. 4 (July/August 1993), pp. 303–318.

9. David Carnevale, *Trustworthy Government* (San Francisco: Jossey-Bass, 1995).

10. Bruce L. Payne, op cit., p. 192.

11. For an excellent empirical study that examines "new" values and their concomitant control mechanism, see Dennis O. Grady and Paul Tax, "Entrepreneurial Bureaucrats and Democratic Accountability: The Experience at the State Level," *Review of Public Personnel Administration* 16, no. 4 (Fall 1996), pp. 5–14.

12. Arie Halachmi, "The Challenge of a Competitive Public Service," In *The Enduring Challenges in Public Management,* Arie Halachmi and Geert Bouchaert, eds. (San Francisco: Jossey-Bass, 1995), pp. 220–246.

13. Montgomery Van Wart, "'Reinventing' in the Public Sector: The Critical Role of Value Restructuring," *Public Administration Quarterly* 19, no. 4 (Winter 1996), pp. 456–478.

14. Dennis Thompson, "Paradoxes of Government Ethics," *Public Administration Review,* vol. 52, no. 3 (May/June 1992), pp. 254–259; Sheldon S. Steinberg and David F. Austern, *Government, Ethics, and Managers: A Guide to Solving Ethical Dilemmas in the Public Sector* (New York: Praeger, 1990).

15. Montgomery Van Wart, "The First Step in the Reinvention Process: Assessment," *Public Administration Review* 55, no. 5 (September/October 1995), pp. 429–438.

16. Beverly A. Cigler, "Public Administration and the Paradox of Professionalism," *Public Administration Review* 50, no. 6 (November/December 1990), pp. 637–653.

17. Terry L. Cooper, *The Responsible Administrator* (San Francisco: Jossey-Bass, 1990), p. 167.

18. In systems where individual values and character have broken down, systems of corruption are accepted as standard. The problem applies equally to Tammany Hall, repressive regimes, or developing countries in which the familial or tribal loyalty far outweighs internalized, national-level, or civic values.

19. Kathy G. Denhardt, "Unearthing the Moral Foundations of Public Administration: Honor, Benevolence, and Justice," In *Ethical Frontiers in Public Management,* James S. Bowman, ed. (San Francisco: Jossey-Bass, 1991), pp. 91–113.

20. James S. Bowman, "Ethics in Government: A National Survey of Public Administrators," *Public Administration Review* 50, no. 3 (May/June 1990), p. 346.

21. While not directly antithetical, entrepreneurialism and the traditional concept of public service clearly have contradictory elements currently. It seems likely that the concept of public service will undergo significant changes as current trends continue. See Chapter 8 for an extended discussion of these points.

22. Stephen J. Bonczek, "Ethical Decision Making: Challenge of the 1990s—A Practical Approach for Local Governments," *Public Personnel Management* 21, no. 1 (Spring 1992), pp. 75–88.

23. Stephen Bailey, "Ethics and the Public Service," *Public Administration Review* 24 (1964), pp. 234–243.

24. Henry Mintzberg, *The Structuring of Organizations* (Englewood Cliffs, NJ: Prentice Hall, 1979).

25. However, John Rohr ("The Problem of Professional Ethics," *The Bureaucrat* [Spring 1991], pp. 9–12) points out that professional groups can also manipulate standards to their own ends, rather than society's.

26. Al Gore, *Creating a Government That Works Better and Costs Less: The Report of the National Performance Review* (New York: Plume, 1993); Al Gore, *Creating a Government That Works Better and Costs Less: Status Report* (Washington, DC: U.S. Government Printing Office, 1994).

27. Harry Hatry, ed., *Service Efforts and Accomplishments Reporting: Its Time Has Come.* (Norwalk, CT: Governmental Accounting Standards Board, 1990); Marc Holzer, ed., *Public Productivity Handbook* (New York: Marcel Dekker, 1992); Geert Bouchert, "Measurement and Meaningful Management," *Public Productivity and Management Review* 17 (Fall 1993), pp. 31–44.

28. Katherine Barrett and Richard Greene, "The Roll Call," *Financial World* (April 17, 1990), pp. 30–36; Katherine Barrett and Richard Greene, "The States—A Special Report," *Financial World* (May 28, 1991), pp. 30–48; Katherine Barrett and Richard Greene, "The State of the States," *Financial World* (May 12, 1992), pp. 24–43, 54–55; Katherine Barrett and Richard Greene, "Tales of 30 Cities," *Financial World* (May 12, 1992), pp. 28–47; Katherine Barrett and Richard Greene, "The State of the States—How We Rank Them," *Financial World* (May 11, 1993), pp. 44–61; Katherine Barrett and Richard Greene, "State of the States—Tick, Tick, Tick," *Financial World* (September 26, 1995), pp. 36–39.

29. Paul Vevers, "Learning From Abroad: New Zealand and Great Britain," a talk delivered at the conference *Managing for Results: Advancing the Art of Performance Measurement,* in Austin, Texas, November 2, 1995.

30. Keven Tate, "Learning From Abroad: New Zealand and Great Britain," a talk delivered at the conference *Managing for Results: Advancing the Art of Performance Measurement,* in Austin, Texas, November 2, 1995.

31. Sandy Kress, "Accountability in Public Education," a talk delivered at the conference *Managing for Results: Advancing the Art of Performance Measurement,* in Austin, Texas, November 1, 1995.

32. Fred Thompson, "Matching Responsibilities With Tactics: Administrative Controls and Modern Government," *Public Administration Review* 53, no. 4 (July/August 1993), p. 313; for an alternative view, see Kenneth R. Mayer, "Policy Disputes As a Source of Administrative Controls: Congressional Micromanagement of the Department of Defense," *Public Administration Review* 53, no. 4 (July/August 1993), pp. 293–302.

33. Michael W.J. Cody and Richardson R. Lynn, *Honest Government: An Ethics Guide for Public Service* (Westport, CT: Praeger, 1992), p. 2.

34. Gore, *Creating a Government That Works Better and Costs Less: The Report of the National Performance Review; Status Report.* The companion study for state and local reform is called the Winter Commission, after its chair. See the First Report of the National Commission on the State and Local Public Service, *Hard Truths/Tough Choices: An Agenda for State and Local Reform* (Albany, NY: The Nelson A. Rockefeller Institute of Government, 1993).

35. Project SLIM, 1993, State of Arizona, Section on the Department of Economic Security.

36. Sandra Hale and Albert Hyde, "Symposium on Reengineering," *Public Productivity and Management Review* 18, no. 2 (Winter 1994); see symposium of articles on reengineering in this issue.

37. Edward W. Deming, *Out of the Crisis.* (Cambridge, MA: MIT Center for Advanced Engineering Study, 1982).

38. Joseph Juran, "The Upcoming Century of Quality," Address given to the 1994 ASQC Annual Quality Congress in Las Vegas on May 24, 1994.

39. Philip B. Crosby, *Quality Is Free.* (New York: Mentor, 1979).

40. David Osborne and Ted Gaebler, *Reinventing Government: How the Entrepreneurial Spirit Is Transforming the Public Sector* (New York: Penguin, 1993); Martin A. Levin and Mary Bryna Sanger, *Making Government Work: How Entrepreneurial Executives Turn Bright Ideas Into Real Results* (San Francisco: Jossey Bass, 1994).

41. Philip K. Howard, *The Death of Common Sense: How Law Is Suffocating America* (New York: Random House, 1993), especially his bibliography; Volcker Commission, *Leadership for America: Rebuilding the Public Service* (Lexington, MA.: Heath, 1989); Don Kettl, *Sharing Power: Public Governance and Private Markets* (Washington, DC: The Brookings Institution, 1989); Robert N. Roberts and Marion T. Doss, "Public Service and Private Hospitality: A Case Study in Federal Conflict-of-Interest Reform," *Public Administration Review* 52, no. 3 (May/June 1992), pp. 260–269.

42. Terry L. Cooper and N. Dale Wright, eds., *Exemplary Public Administrators: Character and Leadership in Government* (San Francisco: Jossey-Bass, 1992).

43. David K. Hart, "To Love the Republic: the Patriotism of Benevolence and Its Rhetorical Obligation," *International Journal of Public Administration* 17, no. 12 (1995), pp. 2231–2258.

44. Kathryn G. Denhardt, "Character Ethics and the Transformation of Governance," *International Journal of Public Administration* 17, no. 12 (1995), pp. 2165–2194.

45. U.S. Bureau of the Census, *The Statistical History of the United States: From Colonial Times to the Present* (New York: Basic Books, 1976); U.S. Bureau of the Census, *Statistical Abstract of the United States: 1994* (Washington, DC: U.S. Printing Government Office, 1994).

CHAPTER 13

Conclusion

In this book, I have tried to make a substantial contribution to the science of values for public administration. The text extended two comprehensive analytic perspectives. The first identified value clusters according to an individual administrator's outlook. Accordingly, values in Parts I and II were divided into five well-established and well-regarded value domains in public administration: individual, professional, organizational, legal, and public interest. Part I reviewed the five domains as background for the American Society for Public Administration's Code of Ethics, whose organization is based upon them. Next, Part II looked at each value domain in chapter-length treatments that discussed three or four basic assumptions for public administration. This resulted in a total list of 17 basic assumptions. This list, and the ASPA Code, are complementary but not identical analyses, then, using the same analytic framework.

The second perspective of this text looked at values from a cultural perspective. The values that public administrators possess are dependent on the overall culture and society of which they are part. The broad choices embedded in the social, economic, and political structures of societies form the context for the basic assumptions of public administrators. These overarching values are further centralized in systems of beliefs about how public administration and public administrators should function. These beliefs lead to relatively consistent patterns of actions, as administrators tend to employ similar types of rationality to similar types of situations. Twelve types of rationality were reviewed, six of which are clearly emphasized, but only one of which is explicitly absent. Finally, the specific decisions administrators make were discussed, using a reasoned choice rationality as the typical example.

Part IV looked at values not so much from an analytic perspective but from an active perspective: What do administrators need to do to clarify, change, educate, monitor, and control values? Trends with which public administrators must deal included increased value system changes at all levels, resulting in tremendous values confusion in many public agencies, and the need for administrators who are more adept at values management.

A Summary of the Main Points of the Book

This book has emphasized the science of values, and has taken the position that ethics is a subfield of values, at least in its non-normative or nonmoralistic mode. In recapitulating the major points of the book, I will start with the narrower ethical core and expand the scope to include all values.

Ethics is doing the right thing, that is, acting on right values. This also means not acting on the wrong values. At a minimum, being ethical means following reasonable social, legal, and moral norms. For public administrators, legal norms are especially important, since they are themselves agents and executors of the law. And when it comes to their special areas of jurisdiction, public administrators are expected to be fully and faithfully compliant with the law. Ethical behavior can also be seen as meeting and exceeding the standards of society and one's profession. The term *ethical*, as used in normal parlance, signifies someone who is an exemplar of ideal behavior. This means that the individual not only complies with general legal and organizational norms but also achieves a high standard of excellence and works hard to fulfill social, organizational, and altruistic ideals. The term also generally implies a high standard of personal morality with regard to behaviors that are consistent, coherent, honest, and reciprocal.

Yet determining what the right values are is often not a simple matter, especially for public administrators. Even meeting minimum standards can be difficult in times of great values turmoil, which can be experienced as changes in agency legislation, organizational rules, working philosophy, and working norms. Meeting high standards is especially difficult in such times, because of values *competition, complexity,* and *change.*

Components of value systems often compete with one another, since value systems are constructed to balance many elements: the needs of society with those of the individual; the values of change with those of constancy; principles of individual initiative with those of social contribution; and so on. Public agencies, for example, are generally not supposed to make a profit in any of their operations, yet they are expected to minimize expenses and stay financially solvent. Thus the values of noncompetition and financial stability often compete. Only simple decisions are without values competition, and then only apparently so because the values in such decisions have been largely agreed upon and internalized. Values competition may be relatively quiescent for long periods but the potential for conflict is always there.

A second important point is that values in value systems are often complex. This is especially true in the public sector, where the emphasis on nonprofitable goals—social equity, due process, the appearance of propriety, openness, financial conservatism, rigorous standards of legally defined fairness to employees, notions of contribution to the common good and so on—is far greater than in the private sector. In the public sector, for example, filling a staff opening from a pool of internal and external candidates, all nearly equally qualified, means deciding on the right mix of organizational loyalty, affirmative action, and external infusion of expertise because the choice occurs within a system that scrupulously monitors due process, employee rights, and legal requirements for social equity.

Such choices are made even more difficult because values in value systems often change, either slowly and quietly, or dramatically and turbulently. Recently Georgia's Governor Zell Miller signed a law retiring the merit system for incoming employees. Unless it is successfully legally challenged, this law will change the merit system in that state to an at-will system. The values changes that this can potentially trigger are enormous, both for good (managerial flexibility) and for ill (old-fashioned corruption and political patronage). Although it is too early to tell, the pendulum may be swinging back toward political and organizational responsiveness because of perceived abuses in tenurelike merit systems that have implicitly guaranteed lifetime employment in an economy that has moved onto another phase in employment relations.[1]

The fact that determining the right values on which to base decisions is not simple does not make determining them less important. Quite the contrary, the difficulty means that public administrators have important responsibilities with regard to values. They have the responsibility to *understand values, to find values consensus,* and *to monitor and control values consistency.*

Public administrators make many decisions. While some of these decisions involve few parameters or little controversy, many involve complex and competitive values that are quite controversial. But no matter whether the decisions are seemingly simple or difficult, public administrators have a cardinal responsibility to understand the values underlying their decisions. For example, many municipalities, counties and states are encouraging their staff to become deeply involved in economic development. Administrators are now increasingly asked to come up with ideas to promote economic potential in both urban and rural areas that are experiencing decline or likely to do so in the near future. They are highly involved in making recommendations about sports arenas, convention complexes, resort and convention hotels, gambling facilities, and unusual attractions and family vacation centers that may or may not be publicly owned but that may have public financing. This means that administrators must understand subtle differences between a declining socially activist (often called positive) government that emphasizes social equity, and a smaller but more focused entrepreneurial government that emphasizes economic competitiveness. Because of the difficulty of understanding values in competing, complex, and changing situations, this book focused much of its attention on the need for understanding. Yet even understanding is not enough, for public administrators ultimately must act.

Public administrators must use their understanding to encourage and cultivate values consensus. They must steer the fine line between leading elected officials and the public to areas of commonality and needed change on one hand, and manipulating them with their often superior knowledge, expertise, and professional position. Public administrators must have their own compelling visions of excellence, but they must not superimpose them on others who have other visions of the common good. Finally, public administrators must be conscientious in screening their values for excessive self-interest, using the public good as a cloak for their personal preferences or even their personal advantage. This is a difficult task indeed, but necessary if the public sector is to achieve the level of trust necessary for an empowered government in the new order.

Finally, public administrators must monitor the values used in public organizations and systems and exercise control where so authorized. This control may be direct but it may also be indirect. For example, the control of public administrators themselves is directly accomplished through laws and rules. In the new era, however, direct, structural means are generally declining in importance as forms of control and indirect types of control are increasing. The enhanced role of public opinion, the place of virtue, and the use of professional norms and standards is moderately on the rise. Steeply rising are the use of competition and comparison; so much so that many areas of the public sector are being transformed into very different value systems. Charter schools and voucher funding for private schools are not only changing the way business is done in the new schools, but are accelerating the pace at which public school systems must make appropriate changes to respond to public demands for better results.

The art of values management for practitioners has already become the leading skill necessary for managers and leaders of public sector organizations. Managers and leaders are poorly equipped for today's environment if they lack the ability to assess current values deeply, to draw out the appropriate values that should be retained and the new values that will be instilled, to motivate and empower employees to collaborate in refining a values consensus, and concretely to encourage some values systematically while discouraging others. Furthermore, other stakeholders—no matter whether they are taxpayers, clients, legislators, or private sector partners—now expect *all employees* with whom they come in contact to be as attuned to a consistent set of values as their counterparts in the private sector. This will require far, far more management effort than in the past, as well as more employee input and vastly more values clarification and support training than in the past.

The science of values for academics and students of public administration has likewise become a cardinal area of study for those interested in the changing world of public management or for those interested in the ramifications of many of the major policy changes that are now almost routinely suggested. The vast changes that have occurred and that are going to occur need to be studied, not only for their technical trappings, but for their deeper value meanings and systems, which are often disguised as they are in any new movement or initiative. Only when the value systems of proposed changes have been exposed in a dispassionate and thoughtful fashion can scientific studies and practical advice be genuinely useful. Although how-to's and assessments of the appropriateness of these changes are useful to a degree, too much normative and prescriptive work, on too narrow a theoretical base, has been done. This book is aimed at helping to establish that base in its examination of changing values in public administration.

Notes

1. I use this example with some trepidation because my colleagues, both within the public sector at large and in the university world revere merit systems so vehemently. Being a member of an extremely strong tenure system myself, I appreciate its virtues and would never willingly give up its cloak. However, tenure systems and tenurelike systems are under attack. Further, while some of the reasons for these changes may be perceived as wrong (*excessive* political responsiveness), it is simply absurd to say that such systems have not made themselves somewhat more vulnerable by the frequent abuses and systemic inbreeding that have occurred during the twentieth century.

INDEX

Page references for primary discussions of a topic are in **boldface**; page numbers for illustrative material are in *italic*.

A

action:
citizen, 176
government official, 176–77
individual, 171
patterns of, 171
Acton, Lord, 140
Adams, John, 138
adaptive cultures, *89*, 90–91
adaptive style, 82
Air Traffic Controller strike, 72
Allaire, Y., 166
alternatives, generating, 242
altruistic culture, 200
altruistic rationality, **214–15**, 223, 227
anarchic culture, 201
anarchic rationality, **221–22**, 224–25
decisionmaking, **222**, 226
appearances, 11
concern for, 41
Argyris, Chris, 46, 168
Arizona, 300
Articles of Confederation, 139
artifacts and actions level of culture, 167
ASPA Code of Ethics, 5, 299, 315
Section I, 22–23
Section III, 11–12, 19–20
Section IV, 17
Section V, 13–14
aspirational values, 282
assumptions. *See* basic assumptions
Austern, David, 278
awareness, 273–74

B

Baier, Kurt, 201
Bailey, Stephen, 48, 298
Balk, Walter, 126
basic assumptions, 170
flowing from ethical subsystem, 176–77
flowing from general philosophy, 172–74
flowing from political philosophy, 174–75
inconsistency with beliefs, 259
about legal values, 119–22
basic assumptions level of culture, 168
as determinant of action, 172–77
beliefs, 170
inconsistency with basic assumptions, 259
beliefs level of culture, 168
benchmarking, 268
Berman, Evan, 5
Bill of Rights, 140
Blacksburg Manifesto, 189
Blacksburg school, 188
Block, Peter, 126–27
body of knowledge, systematic, 62, **70–72**
Bogan, Christopher, 268
Bonczek, Stephen, 5, 40–41, 297–98
Boone, Daniel, 221
Bowman, James, 258, 297
Box, Richard, 21
British Audit Commission, 302
Brown v. Topeka Board of Education, 295
Bruce, Willa, 22
Brumback, Gary, 23
bureaucratic culture, 200
bureaupathology, 14–15, 150

C

Caiden, Gerald, 15
California Franchise Tax Board, 124
Campbell, J.P., 85
Canada, 61, 305
capital punishment, 210
capitalism, 137, 142–43, 175

Caplow, Theodore, 64–65
Carnevale, David, 47
Cava, Anita, 5
Census Bureau, 70, 143
Champy, James, 45
change-oriented culture, 200
chaos, 206–7
China, 220
choice, 242
Chrislip, David, 101
citizen-review boards, 296
citizen surveys, 263, *264*, 306
civic integrity, 9, 33, **46–47**, 52
    and belief in representative-democratic
        social contract, 39
    and belief in universal ethical principles,
        40–41
    conflicting and complementary beliefs of,
        41–42
    need for in public employees, 38–39
Clay, Joy, 194
client, 64
    satisfaction of, 75
Clinton, Bill, 305
code of ethics, regulative, **63–64**, 73
Cody, Michael, 21
coercive rationality, **209–10**, 224
    decisionmaking, **210**, 226
coherence, 9, 40
commitment, 40
community visioning, 265
comparison:
    comparative unit costing, 301
    control by, 301–3
    current shifts in, 308–9
    outcome assessment, 302–3
    public review of comparable data, 302
competence, 40
    heightened levels of, 74–75
competing values framework, 82
    culture types, 87–91, *89*
    effectiveness criteria, 85–87, *86*
    environmental conditions, 83–85, *84*
    leadership types, 91–93, *92*
competition:
    contracting out, 300
    control by, 299–301
    current shifts in, 308–9
    government corporation, 300
    privatization, 300–301
    public-private, 300
    public-public, 299
confrontational culture, 200
consensual style, 82
consensus, 136

prerequisite for, 273–74
    on values, 270–73, *272*
conservatives, 172
consistency, 9, 40
contingency approach, 243
contracting out, 300
contribution, personal, 34
controls, 289, 310, 319
    by comparison, 301–3
    by competition, 299–301
    current shift in emphasis, 303, *304*, 305–9
    external, reliance on, 47
    functions of, 290–91
    by laws, 294–95
    by norms, 298–99
    by public opinion, 296–97
    by rules, 295–96
    types and sources of, 292, *292*
    by virtue, 297–98
conviction, personal, 10–11
Cooper, Terry, 5, 8, 148, 150, 164, 274, 307
creative mover, *92*, 92–93
Crosby, Philip, 271
cultural framework, 161, 163–65, 177–79,
    178
    basic assumptions as determinant of
        action, 172–77
    four levels of, 165–70, *169*
        as determinants of actions, 170–72,
        171
culture:
    defined, 165–66
    four levels of, *169*
        artifacts and actions, 167
        basic assumptions, 168
        beliefs, 168
        as determinants of actions, 170–77,
        171
        patterns of behavior, 167
    organizational, transmittal of, 279–80
    professional, 62–63
    team, *89*, 90
    types of, 87–91, *89*
        altruistic, 200
        anarchic, 201
        bureaucratic, 200
        change-oriented, 200
        confrontational, 200
        democratic, 200
        elite, 200
        hedonistic, 200
        legalistic, 200–201
        market, 200
        religious, 200
        traditionalistic, 200

customer:
  complaint resolution, 263, 265
  focus groups, 263
  identification, 263
customers, 64

D

Dahl, Robert, 243
Death of Common Sense (Howard), 307
decisionmaking, **3–4**
  altruistic rationality, **214–15**, 227
  anarchic rationality, **222**, 226
  coercive rationality, **210**, 226
  decision defined, 233–34
  democratic rationality, **218–19**, 225
  elite rationality, **217**, 226
  human needs rationality, 208
  legal rationality, **220**, 225
  models, 237
    instinctive, 238
    simple, 238–40
  nonlinear systems rationality, **207**, 226
  rational choice, **203**, 225–26
  reasoned choice rationality, **205**, 225
  religious rationality, 213
  traditional rationality, **211–12**, 226
  values in practical decisions, 234–37
  See also decisionmaking paradigms;
    . . . sources;
    reasoned choice decisionmaking
decisionmaking paradigms, 187–89, 196–
    97
  comparison of
    achieving democracy through
      dialogue, 193
    ensuring social equity and fairness,
      194
    using professionalism to achieve
      public good, 195
    valuing public agencies as social assets,
      194–95
  mixed administration, 189–90, *192*
  strong administration, 190–91, *192*
  weak administration, 189, *192*
decisionmaking sources:
  definition, 6
  individual values, 8–12
  key, 4–5
  legal values, 18–20
  organizational values, 14–17
  precedence in, 7–8
  professional values, 12–14
  public interest values, 20–23
Deming, W.E., 45, 307
Deming Award, 270

democracy:
  achieving through dialogue, 193
  direct, 138
  Jacksonian, 147
  loop theory of, 103
  representational, 137
  types of, 175
democratic culture, 200
democratic rationality, **218–19**, 224–25
  decisionmaking, **218–19**, 225
Denhardt, Kathryn, 5, 34, 274, 307
Denhardt, Robert, 16
deregulation, 305
discretion:
  excessive, 249
  insufficient, 249–50
  moderate, 250–51
disequilibrium, 206
disinterest, 22
dissent, 11
Dobel, Patrick, 5, 19
Doig, Jameson, 259–60
domain-enhancing behavior, 50
downsizing, 95
Drucker, Peter, 15
Dudley, Larkin, 194
due process rights, 18, 43
Durkheim, Emile, 61, 67, 211

E

effectiveness criteria, 85–87, *86*
efficiency, 15–16
ego-enhancing behavior, 50
elite culture, 200
elite rationality, **215–17**, 224
  decisionmaking, **217**, 226
empirical expert, 91, *92*
employee
  as expenses vs. as assets, 105
  focus vs. manager focus, 105–6
  needs of vs. system indifference, 105
employee assessments, 265–66, *266*
  focus groups, 266
  opinion surveys, 265, *266*
  value sorts, 266
English, Michael, 268
entrepreneurial government, 190
environment:
  ambiguous, *84*, 84–85
  competitive, 83, *84*
  conditions of, 83–85, *84*
  of current values, 260–70, *261, 264,
    266*
  interactive, 84, *84*
Era of Good Feeling, 136

ethics, 316
ethics assessments, 260–61, *261*
  audit perceptual assessment, 260–61,
    261
  audit structural assessment, 260
ethics legislation, 294
evaluation, 243
expertise, 16

F
fairness, 194
federal budget, 308
federalism, 138–39
Financial World, 302
Firsirotu, M.E., 166
Fleishman, Joel, 19, 273
France, 51, 305
Frederickson, George, 5

G
Gaebler, Ted, 188
Gardner, John, 258
Gawthrop, Louis, 45
General Motors, 88
Ginsberg, Benjamin, 139
goal identification, 241–42
Goodsell, Charles, 135, 250
Gore, Albert, 126, 272, 305
Gortner, Harold, 5, 124
governance, systematic, 137
government corporation, 300
Great Britain, 305
Great Depression, 95, 136
Green, Richard, 34, 126, 194
Greenwood, Ernest, 62
gross domestic product, 143
group cultures, *89, 90*

H
Hamilton, Alexander, 8, 49
Hammer, Michael, 45
Hargrove, Erwin, 259–60
Harmon, Michael, 42, 45
Hart, David K., 164, 307
Hatch Acts, 10
Hawthorne Plant, 48
hedonistic culture, 200
Hejka-Ekins, April, 5
Henry, Nicholas, 22, 75
hierarchical cultures, 88–90, *89*
  evolution of in public sector, 94–95
  movement away from in private sector,
    95–96
hierarchical style, 82–83
Hobbes, Thomas, 117

honesty, 9
Howard, Philip, 47, 75, 119, 127–28, 249–51,
  307
Hubbell, Lawrence, 126, 194
human needs:
  decisionmaking, 227
  rationality, **208–9**, 223
human relations model, 85, *86*
humanity, nature of, 173–74
Hume, David, 208

I
ICMA, 299
ideal profession, 62
  community sanctions, 63
  professional culture, 62–63
  regulative code of ethics, 63–64
  substantial professional authority, 64
  systematic body of knowledge, 62
implementation, 242
incentive plans
  common elements of, 280–82
  goals of, 278–79
incrementalism, 244
individual values, 8–12, **33–34**, 52–53
  environment in America, 34–38
  excessive reliance on, 48–51
  potential contributions of, 46–48
  in public sector, 38–46
individualism, 139–41
individualist, 21
inflexibility, 126
initiatives, 297
innovation, 75
instinctive decisionmaking model, 238
internal process model, *86, 86*
IPMA, 299
ISO 9000, 270

J
Jacksonian democracy, 147, 303
Jefferson, Thomas, 142
job:
  satisfaction, 75
  security, right to, 43
  simple vs. multidimensional, 104
Juran, Joseph, 307

K
Kanter, Rosabeth Moss, 272
Keesing, Roger, 166
Kennedy, John F., 139
Kettl, Donald, 76
Kluckhohn, Clyde, 166
knowledge, 273–74

Kohlberg, Lawrence, 9–10, 117, 273–74, 277
  on civic integrity, 39–40
  on moral development, **3538**, 51—52
Kroeber, Alfred, 166
Kuhn, Thomas, 187–88

L
laissez-faire capitalism, 175
Lane, Larry, 187
Larson, Carl, 101
laws:
  control by, 294–95
  current shifts in, 303, 305–6
leadership:
  style of, 17
  types of, 91–93, *92*
legal rationality, **219–21**, 225
  decisionmaking, **220**, 225
legal values, 18–20, **117–18**, 129
  contributions of in public sector, 124–25
  problems of in public administration,
    126–28
  role in public administration, 118–24
legalism, 126–28
legalistic culture, 200–201
legislative controls, 294
Leninism, 175
Levin, Martin, 262, 271–73
Lewis, Carol, 5
Leys, Wayne, 279
liberalism, 175
liberals, 172
Liebman, Lance, 19, 273
Lipsky, Michael, 45
Lowi, Theodore, 139, 249
Lynn, Richardson, 21

M
machine bureaucracies, 66
Madison, James, 47–48, 140
Malcolm Baldrige Awards, 269–70
Manz, 105–6
market culture, 200
market rationality, 202–4
Marsick, Victoria, 74–75
Marx, Karl, 48
Marxism, 175, 214
Maslow, Abraham, 208
Mayer, Kenneth, 127
Medicare, 214
micromanagement, 126–27
Miller, Zell, 317
minority rights, 140
Mintzberg, Henry, 66, 81–82, 87
Miranda v. Arizona, 294–95

mission statements, 262
mixed administration paradigm, 188, **189–
  90**, *192,* 193–97
Monroe, James, 136
Moore, Mark, 19, 164, 273
moral development:
  conventional level, 36
  postconventional level, 36–38
  preconventional level, 35–36
Mother Teresa, 307
municipal clerks, 70–71

N
National Assessment of Educational
    Progress, 290
National Performance Review, 127, 272
New Deal, 143, 249, 290, 303
New Public Administration, 147, 190
New Zealand, 302
Nigro, Lloyd, 70
Nixon, Richard, 11
nonlinear rationality, 206–7
  decisionmaking, **207**, 226
norms:
  control by, 298–99
  current shifts in, 308
  importance for administrators, 316
Norton, David, 38, 41
Nuremberg trials, 10

O
open systems model, 86, *86*
optimism, 40
Oregon Benchmarks, 302
organizational culture, transmittal of, 279–
    80
organizational values:
  environment of, **81–93**, *84, 86, 89, 92*
  excessive reliance on, 107–8
  leadership style, 17
  organizational design, 15–16
  organizational health, 14–15
  potential contributions of, 107
  in public sector, 94–106, *98–99*
Osborne, David, 188
Ott, Steven, 279–80
Ouchi, William, 47
overhead democracy model, 187

P
Parsons, Talcott, 61, 64
patterns of behavior level of culture, 167
pay, right to adequate, 43
Payne, Bruce, 291
performance assessments, 266–68

personnel systems, 65
  at-pleasure, 65
  merit, 65
  professional, 65
Peters, B. Guy, 97, 106
Peters, Tom, 18, 45, 106, 151
physical safety, right to, 43, 52
pigeonholing process, 71
planning statements, 262
political rights, 42–43
Posner, Barry, 5, 258–59
President's Award for Quality, 270
press, 297
privatization, 300–301, 305
problem/issue identification, 240–41
productivity, 15–16
professional administrative class, 69–70
professional authority, substantial, 64, 73–74
professional culture, 62–63, 72
professional values, **12–14**, 61
  environment of, 62–68
  excessive reliance on, 76–77
  potential contributions of, 74–75
  in public sector, 68–74
professionalism:
  determinants of and public sector, 70–74
  using to achieve public good, 195
professions:
  evolution of, 64–68
  ideal, 62–64
program consolidation, 305
Progressive Era, 195, 303
project organizations, 100
public administration, 201
  decisionmaking in, 246–51, *247*
  role of legal values in, 118–24
public administrators:
  contributions of public interest values for, 151
  decisions of, 318
  initiative in management issues, 123
  initiative in policy issues, 123–24
  need for efficiency and effectiveness with public's resources, 146–47
  need for implementing policy without usurping power, 144–46
  need for supporting public's right to be involved, 149–51
  need for supporting public's right to know, 148–49
  potential problems of public interest values for, 151–52
  subordination of to law, courts, legislative intent, politicians, 119–22
  unique contributions of, 45–46

public employees, 10
  basic rights as citizens, 42–43
  need for civic integrity in, 38–39
  work-related rights, 43–45
public interest values, 20, **135–36**, **153–54**, *154*
  contributions of for public administrators, 151
  environment of, 136–43
  potential problems of for public administrators, 151–52
  practical definitions, 21–23
  and public administration, 144–51
  theoretical definitions, 20–21
public opinion:
  control by, 296–97
  current shifts in, 306–7
public sector:
  controls in, 291
  determinants of professionalism, 70–74
  example of decisionmaking and values in, 236–37
  individual values in, 38–46
  legal values in, 124–28
  organizational values in, 94–106, *98–99*
  professional values in, 68–74
public service, 298
Pugh, Darrell, 5

Q
quality assessments, 269–70
Quality Improvement Prototype Awards, 270
Quinn, R.E., 82, 85

R
rational achiever, 91, *92*
rational choice decisionmaking, **203**, 225–26
rational cultures, 88, 89
rational goal model, 85, *86*
rational style, 82
rationality:
  altruistic, **214–15**, 223
  anarchic, 221–**22**, 224–25
  coercive, 209–**10**, 224
  in cultures, 200–202
  defined, 199
  democratic, 218–**19**, 224–25
  elite, 215–**17**, 224
  human needs, 208–**9**, 223
  legal, 219–**21**, 225
  market, 202–4
  nonlinear systems, 206–7
  reasoned choice, 204–5
  religious, 212–**14**, **223**

traditional, **211–12**, 223–24
types of, 224
Reagan, Ronald, 72, 147
reasoned choice decisionmaking, **205**, 225
  at agency level, 244
  at policy level, 244–46
  in public administration, 246–51, *247*
  contingency approach, 243
  decision defined, 233–34
  models, 240
    choice, 242
    evaluation, 243
    generating alternatives, 242
    goal identification, 241–42
    implementation, 242
    problem or issue identification, 240–41
  values in practical decisions, 234–37
reasoned choice rationality, 204–5
recalls, 296
reciprocity, 9, 40
Redford, Emmette, 187
referenda, 297
Refounding Democratic Public Administration, 189, 193
refounding project, 188
Refounding Public Administration, 189
reinventing government, 190
Reinventing Government (Gaebler & Osborne), 188
religious choice, 141–42
religious culture, 200
religious rationality, 212–**14**, 223, 227
  decisionmaking, 227
representative-democratic social contract, 39
review, outside, 75
Richardson, Elliott, 10–11, 19, 48, 50
Richardson, William, 70
right values, 257, 283
  consciousness of values, 274–77, *275*
  consensus about, 258–60
    establishing when disagreement exists, 271–73, *272*
    prerequisite for, 273–74
    supporting when it exists, 270–71
  environment of current values, 260–70, 261, *264, 266*
  incentive plans for values, 278–79
    common elements of, 280–82
  organizational culture transmittal, 279–80
rights:
  basic, 33
  minority, 140

Rohr, John, 5–6, 21, 67, 117, 124, 139, 164, 191, 277
Rohrbaugh, J., 82, 85
Rokeach, Milton, 6
role morality, 6
Rosenbloom, David, 120, 201, 220
rules, control by, 295–96
Russia, 305

S
sacrifice, 40
sanctions, community, **63**, 72–73
Sanger, Mary, 262, 271–73
Schein, Edgar, 166
Schmidt, Warren, 5, 258–59
Schon, D.A., 46
Schubert, Glendon, 135
Scott, William G., 164
self-actualization, 44
Senate Productivity Award, 270
Senior Executive Service, 69
Simon, Herbert, 189, 202
simple decisionmaking model, 238–40
Sims, 105–6
Skinner, B.F., 211
Smircich, L., 166
Smith, Adam, 200
social equity, 194
Social Security, 214
socialism, 175
socialists, 172
society, organization of, 174–75
Soviet Union, 221
  independent states of former, 301
special interest groups, 296
stable environment, 83–84, *84*
states' rights, 139
statism, 51
status quo bias, 244
Steinberg, Sheldon, 278
Stever, James, 13, 74
strong administration paradigm, 188, 190–**91**, *192*, 193–97
sunshine laws, 290
surveys, 296

T
team builder, 91–92, *92*
technical decisions, 248
Tennessee Valley Authority, 300
Texas, 303
theocratic state, 174
Thompson, Dennis, 11, 48
Thompson, Fred, 127, 303–4
Tocqueville, Alexis de, 141, 214

Total Quality Management, 16, 190, 306
traditional rationality decisionmaking, 211–
    12, 223–24, 226
traditionalistic culture, 200

U
United States, 51, 61, 69, 136–37, 191, 220
    religious choice in, 141–42
    value shifts in, 164
universal ethics principles, 40–41
universe, nature of, 173
U.S. Constitution, 121
U.S. military, 69–70
U.S. Postal Service, 300
U.S. Supreme Court, 121

V
value adjustments, 164–65
value sets, 4–5
value shifts, 164
values:
    cultural framework perspective for
        analyzing, 161–79, *169, 171, 178*
    individual, 8–12, 34–**51**
    legal, 18–20, **117–29**
    organizational, 14–17, 81–**108**
    in practical decisions, 234–37
    professional, 12–14, 61–**78**
    public interest, 20–23, 135–**54**, *154*

"right" values, 257–83, 261, *264, 266, 272*
    in value systems, 317
values statements, 262
virtue:
    control by, 297–98
    current shifts in, 307
vision statements, 262–63
voting, 296

W
Waldo, Dwight, 5
Walker, David, 139
Wamsley, Gary, 193–94
Warwick, Donald, 5
Watergate, 11
Waterman, Robert, Jr., 45
Watkins, Karen, 74–75
weak administration paradigm, 188, **189,**
    192, 193–97
wealth, 216
Weber, Max, 67, 199, 211
welfare, 214, 302
West, Jonathan, 5, 190
Western civilization, 34–35
Wilson, James Q., 146
Wilson, Woodrow, 187, 189, 246
Wolf, James, 193–94
World War II, 67–68, 95, 136, 215
Wright, N. Dale, 307